# Methods for teaching the mildly handicapped adolescent

GEORGE E. MARSH II / BARRIE JO PRICE

**Methods for teaching
the mildly handicapped adolescent**

# Methods for teaching the mildly handicapped adolescent

## GEORGE E. MARSH II, Ed.D.
Assistant Professor, Department of Special Education,
University of Arkansas, Fayetteville, Arkansas

## BARRIE JO PRICE, Ed.D.
Department of Special Education,
University of Arkansas, Fayetteville, Arkansas

*with 67 illustrations*

## The C. V. Mosby Company
ST. LOUIS • TORONTO • LONDON    1980

To
**Kama** and **Meredith**

**Copyright © 1980 by The C. V. Mosby Company**

All rights reserved. No part of this book may be reproduced in any manner without written permission of the publisher.

Printed in the United States of America

The C. V. Mosby Company
11830 Westline Industrial Drive, St. Louis, Missouri 63141

**Library of Congress Cataloging in Publication Data**

Marsh, George E     1942-
    Methods for teaching the mildly handicapped adolescent.

    Includes bibliographies and index.
    1. Mentally handicapped children—Education (Secondary).   I. Price, Barrie Jo, 1947- joint author.   II. Title.
LC4604.M37     371.92′82     80-13396
ISBN 0-8016-3115-7

GW/CB/CB   9   8   7   6   5   4   3   2   1     02/A/244

# PREFACE

We have a long-standing interest in the educational needs of mildly handicapped adolescents and have shared the frustrations of students, parents, and secondary teachers who have struggled with the myriad problems created by the interaction of learning handicaps with the demands of the secondary curriculum and the pressures of socialization. The scope of secondary services has been narrowly conceived, and these services lack the qualities necessary to meet the unique needs of older students. Only a few books, monographs, and articles have been devoted to the issues of secondary education for mildly handicapped adolescents. Currently there is no truly comprehensive source that attempts to embrace the methodologies of teaching these students. Therefore our purpose is to provide a text that will be useful both for the preparation of secondary special educators and for practicing teachers and ancillary personnel who are daily faced with the problems we address in this volume.

The influence of parents and peers on adolescents is clearly much greater than that of teachers or the structure of the secondary school environment. In recognition of this fact, we approached the development of this text with the view that the total social context of the adolescent must be considered. Hence we have not limited our focus to only remedial aspects of teaching but have a broader, more inclusive strategy for education of mildly handicapped students in the junior and senior high school; this was accomplished by utilizing a systems approach to organization of the writing. The product consists of four sections: The Learner, The School, The Teacher, and The Program.

We have used three chapters to consider the learner who may be regarded as learning disabled, emotionally disturbed, or mildly mentally retarded. But first the student must be understood as an individual who is passing through a significant stage of development that transforms the child into an adult. Adolescence is an important period of development that produces stress and conflict for nonhandicapped children. The maturation of the child, influences of the family, and the love and tyranny of the peer group are endemic to a complete understanding of the mildly handicapped student and essential for educational planning.

In the second section, The School, emphasis is placed on the important features of school administration and functioning. The special education program must interact with the other school components to succeed as a programmatic element and as a service to students. The principal, teachers, curriculum, policies, teaching styles, and formal and informal relationships of school personnel constitute a social context into which special education must "fit." Ignoring the formal and informal systems of the school environment prevents the special educator from making pragmatic plans necessary for securing acceptance of the program, mainstreaming students, and meeting the needs of students outside the special classroom.

We envision the responsibilities of the special educator as including direct instruction and indirect services, such as organizing peer and volunteer tutoring programs, teacher consultation, and in-service programming. Interactive roles of the special educator with the principal, classroom teachers, ancillary personnel, parents, and students are as important to successful teaching as a firm knowledge of remedial strategies. Two chapters in this section have been devoted to the many roles of the special educator, who may function as a resource teacher, a vocational educator, or a traditional remedial expert.

The final section of the text encompasses those aspects traditionally conceived as educational methodology. Discussion centers on the mechanics of program development, compensatory teaching, remedial programs, and vocational training. It is our contention that most mildly handicapped students should be educated in the regular school curriculum. To that end we have strongly emphasized accommodation and other strategies to ensure the academic survival of students.

The preparation of a textbook of this scope is an arduous undertaking. We are indebted to many people for their advice, criticisms, and contributions. We are grateful to our Dean, Fred Vescolani, whose insights as a former teacher, principal, and superintendent have shaped our ideas into a practical approach to teaching. We are greatly indebted to Carol Coffman and Barbara Ireland, who spent many hours in the preparation of photographs used to illustrate this volume. The influence of Thelma Fleischhauer on the conceptualization of individualization will be evident to those who know of her successful career in education and unheralded teaching innovations. We are also indebted to the many students whose lives have influenced our thinking. We earnestly hope that our concepts will be found to improve the education and lives of others.

**George E. Marsh II**
**Barrie Jo Price**

# CONTENTS

### SECTION ONE
### THE LEARNER

**1 Overview,** 3

Modern issues in secondary education, 6
Educational tracks of the secondary school, 7
Mildly handicapped adolescents, 7
   Prevalence of mildly handicapped adolescents, 8
   Educational models for special education at the secondary level, 8
   The legal bases for educating the mildly handicapped, 9
Issues in special education, 10
   Importance of basic skills, 10
   Noneducational therapies, 11
   Special curricula, 11
   Mainstreaming, 11
An educational model, 12
   Personal development, 14
   Interpersonal relationships, 14
   Cognitive development, 14
A model for individualized instructional planning, 15
   Components, 16
   Installation of the program model, 19
Scope of the text, 23
Summary, 23

**2 Mildly handicapped adolescents,** 25

   Curriculum considerations in special education models, 26
   Curricular planning, 26
Adolescence, 27
   The major tasks of adolescence, 28
Theories of adolescence, 28
   An evolutionary view, 28
   Psychoanalytic theories, 29
   Field theory, 29
   Cross-cultural view, 29
   Socialization, 29
   The adolescent subculture, 30
   Cognitive structures of adolescence, 30
   The modern social context of the adolescent, 31
Learning disabilities, 33
   Definition, 33
   An operational approach, 34
   Specific characteristics, 35
Educable mental retardation, 36
   Definition, 36
   Characteristics, 37
Emotional disturbance, 38
   Definition, 38
Commonalities of mildly handicapping conditions, 38
   Some major problems of noncategorical classification, 42
   Program development, 42
Summary, 43

**3 Interpersonal relationships,** 45

Family influences, 46
   Parent-child relations, 46
   Parental values, 49
   Serious conflict in the family, 49

Parental attitudes, 52
Peer influences, 55
  Formal groups, 56
  Informal groups, 59
Special problems in adolescence, 63
  Fear of school, 63
  Depression and suicide, 64
  Dropping out of school, 65
  Stealing, 65
Counterculture, 66
  Delinquency, 66
  Alcoholism, 67
  Drug abuse, 67
  Running away, 70
How students behave: an anthropological view, 70
Summary, 71

**SECTION TWO**

**THE SCHOOL**

**4  Organization and administration of the school,** 77

Organization of the school, 78
  Typical organizational arrangements, 79
  Organizational patterns of special education, 81
  Supervisory personnel in special education, 81
  Qualifications of special education management personnel, 82
  External organizational structure, 82
  Federal legislation, 82
Characteristics of administrators, 84
The power structure, 84
  Formal power, 84
  Informal power, 85
  Pressure groups and power, 86
Administrative issues that concern the special educator, 87
  Discipline, 87
  Suspension and expulsion, 88
  Searching students and lockers, 88
  Records of students, 88
  Tort liability, 88
  Tenure, 89
  Dismissal, 89
Summary, 89

**5  Curriculum and instruction in the secondary school,** 91

Curriculum of the secondary schools, 92
  Curricular patterns, 92
  The nature of subject matter, 93
Subject areas, 93
  Social studies, 93
  Science, 94
  Mathematics, 95
  Language arts, 95
The special educator and mainstreaming, 96
  Instructional techniques, 97
  Memory, 98
  Input organization, 98
  Verbal learning, 98
Regular classroom teachers, 99
  Instructional interface, 99
  Behavior of regular teachers, 100
  Student behavior and interaction, 101
  Subject matter influences, 101
  Attitudes of teachers, 102
  Influence of unions and teachers' organizations, 102
Course requirements, 103
  Attending to lectures, 103
  Note-taking, 103
  Homework, 104
Grading practices, 104
  The curve, 104
  Test scores, 105
  Attendance, 105
Extracurricular activities, 105
Graduation requirements, 106
  Competency examinations, 106
Summary, 107

**6  Support services,** 109

Assessment, 112
  Learning disabilities: assessment issues, 112
  Mental retardation: assessment issues, 115
  Emotional disturbance: assessment issues, 116
  General procedures in assessment, 118
  Additional assessment procedures in learning disabilities, 118
  Conclusion, 120

Support personnel, 121
   School counselor, 121
   Speech and hearing clinicians, 132
   School nurse, 134
   Other support personnel, 138
Summary, 142

## SECTION THREE
## THE SPECIAL EDUCATION TEACHER

### 7 Roles of the special education teacher, 147

Responsibilities of the special educator, 148
   Direct pupil services, 148
   Administration, 152
   Teacher consultation, 153
   Public relations, 156
   Advocacy, 157
   Other role functions, 159
Personality variables and the special educator, 160
   Tolerance for frustration, 160
   Temperament and attitude, 161
Training and professional growth of the special educator, 162
   Course work, 162
   Additional training experiences, 163
   Professional organizations, 163
Concerns and issues related to roles, 164
Summary, 168

### 8 Role relationships and interactions of the special educator, 170

Relationship with administration, 171
Role to parents, 173
   Parent conferences, 173
   Other types of parent communication, 176
Relationships with paraprofessionals, 180
   Selection, 180
   Training, 181
   Supervision and utilization, 182
Peer tutors, 183
Role to support personnel, 183
   Counselors, 183
   Educational or psychological examiners, 185

   Speech therapist, 185
   School nurse, 185
   Role to regular teachers, 185
Specialized roles of special educators, 188
   Vocational adjustment coordinator, 188
   Facilitator, 188
   Vocational rehabilitation counselor, 189
   Resource-consultant, 189
Relationships in the community, 189
Summary, 190

## SECTION FOUR
## THE PROGRAM

### 9 Coordination of the program, 193

Organization and scheduling, 195
Daily planning, 197
   Considerations in comprehensive planning, 198
   Process, 203
Monitoring and record keeping, 216
   Student tracking, 216
   Grading, 217
   Program evaluation, 218
   State and federal requirements, 218
   School policies, 218
   Student outcomes, 219
   Communications, 219
   Computers, 224
Classroom management strategies, 225
   Reinforcers, 225
   Common systems utilized in classrooms, 226
Summary, 230

### 10 Compensatory programming and accommodation, 231

Current notions about secondary LD programs, 232
Alternative learning models in the regular class, 234
Information flow and information processing, 236
Types of accommodative and compensatory techniques, 238
   Administrative options in accommodation, 238

Accommodation: regular class
  techniques, 242
Teacher-controlled variables, 243
  Topical outline, 244
  Study guides, 244
  Technical vocabularies/glossaries, 244
  Advance organizers, 245
  Summaries of concepts, 246
  Audiovisual aids, 246
  Use of tape recorders, 246
  Special texts, 246
  Alternative responding, 247
  Talking books, 247
  Milieu, 247
Approaches to individualization in the
  mainstream class, 249
  Programming with a bivalent system, 251
  Assessing objectives of content
    courses, 253
  Selecting approaches to support students
    in the mainstream, 253
  Developing alternative learning units, 254
  An interactional-learning model, 256
  Modified lecture, 259
  Guiding thoughts in developing
    individualized instruction, 260
Accommodation: resource room
  techniques, 261
  Teacher consultation in
    accommodation, 261
Summary, 266

## 11 Remedial programming, 268

Reading, 269
  Characteristics of disabled readers, 269
  Planning concepts in remediation, 272
  Reading approaches, 272
  Assessment of reading, 280
  Practical reading, 284
Study skills, 284
  Application of study skills, 287
Arithmetic and mathematics, 287
  Causes of arithmetic failure, 287
  Characteristics of adolescents with
    arithmetic disabilities, 288
  Erecting arithmetic competencies, 288
  Assessment of arithmetic disorders, 291
  Instructional approaches, 293
Written language disabilities, 293
  Goals of written expression, 293
  The comprehensive language arts
    continuum, 295
Summary, 299

## 12 Vocational programming, 301

Vocational education, 302
  Objectives for planning vocational
    education of handicapped students, 303
  Planning the vocational program for
    handicapped students, 304
Career education, 307
Career preparation, 307
  Goals of vocational training, 308
  Vocational and career information, 308
  Vocational training, 311
  Role of the resource teacher, 313
  Role of vocational rehabilitation, 314
  Vocational education and the future, 314
Postsecondary training, 314
  Employment in the work force, 315
  Attendance at vocational technical and
    two-year colleges, 316
  College programs as an option, 317
  Military enlistment, 318
  The counterculture as a "career"
    opportunity, 318
Summary, 318

**Appendix A** Assessment, 321

**B** Suggested forms for compliance
with P.L. 94-142 for individual
protections and procedural
safeguards, 325

**C** Instructional materials for
mildly handicapped
adolescents, 339

# SECTION ONE

# THE LEARNER

The mission of the school is determined by society. School boards and educators respond to the pressures of interest groups, the legislature, and the courts and to perceptions of societal values. In the most fundamental sense, the purpose of education is to transmit the values of the society to the young, to acculturate them. In a more practical sense, the experiences of schooling provide the child with some of the skills and competencies necessary to function independently of parents, to become gainfully employed, and to assume adult responsibilities.

The purpose of education is typically presented rhetorically and defended or attacked on philosophical grounds. Philosophy, like theory, gives us direction, a frame of reference, and a sense of justification for our actions. Some 300 years ago there was philosophical unanimity about the purpose of education, that is, to improve the lives of children by teaching specific academic skills and inculcating religious precepts. Subsequently, the purpose of education has become manifold and sometimes unclear, reflecting change and confusion in society.

The goals of secondary education have been the subject of continuous debate and considerable thought among educators and critics. The Seven Cardinal Principles of Education, established in 1918 by the Commission on the Reorganization of Secondary Education and reexamined in each succeeding decade by one professional group or another, have served as the philosophical underpinning of American secondary education, as the framework for teacher training, and as the basis for school curricula. But, beneath it all, the secondary school has remained insulated within its original academic dress and devoted to its traditional purpose as custodian of college-bound students. In spite of the inclusion of social, vocational, and affective goals, the liberal arts curriculum continues to be extolled. Schools give preference to academically talented students for whom the process of education is thought to be most beneficial. Those who lack skills, talent, or motivation are not very welcome in the liberal arts curriculum. Conventional standards of academic achievement remain as the ultimate focus of the curriculum, the gauge of school excellence and teaching performance, and the means to classify students into an instructional caste system.

School systems and their bureaucracies have been resistant to change, have slowly responded to public pressure that would effect major alterations, and have only made significant changes when dictated to by the legislature or the judicial system. Many apparent changes are merely add-ons, curricular or programmatic cosmetics that are of little substantive import. But in defense of the schools it must be said that society does not speak in a unified voice: it expects teachers to serve many functions that have been forfeited by the family yet does not provide adequate financial resources to meet its multiple goals. Schools, and what they teach, react to pressures of society; pressures that are often ill founded, shifting, and variously imposed by conflicting groups, all urging the school to move in this or that direction without a prevailing, dominant philosophy.

Fitting the special education program into the secondary system is a formidable task, much more difficult than at the elementary level. The resource room in a junior or senior high school is not a natural extension of regular classes, many teachers are not necessarily understanding or sympathetic with its purpose, and it is likely that students who attend the class will have been branded by the regular faculty as "lazy" or "incompetent" in the learning environment. Because of the complexity of issues surrounding secondary education in an age of accountability and reification of conservative educational policies (back to basics), we must be pragmatic, rather than idealistic, in proposing a philosophy for the secondary special education program.

The program will be a new concept in many schools, and any innovation that disturbs the status quo will be resisted and criticized. Many of the objectives of special education are at odds with current trends and sentiments about education. The mainstreaming movement clashes with the back-to-basics backlash. Compensatory education, accommodation, and other methodologies perceived as "soft" on learning and of inferior standards will be viewed skeptically. Teachers in the various departments of the school may jealously regard the special program as a competitor for limited financial resources. Expectations for mildly handicapped students may be unrealistic, and progress may be measured against the achievement yardstick. Any effort to introduce individualization may be unhappily greeted as an attempt to impose extra burdens on teachers. These and other more pervasive problems must be accounted for in program plans and the philosophy of special education.

Chapter 1

# OVERVIEW

Carol Coffman

American secondary schools are currently being scrutinized by legislators, criticized by educators and lay persons, and generally reexamined for their efficacy in the midst of a technological and automated age. There seem to be two major themes of criticism; namely, schools are not attuned to the realities of the "world of work" because the traditional liberal arts curriculum prepares no one for an occupation, and schools are failing to maintain standards of literacy enjoyed by preceding generations of secondary students. As the major socializing agent in contemporary society, the school is also found lacking in the prevention of social deterioration, as evidenced by high rates of drug abuse, suicide, and delinquency among the young. To remedy these shortcomings, accountability systems have been applied to education, and schools are prodded to get "back to basics," which is to be monitored by means of competency examinations. Moreover, career education has been heralded as a curricular concept that will embrace the entire school curriculum, suffusing and transforming it so that all students will leave school with pragmatic knowledge and skills for employability.

In his thorough examination of adolescence in America since 1790, Kett (1977) challenges the romantic conceptualization of the "good old days" by revealing that the present image of the past, of adolescence and schooling, is not accurate. Until the passage of compulsory attendance laws, which were partly designed to keep teenagers out of the work force during a time of strong competition for jobs, few students attended secondary schools or college. Those who did were either middle-class and upper-middle-class youth preparing for a profession or lower-class youth attempting to avoid a life on the farm. Violence in the form of dueling, fighting, and riots was commonplace in many secondary institutions and colleges, with attacks on teachers and professors not an infrequent occurrence. The family was not the tightly knit institution that has been imagined. Soon after the age of 7, many children were sent away from home to assume jobs in homes or on farms, with the substantial part of the wages returned to the family. Disease and accidents contributed to a short life span, which suddenly and dramatically destroyed family stability. There is ample evidence that child abuse, as it would be characterized today, was commonplace. Preparatory schools, the district school, and the academy had no unified system of instruction and no unified curriculum. Nor were there examinations, diplomas, or standards for completing secondary school. Colleges had very loose entrance requirements. Until 1900, there was no real sense of a period of adolescence. The elite and wealthy families were able to finance a college education, which was typically complete by age 19 or 20. Less affluent students attended schools haphazardly, as they could afford it and to coincide with seasonal employment. Therefore many young persons attended schools off and on well into their late 20s. As Kett pointed out, young people were not firmly in their place, subordinated to the wise exercise of authority, and bound tightly by affective relationships to family and community (p. 60).

It was the development of industrialization and the symbiotic growth of high schools and professions that replaced on-the-job training and apprenticeships with formal training, which created a definable period of adolescence, elevated the high school as the primary institution for socializing youth, preparing them for occupations, and created goals for students that were rarely assumed by many families as important child-rearing responsibilities. As students wished to enter the professions, primarily the ministry, law, medicine, pharmacy, dentistry, and veterinary science, it became increasingly important to have sound academic training since colleges began to establish formal entrance requirements. Subsequently, a structured curriculum appeared in high schools, which was linked to postsecondary education by a certificate or diploma that helped to assure college entrance.

The general or liberal arts curriculum of today was originally a genuine innovation and an improvement over inconsistent offerings in academies, and the certificate or diploma became important as evidence that one had sustained rigorous training. These traditions were laid down at a time when a relative minority of young persons were enrolled in school.

With industrialization came the burgeoning of occupational opportunities for many young men and women, who could escape life on the farm and who need not enter into an apprenticeship to secure a career. School was not necessary either, for most youths, but professional schools emerged to train students for business and engineering occupations created by the changing economy. These new schools tended to imitate the high schools that trained students for the traditional professions. Gradually, it became important to remain in school longer if one were to find success in one of the professional avenues. This prolonged the period that boys and girls remained in the home and placed an economic burden on the family. Children had previously left the home after the age of 7 to enter into an apprenticeship and to earn money for the family (sometimes working for their families even into their mid 20s and providing a substantial portion of the family income). Now, however, the necessity for an education to "get ahead" caused children to remain in school rather than earning money. Ultimately, the compulsory attendance laws forced children of the lower classes and immigrants to attend secondary schools.

A different population of students attended the high school than the formerly elite, middle-class to upper-middle-class student bent on a career in a profession. Nonetheless, the tradition of the secondary school with its emphasis on classical learning was firmly entrenched, a curriculum unsuited to students who were not well grounded in basic literacy and who were more desirous of employment in the community than in the pursuit of a college education. At the same time, the period of adolescence was created by economic pressures because young persons were unable to assume adult roles and they were gradually set apart from adults as a distinct group, a distinction that had not been made in earlier times. Trade training was introduced in schools to prepare working-class youth, the liberal arts curriculum remained for those with professional goals, vocational guidance emerged in the early 1900s to assist students in career choices, and the secondary school became responsible for containing all youth of all classes and for perpetuating adolescence, a by-product of postindustrialization and economic influences.

Adolescence in America is an extended period that is primarily shaped by economic factors. Most young persons are unable to find employment with ample economic rewards. They are economically tied to the family and are today an economic liability. Prior to industrialization the young person was expected to work and to provide economic support to the family. Today this is an impossibility, especially if a teenager is expected to enter a profession or a trade, all of which require prolonged formal training during which time the parents must supply economic support. Puberty occurs much earlier today than it had previously so that young persons become physiologically and emotionally capable of adult roles, if not adult responsibilities. An adolescent subculture flourishes because it has been created by socioeconomic factors that prevent students from becoming adults, by distinguishing adult and adolescent roles. The peer culture of the adolescent is the primary means of child socialization, and the junior and senior high schools provide the meeting grounds for the rites of passage.

## MODERN ISSUES IN SECONDARY EDUCATION

The problems confronting youth, their parents, and schools today are different in degree than in previous generations. The belief that the family of the past was more close-knit and stable is a myth. Although families may be in turmoil by divorce, alcoholism, and desertion, the family of yesteryear was destroyed by the early death of one or both parents or incapacitation by disease with no governmental subsidies to the major wage earner. Although youth may run away from home or emotional strains between children and their parents may result in conflict and suffering, children were formerly separated from their families at a tender age to slave in a shop or labor on a farm to support the family. Drinking, fighting, vandalism, and general disobedience of young persons have been chronicled in all generations, especially among students attending secondary schools and colleges. Gangs of immigrant boys occupied street corners in several generations. The vices and crimes of today's youth reflect a recurrence of rebelliousness that seems to be played out in each generation in some form. The problems of the contemporary teenager are different partly because we live in an era that is, in many ways, more complex and unsettled. There are pressures that did not exist before. In many respects, the adolescent is much more serious because families are more child centered today than they have ever been, teenagers in most middle-class families approach a certain equality with parents rather than being totally dominated by them, and the concentration of youth in secondary schools and colleges focuses attention on adolescents as a distinct group. Sharing their concerns and interests in the adolescent subculture and having many of the symbols and freedoms of adulthood, the youth of today may be more concerned and preoccupied with the youth culture and less concerned with challenging the authority of adults, authority that has waned. The youth of today are more indifferent to adult values because it is no longer necessary to challenge authority and conventions. The subculture has its own values, it disdains competing values, and many of the concerns that society has about teenagers relate to a culmination of the socialization process that was created by society. The major problems of youth are not caused by schools, although they may be best resolved in school in as much as resolution is feasible.

As secondary schools were once shaped by the demands of society, in particular a certain segment of society, they have always responded to pressures for change as social attitudes and economic conditions change. Actually, the major issues in secondary education are not that different than they have been at different times throughout history. Schools have for many years been faced with the problem of educating a diverse population of students while at the same time being held accountable for the highest standards of academic excellence and achievement. Diversity of students is the greatest problem. Not all students are academically talented, yet achievement scores are uniformly regarded as the standard for comparing school districts. Not all students will attend college, but state certification requirements and national accrediting agencies rigidly reinforce the liberal arts curriculum. Not all students can benefit from the general curriculum and many will perform poorly in courses, but entrance examinations for college-bound students are used to verify the quality of education in a school district.

There are many problems facing secondary education in the public sector; because the

special education program will be only one small part of the system, anything that affects the system will have implications for the program. The major issues to consider are:
1. Criticism of schools and the demand for improvement
2. The conservative reform movement (back to basics)
3. Struggle for control of power in the school between the administration and teachers
4. The complications brought about by increasing student and parental rights
5. The reduction of financial resources to support schooling
6. The disaffection and alienation of youth

Each of these factors causes schools to carefully develop policies that will appease critics and patrons. Considerable public attention is focused on schools, which must defend themselves against allegations that there is a lack of discipline, poor instruction, lagging achievement among students, and that the school is failing in its mission. The criticism is strong. Television documentaries and national publications devote attention to the subject of "school failure."

Part of the problem can be explained by the fact that schools have been expected to do too much, accepting responsibilities without adequate resources. The lack of financial support is a central issue relating to increased teacher activism as teachers demand higher wages and a voice in the control of the school and its policies. The anti-intellectualism of students and their disenchantment with society and its institutions contribute greatly to the discouragement of teachers and to negative public opinion.

## EDUCATIONAL TRACKS OF THE SECONDARY SCHOOL

The junior and senior high school curriculum may be conceived as a *general* curriculum (the traditional liberal arts curriculum), a *basic* curriculum, which is a watered-down version for less academically talented students, and *vocational* education. College entrance requirements have remained relatively constant, but requirements for immediate entry to the job market on completion of secondary school have changed dramatically. The vocational component of the secondary curriculum must be more immediately responsive to trends in the economy, to the disappearance and emergence of different types of jobs, and to the requirements for successful entry. The vocational options of a school can theoretically be endless and must be altered and updated. The fact is that in most schools there is a dependence on traditional vocational areas. The basic or watered-down curriculum seems to be the least effective servant of students unless it is balanced with some vocational training. Special education arrangements for mildly handicapped students have been worked around these three basic tracks in education.

## MILDLY HANDICAPPED ADOLESCENTS

Public secondary schools are confronted with the demand to develop educational programs for *mildly* handicapped adolescents who have been commonly labeled as *educable mentally retarded* (EMR), *learning disabled* (LD), and *emotionally disturbed* (ED). Special educational programs at the secondary level have been unavailable or very restricted in scope; however, the mandates of The Education for All Handicapped Children Act (P.L. 94-142) and companion legislation of the various states give specific impetus to the development of a free, appropriate public education for handicapped students, which emphasizes special education and related services. In spite of the mandate, the dearth of program models, research, and usable materials leaves practitioners confused about what approaches to pursue and without a sense of common purpose or direction.

Essentially, the problems confronting special educators and curriculum developers at the secondary level are:

1. What kinds of special education services should be delivered?
2. What should be the balance between special education and the general curriculum?
3. How should the special education program be organized for effective and efficient instruction of the mildly handicapped?
4. What should be the educational outcomes for mildly handicapped students?

Although the problems can be identified rather easily, solutions are very elusive. There is professional disagreement about many issues, provision of certain services would significantly alter the secondary school system, which resists radical change, and the realization of the most egalitarian goals of special education would require a restructuring of the social order to assure vocational opportunity and acceptance in the mainstream of society. For now, there seem to be limited approaches to special education at the secondary level.

## Prevalence of mildly handicapped adolescents

A distinct segment of the secondary school population is unable to benefit from the general curriculum of the school without substantial assistance from special educators. These students, the mentally retarded, the learning disabled, and the emotionally disturbed, are regarded as mildly handicapped. They are capable of performing in school with considerable support through individualized educational programming. Although incidence figures may vary from one setting to another and there is a basis for disputing prevalence figures due to problems in defining the populations, the U.S. Office of Education provides estimates on the prevalence of mildly handicapped students (Table 1).

**Table 1.** Prevalence of mildly handicapped students*

| Type of handicap | Percent of population |
|---|---|
| Mentally retarded | 2.3 |
| Learning disabled | 3.0 |
| Emotionally disturbed | 2.0 |

*From U.S. Office of Education. *Estimated number of handicapped children in the United States, 1974-75.* Washington, D.C.: Bureau of Education for the Handicapped, 1975.

The number of students who might be considered to be mentally retarded will be much lower than the prevalence figures in Table 1 because these numbers include more severe conditions as well as the mild group. The same can be said for the emotionally disturbed. Moreover, some students will drop out of school at the secondary level, further reducing the number that will be expected to comprise the mildly handicapped population.

## Educational models for special education at the secondary level

The various special educational models or approaches at the secondary level for the mildly handicapped may be classified in the following categories.

1. *Compensatory models.* Compensatory models include any approach to education of the handicapped that stresses coping strategies, accommodation, and compensatory teaching to circumvent the learning deficit of the learner and modify the learning environment to promote learning. Students are taught very direct, pragmatic approaches to coping with instructional demands.

2. *Remedial models.* Remedial models include those activities, techniques, and practices that are directed primarily at strengthening or eliminating the basic source or sources of a weakness or deficiency that interferes with learning. The focus is on changing

the learner in some way so that he or she may more effectively relate to the educational program as it is provided and administered for all students. At the secondary level, remediation is commonly directed at the skills of basic literacy and reading, arithmetic, and expressive language.

3. *Vocational models*. Vocational models include prevocational and vocational training programs, such as work-study, which are specifically designed for handicapped students and which lead to immediate or short-range employment in the work force. Although remedial and compensatory strategies may be combined in vocational models, the emphasis is clearly on vocational training.

In recent years the delivery of special education has been conceptualized as a continuum of services ranging from regular classroom placement with little or no special support to removal from the regular setting in some form of self-contained service. The most popular approach to emerge at the elementary level is the resource room model. However, there is wide variation in the types of programs that are currently permissible in various states. The mainstreaming movement and training of generic special educators create inconsistent special education arrangements and teacher certification. Thus in some states all mildly handicapped may be served in cross-categorical or noncategorical resource rooms, while in other states the arrangements remain strictly categorical. Therefore the practitioner may find a number of arrangements at the secondary level that are variations of the resource room (i.e., categorical or noncategorical, and those which are essentially self-contained), all of them reflecting one of the basic models—compensatory, remedial, or vocational. As diverse as these approaches may be, there are practices that may have the widest possible application and that recognize commonalities in all settings.

## The legal bases for educating the mildly handicapped

Provision of services for mildly handicapped adolescents is based on specific federal legislation. Of course, the most notable is The Education for All Handicapped Children Act (P.L. 94-142), which assures that all handicapped children shall have a free, appropriate public education. Furthermore, specific procedures for assessment are enumerated, due process procedures for placing students into special education are clearly outlined, and many other aspects of educating the handicapped are included. The heart of the act pertaining to education is the requirement to write an individualized education plan (IEP) for each student who receives special education. The IEP must contain the following elements:

1. A statement of the present levels of educational performance of the student
2. A statement of annual goals, including short-term instructional objectives
3. A statement of the specific educational services to be provided to the student and the extent to which the student will be able to participate in the regular educational programs
4. The projected date for initiation and duration of services
5. Appropriate objective criteria and evaluation procedures and schedules for determining, on at least an annual basis, whether instructional objectives are being achieved

Another important piece of legislation is P.L. 94-482, The Education Amendments of 1976, which provides for vocational services to disadvantaged and handicapped students. The term "special needs," found in various documents and professional literature, is used by vocational educators to describe this population. The traditional categories of exceptionality are recognized in this legislation. Vocational education funds to the states are set aside for students with special needs.

Schools are encouraged to include handicapped students in the regular vocational education programs of the curriculum as much as possible, although specialized arrangements are certainly practical for students who cannot benefit from regular course offerings.

P.L. 93-112, The Rehabilitation Amendments of 1973, assures equal opportunity to handicapped workers in the labor force. Hiring, training, and promotion practices of employers must respect the status of qualified handicapped workers; affirmative action plans must be developed; and provisions also assure that postsecondary education must not discriminate against handicapped students. Buildings are to be barrier free to accommodate handicapped persons; new facilities are to be designed to be barrier free and older buildings must be modified.

The impact of these pieces of legislation and companion legislation of the states is profound. The legal foundations of special education for the handicapped provide the practitioner with remarkable flexibility and certainty that programming can be developed. What remains is the establishment of viable programs.

## ISSUES IN SPECIAL EDUCATION

Within the field of special education there are a number of factors deserving consideration because they add to the dilemma. Primarily, there has been a total lack of concern, thought, and planning for secondary special education students. With so much emphasis on the elementary school, very few model programs have been conceived or tested for use at the secondary level. The only detectable trends that have emerged have the characteristic emphasis on remediation; there is little attention to the daily needs of students in their classes and interactions with peers. Viewing the education of the secondary special education student as a simple continuation of elementary level remedial reading and arithmetic, or perceptual motor training, is narrow and unrealistic. Even if students can make significant gains in achievement, it is unlikely that they will be able to apply these skills to the demands of the curriculum in the same manner as non-handicapped students. They need help passing classes in content areas as well. With this in mind, we will consider some points more closely.

### Importance of basic skills

Reading is the basic tool for all academic pursuits, for independence in learning and thinking, and for vocational success and advancement. This is an indisputable fact in all Western societies. There is a full range of activities and pragmatic uses served by reading. One can become educated, acquire a job, prepare for advancement, participate more competently in fulfilling one's role as a citizen, and protect or amuse one's self through the power of reading. But, what if a person cannot read after years of sincere effort?

This is the fundamental question facing most mildly handicapped students and their teachers at the secondary level. Frustrated by years of failure, their motivation undermined by discouragement, and placed into classes of ever-increasing difficulty, students rightly view their prospects of success at the secondary level as rapidly diminishing. The promise of the elementary resource room for many children is not realized. There is no panacea for reading difficulties, one of the most debilitating of all learning disabilities. With all the empirical inquiries, there is still little agreement among authorities about the correlates of failure and successful interventions. Therefore the most critical problem facing the secondary specialist is what to do about basic skills. How much of the program should be devoted strictly to remediation of reading, mathematics, spelling, and writing disorders?

## Noneducational therapies

Programs for the mentally retarded and the learning disabled have introduced noneducational therapies directed at underlying processes thought to be essential to academic learning. The variety of programs used to improve motor and perceptual functioning are well known. However, after widespread use in public school programs, many of these approaches have fallen into disfavor with many authorities, especially in the learning disabilities literature, because they have supplanted the traditional remedial programs and have been disappointing to those who had hoped that such activities would lead to improved academic functioning.

The practitioner may consider the use of process training in secondary programs, especially with LD students, but careful analysis of the anticipated benefits, the amount of time to be devoted to such endeavors, and the choice of approaches that might be used may lead to the conclusion that other educational goals would be more appropriate. Depending on the special educational arrangements, the orientation of teachers, and the philosophy of the district program, this issue may confront the practitioner as a secondary program is developed.

## Special curricula

Although specific, segregated LD programs are being developed in some settings and similar programming exists for ED students, EMR students have enjoyed a longer history and more widespread services in junior and senior high schools. The secondary program for mildly retarded students has frequently taken the form of a prevocational and vocational training sequence as a separate curriculum. These programs have been reported by Kolstoe (1972) and considered to be an effective approach to the education of these students. Similar programming for LD and ED students has not developed as rapidly or to the same extent. The eligibility of LD students for special vocational arrangements was previously questioned, although all could participate in the regular vocational program of the school and receive support in a resource room. However, most authorities maintain that EMR students require a special vocational sequence to assure transition to the work force. Unfortunately, work-study is not recognized as a vocational program in some locations unless it is under the direct supervision of a certified vocational educator.

Another problem confronting practitioners in some settings is whether or not to group the mildly handicapped (EMR, LD, and ED) together in an arrangement such as a special vocational curriculum, a remedial program, or any other arrangement. Although this may be precluded by mandatory organizational arrangements in some states, it is an issue that deserves attention. This approach has strong support from some authorities who maintain that there are little differences between the three groups in terms of characteristics, needs, and instructional methods (Hallahan & Kauffman, 1975).

## Mainstreaming

Should adherence to the mandates of P.L. 94-142 be carried to the fullest intent, that is, attendance in regular classes with nonhandicapped students to the maximum practicable extent? If the student cannot read well enough to handle elementary school texts, how can he or she be expected to function in an upper-level classroom with advanced textbooks, outside readings, written papers, essay tests, and extensive homework? If the students are mainstreamed, then how would it be possible to adhere to a separate curriculum? Should students come to a resource room just for the purpose of training in special curriculum but not receive any help with the work they are expected to accomplish in their regular classes? If this is done, when will they receive help in remediation of reading and mathematics? Can mainstreaming and special vocational programs coexist? These and other issues will be considered in this text, but it is certain that many problems will remain unresolved for a long time to come.

## AN EDUCATIONAL MODEL

Now that we have identified some of the issues and noted the lack of research and model development, an educational prototype for secondary special education will be proposed. The necessary ingredients to make it function and to refine it exist in the typical school. At the present time, there are few materials, that is, hardware and software, to be enthusiastically endorsed; but as a foundation the model (Fig. 1-1) should be appropriate for the broad curricular endeavors in any of the approaches (i.e., compensatory, remedial, or vocational) and under any condition of service delivery (i.e., resource room or self-contained classroom).

We have combined the developmental tasks of adolescence identified by Erikson and Havighurst (see Chapter 2) and developed general goals that are associated with three broad components of a special education program, namely, personal development, interpersonal relationships, and cognitive development. The tasks and educational goals for each of these components are as follows:

| Developmental tasks | Goals |
| --- | --- |
| *Personal development* | |
| Develop a sense of identity | Have awareness of familial and cultural heritage |
| Develop a sense of sexuality | Have knowledge of physiological changes associated with adolescence |
| Accept and adjust to bodily changes | Be able to identify personal abilities |
| Understanding personal strengths and weaknesses | Develop individual areas of interest in accordance with abilities |
| Attain emotional independence | Adjust to physical and mental limitations |
| Define personal interests and talents | Learn to compensate for physical and mental limitations |
| | Understand and accept sexual development and interests |
| | Develop an appropriate sexual role |
| | Develop control of emotional responses |
| | Develop an appropriate emotional repertoire |
| | Develop a positive self-image |
| | Be able to identify personal needs |

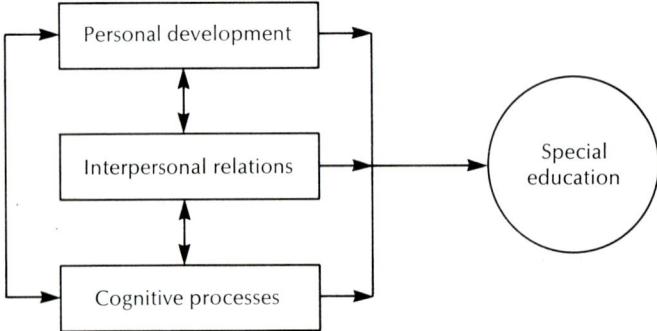

Fig. 1-1. Basic planning model for secondary special education.

| Developmental tasks | Goals | Developmental tasks | Goals |
|---|---|---|---|
| | Develop acceptable standards of dress and appearance | Adopt societal values | Complete formal schooling and earn a diploma |
| | Develop awareness and knowledge of personal self-care | | Develop occupational awareness |
| | Develop life-long personal hobbies and recreational interests | | Establish realistic occupational goals |
| *Interpersonal development* | | | Secure employment or develop short-term plans for employment after graduation |
| Develop self-assurance and confidence in social interaction | Understand the attitudes and values of one's peer group, family, and community | | Understand and resolve personal and group values with societal values |
| Attach sexual interests to persons outside the family unit | Identify responsibilities and role relationships within a family unit | | |
| Develop relationships with peers | Achieve status outside the family | | |
| Develop social and moral maturity | Develop an awareness of social interaction | | |
| Prepare for marriage and parenting | Understand social groups | | |
| | Relate to peer groups in appropriate ways | | |
| | Identify conventions associated with dating behavior | | |
| | Have awareness of the responsibilities of a marital relationship | | |
| | Have knowledge of sexual activity and birth control | | |
| | Understand motives and needs associated with the behavior of others | | |
| | Be able to accept differences of others (opinions, beliefs, values, etc.) | | |
| | Be able to adjust behavior appropriately to different settings | | |
| | Be able to evaluate the consequences of antisocial activities (gangs, drugs, etc.) | | |
| *Cognitive development* | | | |
| Consider vocational interests | Participate in regular curricula of school as much as possible | | |
| Complete formal education | | | |
| Explore suitable occupations | Develop basic literacy skills as a minimum academic goal | | |

Within the conceptual framework of Fig. 1-1 we have attempted to capture all the elements of individual development to which curricular goals should be addressed in a comprehensive program. The breadth of the model is such that any educational effort may be encompassed for any student, handicapped or not. Personal development and interpersonal relations are stressed because there is narrow attention to cognition, which casts personal development and interpersonal relations into a category of relative unimportance, although these areas are recognized and heralded by educators. They have a place in the curriculum but typically very little attention is directed to them during instruction.

Strong personal development and good interpersonal relationships may augment traditional educational efforts. Students who have affective disorders, a likelihood among LD and ED adolescents, will be unable to effectively cope with social-emotional stress. Cognitive growth, learning, and academic achievement are hampered by personal conflict. Inhelder and Piaget (1958) have clearly indicated that there is no behavior pattern, no matter how intellectual, that does not involve affective factors. They state that affect and cognition are inseparable and irreducible. Elkind (1970) maintains that the majority of adolescent experiences must be understood within the context of new mental capacities *and* affective transformations. How then can we regard the instruction of mildly handicapped students as only a matter of remediation or achievement?

The model is intended to give shape and direction for the goals of a program, for educational strategies, for utilization of the existing school curriculum and for resourceful use of support services. It should be reiterated that we are not advocating the development of a special curriculum with the proposition of this model. A special curriculum is incompatible with the goals that are proposed as well as with a vocational program, resource room, or approach that supports integration in the existing educational system. Emphasis in the model is on methods of meeting the major developmental tasks of adolescence (described in Chapter 2) by organizing resources of the school and adding to them in a comprehensive effort. The model is a nonhierarchical triad of the three major components essential for a broad-scoped educational program. Each constituent part may be hierarchically arranged and cross-related and otherwise adapted for local use.

## Personal development

Included in the personal development component are any educational or counseling efforts that assist the student in personal development. The major tasks of adolescence and the programmatic approaches are as follows:

| Major developmental tasks of adolescence | Programmatic approach |
|---|---|
| Develop a sense of identity to include a sense of sexuality | Personal counseling |
| Accept and adjust to bodily change | Sex education |
| Understand personal strengths and weaknesses | Health education |
| Attain emotional independence | Goal setting |
| Define personal interests and talents | Decision making |

## Interpersonal relationships

Another major component of the planning model singled out for special consideration is the area of interpersonal relationships. Attention to this area in the curriculum is important especially because of the adolescent's problems in relating to others (see Chapter 3). There must be attention to the interpersonal needs of mildly handicapped students to promote better functioning in the school setting, with the family, with peers, with teachers, and ultimately in society. Elements of the existing curriculum, and specific efforts identified and stressed by the authors, would be included in the programmatic approaches assisting the adolescent to meet corresponding developmental tasks.

| Major developmental tasks of adolescence | Programmatic approach |
|---|---|
| Develop self-assurance and confidence in social interactions | Training in social skills |
| Attach sexual interests to persons outside the family unit | Sex education |
| Develop relationships with peers | Extracurricular activities |
| Prepare for marriage, parenting, and more mature social interaction | |

## Cognitive development

Cognitive development is the most familiar, commonly recognized component of education and special education. Concern is with regular course work, remediation, accommodation, compensatory teaching, and any other major activity that promotes thinking and reasoning. The model of teaching used in the classroom should, where possible, emphasize attainment of higher cognitive skills rather than low-level abilities.

| Major developmental tasks of adolescence | Programmatic approach |
|---|---|
| Select vocational interests | Regular courses (vocational and academic) |
| Complete formal education | Remediation |
| Explore a suitable occupation | |

| Major developmental tasks of adolescence | Programmatic approach |
|---|---|
| Adopt societal values | Accommodation and compensatory teaching |
| | Study skills |
| | Career education |
| | Counseling |

## A MODEL FOR INDIVIDUALIZED INSTRUCTIONAL PLANNING

So that we will not be misunderstood nor lead the reader to confusion by the liberal use of the term "model" in this text, it should be noted that "model" is an ambiguous term, especially in education. As Nuthall and Snook (1973, p. 47) have said, "a model may be used for imitation, description, explanation, prediction or persuasion. . . . Within education the term 'model' is used in similarly diverse ways." There are two models generally described in this chapter, suggested for imitation, and included for descriptive and persuasive purposes.

The two types of educational models in this chapter are (1) a model for individual instructional planning and (2) a general program model for secondary special education (already discussed). In education there is an emphasis on models of teaching such as the behavioral or discovery learning types. In special education there is pragmatic concern with which teaching strategies should be used with certain categories of students and, to a lesser degree, what curriculum should be used, as well as the setting for instruction (mainstreaming vs special class). Hence, the process may degenerate to that of planning a *unitary* curriculum for a *group* of secondary students who share a diagnostic label. The process is characterized by the simplistic notion that "all LD students should receive intensive remediation in basic skills." Individual characteristics and needs of "LD" students are ignored or confused by the single purpose of special education. Consequently, teachers are implored to use behavior modification or to reject it, to use one specific instructional program instead of another, or to place all students into limited types of instructional settings.

Such choices should not be made with the institution as the referent point; rather, they should be made with attention to a specific set of needs expressed on behalf of an identified student who is to benefit from special education. This should be the work of an IEP in defining the needed educational plan from the student's point of view, even to the extent of planning programs and services for a student that may be presently beyond the school's capability to deliver! If a student's needs indicate that certain types of special education are required and that related services are necessary to augment special educational interventions, then they should be designed rather than compromising a student's education by deferring to the institution's needs and limitations.

To truly individualize the education of a particular student, it is mandatory that the focus be placed on the unique characteristics and needs of a specific student and that all instructional elements be arranged around those traits. The predominant practice of creating educational programs based on preconceived or hypothetical needs of classes of students (classified by diagnostic label) must be dismantled. The prevalent best practices of education that enjoy popularity in special education, such as diagnostic-prescriptive teaching, task analysis, and applied behavioral analysis, are excellent but incomplete approaches to the challenge of individualization. An educational model of individualization that fulfills the promise of the Individualized Education Plan (IEP) is needed, that is, a model that enables educators to utilize the IEP as a *process* instrument rather than a *product*. It is illuminating, indeed essential, to examine the characteristics associated with handicapping conditions and those of adolescence; but it is ultimately necessary to

**16** THE LEARNER

|  | SERVICES | | | | |
|---|---|---|---|---|---|
|  | Teacher variables | Instructional procedures | Placement | Related services | Other |
| **NEEDS** Level of educational functioning |  |  |  |  |  |
| Personal-social-behavioral functioning |  |  |  |  |  |
| Sensori-physical functioning |  |  |  |  |  |

**Fig. 1-2.** Individualized educational planning: a model. *I.E.P.*

narrow the focus on idiopathic characteristics of a particular student, regardless of the label, and orchestrate an individualized educational program around the identified needs. Educational plans should be erected *only* on individual needs and characteristics. The shortcomings of current models seem to be that important elements of student needs or educational planning are ignored or overlooked in planning. In an initial attempt to propose a workable approach that will capture these elements in planning, we are proposing the model shown in Fig. 1-2.

## Components

The following descriptions of the components of the model (Fig. 1-2) provide explanations of the use of each part and the interaction of components in the matrix that should be considered. As will be seen by contrast, the utility of this matrix is that it can serve as a more uniform and systematic approach to the identification of needs and educational plans than existing approaches that focus on only one aspect or another. For example, the continuum of services in special education (e.g., Deno's model) conceptualizes the service for a child in terms of types of settings, such as self-contained, resource, or itinerant. If a multidisciplinary team focuses only on the label of a student and makes a selection about placement from options in the continuum, other aspects of planning may be ignored. Specific instructional approaches and precise needs of the student may be masked by the diagnostic category that only implies needs. Unfortunately, it is all too often true that once a label, such as emotionally disturbed or learning disabled, is agreed on, and a program option, such as a resource room, is chosen, the process is considered to be completed. Attention to more subtle and important aspects such as the nature of the curriculum, the teachers, instructional goals, and instructional techniques is missing. The process should culminate in a *dispositional* placement with planning decisions based on as many characteristics and needs of the student as may be feasibly met in the total school environment, and beyond if necessary.

**Teacher variables.** Included within the general category of teacher variables are such variables as the specialization of a teacher (e.g., science, history, special education), instructional style (e.g., lecturing, program directed, permissive, task oriented), temperament (e.g., willingness to accept and adapt a program for a student), and any other dimension of perceived importance for a particular student. The teacher should be matched to a student in terms of identified student needs rather than simply scheduling a student into a particular class because it is convenient. An impressive body of research has emerged to indicate the importance of teacher variables in promoting learning. These should be seriously considered within the context of each handicapped child's educational plan. If it is found that certain characteristics are needed, it may be determined that in-service training or consulting activities will be necessary to improve the prospects of suiting teachers to a student.

**Instructional procedures.** The category of instructional procedures includes a variety of teaching strategies, for example, specific remedial approaches, compensatory techniques, the use of instructional aids (films, tapes, hardware, etc.), accommodations (e.g., reduced reading requirements and extended times for examinations), types of behavioral approaches (e.g., primary reinforcement, token economy, applied behavioral analysis), curriculum, materials, and any other instructionally related activity. Frequently, in many settings, this area is the primary focus of the assessment team and the IEP. As important as instructional procedures are for a handicapped student, other factors can enhance or subvert the best conceived instructional procedures.

**Placement.** The placement category includes the placement decisions that are ordinarily put into the form of a continuum. Since the advent of mainstreaming, the resource room tends to be the most popular special education placement. In a secondary setting there will be many other factors that should be considered, especially the types of regular classes, the type of vocational programs, and the milieu of classes. Placement may need to adhere to certain physical considerations for particular students such as acoustical properties, type and arrangement of seating, and lighting. Some students are not able to function well in open classes. The special class should be located near the center of activities and near the library or media center but still retain the qualities of a relatively quiet environment.

Milieu considerations might include the involvement, leadership, and support of a teacher (which are also teacher variables), and they must be verified by observation in the class. Teachers who claim to be supportive may not perform in that manner. Information that must be considered in terms of the needs of a student includes the following: does the class permit interaction between students, herald competition, or have specified roles of conduct; is it teacher controlled or program directed, innovative or rigid?

**Related services.** Any legally defined related service such as physical therapy or counseling may be important to a particular student as an aid to the major special education activities, and any such service may have an impact on personal and interpersonal functioning of a student. Services to parents or services outside the school may be included here but it would be more effective to introduce a discrete category for this purpose. Schools, however, have little control on activities beyond the school's responsibility.

**Level of educational functioning.** The level of educational functioning component includes many of the standard measures typically used in assessment, for example, standardized tests of intelligence, achievement tests, diagnostic achievement tests, criterion-referenced tests, and process tests. By informed decision of the team or by using a system of refined statistical data in conjunction with more subjective impressions, the magnitude of interaction between the level of educational functioning and components in the services may be determined. For example, it may be decided by the team that the nature of intellectual functioning gives little direction to the planning effort, although a cognitive task assessment (e.g., Piagetian) may offer some guidance in determining some aspect of instructional procedures. Measures in the area of academic achievement, especially criterion-referenced measures, provide a clear picture of the tasks that are achieved and that must be met in the next sequence of instruction if the student is to progress academically. It may be determined by the team that a low score on a process measure (e.g., in the area of visual perception or auditory discrimination) should receive minimal attention in the educational plan because of the unlikelihood that improvement will result from intervention. In any event, it is within this dimension that a number of educational goals and task analyses can be used, to include the process typically referred to as diagnostic-prescriptive teaching. Specific instructional objectives in reading and mathematics may be precisely determined and the needs related to teacher variables (what kind of a teacher is needed in terms of experience and temperament), instructional practices (types of instructional methods to be used and curricular sequences), placement (type of settings and duration in special and regular education placement), and related services. It is possible that a variety of decisions might be made, depending on a particular constellation of needs based on level of educational functioning. In one case it may be determined that a student needs a supportive but task-oriented teacher who is skilled in a specific instructional technique to occur in the mainstream with consultation service from the special education teacher. Another student may require much more intensive intervention, to include related services. In any event the level of educational functioning is only one part of the process in this model and should be weighed against other factors in the personal-social-behavioral and the sensoriphysical dimensions.

**Personal-social-behavioral dimension.** The personal-social-behavioral dimension includes a variety of measures and impressions provided by personality assessment (such as the Thematic Appercention Test or similar instrument), measures of adaptive behavior, impressions of social interaction with peers and in the community (such as those proposed by Mercer in conjunction with the SOMPA assessment approach), behavioral checklists, and observational techniques (such as the Flanders or Spaulding technique). Although the use of such instruments must be defended on the same grounds as the use of any test device (it should be noted that the authors do not necessarily agree with the philosophy and uses of some instruments), if information is gathered that can be utilized in educational planning in the various components, some important decisions can be made. For example, the skills and personality of a particular teacher may be better suited to students with certain characteristics. There is ample evidence from research to indicate that matching teachers to students is a fruitful approach to education. In the same way, the structure of the classroom necessary may be dictated by the student's needs, specific instructional procedures may be employed (e.g., a type of behavioral approach to modify aggressive behavior), and related services may be recommended (e.g., counseling). There are undoubtedly many interactions that can be examined along this dimension, and much more research needs to be accomplished to center on significant issues of education related to a student's personal, social, and behavioral pattern in terms of educational needs, which may be categorized under teacher variables, instructional procedures, placement (i.e., the mix of special and regular programming and type of structure and interaction with peers), and related services. For the time being, there are apparently some useful approaches to education that can be derived from examination of these interactions if we are willing to look for them and to plan accordingly.

**Sensoriphysical dimension.** The sensoriphysical context refers to a sensory or physical condition (e.g., deafness, blindness, orthopedic condition) that might have implications for programming. This may not have much relevance to mildly handicapped students per se but can be a good approach to any child, including one with a temporary condition such as a broken leg. A student who has seizures may need to have special programming because of interactions with various components along the needs axis. There may be teachers totally unsympathetic to students with seizures or who are frightened to the extent that it would interfere with the student's progress and self-concept. Specific related services such as counseling and medical supervision may be necessary. Placement considerations might dictate a classroom arrangement devoid of fluorescent lighting due to susceptibility to photophobically induced seizure activity.

It is apparent that interaction may not occur between variables and it would not be necessary to develop a program element for each cell (12 interactions). It should also be apparent that there is vertical interaction (e.g., behavioral or personal with physical). We are proposing this as an educational model that may be useful in comprehensive programming. It appears to capture most of the important considerations necessary in such programming so that its application is best conceived as a planning matrix for probing individual needs more carefully. General program models are designed for special populations and are shaped by laws, regulations, and available resources. Within the parameters of a general program model it should be required that an individualized approach be used, as proposed herein, so that educational options are actually determined by *student needs* rather than by tracks designed for large number of students who are placed on the basis of a label.

## Installation of the program model

Analysis of the program components reveals that the secondary special education program, regardless of the type, may be integrated with the regular program of the school or treated as a self-contained program, if suitable. Resources of the school are finite and the specialist can only be expected to accomplish a certain amount of successful intervention before becoming overburdened. To a certain extent, administration of the program will be a juggling act. For efficiency, wherever possible the three components should utilize existing courses and services of the school, unless a segregated program is required or deemed necessary.

**Coordination.** The concept herein proposed will be functional only as long as the program is viewed as *dynamic*. By contrast, a *static* program is one in which the content, curriculum, materials, and scheduling are structured the same way for all students who participate. For example, each student should not have remediation in reading *at the same time* and with the *same* materials as all other students. A special curriculum will also deteriorate to a static program if structure does not account for individualization. A dynamic program provides a full range of services and a vast array of individually determined activities.

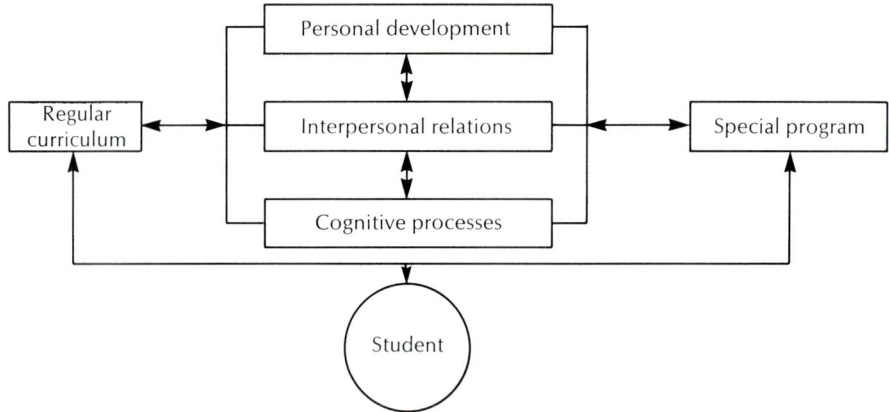

**Fig. 1-3.** Program relationships.

Because many secondary programs will be modeled after the resource room, the relationship of the *resource room* to the regular curriculum is depicted in Fig. 1-3. Except in strictly remedial programs, part of the responsibility of a resource teacher is to select the appropriate placement in regular classes (type of course and teacher), the focus in the resource room, the amount of remediation, and other services. Actually, major decisions such as intake, placement, and scheduling are reached through cooperation between the student/parent, counselor, specialist, and other important persons and committees in the school setting. It is essential that each student have one key person who is responsible for coordinating and monitoring the individual program.

The most logical person in the school to assume the role of coordination is the specialist, although many functions would be assumed directly by other professionals (principal, special education supervisor, counselor, etc.). Nonetheless, because programming for mildly handicapped students should not be left to chance, the specialist can assure program integrity by coordinating student services.

**Variables of the system complicating program development and functioning.** There are, unfortunately, a great number of complications within the system, which can significantly interfere with the program success. Fig. 1-4 depicts the major areas into which these variables may be classified. The reader should be aware that circumstances will be different from one district to another and, often, quite different between schools within the same system. The most important person in the system is the principal, whose support or opposition can be critical.

***Student attitudes.*** Of the many problems that might have an adverse effect on the special program, some that involve student attitudes are listed below:

1. Resistance of students to identification with a special program
2. Emotional problems of students
3. Problems of students assuming responsibility for self-direction and handling relative freedom of secondary school setting
4. Failure expectancy and failure avoidance
5. Attraction of students to alternative social status and counterculture activities

Secondary students are extremely conscious of the social structure of the adoles-

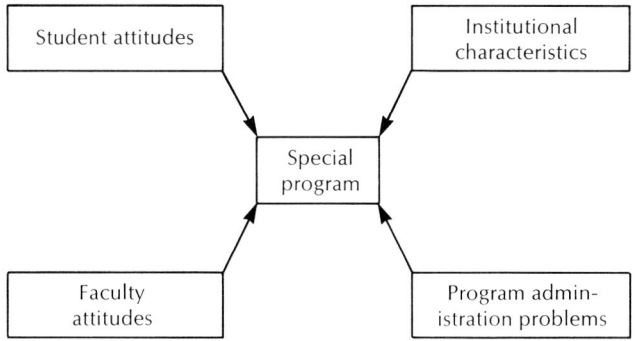

**Fig. 1-4.** Systems variables influencing the special program.

cent peer culture. As such, the stigma associated with being labeled as "different" in some unacceptable way is abhorrent. As a consequence, the secondary program may encounter difficulties in getting students to accept the services of a resource room or vocational program. This should be obvious. Every effort to prevent embarrassment through stigmatization should be made.

The emotional disorders of mildly handicapped students will cause problems for the program. Emotional outbursts, fights, and other antisocial acts will call attention to the students, especially with the faculty. If unfortunate incidents become consistently associated with the class because special students are involved, then the principal and teachers may develop negative attitudes about the class. These same conflicts will cause some students to waste a lot of valuable class time in anger and frustration.

The relative freedom of secondary school is a problem for some students. The freedom to walk out of the building and not return can lead to habitual truancy. Tardiness, truancy, and the lack of discipline to use study periods fruitfully are factors associated with a complex of difficulties with teachers, the administration, and poor grades. Failure experiences over the years make school attendance aversive to students.

A potentially significant problem for some students is the attraction of the counterculture. Students who take drugs or use alcohol will not have good attendance and may be most noticeably "out of it" while in school. In addition to the impact such behavior has on learning, incidents of this type may become associated with this group of students and, subsequently, with the specialist who is their teacher and most notable advocate.

***Institutional and bureaucratic inflexibility.*** An irritating source of complications arises from the sphere of institutional policies and procedures. Many regulations interfere with the program. Some requirements of the state or local school board are impossible to change, but some can be altered. Building regulations established by the principal are frequently subject to change. Part of the problem for any new program is that newness creates change in the system, and a smooth functioning system resists change. Some of the factors or variables in this category are:

1. Specific course requirements interfere with programs that might be necessary for some students to survive.
2. Accommodatory and compensatory approaches will not be fully understood and may be resisted.
3. The curricular opportunities are restricted for low-achieving students.

4. Special education will be isolated or unattached at the secondary level where teachers and their subjects are commonly identified with departments.
5. Financial support will be partly discretionary (by the principal) and in competition with other areas. Some departments will have a line budget; special education may not.
6. Competency tests and other requirements for a diploma may be rigidly enforced without allowances for specific learning disabilities, even though the student may possess the knowledge to pass the tests.
7. Informal sources of power within the faculty may influence rejection of the program and noncooperation.

*Faculty attitudes.* Next in importance to the principal's attitude about the program are certainly those of the faculty. The teacher of mildly handicapped students should do everything possible to earn the respect and cooperation of the faculty. Some of the most significant considerations are as follows:

1. Many secondary teachers have negative attitudes toward "slow learners"; this group of students will be known to teachers as inefficient learners and perhaps tagged as "dummies," unmotivated, and lazy. The bias and the stereotype will interfere with many plans of the specialist.
2. Any attempts to secure assistance, cooperation, and deviation from standard operating procedures may cause some teachers to feel that their work loads will be unnecessarily increased with students for whom they feel little respect.
3. Individualization is foreign to the secondary school in most regular classes. The teachers are not trained for it, do not understand it, and will have great difficulty in making the transition because the class periods are less than an hour in length and the teachers will find it difficult to make special accommodations for individuals under these circumstances.
4. Any activity that detracts from class time or interferes with the routine will be resisted.

**The special program.** Although all of the problems listed above have an impact on the resource room, there are certain complications that are endemic to the program itself. One major problem was identified above; the special education program will be a "floater" in a system that has clearly defined departments. The special education program does not belong anywhere and is yet too small to exist by itself. Additionally, in the pecking order, other departments will have status as components of the predominant system. The special education program will be unequal, inferior, and lacking in the qualities that confer traditional respectability in the minds of many teachers.

The problems associated with a special program are:

1. In addition to the special program's isolation among a departmentalized system, there will be few other special educators with whom the teacher can associate. Special effort to make contact with counterparts in other schools is difficult.
2. There is also significant discontinuity in many school systems between levels. If there is no official link and planning between elementary schools and junior high, and between junior and senior high, the adjustment for students is problematic due to significant changes in curricula, scheduling, and routine.
3. Time is a factor affecting the mobility of the specialist. There just is not enough time to accomplish all that is desired. There will be many more per-

sonal problems of students brought to the teacher, and these can become emotionally abrasive and draining. To meet the needs of the students in class, to coordinate and to sell the program to others in the building, and to keep up with other aspects is taxing.

4. Lack of materials is a current, although temporary problem. As the field grows, acceptable materials will become available. For the present, the lack of them causes a great deal of time to be spent in making adaptations.

## SCOPE OF THE TEXT

This text has been written to assist practitioners in the development of secondary special education programs for the mildly handicapped. This is a challenging and complicated effort for several reasons. First, there is a general lack of agreement among authorities about the intended purpose of the secondary program. Some maintain that achievement of basic literacy skills is the primary objective, others advocate maximal mainstreaming, and some recommend a separate vocational track. Second, there is wide variation in the types of programs that are currently permissible in various states, due to different formulas for funding special programs, different certification requirements of teachers, and other legal or regulatory peculiarities. Finally, the operational criteria for identification of adolescents as mildly handicapped and the possible diversity of this population of exceptional students clearly indicate that a variety of special educational arrangements should be considered, but there is little certainty about the validity of specific approaches for populations of exceptional learners or for individuals.

Nonetheless, the reality is that secondary students with mild handicaps will be served in many settings in a variety of ways. If the special educator is required to select a particular approach or has the freedom to choose, there are certain commonalities about the education of mildly handicapped that may be recommended. The following chapters are presented as a systematic approach to comprehensive programming for mildly handicapped adolescents.

## SUMMARY

This chapter has been an overview of many issues in secondary education and special education of mildly handicapped students. The point was made through review of the historical record that adolescence is a relatively recent creation of society brought about by economic factors in the postindustrialized nation. The problems experienced by young persons have been similar throughout several generations although they may be more keenly observed today because the high school is the primary institution responsible for the socialization of teenagers. Similarly, the problems of high schools are only different today because of a need to be responsive to students in a more complex, technological society. Schools have always been affected by pressures of the times and demands to respond to many needs. The greatest problem of schools today is the same as it was at the turn of the century—the need to provide for an extremely diverse student population. One small segment of that large group of students is made up of the mildly handicapped: the mildly retarded, the learning disabled, and the emotionally disturbed.

It was noted that the mildly handicapped may be served in a variety of settings at the secondary level, a circumstance created by trends toward generic certification of teachers in some states, categorical certification in others, and a generally lower level of program development for this population of students in secondary schools. In spite of these complexities, it was noted also that sufficient commonalities exist to make recommendations that have wide application to the education of mildly handicapped adolescents despite the setting, the size of the school, or the organizational arrangement. The common models for classification of instruction are the compensatory, the remedial, and the vocational. However, these apparently exclusive approaches have common ends if not processes. Each should be based on curricular aspects, either in the regular curriculum or in the special education program, which account for the personal development, interpersonal relationships, and cognitive training of mildly handicapped students. It was noted that the purpose of the text was to assist the secondary special educator to develop a comprehensive program.

Programming must be based on the unique needs of adolescents, reflect the differences between elementary and secondary schools, account for the disabilities of mildly handicapped students, and be rationally tied to objectives of postsecondary adjustment. There are many practices and ideas that might be implemented in a secondary special education program, but they should be tested for reasonableness before they are used. Programs that ignore the developmental tasks of adolescence and the learning characteristics of mildly handicapped adolescents, and that simply extend the typical resource room of the elementary school, will not serve students well.

## REFERENCES AND READINGS

Elkind, D. *Children and adolescents.* New York: Oxford University Press, 1970.

Hallahan, D. P., & Kauffman, J. M. Research relevant to the education of distractible and hyperactive children. In W. M. Cruickshank & D. P. Hallahan (Eds.), *Perceptual and learning disabilities in children* (Vol. 2: *Research and theory*). Syracuse, N.Y.: Syracuse University Press, 1975.

Inhelder, B., & Piaget, J. *The growth of logical thinking from childhood to adolescence.* New York: Basic Books, 1958.

Kett, J. F. *Rites of passage.* New York: Basic Books, 1977.

Kolstoe, O. P. *Mental retardation.* New York: Holt, Rinehart & Winston, 1972.

Marsh, G. E., II, Gearheart, C. K., & Gearheart, B. R. *The learning disabled adolescent: Program alternatives in the secondary school.* St. Louis: Mosby, 1978.

Moos, R. H. *Evaluating educational environments.* San Francisco: Jossey-Bass, 1979.

Nuthall, G., & Snook, I. Contemporary models of teaching. In M. W. Travers (Ed.), *Second handbook of research on teaching.* Chicago: Rand McNally, 1973.

U.S. Office of Education. *Estimated number of handicapped children in the United States, 1974-75.* Washington, D.C.: Bureau of Education for the Handicapped, 1975.

Chapter 2

# MILDLY HANDICAPPED ADOLESCENTS

Effective programming for mildly handicapped adolescents results from sound teaching practices that follow a relevant curriculum of study. The curricular components of the secondary program should be based on the needs (developmental tasks of adolescence) of mildly handicapped adolescents. The curriculum would account for the learning styles and differences of students, which are extremely important considerations with regard to handicapping conditions; it would address the needs of students along a continuum toward maximal competencies in personal, interpersonal, and cognitive functioning, areas identified in Chapter 1. Curriculum development for mildly handicapped students may focus on a complete, isolated curriculum for self-contained programs or it may be a hybrid of available components in the regular and special curricula, including the general and vocational curricula of the school. Programs that are developed specifically for a categorical group, such as the learning disabled or mentally retarded, may focus on specific types of curricular concerns deemed appropriate for the student population under consideration.

## Curriculum considerations in special education models

As indicated in Chapter 1, there are three general models used by schools in secondary programs to provide special education to mildly handicapped students—compensatory, remedial, and vocational. The personal, interpersonal, and cognitive competencies for mildly handicapped students would be developed at the school level and might include a variety of existing recommendations of authorities and commercially available materials. To a certain extent, the general model used by a school dictates the aspects of the curriculum to be included in the special education program; the types of models may be conceptualized as follows.

**Compensatory model.** The major goals and competencies in the personal and interpersonal components of the curriculum are primarily the responsibility of the special educator, although support from the school counselor and peer counselors is expected. Cognitive competencies in general and special education classes are shared by the special educator and mainstream teachers.

**Remedial model.** Most remedial programs have a narrow focus on reading and may include remediation of arithmetic disorders and written expressive disorders. As a result, the concerns of personal and interpersonal development and many other cognitive competencies are left entirely to the mainstream teachers. As described later, the concept of direct, remedial instruction advocated by some authorities specifically excludes any attention to problems of personal adjustment, interpersonal relationships, affective education, and assistance with functioning in the mainstream class. The role of the remedial specialist is conceived as being mainly concerned with reaching functional literacy objectives.

**Vocational model.** The variety of vocational approaches to education of mildly handicapped adolescents are so plentiful that numerous plans for including personal, interpersonal, and cognitive goals and competencies exist. For example, work-study programs place the major responsibility for education in all three areas on the special education staff. Programs that emphasize integration of students in regular vocational courses provide direct services in personal and interpersonal growth in the special education class, but educational goals and teaching activities in the cognitive area are shared with vocational educators.

## Curricular planning

The task of the local district and special educators is to identify goals that address the major areas of the curriculum under the headings of personal, interpersonal, and cognitive development and locate courses in the general and special curricula that can include them. The development of the curriculum would adhere to the following general steps:

1. Selection of general goals
2. Assignation of goals to regular and special education areas in accordance with the type of model (compensatory, remedial, or vocational) and type of delivery system (self-contained, resource room, etc.)
3. Development of functional curriculum sequences for mildly handicapped, respecting their needs and learning characteristics
4. Development of logical instructional procedures

In order for a curriculum to be developed and for instructional activities to emerge that relate to the needs of adolescents who are mildly handicapped, it is necessary to investigate thoroughly the characteristics of adolescents and the characteristics and needs of *handicapped* adolescents.

## ADOLESCENCE

Adolescence is a period of human development in which a transition is made from childhood to maturity. It is a time during which the individual experiences sexual maturation and must attempt to gain emotional and economic independence from parents. Emancipation from the primary family unit is a major task that must be accomplished before it is possible for one to fully assume adult roles. A variety of social, psychological, and emotional changes accompany the physiological transformation of the child. Although biological factors account for glandular changes in the body of the adolescent, it is the interaction of biological factors with cultural imperatives that is most important in the conceptualization of adolescence.

Emerging intellectual, sexual, social, emotional, and physical characteristics interplay with the social environment of the culture, which determines patterns of acceptable behavior, defines opportunities, and dictates the consequences of nonacceptance or maladjustment. Therefore the society into which one is born is of utmost importance because it is within this context that standards are established, values are attached to human characteristics, and patterns of life are shaped.

In primitive and less complex societies, the child who enters adolescence is secure in the knowledge that the onset of puberty will immediately assure him or her the status of adulthood. The role of the adult is clearly defined, responsibilities are known, and society will readily embrace the *new* man or woman who may comfortably adhere to the prescriptions of social roles. It is true that the demands of any culture may tax the innate abilities of certain individuals to adjust to cultural imperatives. A given complex of physical anomalies or behavioral deviations may complicate one's life. In fact, the record of history stands as testimony to the efforts of mankind to adjust to the physical environment and cultural demands. But it was not until the development of modern Western societies that adolescence per se became an especially complicated state of development.

Unfortunately, the nature of Western societies causes the transition from puberty to adulthood to be prolonged and creates a need for an artificial subculture because persons who are not children are prevented from becoming adults. A natural antipathy develops between adolescents and adults as the attempts to break childhood ties are stifled by numerous restrictions. Because of rejection by the adult world, the adolescent experiences stress and anxiety from conflict with established authority. Having the sexual and intellectual capabilities of adults but unable to gain financial independence or to develop mature sexual relationships, the adolescent must rely on the peer group for security, recognition, and esteem.

### The major tasks of adolescence

As a major stage in human development, the adolescent period is characterized by several major developmental tasks, which have been identified by authorities and which may be summarized as follows (Erikson, 1950; Havighurst, 1951):

1. Development of a sense of identity to include a sense of sexuality
2. Development of self-assurance and confidence in social interaction
3. Acceptance of adjustment to bodily changes
4. Understanding of personal weaknesses and strengths
5. Attachment of sexual interests to persons outside the family unit and development of relationships with peers
6. Attainment of emotional independence
7. Development of moral and social maturity
8. Definition of personal interests and talents
9. Consideration of vocational interests
10. Completion of formal education and exploration of a suitable occupation
11. Preparation for marriage, parenting, and mature social interaction
12. Inculcation of societal values

Examination of the developmental tasks adapted from the classic works of the 1950s reveals a remarkable similarity to tasks that confront the adolescent today. Perhaps the major change in the American culture that complicates adolescence some 30 years hence is the instability of early adulthood. The feminist movement, cohabitation as an alternative to marriage, and other dramatic changes in the cultural fabric increase the potential for turmoil because role models are less well defined, career choices are not clear-cut, and there is generally more indecisiveness about the future in a changing society.

## THEORIES OF ADOLESCENCE

A number of theories have been developed to explain adolescence. There is agreement that adolescence is a period of significant physiological transformation due to an alteration in glandular activity that causes a change in metabolism, stimulates growth, and brings about the development of secondary sexual characteristics and sexual drives. Adolescence is typified biologically by growth and a change in bodily proportions and psychologically by cognitive and emotional changes. The apparent changes of adolescence can be categorized as (1) glandular, (2) growth, (3) cognitive, (4) emotional, and (5) social. Adolescence is therefore generally regarded as a period of biological change marked by the onset of puberty. There is, however, considerable disagreement in psychological thought about this period of development.

### An evolutionary view

Hall (1904) is recognized as the first psychologist to undertake a scientific investigation of adolescence by employing the theory of Darwin. He proposed that each individual passes through stages of development that recapitulate the developmental stages of the human race. Each stage of individual development (infancy, childhood, etc.) is likened to stages in the long evolution of the race to its present state of civilization—the infant is compared to a primitive animal; and, ultimately, the adolescent represents the transition from a savage to a civilized human being. Because the transition from savagery to civilization was regarded as a period of oscillation between base pursuits and lofty human ideals, so also is the period of adolescence depicted as a time of "storm and stress." Although Hall's speculations are not accepted today, the depiction of storm and stress remains a popular characterization of adolescence in Western society.

## Psychoanalytic theories

Adolescence was viewed by Sigmund Freud as a period of turbulence, or storm and stress, but for different reasons than those of Hall. According to Freud's theory, the greatest adjustment problem of the adolescent is to accommodate to the reemergence of suppressed sexual instincts initially arrested by resolution of the Oedipal complex. Glandular activity stirs primitive instincts that must be once again resolved. It is normal for the adolescent to be troubled, aggressive, uncertain, and to have conflict with adults because of the turmoil over sexual instincts and the need to seek emancipation from adults. Freud viewed this pattern of behavior as genetically determined and little influenced by the environment. Sexual drives become displaced to appropriate persons outside the family because of the repression of incestuous feelings. Anna Freud extended the views of her father by emphasizing that sexual drives stimulate aggression and fantasies in reaction to the feelings of guilt and anxiety caused by them.

The neopsychoanalytic view of Erikson (1950, 1968) recognizes the importance of one's culture in addition to sexual drives. According to this view, the individual must develop a sense of ego identification and autonomy that permits social relationships with others. The adolescent must also accept a system of values, learn to engage in intimate relationships with others, and develop a sense of identity that can relate meaningfully to the world.

## Field theory

In field theory, the life space of the individual is the important psychological dimension (Lewin, 1951). The psychological, biological, and social forces of the environment affect the life space so that the individual is gradually able to more easily understand reality and to engage in mature social interaction. Vacillation between adult and childhood groups disturbs the life space, which explains the turmoil created by conflict between old and emerging ideals and value systems. The nature of such conflicts as they alter the external and internal life space of an individual is, in essence, the nature of adolescence according to this theory.

## Cross-cultural view

Mead (1928) observed that the Samoan culture evidenced little difficulty in transition from childhood to adulthood. Physiological changes, sexual identity, and adjustment to the demands of adult roles are universal characteristics of adolescence; however, it is not necessarily true that conflict or "storm and stress" of adolescence proposed by other theorists is a universal trait.

The influences of a particular culture dictate the nature of sexual roles and the status of individuals; mores define and shape acceptable behavior. The socialization process from childhood through adolescence can be placid or turbulent depending on cultural influences.

## Socialization

A pragmatic view of adolescence has been proposed by Havighurst (1951), who stresses the importance of developmental tasks as a process of socialization necessary for becoming an adult. A synthesis of these tasks was listed previously in this chapter. There is considerable merit to this viewpoint because the tasks defined are clearly necessary for adjustment, they can be ordered, and they can be used as a rough yardstick for developmental comparisons. We have relied on them heavily for these reasons. Although it may be interesting to know that there are various explanations for the emergence of adolescence, it is extremely useful to know the major developmental tasks of the adolescent on which it is possible to erect educational plans that may facilitate the attainment of goals related to each major task.

These viewpoints represent the major approaches to adolescence, although other minor views (e.g., social learning theory) are helpful in the study and interpretation of adolescent behavior. A more complete discussion of these minor elements may be found in another volume (Marsh et al., 1978). Two other concepts deserve consideration although they are not recognized as major theories of adolescence. These are the adolescent subculture and the cognitive theory.

## The adolescent subculture

Coleman (1971) portrays the relationships of peers as detrimental to major societal goals for adolescents. The values of students differ greatly from those established by society for the schools because of the significant impact of peer influence, which elevates athletic prowess, popularity, and attractive physical attributes to higher status than academic pursuits. The stress on conformity in the peer group causes students to mask abilities praised by teachers, and energies of young men and women are channeled into activities that detract from the process of making the transition to adulthood.

Although the assertions of Coleman may be true, in fairness to the adolescent it is quite clear that industrialized and technological Western societies create the circumstances that propagate the subculture and cause it to flourish. If adolescents are barred from rapid and unrestricted achievement of adult status, then the group that attracts, supports, and befriends them will be comprised of peers. Although the values of the peer group may seem immature and shallow to many adults, positive gains can be acquired through interaction with it.

The peer group provides the adolescent with a frame of reference, emotional support, and social feedback. Bodily changes, replete with pimples and motor awkwardness, are shared with others and implicitly understood with varying degrees of sympathy. Acceptance provides some security, and the social activities of the peer group provide valuable experiences that will be applicable to later adult social roles. Unfortunately, the dominant peer group or clique in a social setting of a particular school will not tolerate too much deviance in terms of "acceptable" behaviors, dress, appearance, and rituals. Students in a school may be cruelly rejected and ridiculed for many reasons, including unattractiveness, variant social or personality characteristics, and social class of the family. This rejection may have long-term consequences for the adolescent social pariah.

## Cognitive structures of adolescence

Another useful approach in the study and appreciation of adolescent development is the cognitive theory of Piaget. According to Piagetian theory (Ausubel and Ausubel, 1971; Elkind, 1975; Inhelder & Piaget, 1958), the adolescent becomes capable of attaining the highest level of cognitive development, which is *formal operational* thought. The adolescent gradually becomes able to use a combination of facts (combinatorial thinking) and a refined system of symbolism, both of which reflect the theoretical structures of formal operational thought. The cognitive structures of one who performs at this level permit indulgence in flights of mental fantasy, indulgence in hypothetical problems, the ability to recognize many different viewpoints and abstract complexities of a variety of issues, and freedom from the concrete world of the child. The emergency of formal thought parallels the development of other mental structures relating to moral concepts and a generally more mature view of the world and social interactions. Elkind stresses the importance of cognitive development in the adolescent by asserting that the adolescent is able to invent ideal (conceptually) situations, which leads to self-dissatisfaction as one compares one's self with the invented ideal. Conflict with adults and disillusionment with the world result from comparison of reality with pure, abstract idealism. The increasing development of adolescents toward the formal operational period provides a theoretical explanation for the ability to handle a more abstract curriculum, prepare for responsible adult roles, and achieve the highest levels of concept attainment.

• • •

The taxonomy of approaches to the investigation of adolescence presented above includes most of the major influential theories. The student is directed to original sources for a more complete examination of theoretical formulations. For our purposes in this volume we find the socialization theory to be the most useful and have adapted the *developmental tasks* of Havighurst and augmented them with the work of Erikson as a means of conceptualizing the personal-social achievements that bring the child to the brink of adulthood. This sequence of tasks is also useful to the school and the resource teacher as a form of criterion reference in marking the milestones of development, understanding the needs of the adolescent, and defining educational responses to those needs. Combining this information with the characteristics of mildly handicapped adolescents completes the necessary process for developing a framework for educational planning. Rather than merely extending the elementary school resource room, the school can effectively martial its resources to serve this population of students according to their characteristics.

Programmatically it is possible to plan in accordance with the broad range of behavioral characteristics, but the practitioner is cautioned not to accept characteristics of adolescents or handicapped students literally. There are wide individual differences, and no student will fit the "typical" pattern. Perhaps the best approach to planning is to compile as much relevant educational and personal data as possible for each individual student. Although the definition and diagnosis of handicaps are rooted in medical and statistical (psychological) models, the educational effort must focus on cognitive, social, emotional, and school-related (ecological) variables impinging on the student. A systems view of the secondary school from the adolescent's perspective leads to the conclusion that a program must encompass many facets, not just remediation of reading and arithmetic. Therefore the characteristics of the group of mildly handicapped adolescents dictate the general parameters of the special program, while adherence to an educational scheme incorporating regard for idiosyncratic variables of each student will assure the ultimate benefit of special education.

## The modern social context of the adolescent

A rather sterile discussion of the theories of adolescence, characteristics of the adolescent, and the need for program development is meaningless without consideration of the total social perspective wherein all pieces fit and interact. It is truly impossible to isolate a student or a student's learning problem and treat an underlying disorder without consideration of the many influences surrounding the learner.

In general and special education, we have been guilty of ignoring the broad social arena of the learner and the ecological factors of the classroom. We have investigated instructional methods and curriculum materials in a vacuum with little attention to the culture of the learner. There is indeed a culture. There is a youth culture, a culture of peers, and a classroom culture. Many teachers are unaware of these myriad influences and the impact they have on learning. We must investigate the interaction between students and between students and teachers in the learning environment rather than searching for "something" that works in the form of a kit or new methodology.

We must consider the society in which the adolescent lives. We all live in that society, but there are differences in the lives of adolescents that are unknown to the adult who passed through childhood in another age. The youth culture is much different than a decade ago and certainly greatly transformed since the 1940s and 1950s when many of today's teachers and educational leaders were adolescents.

Today's youth are faced with problems of major importance never before confronting a generation entering adulthood. It is not that other generations did not face serious problems, it is that the problems of today seem to be so many and so different. There are many issues in the society at large and within the youth culture that must be considered. Our efforts to teach will be less successful if we are alienated from the youth culture and do not empathize with the conflicts of youths. We provide the following list of social issues to gain perspective and to identify factors that might influence the nature and scope of the resource room in a high school. To some extent, these issues affect all of us in our daily lives.

1. *Changing adult roles.* The most immediate effects of changing social patterns in our society are evident in the culture of young adults. The effects drift down as cultural changes of our time, leaving us with few traditions and an uncertain future. There are no clearly defined sexual roles anymore, and this is perplexing to adults and youth. Young adults cohabit rather than marry, children are unwanted, and the "singles' scene" appears to be an experiment to find new roles. As the young adult experiments within the changing social structure, the adolescent looks on with no clear-cut role models and with uncertainty.

2. *Sexual relations.* The changing sexual mores of the adult society have reached the adolescent culture. There are several million teenagers who have sexual intercourse each year, and abortions, miscarriages, births, and venereal disease among unmarried adolescents are increasing dramatically. All of this occurs while many schools continue to debate the need and extent of sex education.

3. *Anti-intellectualism.* The youth culture of today is quite different from preceding generations, not only because young people mature more rapidly and are taller and heavier, but because they are more sophisticated as a result of the tremendous bombardment of information and frank knowledge about subjects that would have once been taboo. The classroom cannot match the appeal of the media, which entertain students. Youth are more interested in social prestige than learning, and there is a general disdain for academics.

4. *Environment.* Industrialization and technology have enabled mankind to reach a level of achievement and a standard of living never before known. Just as rapidly, the society may deteriorate because of pollution and the scarcity of energy. The economic factors associated with the environment may lead to higher levels of unemployment, increased prices of goods and services, and

economic turbulence. Inflation and recession pose a constant threat.

5. *Alienation and crime.* Depression and suicide have increased dramatically among the young. Suicide is the third leading cause of death among adolescents. There has been a significant increase in juvenile delinquency, violence in schools, vandalism, crimes against persons, drug use, and a variety of other maladies.

6. *Back to basics.* There has been a conflict for control of the schools caused by the definition of student rights, the demand for power by teachers' unions, and the increasing control of the federal government. The school has become, in many places, an adverse environment administered with an eye to legal guidelines. In the midst of this turmoil has come the cry for a return to accountability in terms of student achievement. There will be a renewed emphasis on academic competition with a lessening concern for affective development. Secondary students will likely find this trend even more unpalatable as they anxiously face the future with trepidation and a need for personal and social guidance and support.

Bloom (1978, p. 574) depicts our schools as rather lonely places for students. Competition for grades and teacher attention is emphasized. He states, "Our teachers devote so much time to controlling, teaching, and judging students, that our students are given little opportunity for either independence or the assumption of responsibilities for each other." Any such effects are only magnified for the mildly handicapped adolescent. Therefore the importance of other factors in the education of mildly handicapped students must be stressed in addition to concern for remediation of academic weaknesses.

The needs of mildly handicapped adolescents must first be identified as the needs of any adolescent. Subsequently, the additional problems of being a learning disabled, mentally retarded, or emotionally disturbed student must be accounted for because the outgrowth of handicapping conditions is translated into the social arena of students; that is, in interpersonal relationships with parents, peers, and teachers and later with employers. Perhaps we seem to be asking too much of the specialist, who might reasonably be expected to have enough to do by providing assistance directed at learning problems; however, when one considers the social forces impinging on the handicapped adolescent, remediation is just not enough.

## LEARNING DISABILITIES
### Definition

Although there has been considerable controversy over the definition of learning disabilities because of its lack of specificity, and although many authorities continue the important debate over alternatives and variations, there is little practical need to consider the scope of the controversy or reiterate discussions of semantical and taxonomical confusion in this volume. There is an official definition that has been established through federal regulations issuing from P.L. 94-142. Regardless of its inherent weakness, it is the definition affecting most public school programs. The definition is as follows:

"Specific learning disability" means a disorder in one or more of the basic psychological processes involved in understanding or in using language, spoken or written, which may manifest itself in an imperfect ability to listen, think, speak, read, write, spell, or to do mathematical calculations. The term includes such conditions as perceptual handicaps, brain injury, minimal brain dysfunction, dyslexia, and developmental aphasia. The term does not include children who have learning problems which are primarily the result of visual, hearing, or motor handicaps, or mental retardation, of emotional disturbance, or of environmental, cultural, or economic disadvantage. [Section 121a.5, *Federal Register*, August 23, 1977.]

The difficulty with the preceding definition is that as it is being employed at the local district level, there arise some very real, practical problems. The school district cannot engage in heuristic endeavors to discover the nature of learning disabilities. This is the role of scholars and research investigators. On the firing line it is necessary to develop programs for LD students, employ teachers, order materials and equipment, and make other pragmatic decisions that are accountable in terms of prevailing laws and regulations. It is necessary to identify, assess, and classify students as learning disabled. Federal and state guidelines pertaining to these matters are typically not very useful to school officials who require more specificity; and there is little guidance to be found in the pages of professional texts, which either skirt the issue of specificity in assessment and classification or unfold theoretical discourses that have the same effect.

Schools can be excused for their confusion, and it is little wonder, as Bryan and Bryan (1978, p. 24) have noted, that "school districts are increasingly defining children as learning disabled if the children manifest any signs whatever of underachievement in academic subject areas, whether or not the individual has potential for learning." Evidence of this phenomenon can be found in one of the few secondary programs of the CSDC network of model programs reported by Zigmond (1978), which enrolls students with IQ scores as low as 80 as well as those who have trouble "making it" in the regular curriculum. Whether or not the term "learning disabilities" should be expanded to encompass the traditional categories of mental retardation and emotional disturbance, as some have proposed (Hallahan & Kauffman, 1975), is an important issue to be debated in a different forum than the public school classroom. For the present, we agree with Kirk (1976, p. 258), who states:

. . . Indeed all exceptional children—the deaf, the blind, and others—have learning problems. But these children are not children with a *specific learning disability*, that is, a learning disability in one area when all other functions are intact. Many fail to heed this major criterion of a learning disability: namely, major discrepancies between the deficit area (or disability) and other areas (or abilities).

How one defines the condition of learning disabilities in secondary students and what characteristics are attributed to them have important implications for the type of services that will be designed. Responsible officials in local schools should approach the secondary program conservatively and restrict the number of students served in this category in junior and senior high schools.

## An operational approach

In order to restrict the number of students classified as learning disabled at the secondary level the school will need to rely on some index of identifying characteristics that is operationally defined. We certainly agree with Hammill (1978), who maintains that school administrators cannot wait until there is full resolution of definitional questions.

It would seem that there is little support for the use of process tests, especially at the secondary level, in the identification of LD students. The constructs are suspect, the tests are unreliable, and very few instruments can be considered appropriate for older students. Although this may be true, schools will likely be required to include a variety of such measures in the assessment process because of the need to support reasons for classification of students and the requirement for multifactored assessment.

In spite of the controversy over the use of norm-referenced tests (and we heartily support the use of criterion-referenced tests and ecological assessment), *the most defensible position relating to the key concept of a major discrepancy between a deficit area and other areas rests on, as a minimum requirement, statistical proof of the discrepancy.*

School districts in many states should be able to introduce this element into the identification and assessment (diagnostic) process because of the latitude in existing procedures promulgated by the states. Some states only institute the federal regulation (there is certainly a great deal of latitude in that definition), while others attempt to clarify the definition through inclusion of cut-off points or scores from various psychoeducational tests. Evidence of a disparity between a deficit area and other areas (abilities) should be determined by means of calculating statistically significant differences between the deficit area and abilities on the basis of obtained scores with established confidence levels.

If schools are required to use psychoeducational tests in the process of classification then they should also adhere to the conventions of assessment and principles of standardization; namely, (1) tests should be selected for their appropriateness, (2) the limitations of the instruments should be recognized, (3) statistical properties should be appreciated, and (4) small deviations that are not statistically significant should not be regarded as important because deviations of such magnitude can occur by chance.

Unless statistically significant differences can be found, further consideration of the student as a candidate for LD programming should not be pursued. It is true that this will not totally resolve the problem of trying to separate the learning disabled from among the large group of low achievers and educationally retarded students (i.e., the poorly instructed, poorly motivated, etc.); but at least it should abate the trend to simply label many or all students who fail to keep pace with the school curriculum or who may, in the least scientific sense, be said to have trouble "making it" in school.

**Specific characteristics**

Obviously, if the definitional problems have led to confusion then it follows that the characteristics of a poorly defined group will also be muddled. Perhaps it is superfluous to mention that there has been a myriad of characteristics associated with the learning disabled population. However, it is precisely because of the numerous characteristics perceived by various professional groups that ultimately there was the recognition of a taxonomy and a name for children with inexplicable learning difficulties. Subsequently, the characteristics of LD children have been repeatedly considered in every major volume devoted to the subject. Some of the most common characteristics have been attention and memory disorders, perceptual-motor disturbances, awkwardness in motor coordination, emotional disorders, hyperactivity, thinking disorders, disorders of language, abnormal neurological signs, and, of course, learning disabilities related to academic subjects and fundamental literacy skills.

Additionally, it may be said that two major points of view or trends of thought are present concerning the characteristics and the nature of the LD adolescent, which are based on sparse research and authoritative opinion (Marsh et al., 1978, p. 20) and can be summarized as follows:

1. One major point of view is that many adolescents seem to overcome learning disabilities as a result of maturation of the central nervous system.
2. A second major point of view is that learning disabled adolescents exhibit vestigial remains of characteristics recognized in childhood that can be attributed to central nervous system damage or dysfunction that does not appreciably improve.

There is also evidence, or at least the opinion of some authorities, that there are characteristics unique to the LD adolescent which, in most instances, seem to appear due to an interaction between the condition of learning disabilities and the maturational processes of pubescence. These unique characteristics are listed here, although a more complete discussion of them and their sources will be found in reference to other handicapping conditions.

1. Poor self-concept
2. Inadequate social skill
3. Unstable family relations
4. Peer dependence
5. Physiological disorders
6. Greater anxiety, depressions, and mood swings than peers
7. Attraction to the counterculture (delinquency, drug and alcohol addiction)
8. Faulty social feedback mechanism
9. Uneven development of cognitive skills
10. Inferior conceptual ability
11. Aggressive tendencies
12. Unrealistic career and life goals

We do not necessarily support or dispute these so-called characteristics of the LD adolescent but report them because some investigators have listed them as conclusions from research data or because they appear with regularity as manifestations of students who have been classified as learning disabled. The reader is cautioned that any constellation of characteristics related to learning disabilities does not necessarily represent *true* characteristics, the characteristics are not necessarily group characteristics, and they may be best examined and authenticated on a student-by-student basis. The existence of the characteristics in the literature, however, gives impetus to the development of broad programmatic planning because of the belief that many of these characteristics are *associated* with LD adolescents as a result of environmental stress rather than because they are true correlates of learning disabilities. For the most part, these characteristics are best considered within an ecological framework and must be incorporated along with the traditional correlates of learning disabilities because of the enhanced significance of the social environment of the adolescent.

## EDUCABLE MENTAL RETARDATION
### Definition

According to federal guidelines the definition of mental retardation is "significantly subaverage general intellectual functioning which exists concurrently with deficits in adaptive behavior and is manifested during the developmental period, which adversely affects the child's educational performance" (Section 124a.5, *Federal Register*, August 23, 1977). This is, of course, a variation of the definition of the American Association on Mental Deficiency (AAMD) reported by Grossman (1977). It is within the area of mental retardation that definitional problems caused much of the litigation that ultimately affected the entire field of special education. Among the issues are labeling students, due process, multifactored assessment, the right to fair classification, and the right to treatment. At the heart of the controversy was the underlying concern about identification and placement of mentally retarded pupils on the basis of a single IQ score. To offset the effects of a single score in cases of potential misclassification, the AAMD lowered the IQ score on standard deviation to below 70 on an individualized intelligence test and included measures of adaptive behavior to provide additional data to assure that candidates are probably functioning within the range of mental retardation. Because of the emphasis on multifactored assessment by a multidisciplinary team, no mention is made in assessment guidelines about a cut-off score for diagnosis of mental retardation. Consequently, it is certain that many students in the range of 70 to 85 are consistently identified as mentally retarded. The use of adaptive measures, which are frequently highly correlated with intelligence measures in some samples, has not clarified identification but has added a complicating factor.

In spite of a tradition of research, far exceeding that of learning disabilities or emotional disturbance in American education, the definition of mental retardation is unclear, classification systems are controversial, and professional reluctance to stigmatize students with an undesirable label leads to as much consternation for practitioners as in the case of learning disabilities. Other alternatives to the IQ-centered approach have not been vigorously supported by professional groups, although superior information might be gained not only for diagnosis and classification, but also for programming. Systems that emphasize behavioral information and multiple-setting ecological assessment procedures have been confusing. An example of an alternative approach is that of Kolstoe (1972), who originally proposed the use of a Piagetian framework that would have the benefit of centering on what students *can* do rather than how they deviate.

Nonetheless, most accepted assessment procedures systematized in school-based programs tried to follow general guidelines that require the use of an IQ measure, a measure of adaptive behavior, and other information. Clearly the factor that many critics find to be most unsatisfactory is heavily relied upon, namely, an IQ score. As a result, there is considerable variation in the students that may be identified as EMR. In some settings they will be regarded as learning disabled and if undesirable behavior is observed, they may be regarded as emotionally disturbed. Considerable overlap may occur.

## Characteristics

Numerous writers have attributed various characteristics to the mentally retarded. Kolstoe (1972, pp. 105-106) has succinctly summarized learning characteristics; these are adapted as follows:

1. Learning is mental age specific.
2. Initial learning is haphazard but learning rate is similar to that of nonhandicapped students after the initial learning problem is resolved.
3. The learning style is concrete.
4. Learning is subject to the same interferences as with nonhandicapped learners.
5. Transfer of learning occurs but it is accomplished on the basis of identical elements rather than principles.
6. Incidental learning of the retarded is similar to that of nonhandicapped students.
7. The learning style of older students is likely to be characterized by failure-avoidance, that is, a reluctance to attempt new learning because of a history of failure.
8. Social inadequacy is a pervasive corollary.

The most common characteristics reported by writers, and central to those listed above, relate to memory, attention, and conditions of learning. The contention is that most mentally retarded students will have a significant academic deficiency, compared with normal age peers, with the expectation that ultimate levels of academic achievement will fall somewhere between second and sixth grade levels. The inability to deal with increasingly complex concepts and abstractions, coupled with a lower level of basic skill achievement, diminishes the potential for successful performance in many secondary classes, which are steeped in comprehensive reading assignments and demands on higher cognitive abilities. Those who advocate a noncategorical approach most vehemently, for example, Lilly (1979), would take issue with these assumptions. Their point is well taken, especially in view of the fact that citing such general characteristics may influence lowered expectations of students who might be more capable. In any event, it is certain that many students will not be able to benefit from the general school curriculum without considerable intervention and support, and others may find it totally unsatisfactory and may need highly unique special educational programming.

## EMOTIONAL DISTURBANCE
### Definition

It is common to find reference to children who are behaviorally disordered (BD), emotionally disturbed (ED), socially maladjusted, aggressive, acting out, and antisocial. The terms are used without any clear indication that similar groups are being described. The legal definition refers to *seriously* emotionally disturbed and is phrased as follows:

> Children . . . exhibiting one or more of the following characteristics over a long period of time and to a marked degree, which adversely affects educational performance: (A) An inability to learn which cannot be explained by intellectual, sensory, or health factors; (B) An inability to build or maintain satisfactory interpersonal relationships with peers and teachers; (C) Inappropriate types of behavior or feelings under normal circumstances; (D) A general pervasive mood of unhappiness or depression; or (E) A tendency to develop physical symptoms or fears associated with personal or school problems. [Section 121a.5, *Federal Register*, August 23, 1977.]

The term includes children who are schizophrenic or autistic. Children who are socially maladjusted, but not emotionally disturbed, are not included in this category.

As Bryan and Bryan (1979) indicate, there is probably no area of exceptionality more difficult to define and assess than this one. Whereas the LD category is based on deficient academic performance and the EMR category on a subaverage intelligence score, there is no parallel measure for behavior.

Students who might be considered to be mildly emotionally disturbed may have many of the characteristics associated with both the EMR and LD categories, especially since much of the symptomatology will be identical, such as hyperactivity, attentional deficits, and academic retardation. Likewise, because of the transient situational stress of adolescence, many students may develop symptoms of aggression, depression, and other disturbances, which might be clearly thought of as normal behavior for this period of development! This is a complicating factor that can be avoided if diagnosis is restricted to students who have displayed prolonged symptomatology since childhood. Many, if not most, mildly emotionally disturbed adolescents should be expected to attend and perform satisfactorily in regular classes. As in other instances, this must be determined on a student-by-student basis due to the wide range of behaviors that may be found and the variable levels of academic achievement necessary for success in mainstream classes.

## COMMONALITIES OF MILDLY HANDICAPPING CONDITIONS

Although his definition is restricted in practical utility, Lilly (1979, p. 102) has proposed a noncategorical definition of learning and behavior problems that encompasses the categories of mental retardation, learning disabilities, and behavior disorders but that he admits is lacking in precision. Lilly's definition is as follows.

A child with learning and behavior problems is a child (1) whose regular classroom performance, in terms of academic and/or social behavior, is perceived to be inadequate, by a teacher, parent, or the child himself; and (2) for whom a team consisting of professional educators and the child's parents determines that special education services are necessary to provide the child with appropriate educational opportunities.

Accordingly, the common characteristics of children with learning and behavior problems described by Lilly are that they are referred for special education services, they are determined to be eligible, and their educational needs can be met while contact with regular class peers is maintained.

As noted previously, others have advocated elimination of the distinction between the three categories, not necessarily because stigmatization would be eliminated or for the sake of parsimony, but because of the hypothesis that scrutiny of the *behavioral* characteristics of the three categories overlaps so much that the lack of variance reveals a single constituency with more similarity than difference. It is true that the behavioral characteristics of the three categories, especially at the elementary school level, do overlap; this is true along other dimensions such as achievement or instructional modes. It should not be surprising that such similarities would be found because of the imprecision of definitions and the fact that much research in the field uses in situ classes of students, which, although called LD or EMR, may have considerable variability in makeup. Any system that predominantly uses a single IQ cutoff score is likely to result in classification errors (Mercer & Snell, 1977).

It cannot be disputed that similarities between the groups exist along a behavioral dimension. However, if a shift to a qualitatively measured cognitive dimension is made, some differences are found that may have implications for secondary level programming. Notably, the distinction between the EMR and other groups may be made. Of course, reference here is to Piagetian stages and it is clear that mentally retarded subjects do not tend to move from one developmental stage to another as rapidly as others, they tend to fixate at certain stages, and they do not tend to enter formal operational thought, a stage characterized by hypothetical deductive reasoning and the ability for abstraction. There are dramatic differences between the cognitive skills of students at the secondary level due to the unfolding of natural maturational processes, which limits one group and not the other. The most complete evaluation of retarded subjects in a clinical setting is reported by Inhelder (1968), although others have begun to report similar findings indicating that mildly retarded subjects tend to fixate somewhere in the concrete operational stage.

If the distinctions between the categories are collapsed or eliminated because of perceived functional abilities, similarities in perceptual disorders, or commonalities in behavioral characteristics, the benefits to students in the educational setting may or may not be increased. It is certain, however, that regardless of the preferred emphasis on nomenclature and definitions, educators should not lose sight of the fact that differences exist between students and that some students, in spite of academic retardation, are cognitively capable of achieving in the most difficult courses of the general curriculum. Retreating to a system of classification by academic performance may mask differences between students on the basis of cognitive abilities; programs may become narrowly focused on low-level literacy goals for all students or on vocational programming circumscribed by limited objectives.

For the time being, the within-group unity of any of the three diagnostic categories is suspicious because of vague definitions, variation in identification and placement practices of practitioners, and overlapping characteristics. The commonalities of the groups include subaverage academic achievement, specific disorders of the basic skills, behavioral disorders, and other minor characteristics. The implications for programming are clear; namely, the diversity of the group is such that programs cannot be established based solely on commonalities and certainly not on the differences. If possible, a number of options should be available for mildly handicapped students to account for their unique needs as well as the variety of needs among the population identified for special education services.

Of particular concern to the secondary special educator and to planners who would attempt to separate mildly handicapped students on the basis of characteristics to more suitably match them with curricular elements, is the concept of thinking behavior, which can be defined as intelligence; it can be qualitatively described using Piagetian theory or quantitatively defined by intelligence measures. In learning situations teachers may be interested in determining which students are able to manage more complex problems or in teaching students to "think" more efficiently. In fact, this is an increasing area of interest to some learning disabilities authorities, who maintain that teaching techniques can be used to improve the general thinking behavior of adolescents. The theoretical aspects of this endeavor have not been subjected to much empirical investigation, but it is certain that some educators will employ teaching strategies in an effort to improve the cognitive efficiency of students. It should be decided (1) if there is any reasonable expectation that training in thinking strategies will actually benefit students and (2) if such training can be meaningfully integrated into curricula without significantly detracting from other teaching endeavors.

There is a danger that "games" and other activities thought to increase thinking efficiency will consume inordinate amounts of instructional time when the same principles could be applied to actual learning demands in content areas, a more practical purpose of cognitive modification. For example, Fraenkel (1973) recommends the use of strategies to improve thinking in the teaching of social studies content. The operations are observing, describing, developing concepts, differentiating and defining, hypothesizing, comparing and contrasting, generalizing, predicting, explaining, and offering alternatives. The operations of the latter part of the sequence are actually hypothetical or abstract processes included in *propositional thought* of Piagetian theory, which is classified as formal operations.

An efficient way to embrace the theories and approaches described by various writers (e.g., Fraenkel, 1973; Feldhusen & Treffinger, 1977; and Piagetian theory) is to use the factorial theory of Guilford (1959), which describes the *operations* of intellectual activity: evaluation, convergent thinking, divergent thinking, memory, and cognition; two of the *contents:* symbolic and semantic; and two *products:* transformations and implications. These "cells" of the Guilford model can be used to classify what may be regarded as abstract reasoning as well as the numerous terms that apply to abstract reasoning in the writings of educators, psychologists, and theorists.

Another simplified way of considering thinking behavior and looking for means of improving it is to utilize Bloom's (1956) taxonomy. If, for example, a student consistently demonstrates an inability to remember facts (which corresponds to the lowest level of Bloom's taxonomy in the cognitive domain) then it becomes obvious what kinds of instructional strategies should be employed as well as what the chances are that the student

**Table 2.** Determination of thinking behavior, based on Bloom's (1956) taxonomy

| Subdomain | Inquiries | Subdomain | Inquiries |
|---|---|---|---|
| Knowledge | Can the student recall or recognize specific elements in a content area? | Analysis | Can the student use divergent thinking? Can the student identify specific elements of a concept, process, theory, or idea, break them down into a hierarchy, and demonstrate the relations between elements? |
| Comprehension | Can the student accurately transform content into his or her own words? Can the student separate essential from unessential elements? Can the student make inferences about content that are not inherent in it, or is the student bound by concrete literal interpretation? | Synthesis | Can the student use convergent thinking? Given pieces, parts, and elements, can the student arrange and combine them into a pattern or structure? |
| Application | Can the student form and apply ideas, rules, and generalizations to practical problems in the curriculum? Can the student apply general principles and theories in practical problems? | Evaluation | Can the student use standards for making comparisons on the value of purposes, ideas, methods, and so forth? Can the student use a set of criteria to make judgments based on the merit or value of purposes, ideas, and methods? |

will succeed in the regular curriculum. Individual students will demonstrate varying abilities to process information in accordance with the taxonomy. EMR students may not be able to apply, analyze, synthesize, or evaluate as a consequence of deficient internal cognitive structures, which are necessary for envisaging all possible relations and using logical analysis to manipulate ideas in the process of abstract thinking. An informal method of qualitatively determining thinking behavior of a student would be to use the information in Table 2, which is based on Bloom's taxonomy.

Making determinations about the ability of students to think, or to process information and raw data, in accordance with this hierarchy should enable the teacher to make important instructional decisions. At least, the level and nature of learning activities within the student's grasp can be selected. If attempts are to be made to improve the "thinking abilities" of the student they might more properly be based on actual learning opportunities of the curriculum rather than on isolated, irrelevant games that have little relation to the major purpose of educating people and that may not readily make application possible in content areas. The use of convergent and divergent teaching strategies, for example, may be possible in the teaching of basic skills, as in comprehension questions of reading and word problems in mathematics, and in content areas that are open-ended and unlimited in variety. In any event, this approach may clearly illuminate commonalities and differences of mildly handicapped adolescents.

## Some major problems of noncategorical classification

Although the school district may incorporate students from the three traditional diagnostic categories into noncategorical special education programs, the simplicity of the noncategorical approach becomes increasingly complicated as it is activated. First, federal and state guidelines are rigidly categorical, which means that attention to explicit assessment procedures must be observed and labels must be applied to referred students before they are eligible for special education services, even though noncategorical programming may be adopted. Practitioners would be well advised to scrupulously follow all required assessment and due process procedures and not to be deluded by iconoclasts who would compromise procedural safeguards. Second, prevalence figures for a single, broad noncategorical grouping of the traditional categories will be impossible to determine. Lilly (1979, p. 102) estimates that prevalence may range from 0.5% to 50% of the school population. Although it is improbable that half of a school population would actually be so classified, it would indeed be likely that inflated numbers of students would appear in various settings, presenting an unreasonable problem to the school and causing finite resources to be stretched beyond effectiveness. Finally, the tendency to view all children broadly defined as mildly handicapped at the elementary level as a unitary group may have certain genuine advantages; at the secondary level the same view could be disadvantageous because as common programs are established, so will common methods of instruction, common curricula, and common expectations be established.

## Program development

The secondary special education program, the curriculum, and the competencies of teachers should be predicated on the needs and characteristics of mildly handicapped adolescents. Although each student is an individual, and characteristics are so diverse that this population of students is heterogeneous, there are sufficient commonalities to give direction to educational plans. First, there are normal developmental tasks confronting each adolescent in our culture, which should be included in developing educational plans and strategies. Second, there are additional stresses placed on the adolescent who must grapple with the social consequences of a disability. Finally, there are constraints on the nature of the program dictated by regulations and policies as well as the need for the effort to be integrated with the total school curriculum and system of organization. Within this context and from this general framework it is possible to iden-

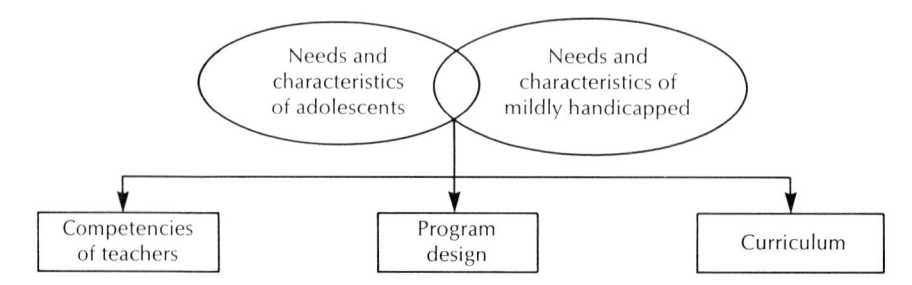

Fig. 2-1. Effects of student needs on secondary programming.

tify the components of a program. Fig. 2-1 represents the relationship between these elements as they lead to program development.

The secondary specialist should be a person who is well trained in the remediation of disabilities, who is familiar with the breadth and extent of the secondary curriculum, who has knowledge and skill in understanding the nature of handicaps and the importance of this period of development, who can assume leadership as an advocate of students, who can act as a liaison between the students, school authorities, and the home, and who can assist in the modification and adaptation of learning experiences in the secondary curriculum. The overriding principle is to plan in accordance with needs identified by examination of handicaps manifested in the adolescent and recognition of the dynamics of the various ecological systems of the adolescent. Hence, the program is planned in accordance with the characteristics and needs of students in as much as we are able to determine them validly. This promises to be a better approach than that which limits special educational intervention to only remediation and which ignores social and emotional states.

## SUMMARY

This chapter stressed that effective teaching and relevant curricula for mildly handicapped students should be based on the characteristics and needs of adolescents and the characteristics of the handicapping conditions that comprise the group of mildly handicapped. Instructional sequences, assignation of educational goals to components of the regular and special curriculum, and other considerations should account for the needs and learning styles of students rather than following preconceived notions about what should be provided in the special education program. The type of model and service delivery system adopted by the school will affect decisions, define options, and otherwise determine how students will be educated.

The major developmental tasks of adolescence were reviewed because they provide the most fundamental commonalities of all adolescents and give direction to curricular considerations. Predominating theories of adolescence were reviewed as were the definitions and characteristics of mildly handicapped students. A discussion of the noncategorical conceptualization of this area of exceptionality was presented, and advantages and disadvantages were considered.

It was concluded that although the traditional categorical groups of mildly handicapped students share certain characteristics in the behavioral dimension, cognitive differences may be increasingly apparent during adolescence, which would support the need for more programmatic options at the secondary level rather than a common special education arrangement. Common goals for all students will be unsatisfactory.

**REFERENCES AND READINGS**

Ausubel, D. P., & Ausubel, P. Cognitive development in adolescence. In M. Powell & A. H. Frerichs (Eds.), *Readings in adolescent psychology.* Minneapolis: Burgess, 1971.

Bloom, B. (Ed.). *Taxonomy of educational objectives: The classification of educational goals* (Handbook 1: *Cognitive domain*). New York: McKay, 1956.

Bloom, B. S. New views of the learner: Implications for instruction and curriculum. *Educational Leadership*, April 1978, 35(7), 563-576.

Bryan, J. H., & Bryan, T. H. *Exceptional children.* Sherman Oaks, Calif.: Alfred, 1979.

Bryan, T. H., & Bryan, J. H. *Understanding learning disabilities* (2nd ed.). Sherman Oaks, Calif. Alfred, 1978.

Coleman, J. S. The adolescent subculture and academic achievement. In M. Powell & A. H. Frerichs (Eds.), *Readings in adolescent psychology.* Minneapolis: Burgess, 1971.

Elkind, D. *Children and adolescents* (2nd ed.). New York: Oxford University Press, 1975.

Erikson, E. H. *Childhood and society.* New York: Norton, 1950.

Erikson, E. H. *Identity: Youth and crisis.* New York: Norton, 1968.

Feldhusen, J. F., & Treffinger, D. J. *Teaching creative thinking and problem solving.* Dubuque, Iowa: Kendall/Hunt, 1977.

Fraenkel, J. R. *Helping students think and value: Strategies for teaching the social studies.* Englewood Cliffs, N.J.: Prentice-Hall, 1973.

Grossman, H. J. *Manual on terminology and classification in mental retardation.* Washington, D.C.: American Association on Mental Deficiency, 1977.

Guilford, J. P. *Personality.* New York: McGraw-Hill, 1959.

Hall, G. S. *Adolescence: Its psychology and its relations to physiology, anthropology, sociology, sex, crime, religion, and education.* New York: Appleton-Century-Crofts, 1904.

Hallahan, D. P., & Kauffman, J. M. Research relevant to the education of distractible and hyperactive children. In W. M. Cruickshank & D. P. Hallahan (Eds.), *Perceptual and learning disabilities in children* (Vol. 2: *Research and theory*). Syracuse, N.Y.: Syracuse University Press, 1975.

Hammill, D. D. Adolescents with specific learning disabilities: Definition, identification, and incidence. In L. Mann, L. Goodman, & J. L. Wiederholt (Eds.), *Teaching the learning disabled adolescent.* Boston: Houghton Mifflin, 1978, pp. 29-46.

Havighurst, R. J. *Developmental tasks and education.* New York: Longman, 1951.

Inhelder, B. *The diagnosis of reasoning in the mentally retarded.* New York: Day, 1968.

Inhelder, B., & Piaget, J. *The growth of logical thinking from childhood to adolescence.* New York: Basic Books, 1958.

Kirk, S. Personal perspectives. In J. M. Kauffman & D. P. Hallahan (Eds.), *Teaching children with learning disabilities: Personal perspectives.* Columbus, Ohio: Merrill, 1976, pp. 238-269.

Kolstoe, O. P. *Mental retardation.* New York: Holt, Rinehart and Winston, 1972.

Lewin, K. *A dynamic theory of personality.* New York: McGraw-Hill, 1935.

Lewin, K. *Field theory in social science.* New York: Harper & Row, 1951.

Lilly, M. S. *Children with exceptional needs: A survey of special education.* New York: Holt, Rinehart and Winston, 1979.

Marsh, G. E., II, Gearheart, C. K., & Gearheart, B. R. *The Learning disabled adolescent: Program alternatives in the secondary school.* St. Louis: Mosby, 1978.

Mead, M. *Coming of age in Samoa.* New York: Morrow, 1928.

Mead, M. *Male and female.* New York: Morrow, 1949.

Mercer, C. D., & Snell, M. E. *Learning theory research in mental retardation.* Columbus, Ohio: Merrill, 1977.

Zigmond, N. A prototype of comprehensive services for secondary students with learning disabilities. *Learning Disability Quarterly*, Winter 1978, *1*(1), 39-49.

Chapter 3

# INTERPERSONAL RELATIONSHIPS

Carol Coffman

The importance of the family environment to the social and emotional development of a child cannot be underestimated because of its implications for school adjustment and adaptation to the culture. The dynamics of family interaction are of intense interest to the secondary resource teacher because of their direct impact on a student's personality, self-esteem, self-concept, daily moods, and approach to learning. The ultimate task of adolescents is to break the emotional and economic ties that subjugate them to their parents. Therefore much of the turmoil of adolescence stems naturally from conflict with parents as the emancipation process proceeds. Although the anguish of adolescence is a normal consequence of role conflict created by our society, it is no less painful for parents and their children. In those instances where family dynamics are complicated by rigid or deviant parenting practices, abuse, or personality disorders of family members, the problems of the adolescent can be exacerbated.

Another important dimension of interpersonal relationships is within the domain of peer contact. The social significance of school is frequently more important to adolescents than traditional goals of the educational system. The attractiveness of the peer group, its power in the establishment of ritual behaviors and modes of conduct, and its influence to harm or help the individual causes this sphere of adolescent activity to be an area of legitimate professional concern.

## FAMILY INFLUENCES
### Parent-child relations

The study of the family has traditionally been within the province of the sociologist or anthropologist, with considerable attention devoted to the types of family units (Burgess, 1926). The predominant family unit in most Western societies is the *nuclear family* consisting of one or both parents (or stepparents) and one or more children. This is markedly different from family groupings in nonindustrialized nations, where a rich variety of interactions can be derived from contact with numerous relatives of all ages. The contemporary nuclear family forfeits many benefits as the interactions of fewer family members are intensified. The change in the economic climate in America has transformed the family from a relatively self-contained and self-sufficient unit to one in which one or both parents are preoccupied with matters outside the home associated with occupations and avocations. Schools have assumed many of the basic functions of the traditional family.

In highly integrated families there are strong bonds, a strict definition of roles and responsibilities, rituals, customs, and cooperation. More loosely integrated families lack these qualities and can cause emotional disturbance, social incompetence, and personality disorders, which are carried by the child into social and educational interactions. Because of a higher incidence of social and behavioral problems of mildly handicapped students and conflict between parents and children, the special education teacher may need to be able to deliver *affective first aid* to disturbed students, and he or she must surely account for personality variables on a daily basis in dealings with students.

Of all major endeavors in adult life, young persons are probably the least prepared for the roles of marriage and child rearing. Although these are important roles if one considers the functions associated with them and the "products" of such endeavors, it is apparently believed that little training beyond modeling oneself after one's own parents is necessary. Perhaps this stems from the belief that people marry because they "fall in love" and raising children is based on "common sense" (Baldwin & Baldwin, 1970). Without a theory and a plan, however, parenting is a series of random, disconnected reactions to events and behaviors beginning with the first fumbling attempts to diaper a baby and ending wherever chance and circumstance lead. Parenting is practiced by amateurs who rely on mechanistic responses learned during their own childhoods. The consequences are that harmful patterns of parenting and damaged personalities can be passed on to each consecutive generation as a dangerous legacy.

Central to the concept of interpersonal relationships are how and why people act in the ways they do. Much of psychology has been devoted to this complex issue and may be classified according to many viewpoints, but most seem to ignore the external structure of the social context and the importance of socialization through the family unit.

The role theory of Mead (1934) may be adapted for use in future research dealing with the investigation of family interaction with the mildly handicapped and may be used here to accent the significance of the family in developing the self-concept, roles, and interaction with the culture. Mead viewed *sociality* as role taking, a process in which the individual not only is a reactor but is also a creator of his or her social environment. An individual assumes a place in the social context by learning to enact a repertoire of roles that are appropriate for specific social situations. This occurs primarily as a direct result of family interactions. Parental roles are very important. One aspect of the development of the self, the "me," is the internalization of the attitudes of parents. Another is the "I," which develops by experiencing social situations and directing one's behavior in such situations. A role is self-directed behavior in interaction with other persons (Lewis, 1976).

It can be seen that the contribution of the family to the development of the *self* in a particular child is much greater than just inherited traits and socioeconomic status. To the extent that an individual creates his or her own self, an atypical characteristic comes to play an important part in the interactional process of the family. If a child is hyperactive, the development of the self is affected by responses of family members to the behavioral differences of the child. The family's attitude becomes part of the child's attitude. The self-concept is a complex structure of gradually acquired assimilations that initially emerge through interaction in the family. An atypical characteristic in a child may come into play as parental concern is directed to the difference of the child as contrasted with a preconceived ideal, with siblings, or with other children outside the family. The characteristic of being different causes parents to react differently to the child than they would if the child were not atypical. This process of adjustment in family interaction over a long period of time may lead to unhealthy self-concepts of a child because the child may symbolize family conflict and distress. Atypical behavior may come to be expected and reinforced. A system of interaction emerges in which parents are frustrated and disappointed (if not rejecting), and the child assimilates these reactions in the development of his or her self-concept. Some possible consequences of a poor self-concept are depicted in Fig. 3-1.

The diversity of naturally emerged child-rearing patterns has been examined and classified by Elder (1962). We have listed his home organizational patterns and attached the possible affective and socioeducational implications for each type in a corresponding column in Table 3. The interaction of the effects of handicaps is not considered in this matrix, although this would be a most interesting approach to research and ecological assessment pertaining to parent-child interactions.

**48** THE LEARNER

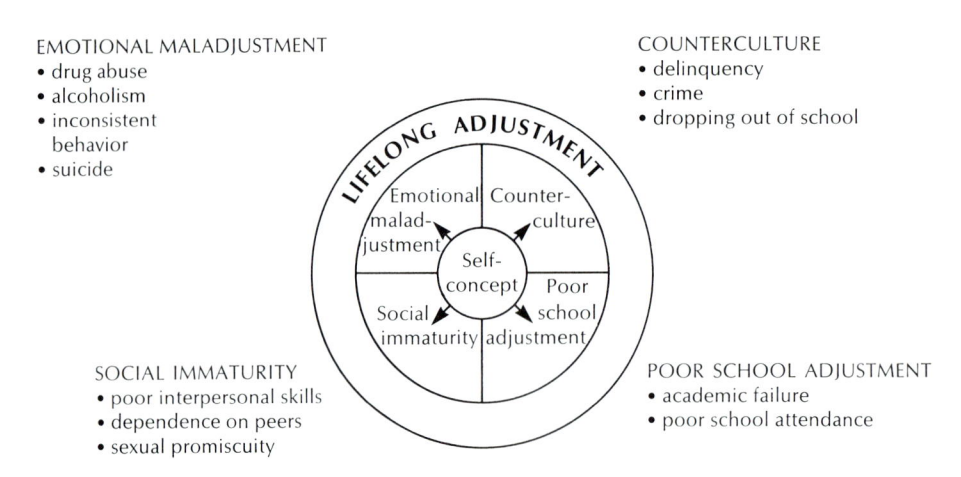

**EMOTIONAL MALADJUSTMENT**
- drug abuse
- alcoholism
- inconsistent behavior
- suicide

**COUNTERCULTURE**
- delinquency
- crime
- dropping out of school

**SOCIAL IMMATURITY**
- poor interpersonal skills
- dependence on peers
- sexual promiscuity

**POOR SCHOOL ADJUSTMENT**
- academic failure
- poor school attendance

**Fig. 3-1.** Possible consequences of poor self-concept.

**Table 3.** Home organizational patterns and possible educational implications

| Type of parenting | Parent-child interaction | Resolution of conflict | Possible educational implications |
|---|---|---|---|
| Autocratic | None | Parents | Peer dependence |
| Authoritarian | Limited | Parents | Lower academic achievement |
|  |  |  | Reduced intellectual curiosity |
|  |  |  | Increased dependence on adults |
|  |  |  | Lower school motivation |
| Democratic | Active | Parents | Higher achievement |
| Equalitarian | Active | Parents-child | More independence |
|  |  |  | Better self-concept |
|  |  |  | Better social adjustment |
|  |  |  | More school orientation |
| Permissive | Active | Child | Increased peer dependence |
| Laissez-faire | Limited | Child | Lower school achievement |
| Ignoring | None | Child | Poor homework orientation |
|  |  |  | Lower self-concept |
|  |  |  | Less interest in school |

We have stressed parenting styles because there is evidence that family interactions have a strong relationship with school success. Poor parent-child interactions have been found to exist in the families of LD adolescents (Erickson, 1978). It cannot necessarily be said that any of the parenting styles of Elder are poor, with the exceptions of the extremes, but the use of a particular style that is successful with children in one stage of life may need to be relinquished at a later period. As emancipation from parents gathers force during adolescence, an autocratic or authoritarian approach may create incredible conflict and resistance in the child. In some instances where domination of the parents is complete, it is possible that the family will foster dependency and exercise overprotection, thus interfering with normal adjustment. If a counselor or counseling agent could impact any family positively it would be to implore the family not to meet the natural rebellion of adolescence with rigidity and increasing control, but to gradually relax and alter old styles.

Adolescents apparently prefer listening as the most acceptable form of parental attention (Erickson, 1978). This may be most effectively employed with gradually diminished parental control as adolescents are permitted to work through their own problems, consider alternatives, and make independent decisions. Parental advice may be accepted when requested but summarily dismissed when volunteered. The regular class teacher and the special teacher may benefit from this insight into adolescent behavior by avoiding the mistakes of parents who admonish, cajole, scold, and threaten rather than simply listen.

## Parental values

Interfacing with parental styles of child-rearing practices are the values of parents, which come to affect the attitudes of children. There is evidence that, in spite of the apparent disagreement between adolescents and their parents (lately referred to as the generation gap), many adolescents retain the basic values of their parents into adulthood. Contrary to earlier research and stereotyped views, Bachman et al. (1978) have concluded from longitudinal research that patterns of values and behavior that adolescents have by the age of 15 are retained into adulthood.

Operationally, a value is a standard comprised of a constellation of related beliefs, opinions, and biases against which the behavior and status of others are judged. Values tend to become entrenched over time and resistant to change. Parents bring their own values into a marriage, and the differences often become synthesized into a unified set or at least into two, noncompeting sets. Conflicting expectations within the family negatively affect a child's attitude toward learning (Freidman, 1978).

Parental values represent the major influence in family life in addition to child-rearing styles. Religion, social class, cultural and ethnic background, educational level of the parents, and other factors are related to the development and crystallization of values. This process is important in understanding and planning for individuals. Learning styles, work habits, values about education (purpose and outcomes), and ways of relating to teachers are initially learned in the family setting (Friedman, 1978). For example, families of low socioeconomic status tend to maintain the belief that it is best to be a generalist in the work force, or trained in many unskilled and semiskilled occupations. Middle-class values dictate specialization in a profession. A family that values high achievement and high-status professions (law, medicine) will likely be disappointed in their mildly handicapped child's lack of academic progress.

## Serious conflict in the family

Some adolescents will be affected by serious forms of conflict and distress in the family: alcoholism, abuse, and divorce.

Depending on family dynamics, there are a number of possible effects of parental alcoholism on a child. There is an obvious financial loss to low-income families as resources are diverted to sustain the addiction; middle-income families are subject to the same jeopardy with the constant threat that the major wage earner's drinking problem may culminate in unemployment.

An alcoholic in the home may prevent normal peer associations from developing because of embarrassment and the reluctance to invite friends into the home. The attention devoted to the problems created by the drinking parent and the emotional drain on other family members may limit the amount of support available to the maturing adolescent. If it is true that handicapped students tend to develop more anxiety because of their personal problems, then the total impact of alcoholism may be most detrimental.

Battering or child abuse is a social malady that is receiving considerable attention along with the increasing awareness that many spouses frequently pummel one another. There are apparently certain characteristics in adults and children that interact to reinforce a pattern of abuse through cues in interaction. Although we are not aware of much specific evidence, it seems possible that handicapped children and adolescents in certain families would be subject to abuse if we can accept the limited evidence that additional stress is placed on the family because of the child's behavior. LD and ED adolescents are frequently perceived by teachers, peers, and parents as offensive because of unacceptable behavioral patterns (rebelliousness, defiance, inattention, obstinance, name-calling, teasing, etc.). A key concept in understanding the genesis of abuse is that the parent's ability to tolerate frustration becomes overloaded. Therefore it would be plausible that there is a higher incidence of abuse with mildly handicapped children because of the additional stress.

Although there has been considerable attention to abuse of younger children, there is currently increasing concern about abuse of adolescents because of emerging evidence of the magnitude of the problem with this age group (Lourie & Cohan, 1976). There is a strong relationship between abuse and other teenage problems, namely, running away, alcoholism, disrupted school performance, and pregnancy (Garbarino & Jacobson, 1978; Rosenstein, 1978). For any child, a violent family environment leads to a deteriorated sense of security, physical and health problems, psychological trauma, absence from school, and many other problems, not the least of which is that this pattern may be repeated in the next generation of children. In suspected cases of abuse, the teacher is obligated, in many states, to report incidents to legal authorities (DeFrancis & Lucht, 1974; Theisen, 1978).

As with other types of adjustment problems, the effects of a divorce on children will vary with many factors influencing family unity and relationships. Traditional values of the culture have maintained the sanctity of marriage (originally for religious reasons); therefore divorce is generally regarded as undesirable, an index of immaturity on the part of the partners, a social failure, and a detriment to child development. Aside from popular beliefs, it is clear that the potential for harm to any particular child as a result of divorce depends on a complex of factors, which include the circumstances leading up to the divorce, the maturity of the children, and the attachment of the children to one or the other parent. Therefore the possibility of harm to a child is a variable factor related to idiosyncratic patterns of development and adjustment.

It is interesting that very little research has been conducted in this area, and it is certain that there has been no attention to the effect of divorce on mildly handicapped adolescents. Studies indicate that, in some instances, adolescents from broken homes exhibit better adjustment in aspects of daily living, have more privacy, take a greater part in making family decisions, reach economic independence more quickly, are not

**Table 4.** Resource teacher: professional responses to adolescents from troubled families

| Problem in the family | Resource teacher's responses ||
|---|---|---|
| | **Educational** | **Other** |
| Alcoholism of a family member | Provide support to adolescent<br>Avoid involvement in family situation<br>Avoid making judgments<br>Assist in getting part-time job if needed by student | Possible referral to Al-anon<br>Referral to family service agencies |
| Abuse/battering | Recognize health status<br>Recognize social embarrassment for the student<br>Provide support in a matter-of-fact manner<br>Avoid overreaction<br>Understand reluctance to confide details | Referral to legal authority<br>Reporting to school authorities<br>Referral to school counselor |
| Divorce or broken home | Understand temporary emotional trauma<br>Recognize importance of reactions of those around student<br>Provide genuine support | Possible referral to school counselor if trauma persists or is extreme<br>Referral to counselor in case of absenteeism |

more prone to delinquency, and do not, as a group, reveal patterns of serious maladjustment (Burchinal, 1964; Landis, 1953).

Table 4 is intended to assist the special teacher in responding to the needs of the adolescent. In those instances where problems arise, it would be advisable to clear certain actions with the school administration and to contact the school counselor. For the most part, the teacher is limited to (1) providing support to the student that is noninterfering, (2) providing information and support to parents, (3) requesting support and active involvement of parents, (4) making appropriate referrals and recommendations to students and parents, and (5) reporting incidents that involve abuse of a student to school or legal authorities.

One important dimension in consideration of the problems that complicate the life of an adolescent pertains to the range of parenting styles, especially as the child's personality, motivation, and affective development are concerned. The preceding section has been presented as a brief overview of the factors to be considered in understanding parenting styles, values, attitudes, and the conflict that may exist between an adolescent and his or her family. *It is important to reiterate that the influences we have outlined may be interactive variables in the life of any adolescent while the imposition of a handicap may or may not alter parental practices of child rearing or parental attitudes toward children.* In all families it is certainly true that the unalterable process of biology compels the adolescent to seek independence. The school may not have much influence on the family nor be able to assist in the event of conflict. It is a fact that the teacher cannot be expected to do everything. However, it is essential that the emancipation process be understood, that problems be identified, and that counseling and educational strategies take familial factors into account. This is especially true because affective development is originally structured in the family and later influences motivation, selection of life goals, attitudes, values, and relationships with others. The special education field is gradually coming to the recognition that emotional development and the self-concept of a mildly handicapped adolescent may be of paramount importance.

## Parental attitudes

Parental attitudes are affected by expectations relating to parental behavior and to the behavior of children. Parent-child relationships are governed to a maximum extent by such expectations (Baldwin & Baldwin, 1970, 1974). As adolescence progresses the conflict between parents and children arises in part because of the differences in expectations and values. Parents convey their expectations to adolescents explicitly or through role functions. Parents may not actually be conscious of their plans and goals for their children and may not verbalize them. Some life-long expectations may begin when the child is in the crib. If the behavior of the child diverts from tacitly conceived expectations, the parents may show increasing concern. Therefore the totality of goals, dreams, and hopes of parents represents a source of stress that can be intensified during the adolescent period.

One factor that can cause a clash between parents and the child is the existence of a handicap or a perceived handicap. If the parents value school success and the child does not achieve in accordance with parental wishes, attendant disappointment can be most distressing and interfere with emerging parent-child interactions. A formal process of testing and labeling a child can result in a more pronounced effect. Nonbehavioral labels (dyslexia, minimal brain damage) elicit more parental reaction than task-related terminology (Johnson & Morasky, 1977). The diagnosis of a learning disability may result in an intense response from among a full range of emotions. The reactions of parents to the label and to the child constitute an area of importance to the school because of the impact on parent-child relationships and school adjustment. There is certainly evidence to indicate that a teacher's perception of a label creates a negative bias in the classroom (Foster et al., 1976), and this effect may also be found in some parents.

Although much depends on the definition that is used in research, there is evidence leading to the conclusion that behaviors of mildly handicapped children cause them to be viewed negatively by their parents, to place additional stress on the family, and to adversely affect the interpersonal relationships of family members (Wender, 1971). In reference to LD children, Bryan and Bryan (1978, p. 120) summarize this point when they say, "The difficulty is not simply that such children are not reading, but that they are not pleasant." Therefore the concept of a social learning disability proposed by Johnson and Myklebust (1967) might need to be resurrected and examined more carefully. The learning disabled may need to know how to interpret the social actions of others, to understand their own behavior and its effects on others, and to develop acceptable social interaction with their parents, siblings, teachers, and peers. Social acceptability, more than all other skills and capabilities, is a significant prerequisite for vocational adjustment and integrated adult roles.

Farber (1968) has demonstrated that persons who deviate from conventional standards in meaningful ways are viewed by society as incompetent or deviant. Deviancy is threatening to society, hence, those who are placed in this category, either legally as in criminal justice, or as a consequence of social stigmatization, receive the most rejection. To a great extent, many people fear and reject the mentally retarded and emotionally disturbed because of perceptions about the labels or as a result of unsatisfactory social interaction. It is well known that the behavior of ED students cause them to be socially unacceptable to peers, parents, and teachers. Bryan and Bryan (1979, p. 166) state that, "It is clear that normal children do not like retarded ones." However, it is much more likely that retarded students will simply be ignored or ridiculed.

Although suppositions may be made that mildly handicapped students are not liked and accepted because of social and behavioral deviance, or as a consequence of deficient academic or intellectual functioning, there are undoubtedly many intervening variables that have yet to be rigorously investigated. For example, physical appearance, socioeconomic status of the family, race, and other factors certainly influence reactions of others.

Although there has been some research into the dynamics of parental reaction to the diagnosis of a handicap, primarily in young children with more severe handicaps, very little actual research has been conducted with parents of the learning disabled. Much more has been done with parents of MR and ED students, and most of it has been concerned with parents of younger children. Theoretically, it is possible to outline the dimensions of possible parental reaction to any label used to describe handicapped children. Fig. 3-2 represents an outline of the process. It should be reemphasized that the adolescent who is labeled for the *first time* is not likely to elicit intense reactions because of the long-standing knowledge that "something has been wrong." Parents may find relief in finally getting an explanation.

The reactions and perceptions related to the problem behaviors of children with handicaps may be as important as the actual behaviors in determining the degree or seriousness of a problem (Baldwin & Baldwin, 1970, 1974; Sheppard et al., 1966). This is true in the broader social perspective as well, in that the stereotyped expectations of people are more limiting to an individual than an actual handicap. A deaf or blind person may be prevented from en-

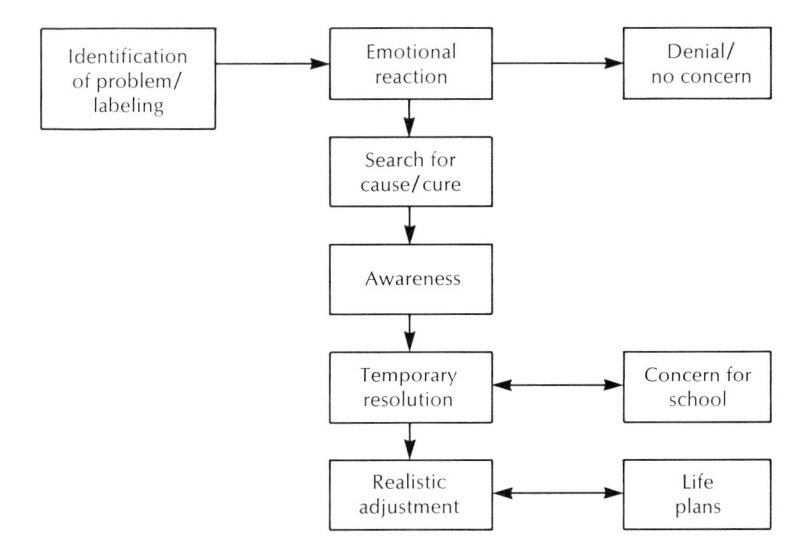

**Fig. 3-2.** Parental reaction to labeling in special education.

gaging in certain activities or from obtaining certain types of jobs because employers *believe* he or she cannot function adequately.

Erickson (1978) asserts that most parents of adolescents tend to underestimate the ability of their children to assume responsibility because of an inaccurate estimation of maturity and self-reliance. This rather normal pattern can be magnified when a handicap is recognized. Parents react to the label with fears and worries about its meaning for themselves and their children. They may begin to attend to behaviors in the child that would ordinarily go unnoticed. Parental anxiety may increase because of the diagnosis, although the children may exhibit emotional and behavioral reactions common to other children of the same age (Johnson & Morasky, 1977).

The label may contribute to parental anxiety and foster overprotection and dependence (Hammill & Myers, 1969; Johnson & Morasky, 1977). Some adolescents with neurological handicaps may need protection, but overall it seems that most mildly handicapped adolescents should be expected to follow more typical patterns of development. The degree of dependence on parents will have important implications for social interaction with other adults, relationships with peers, and realistic preparation for adult life.

The emancipation process is a source of anxiety and stress for any family because the beginning of such a struggle marks the point of cleavage between parental and child authority for what must ultimately terminate in independence. This may be most typical of students in junior high school and may be characterized by conflict over styles of dress, choices of friends, recreational activities, dating restrictions, allowances, and responsibilities. The style of the conflict may be carried into the school setting, where teachers may become unwittingly involved in displaced aggression, especially if nonsupportive, authoritarian teachers provoke unpleasant encounters.

Fig. 3-3 represents the theoretical schema-

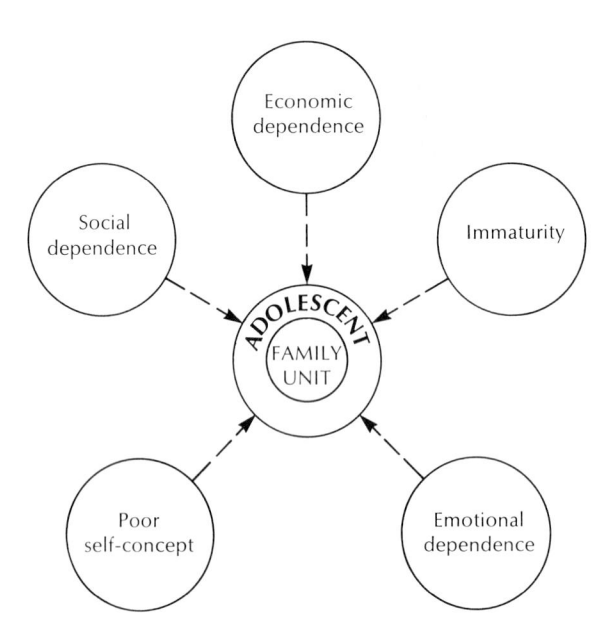

**Fig. 3-3.** Factors impeding normal emancipation process.

tization of factors impeding the normal emancipation process. Ecological assessment may uncover these factors in the relationships of some students to the family unit.

A number of generalizations about parents of special education students can be made, although some points are not necessarily supported by research. They are as follows:

1. The special education teacher is more likely than other teachers in the secondary school to have frequent, direct contact with parents because of a higher incidence of behavioral problems and violation of school regulations among his or her students. The other extreme, which is a general pattern with parents of many teenagers, is also likely; that is, some parents will make no contact with the school in spite of repeated appeals to do so.

2. The relationship between some students and their parents is likely to be more unstable and the conflict between them more volatile because of a suspected higher degree of stress between parents and handicapped children over a long period.

3. The teacher must walk a tightrope between parents and the adult world they represent and the opposing world of the adolescent. The adolescent may be more attuned to the conflict, sensitive to adult criticism, and outraged by "establishment betrayal" and injustice.

4. Family conflict and parenting styles are significant factors in the social and emotional development of adolescents and are of more acute significance to the mildly handicapped.

5. Although there are undoubtedly many mildly handicapped students who have well-adjusted, happy homes, there is a significant tendency for these adolescents to have family lives that are more unsettled because of conflict. However, cause and effect have not clearly been established.

6. Although there are a variety of parenting styles employed with adolescents, two distinct groups appear to exist: the rejecting, critical parent and the overprotective parent.

7. The potential for more extreme reactions to the natural events of adolescence exists in families of handicapped adolescents with the possible consequence of serious adjustment problems, lifelong patterns of personal emotional troubles, and violent overreaction to stress.

8. Ecological assessment should be employed in the secondary program and must logically extend to incorporate information about families.

9. The teacher should be aware of the familial factors that affect a student because of the possible interaction with self-concept, motivation, peer relationships, and general adjustment.

10. The resource teacher is legally and ethically restricted from making direct intervention in the family life of a student but should be prepared to offer support and make appropriate referrals.

11. The school counselor, in cooperation with other personnel in the school, should develop a strategy for delivering support services to families of handicapped adolescents.

## PEER INFLUENCES

The words of an old rock tune summarize the essence of the social strivings of many adolescents and the secure complacency of others:

> I'm in with the In-Crowd,
> I go where the In-Crowd goes.
> I'm in with the In-Crowd,
> I know what the In-Crowd knows.

Although there may be many sociological conclusions reported by observers of adolescent pubertal rites, the most pervasive characteristic of all social interaction between teenagers is the social stratification of individuals. In each school there is a predominant group and those who lack the qualities for acceptance in that group. Adolescents form a society of conformists that demands rigid codes of dress and conduct. However, the basic requirements are acquired by birth into the "right" family and the genetic endowment of an attractive body. Governed by these superficial principles the adolescent attempts to adjust, seek friendships, and gain a sense of identity.

The ritual of pubescence lasts a number of years and is manifested as the quest for status in one's group. Deviating from explicit or subtle standards of the group prevents the achievement of status. The significance of peer influence is sometimes downplayed by authorities, but for most people the memories and lasting effects of the high school experience extend well into adulthood. For this reason it is essential that secondary teachers remember that the power of the peer group has a dominating effect on the moods, attitudes, and motivations of students.

Group identification is important to adolescents because of the need for acceptance in a world where they are shunned by adults and treated "like children." The peer group is an intellectual buffer against the "hypocrisy" of the adult world, a situation caused by a clash between adolescent idealism and reality. Yet, the hypocrisy of the peer group is tolerated, its insincerity overlooked, and its cruelty justified, at least by the "in crowd."

For any adolescent, regardless of his or her status, experiences with the peer group must often be painful. The rigidity of adolescent standards leaves little room for nonconformity, individual expression, or tolerance for idiosyncrasies. A facial blemish can ruin the emotional stability of a girl or boy for an entire week, and the inability to have the latest styles, a car, money for a date, or time to use the telephone to call a friend of the opposite sex or to gratify a variety of immediate wants can relegate every other part of life to a category of unimportance.

Although these natural, egocentric aspects of the adolescent personality may seem unimportant and immature to teachers and parents, the gravity of these matters to adolescents is of utmost concern. Because of this importance, the anticipation of meeting a girl friend after class or taking a date to a basketball game can overshadow all other endeavors such as preparing for a test, taking a clear set of notes, or identifying the critical theme in a literary work. The influence of groups is therefore an important consideration.

## Formal groups

For the most part, formal groups of adolescents are sanctioned by the school or some community organization. Their acceptability and importance to adolescents are determined by the value attached to them by the peer group. Membership in some groups is highly desirable and may vary in accordance with factors peculiar to a community or geographical region. There seems to be an inverse relationship between the importance of formal group activity and the increasing power of the peer group as an influence on individuals. For example, a formal group, such as Boy Scouts, loses its attractiveness to high school students as the activity of the peer group becomes more adultlike and focused on the school setting. Formal organizations within a particular school are classified and ranked by the student body and the predominant group of students. Membership in some groups is highly prestigious and very desirable. This will vary from school to school, but there do seem to be some generalizations that can be made.

Social popularity (e.g., through athletics or student government) is of highest importance and looms above group membership that does not meet criteria for prestige (e.g., Spanish Club). It should be stressed that group membership for any student may be important (even though it may be in an organization of low esteem) because of the social benefit to be derived from such contact. Mildly handicapped students especially need this type of contact.

Having athletic prowess and being popular are more important to boys and girls than academic achievement, and the few who become football stars or cheerleaders will likely be the most popular, most sought after for social interaction, and most admired. Physical attractiveness is a most important social commodity, which in combination with social activity and pursuits confers status.

It is unfortunate that little importance is placed on academic excellence, especially because of the dire consequences for mildly handicapped students who have motivational problems anyway. In some schools it is socially unacceptable to be seen carrying textbooks. Undoubtedly, it is very difficult to interest students in learning in an environment where learning is not rewarded; but there is a kind of double jeopardy for mildly handicapped students. Whereas the typical secondary student can succeed in his or her studies, the handicapped student cannot. A basic requirement for membership in many formal groups of the school is a good grade point average (GPA). The handicapped student is ordinarily unable to earn good grades and is therefore denied membership in many organizations of the school that would be socially rewarding and perhaps motivating to academic achievement through the circular effect of social acceptance and resulting ego strength.

**The special education teacher and formal groups.** Membership in certain formal groups seems to ensure acceptance and peer support. The adolescent struggles with the development of social skill, comfortable peer interrelationships, and identification with others. Membership in *any* formal group of the school may be beneficial to the student's growth and adjustment in other dimensions of development. The special education teacher may be able to assist students to achieve membership in some group for the additional purpose of providing better social skills.

First, it is necessary to know what formal groups exist in the school. This can be easily determined by perusal of a student of faculty handbook. It might be surprising to veteran teachers in large schools to discover just how many organizations actually operate. As a matter of interest it might be possible to determine the social importance or ranking of specific organizations according to a random sample of students. Table 5

**Table 5.** Informal checklist for determining social importance of organized school groups, Prairie Grove High School, Prairie Grove, Arkansas

| Name of group | Low | Moderate | High |
|---|---|---|---|
| Football team | | | x |
| Basketball team | | | x |
| Baseball team | | x | |
| Softball team | x | | |
| Cheerleading | | | x |
| Pep Club | | x | |
| Band | x | | |
| National Honor Society | | x | |
| Future Homemakers | x | | |
| Future Farmers | x | | |
| Future Business Leaders | | x | |
| Future Teachers | | x | |
| Student Government | | | x |
| Chess Club | x | | |
| Drama Club | x | | |
| Art Club | x | | |
| French Club | | x | |
| Science Academy | x | | |
| Choir | | x | |
| Track | x | | |

illustrates this process. This table actually represents the popularity of existing formal groups as ranked by a sample of students in a small high school. The sample included primarily popular students.

Reference to Table 5 reveals that athletics and student government receive the highest ratings, not an unexpected finding. The moderate popularity of some groups can be explained by the personalities of members or sponsors or by unique activities associated with the groups. For example, singing in a choir is not ordinarily a very popular interest but in this case the choir was scheduled to make a tour of Mexico, which heightened its prestige among the student body.

After identifying and determining rankings for the groups, the special educator should investigate the specific requirements for membership. Some groups may have obvious requirements (GPA, athletic ability, skill with an instrument), but the qualifications for others may be less rigorous. Armed with such information the teacher can assist students in developing an interest and gaining membership in a group.

There are a number of groups to which the student can belong and contribute. The teacher should actively assist each student in realistic goal-setting behaviors that could include formal group membership. Many vocational clubs include the handicapped. The teacher should not be surprised to find that some students are so socially isolated that they are not aware of how one achieves group membership or what is required to participate in group functions; assisting students in becoming part of a formal group should be an important priority of the teacher because of the possible benefits to the students. Membership in even low-status groups will provide a sense of belonging that the students need. The most desirable effect would be the improvement of self-concept and social interaction. At the very least, such activities may prevent some students from being attracted to counterculture groups.

The teacher should consider the importance of formal group activity in the school to the social development of all students and the handicapped student in particular. Because a learning disorder cannot be treated in isolation, the total environment of the student must be examined and accounted for in planning and intervention. Enhancement of social development through successful interaction in formal groups is desirable and should be considered a significant step in effecting contingencies for improved self-esteem and social skill and as a foundation for attitudinal change and motivation in the learning environment. In summary, the teacher should follow these steps in incorporating this aspect of school-related functions into the lives of students:

1. Consider social skills training to be an important part of assistance to students.
2. Encourage the participation of students in formal school activities.
3. Identify the types of organizations in the school and examine their nature and functions.
4. Ascertain the requirements for membership.
5. Match up possible groups with talents and abilities or interests of each student.
6. Assist the student to join one or more groups.
7. Provide information and assistance to sponsors of specific groups to facilitate the inclusion of students in organizations they supervise.
8. Recognize that barriers to membership of students may be based on stereotyped responses or policies of the school that discriminate against them.
9. Actively work to remove unfair and

unreasonable policies that restrict the student from active participation in a group.
10. The academic grade point average is likely to be a major hurdle for membership in many groups. This reflects policies that are well intentioned but that should be waived or based on alternative candidacy requirements to accommodate the handicapped.

## Informal groups

Adolescents form small groups or cliques that have considerable contact and interaction. In the junior high school there are a number of such cliques comprised of members of the same sex. This pattern continues into the high school where there may be frequent interaction between specific groups of girls and groups of boys to the exclusion of other groups. Ultimately, dyads or pairs of adolescents develop as dating becomes more a part of social activities, and the time devoted to the dating relationship softens the bonds and reduces the time of interaction with the cliques formed by sexual identification. In cases where students "break up" with one another there is a period during which intensified interaction with one's friends of the same sex occurs until a couple "makes up" or another relationship is formed. This pattern occurs with college students as well. A small group of male or female friends becomes the primary group of contact for a boy or girl, which can be forsaken in the event of a more stable, prolonged relationship with a "love" interest. The following list outlines the constellation of group activity:

1. There are small, primary groups comprised of members of the same sex, which have frequent contact with opposite sex groups.
2. Members of these groups tend to have similar characteristics and are typically formed in accordance with the caste system of popularity; for example, popular girls tend to associate with each other.
3. There may be several groups that interact with one another for certain social activities in the school. These groups will tend to be of relatively equal status and rival one another.
4. These groups or cliques become less important and less active as students begin to interact more intimately across sexual lines or as dating becomes a primary social activity.

Belonging to an informal group means that an adolescent fits in or that the behaviors of the individual are appropriate and consistent with group norms. The physical characteristics, popularity, and social status of the individual permits group acceptance and enhances esteem through belonging. Although groups of like individuals seem to simply evolve, there are certain rather specific requirements recognized by the groups.

Following are some characteristics of group behavior that will be of interest to the teacher:

1. *Dress styles of the group conform to some acceptable patterns.* Each generation of students tends to have a predominant style of dress. What is in vogue, however, may change rapidly. Faddish dress is most important to the secondary student. They may look similar in appearance, but some rather specific differences may demarcate one clique from another (e.g., a symbol worn on clothing, jewelry, and other signs). Depending on the school and location, a particular brand name or style of clothing is essential. Students who naively or willingly deviate from a certain acceptable style will be laughed at and ridiculed. Those who cannot afford the type and quantity of dress styles can be unfortunately penalized. This circumstance is more significant where there

is a polarity of socioeconomic status in the student body.

2. *Slang expressions, unique mannerisms, and inside jokes grow out of the peer group influence and serve to solidify group identification and set the generation apart from younger children and adults.* Adults are alienated from teenagers by ritual behaviors. Adults who attempt to adopt cultish mannerisms and speech patterns tend to look foolish to students. The "cool" behavior of the 1950s is the most familiar example of this behavior, which is remarkable for its popularity and continued longevity through television and movies.

3. *A significant portion of adolescents from a specific school will go to certain locations for the primary purpose of social intercourse—to see and be seen.* Aside from school-related functions, certain places in a community become identified as gathering places for students. Not surprisingly, a drive-in restaurant is "chosen" and students will spend a great deal of time, if not money, meeting there. This underscores the importance of having access to an automobile, a significant social prerequisite since the 1950s.

4. *For many adolescents, an inordinate amount of time is devoted to conforming behavior.* Seeking and gaining attention leads to recognition, which gives one prestige and status. Status in the adolescent subculture is, for the most part, bestowed on the most popular, who have little difficulty in meeting such shallow standards as good looks and adequate financial support from parents. Those who cannot conform by meeting these insipid social criteria will not be as popular and will suffer to varying degrees, at least for the time being. This is the most tragic part of the subculture that flourishes in secondary schools. As Coleman (1971) asserts, the subculture is at odds with the institutional goals established for schools and detracts from the process of socialization. Except for those students for whom "things come easy," there is very little about the subculture that contributes to the development of security in adulthood. There is the danger that rigid patterns of behavior, an inaccurate self-concept, and poor preparation for adulthood will result from the adolescent social experience. A subculture that adheres to such vapid values as good looks, athletic ability, and popularity demands conformity, mediocrity, and the stifling of individual expression and achievement. Part of the disappointment with academic achievement of today's high school youth must be blamed on the adolescent subculture that disdains it and the adults who, because of economic factors at work, have allowed the subculture to exist with its shallow social system.

**Dating and sexual behavior.** It seems reasonable to assume that there may be a diminished level of dating among handicapped students, overall, because of a greater incidence of interpersonal problems. However, for the same reason, there may be a variety of sexual problems experienced by students in this category. Dating and sexual interests will preoccupy students, so we have included some general information that may be useful to any secondary teacher.

1. The sexual revolution has affected the adolescent culture. There are many problems—pregnancy, abortions, miscarriages, and a high level of venereal disease. However, we suspect that this is a pattern that may be related to the demographic and social characteristics of the community.

2. The efforts of the feminist movement notwithstanding, the double standard seems to be firmly rooted in this generation.

3. Male adolescents continue to acquire status through sexual exploits or through lying about them. This topic may preoccupy the conversations and interests of male stu-

dents. That is not to say that females will not be as interested but less verbal about the subject.

4. Parental values may appear to conflict with peer values about sexual matters. In many instances, parents are likely to espouse one set of values for "the good of the kids" and believe in another more liberal set. Due to the lack of guidance, the traditional taboos of the Puritan ethic, and the sensitivity of the subject, the adolescent may suffer guilt, anxiety, fear, and general confusion about sexual thoughts and feelings.

As with other areas of interpersonal relationships, the specialist at the secondary level may need to be aware of possible sources of support and guidance for teenagers who experience some sexually related problem. This may range from timidity about interaction with the opposite sex to a serious problem. Romantic concerns can be most detrimental to learning.

**The role of the teacher in facilitating informal group acceptance.** If self-esteem emerges from interaction with peers (rejection vs acceptance) then this aspect of socialization is a primary influence in the life of a student and must be a concern of the teacher. Modeling can be a boon or a curse to certain students in the program, depending on which individuals and behaviors they tend to imitate. As an instructional technique the teacher may wish to guide students in modeling behaviors that will gain them acceptance in peer groups and improve their status with other students and regular classroom teachers. One reason that this development should not be ignored and left to chance is that many handicapped students are thought to be more suggestible than others.

The possible attractiveness of the counterculture (e.g., drug use, delinquency, crime) may cause some students to reject the school setting and the in group that excludes them. There is the potential for association with other outcasts who can provide a sense of identity and social interaction. The teacher can participate in an *extended counseling*

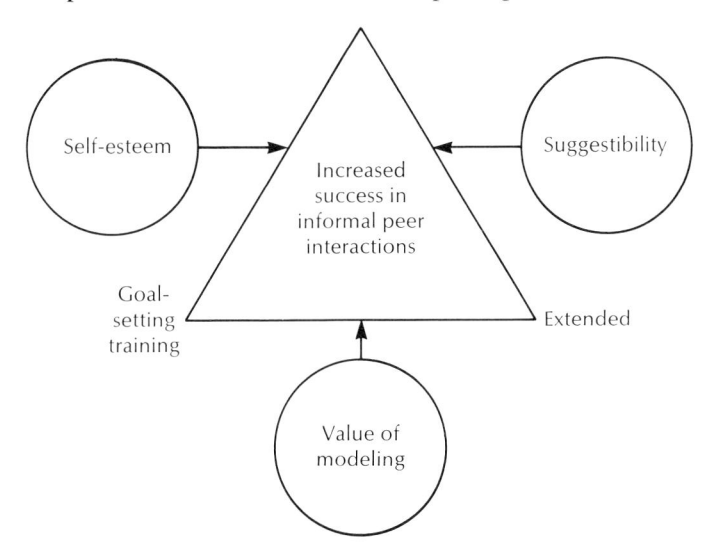

**Fig. 3-4.** Social skills training in informal groups: facilitating an increase in peer acceptance within resource room program. Circled variables represent "soft" influences not controlled by the teacher; these can have a beneficial or detrimental influence on formal training, located at points of triangle.

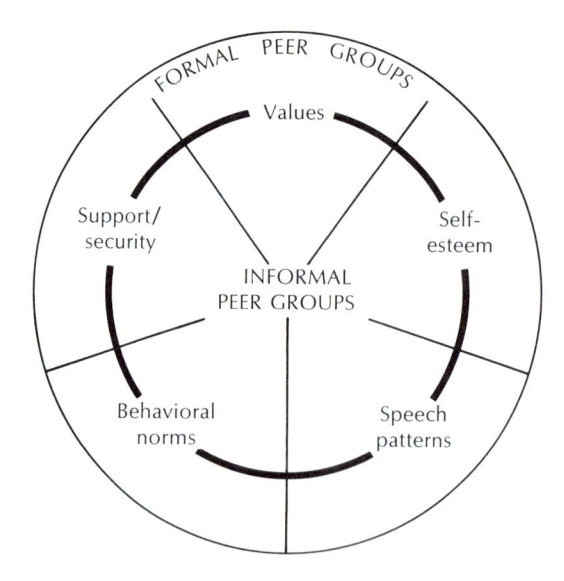

**Fig. 3-5.** Areas of adolescent development in which formal and informal peer groups exert influence.

**Table 6.** Six active strategies that acknowledge importance of peer influences

| Strategy | Explanation |
| --- | --- |
| Accommodation to increase academic success | Assisting students through compensatory teaching and circumventive strategies will help protect them from being identified as "dumb" or "retarded." |
| Indirect intervention in the form of assisting in membership in formal school peer groups | Checklist of formal groups and clarification of membership requirements may lead to increased participation in such groups and increased positive peer interaction. |
| Direct intervention through goal-setting training and social skills training | These two program components address student needs such as accurate self-evaluation, realistic goal setting, and clues within social settings as to appropriate behavior. |
| Assistance in accurate observation and assessment of peer status-gaining behaviors | Students usually have poor social perception so that they may not actually know what being popular means in their school. They may misunderstand and view any attention-gaining behavior as status-gaining behavior. |
| Assistance in selection of appropriate status-gaining behaviors | Clarification of the concept of popularity can be accomplished with these students. Suggesting possible behaviors consistent with their abilities and peer values can facilitate peer interaction. |
| Personal grooming assistance | Accepted modes of dress may not be obvious to the handicapped adolescent. Personal appearance consistent with positive peer codes can ensure greater peer status. |

*program* and assume some responsibility for *social skills training* in an effort to prevent this outcome. Fig. 3-4 depicts the interaction of variables relating to development of better social interaction. Social training may open avenues of interaction to adolescents who do not understand the rules of the social game. This may be a major need if ED, LD, and EMR students repulse others.

The self-concept of the adolescent is partly a composite of the reactions of peers, the family, and other experiences. It is subjective and individual. The characteristics the individual perceives as personally descriptive are particularly important in determination of behavior. The adolescent's perception of his or her own ability is, to a large extent, a mirror of the attitudes and opinions of significant others. Fig. 3-5 depicts areas in which peers exert influence through formal and informal groups.

The tasks of adolescence are facilitated or impeded by peer influence. The teacher must be aware of the effects of peer influence and the added importance it holds for the mildly handicapped adolescent. Total programming for the secondary student cannot be accomplished without addressing the need for peer acceptance and the difficulties that may be encountered in achieving that acceptance. Table 6 lists some strategies that the teacher might utilize in assisting the student in peer relationships. These can be modified to fit the specific population of students and the particular school setting.

## SPECIAL PROBLEMS IN ADOLESCENCE

There are some specific problems that seem to have particular relevance for those working with the mildly handicapped adolescent. Most of these problems are found in the normal-achieving adolescent, so it should not be assumed that they are specifically characteristic of the population. Many adolescents probably develop coping mechanisms to lessen the difficulties of the handicap without encountering inordinate problems.

### Fear of school

A phobia is an unwarranted and uncontrollable fear. There are two factors involved in a phobia: (1) the emotional component and (2) the motor component of compulsive response. Most phobias, including school phobia, are mild and transient in nature. In more severe cases, the emotional and motor components are more intense. School phobia is defined as the refusal to attend school because the student is afraid. This should be distinguished from truancy. The fear of school is so real that it prevents students from attending, unlike truancy where a choice is made. No matter how unwarranted the fear may seem, the feeling is strong enough to prevent the student from dealing with it.

Fear of school is misunderstood by the general public and is abused as a clinical concept. Although school phobia is considered rare, Erickson (1978) indicates that the incidence can be as high as 8% of the school-aged population. More girls than boys are usually represented in prevalence figures. Some mildly handicapped students find themselves in circumstances that may lead to the development of school phobia. Repeated failure is obviously associated with the school setting and may result in withdrawal or noninvolvement (Gardner, 1974). The student's expectation for failure (and perhaps peer rejection) makes school an unpleasant experience. Therefore the potential for school phobia is definitely present in the mildly handicapped student. Typical feelings expressed by students with school phobias include feeling different, less worthy, and withdrawn.

Treatment for school phobia includes correction of problems in the environment of the student, assistance in making social contacts, talking about the problem, and genuine understanding (Bakwin & Bakwin, 1972). Prevention of school phobia can be accomplished with the help of the special education teacher. The overall special education program can serve this purpose by facilitating the achievement of developmental tasks associated with adolescence.

**Depression and suicide**

In America, almost 5000 young people commit suicide each year. That is an average of 13 per day, an epidemic by any standard. Suicide is now the third leading cause of death for individuals 15 to 24 years of age, following accidents and homicides. The annual suicide rate for white youths, aged 15 to 19, increased 171% between 1950 and 1975 (Wynne, 1978). Young suicide victims represent a cross-section of youth from all economic, social, and racial backgrounds.

The reasons for the epidemic of suicide among teenagers, documented and speculated, are as varied as the young victims themselves. The anxiety associated with adolescence appears to be one of the major reasons. As pointed out earlier, the need for identity and self-esteem is great during adolescence. The need for acceptance contributes to anxiety. Adolescents need support at this stage in their development, and some individuals may need more help than adults or peers realize. The need for support, if not fulfilled through family or peer groups, may result in deep depression with which the adolescent is unable to cope. Hopelessness has been cited by would-be suicidal adolescents as a major cause in seeking suicide as an alternative. Many express the feeling that things just cannot be changed and that their whole lives are hopeless. This makes suicide appear to be the only means of relief from despair.

Even if the family setting is secure and comforting, many suicidal youngsters identify the pressures to succeed in school as reason to consider killing themselves. Some news reports on adolescent suicides equate the current atmosphere in America with that of Japan, where career competition is fierce and the suicide rate is high among young people. Of course, suicide in Japan is socially acceptable. Heightened competition in school and for jobs seems to have boosted the suicide rate for young blacks. Previously, the rate for young blacks was one third to one half the rate of young whites (*Newsweek*, August 28, 1978). However, the rates for blacks and whites are currently reported to be about the same. As hope rises, so does pressure, frustration, and the possibility for failure. Mounting pressure contributes to depression and may lead the youth to suicide.

Many mildly handicapped adolescents may be particularly susceptible to anxieties and the pressures of competition. There is awareness that other students are receiving support from their environment. Others are seen gaining status, acceptance, and success, all of which appear to be beyond reach. Peers and family may not perceive the severity of personal problems and may not recognize the resulting depression for what it is. The usual amounts of anxiety and frustration are experienced by the mildly handicapped student because he or she is an adolescent but with an added measure stemming from the nature of the handicap. This may increase the possibility of suicide.

Fatigue and loss of sleep, sudden loss of appetite, mood changes, a significant decline in schoolwork, heavy smoking, writing numerous letters to friends, an increase in drug or alcohol use, and giving away prized possessions are important warning signs. The causes for such behaviors may appear insignificant to adults, but they should not be ignored. It is a standard admonition in the human services fields that any suicide threat or sign should be taken seriously.

There are about 200 independent, locally funded suicide prevention centers in the United States, in addition to 675 federally funded community health centers that have crisis-intervention services (*Newsweek*, August 28, 1978). Hot lines providing emergency support are becoming prevalent. Professional assistance should be sought outside the school setting if necessary, and teachers, as the first line of defense, should be alert to the problems and symptoms.

## Dropping out of school

The mildly handicapped adolescent is vulnerable to dropping out of school. There are a variety of reasons why students fail to complete their school careers. The following facts should summarize general findings about the dropout:

1. In some school districts the incidence of dropouts is as high as one fourth the school population (Grant, 1975).
2. Academic and social *failure* are contributing factors in most cases.
3. More boys than girls drop out.
4. Not all students drop out because of a lack of academic ability (Howard & Anderson, 1978).
5. Academic pursuits are not important to some students, and they see little relationship between school activities and their futures.
6. Rebellion against parents and school authority, dislike for the school setting and its regulations, and academic failure are important causes for leaving school (Hicks, 1969; Howard & Anderson, 1978).
7. The typical dropout is not only uninterested in classes but is not involved in extracurricular activities; he or she is a social isolate. This underscores the importance of peer interaction within the educational context.
8. It has been demonstrated that when parents are brought into the school and involved in the problems of the student the student's tendency to develop a negative, defensive attitude leads to the decision to flee (Hicks, 1969).
9. Peers (age peers) who have dropped out and have jobs and their first real social activity free of the school can make appealing and persuasive arguments to the potential dropout.
10. A combination of limited aspirations, motivation, and accomplishments damages the student's self-concept, making school intensely unattractive.

A host of reasons can apparently cause a student to drop out; namely, academic and social failure, dislike of school, rebellion, costs of school, peer influence, the educational level of parents and siblings, family values toward education, motivation, mental and physical health, the desire for material possessions, gratification of immediate needs, and others. The mildly handicapped adolescent would be a likely candidate due to the high risk of social and academic failure. Any program for secondary students must attempt to meet the direct needs of students on a daily basis.

Related to the issue of the dropout is that of the *push-out*. Some students are known to be displeased with school or to have problems with controlling anger and aggressive behavior when frustrated or both. It is known to the authors that such students have been targeted by certain unscrupulous secondary teachers who want these students to leave school. Therefore they will provoke an unacceptable response, causing the student to violate a school rule, which will lead to suspension or expulsion and ultimately termination. Resource teachers may need to protect certain students from being victimized in this way.

## Stealing

Stealing is a problem of early childhood as well as adolescence. Stealing is often overlooked in young children and dismissed as something that they will outgrow. Reasons for childhood stealing include a desire to possess, lack of a sense of property rights, revenge, and bribery. Parents usually find it difficult to accept. However, adolescent stealing has become a serious problem that cannot be ignored. Parental factors along with the other environmental influences may interact in the degree or frequency of stealing behavior in adolescents. Failure in the academic areas may cause adolescents to turn to stealing as a means of achieving success if peers are impressed by the behavior.

The most common type of stealing among adolescents appears to be shoplifting. Shoplifting is a $1 billion loss to stores annually. Only a small percentage of offenders steal for economic need. Most come from average middle-class families where the necessities of life are readily available. The reasons given include adventure and the challenge involved in the act itself. Here again, attention might be devoted to this problem as it relates to the adolescent's need to succeed.

## COUNTERCULTURE

Of particular interest to the field of mildly handicapped adolescents has been the trend to correlate delinquency with the condition and to assume a causal relationship. In keeping with the theme of this chapter, it is feasible to expect that some students would be attracted to delinquents because of the adverse experiences identified with school. This need not be a cause of delinquency if school programs can become attuned to the needs of such students, can develop accommodative approaches, can permit participation in normal school functions and extracurricular activities, and can generally prevent the development of factors that drive students from school. In fact, alcoholism, drug abuse, running away, and delinquency may all have common roots that grow out of a general alienation from the family and the peer group.

## Delinquency

Adolescents who commit crimes and are adjudicated as law offenders are considered delinquent. Laws vary from state to state so that specific acts considered to be within the definition of delinquency may be somewhat different. The establishment of prevalence figures from statistical data is difficult because of inaccurate or closed records and the tendency for youth of the lower classes to be prosecuted. In any event, the highest rate of delinquency is for youth between the ages of 10 and 15. The highest adult crime rate is in the age group of 20 to 24, an age considered by some to be late adolescence. About 75% of all people arrested for burglary, larceny, and auto theft are under the age of 25 (Thornburg, 1975).

Dating from 1957, the juvenile court case load has shown a steady increase in cases of minors between the ages of 10 to 17 (Wynne, 1978). Erickson (1978) has stated that over 50% of the teenage population has participated in some type of delinquent act. Approximately 80% of all offenders are males, who are usually charged with property offenses. Females engage in sexual misconduct or are status offenders who run away or are considered unmanageable.

The relationship between mildly handicapping conditions and delinquency has not been clearly established, but some writers tend to believe there is a causal relationship between academic failure and delinquency. Alarming reports (Dulling et al., 1970; Jacobson, 1974; Walle, 1972) of extremely high proportions of delinquents with learning disabilities have been used to generate special programs to either prevent or reduce the number of miscreants and felons through remedial education. Whether or not behavioral misconduct masks learning disabilities has not been clearly determined in spite of the dramatic figures reported by some writers. The tendency for some school districts to include any child with a low rate of success in academic subjects in the LD category, the tendency to relabel EMR students as learning disabled, and the confusion about the diagnosis and definition, coupled with an equally poor definition of delinquency and inaccurate reporting methods, can lead to inaccurate conclusions.

In spite of the problems with defining and describing the proper parameters of the mild handicaps and delinquency, it is clear that the potential for becoming a delinquent is inherent in the ED and LD population, not so much because of the inability to succeed in academic subjects, but because of social and emotional factors of which school failure is only one facet. A more successful prevention strategy in the school would entail socialization of the student rather than expecting academic gains to do the job. The reasons, ultimately, that students seek status and prestige from among friends in the counterculture are related to their inability to gain acclaim from peers in the school. Excluding students from clubs, organizations, athletics, and student government because of their inability to earn grades virtually assures the attractiveness of the counterculture. In any event, prevention is more promising than rehabilitation after the fact.

## Alcoholism

Some children begin drinking at an early age, and many have taken a drink before their late teens. Peer pressure figures prominently in the use of alcohol, although parent modeling may also be a strong influence. Over 1 million teenagers drink too much (Unger, 1978). However, very little attention to this problem has surfaced, and some parents seem to be relieved that a child chooses to indulge in alcohol rather than drugs.

Once alcohol is used frequently by a student it can be abused for some of the same reasons as in the adult abuser. It numbs the adolescent to the stresses of growing up and the disappointments of academic and social life, and it reduces anxiety. Unger (1978) cautions therapists who work with the teenage alcoholic to take care in exhorting a drinker to stop suddenly because drinking may mask suicidal tendencies. This, like other social and emotional problems, is impossible to deal with effectively without specific, qualified personnel to assume responsibility. Perhaps the emphasis should be placed on prevention by means of accommodating to students' needs early in the school career, thereby reducing the trend of students to be socially isolated, anxious, and depressed by the stresses placed on them by a school system that unwittingly contributes to their unhappiness through rigid regulations.

## Drug abuse

Drug abuse is the use of drugs inconsistent with medical, social, and legal regulations or norms. Drug abuse occurs in all segments of our society, in all geographic regions, and within all age groups. Some estimates of drug use in high school individuals range as high as 80% (Millman, 1978). Table 7 is a summary of reported drug use adapted from information reported by Shafer (1972), which indicates the incidence of drug experimen-

**Table 7.** Incidence of drug experimentation among persons between the ages of 12 and 25*

| Number of users | Drug used |
|---|---|
| 2.1 million | Heroin |
| 2.6 million | Cocaine |
| 3.7 million | Methamphetamines |
| 4.7 million | LSD, peyote, mescaline |
| 9.3 million | Hashish |
| 24.0 million | Marijuana |

*Adapted from Shafer, R. P. *Marijuana: A signal of misunderstanding.* New York: Signet, 1972.

tation of adolescents and young adults between the ages of 12 and 25.

Incidence figures are difficult to obtain because investigators must rely on self-reporting and legal records of reported usage. Cultural variation, sampling techniques, and legal problems complicate data collection. Survey, the most common method of investigation, may contain inaccuracies. For example, subjects surveyed report two to three times greater prevalence and frequency of drug use for their acquaintances than for themselves (Yancy et al., 1972). Nonetheless, there is a consensus among professionals and law authorities that high levels of teenaged drug use are of such a magnitude as to constitute a significant social problem.

The reasons for the use of drugs in our culture are difficult to ascertain. We reviewed the literature on drug abuse by adolescents and discovered a few common explanations, which are summarized below:

1. Some writers speculate that adolescent drug use correlates directly with the *alienation*, *rejection*, and *isolation* the adolescent feels within his environment (Bronfenbrenner, 1972; Keniston, 1971).
2. *Peer pressure* is considered a more important factor by some researchers (Warner & Swisher, 1975).
3. *Curiosity* aroused by friends' use of drugs or the belief of a higher prevalence of drug use among peers was revealed to be a factor in drug use (Yancy et al., 1972).
4. The adolescent uses drugs in an attempt at *self-treatment* to satisfy and control drives unsettled during puberty (Millman, 1978).
5. *Family dynamics and family stresses* may also contribute to the use of drugs because the adolescent seeks an escape (Biggs et al., 1974).

The personality of the user, popularity of certain drugs among friends, expense of the drug, and physiological effects on the individual are related to use. The types of drugs are briefly described below:

NARCOTICS: opiates, such as opium, heroin, morphine, and codeine act as central nervous system depressants.
SEDATIVE-HYPNOTIC DRUGS: tranquilizers, sleeping pills (barbiturates); commonly known as downers.
STIMULANTS: amphetamines, cocaine and diet pills; stimulate the central nervous system.
HALLUCINOGENS: LSD, mescaline, and peyote.
SOLVENTS: glue sniffing; includes fumes of gasoline, lighter fluid, paint thinner, cleaning fluid, and glue.
CANNABIS: marijuana and hashish.

Drug overdose, more appropriately termed "drug poisoning," is a serious threat to the life of an individual. An overdose or other serious reaction may result from forgetting how much has been taken, from attempting to get a "better high" or "cop a buzz," or from ingesting or injecting substances of unknown origin and consistency. Combining various drugs or mixing drugs with alcohol may result in catastrophic reaction. Due to the increased frequency of drug use among teenagers, a secondary teacher should be aware of types of substances used by students and of signs of toxicity. If indicated, first aid or immediate attention of medical authorities might be necessary. The teacher should be aware of school policies and procedures pertaining to drug possession and use. Table 8 is a list of common street drugs and signs of toxicity.

As with other social and emotional problems we have discussed, *we are not aware of any data specifically relating to the use of drugs among handicapped students*. As in the case of delinquency, which has been related to learning disabilities by some writers, it would be naive to presume a simple cause-and-effect relationship or to blame drug use

**Table 8.** Common drugs and signs of toxicity*

| Drug | Mild toxic signs | Severe overdose signs |
|---|---|---|
| *Opiates* | | |
| Heroin, morphine, meperidine (Demerol), methadone | "Nodding" drowsiness, small pupils, urinary retention, slow and shallow breathing; skin scars and subcutaneous abscesses; duration: 4-6 hours; with methadone, duration to 24 hours | Coma; pinpoint pupils; slow, irregular respiration |
| *Depressants* | | |
| Barbiturates | Confusion, rousable drowsiness, delirium, ataxia | Stupor to coma; pupils reactive, usually constricted; respiration/blood pressure depressed |
| Methaqualone (Quaalude) | Hallucinations, agitation, motor hyperactivity, tonic spasms | Coma, occasional convulsions, bleeding tendency |
| *Stimulants* | | |
| Amphetamines | Hyperactive, aggressive, sometimes paranoid, repetitive behavior; dilated pupils; tremors | Agitated, assaultive, and paranoid excitement; occasionally convulsions |
| Cocaine | Similar to above; less paranoid, often euphoric | Twitching, irregular breathing |
| *Psychedelics* | | |
| LSD, mescaline | Confused, disoriented, perceptual distortions; distractable, withdrawn, or eruptive; wide-eyed, dilated pupils; restlessness | Panic |
| *Antidepressants* | | |
| Imipramine | Restlessness, drowsiness, sweating | Agitation, vomiting, convulsions, sweating |

*Adapted from Millman, R. B. Drug and alcohol abuse. In B. B. Wolman (Ed.), *Handbook of treatment of mental disorders in childhood and adolescence.* Englewood Cliffs, N.J.: Prentice-Hall, 1978.

on academic failure. Many factors contribute to social deviance, not just academic failure. If it is true that many students tend to alienate their peers and families because of unacceptable social skills, the total ecology of the social environment becomes important. Attractiveness of the counterculture becomes heightened if the social setting of the school is undesirable.

We are aware, through personal contact with secondary teachers, that some handicapped students use drugs, especially marijuana. The effects of cannabis on attention, moods, and memory are becoming documented and better understood. As might be expected, the impact of smoking cannabis on the central nervous system of a student is very detrimental to motivation and school performance. One teacher related to us that she was certain that one student made a concerted effort to smoke a marijuana cigarette before his English class because it made him mellow enough to make it through the hour.

## Running away

Some adolescents are so overwhelmed with their lives that they simply leave home. They may be gone for a few days or for longer periods. A few manage to disappear. This is a common status offense. There are only rough estimates of the number of teenagers who run, and they are complicated by reporting problems. Like other problems worsened by learning and behavior disorders, we believe that many students would have good reason to find more promise in a distant and unknown future. Unfortunately, there is considerable danger for a runaway who may fall victim to illness, abuse, or much worse.

The only successful approach to treating the problems of the runaway is to involve the whole family (Gordon, 1975). The act of running involves the whole family unit, not just the individual, because it is a manifestation of a breakdown in family unity and communication. The special teacher is likely to have more personal contact with students than other teachers of the secondary school and will be working with a population of students who may have more severe personal and social problems than others. Consequently, the signs of disaffection and the desire to run may be noticed by the specialist before others.

## HOW STUDENTS BEHAVE: AN ANTHROPOLOGICAL VIEW

We present the following observations without scientific justification but also without apologies to the empiricist. In our professional experiences with students at the secondary level we have witnessed the following behaviors and believe them to be of great importance to the prospective teacher. Veteran teachers will confirm these characterizations and will be able to embellish them. We doubt that much attention is ordinarily given to them in preservice course work except as they are considered problems in need of mass behavioral management.

1. *Junior high students (especially boys) push, hit, and shove one another.* This is an annoying pastime of young teenagers, who joust with one another in the classroom and the hall, on the bus, or anywhere else it seems that two or more may gather. Considering the frequency of such pseudoaggressive attacks it is remarkable that injuries are infrequent and tempers rarely flare up. Junior high students do it because they enjoy it, and typically such interaction does not occur between enemies. It is a good-natured indulgence that is quite normal and is recognizable in the young of other species, such as chimpanzees.

2. *Junior high students (especially boys) attack one another verbally.* Any student who is obese will be called "fat," and a thin student will be called "skinny" or "toothpick." For the most part, it too is intended as a ritualistic insult. The best response is a clever rejoinder. Losing one's temper violates the rules and leaves one vulnerable to more severe attacks, which are sure to be supported by others who learns about one's sensitivity to name-calling. It is important for the resource teacher to recognize this behavior as a puberty rite that cannot be stopped. It is also important to counsel the more socially inept student to understand the behavior, to resist angry responses, and to either absorb the abuse or join the patter. To be oversensitive is to invite merciless teasing, which can become a problem.

3. *Junior high students (especially boys) throw things.* They will throw paper wads, paper clips, chalk, erasers, paper airplanes, and a variety of other objects. This is evidenced by the incredible amount of litter on the floors and soggy paper towels blanketing the restroom.

4. *Junior high students like to go to the restroom.* In addition to the valid reasons for wanting to go to the restroom are an interest in simply getting out of the classroom, the need to sneak a smoke, or the desire to pass

by a friend's classroom in order to make a hideous face in the doorway.

5. *Junior high students like to write on things.* Expressions of love and sorrow, derision of rivals, disrespect for school personnel, and frank vulgarities may be found on toilet walls, desk tops, sides of buses, and other writing surfaces. A tremendous quantity of paper is consumed because of a significant trade in notes.

6. *Junior high students make a lot of noise.* Animal sounds, grunts, groans, squeals, whistles, hoots, howls, and giggles make up a substantial part of the vast repertoire of sounds achieved by teenagers. More elaborate noise making is managed by experts who can stomp a milk carton with sufficient skill to make a loud explosive sound and by risk takers who pull the fire alarm or invoke the aid of fireworks.

This does not exhaust the list of behaviors but should serve to provide neophytes with basic training (in case they have forgotten their own school days).

The older adolescent is more sophisticated and adultlike in behavior, which accounts for the decorum of the high school (by contrast to the junior high).

1. *High school students primp a lot.* Literally hours will be spent in front of a mirror. The purpose is to worry about one's appearance, to keep hair combed or uncombed properly, to fix makeup, and to wish away skin blemishes.

2. *Adolescents fall in love.* One of the problems in high school is that a romance can run smoothly for a while and then fall apart. In either extreme, the moods that accompany the status of the relationship at any point in time can interfere with all others parts of a student's life. It is difficult to consider homework if one is agonizing over a broken romance.

3. *Adolescents are preoccupied with the immediate future.* The class period is an eternity for teenagers who anticipate 5 minutes in the hall with a friend between classes. Monday is a long way off from a weekend date. A lot of time is spent fantasizing about the future. The track coach would be impressed with the quick starts of students as they exit their desks at the sound of a bell.

4. *Adolescents are intolerant.* The attitudes of parents and teachers can be smugly and categorically dismissed. There is a certain sense of egocentrism and cocksure confidence that permeates adolescence. Adolescents are as rigid in their postures and attitudes as the rigidity they perceive and acrimoniously attack in the adult world. They criticize those who are different in thought, speech, and manner and are convinced of their self-importance. Beneath the exterior they are much less confident.

## SUMMARY

In this chapter we presented an overview of the issues pertaining to interpersonal relationships of adolescents. Emphasis was placed on the family unit and the peer group with references to the mildly handicapped adolescent at points where either evidence or theory would seem to warrant special consideration. We stressed that socialization of the mildly handicapped student is essential to understanding the correlates of handicapping conditions as well as planning for the amelioration of problems.

According to some investigators, many students repel parents and peers. Ineptitude in social interaction is a detriment to the development of friendships, the self-concept, academic achievement, and vocational adjustment. If a student is "hard to like" then he or she will be walled off from important contacts, will be socially isolated, and will be viewed unsympathetically by parents and teachers as well as peers. The very persons who can help the student the most may become alienated.

With reference to the families of students, we made the following points:

1. The nature of a student's personality may be such that certain characteristics cause additional stress on the family unit, which may result in a deterioration of family alliances, conflict between the child and parents, and ill effects on the personality development of the child.
2. The student will be more vulnerable to socialization problems in the school and community because of a greater tendency for interpersonal conflict.
3. As a result of a complex set of problems related to the family, the socialization process, and the impact of disabilities on the personality, the student may be more subject to the social disorders of this generation of students.

We freely admit that some of our conclusions may not be warranted because of a lack of relevant research to confirm or to deny certain points. There is reason to believe that some students will be more easily attracted to social deviance, will have more problems with their families and peers, and will generally have more personal and social problems than other adolescents. A great deal of research is necessary in this area before we can be sure. Nonetheless, consideration of the sheer pressure on adolescents from the various social forces in today's world easily leads one to the undisputed conclusion that the needs of the mildly handicapped adolescent far exceed the simple delivery of some form of remedial education. Whether or not the specialist should assume much of this added responsibility is a question that cannot be easily answered, but it seems obvious to us that much more planning to account for the characteristics of adolescents and their unique problems will be mandatory if a complex of special educational strategies is to be successful in meeting the needs and requirements of mildly handicapped students on a daily basis.

## REFERENCES AND READINGS

Bachman, J., O'Malley, P., & Johnston, J. Dogmatic teens. *Human Behavior*, October 1978, 7(10), 32.

Bakwin, H., & Bakwin, R. M. *Behavior disorders in children* (4th ed.). Philadelphia: Saunders, 1972.

Baldwin, A., & Baldwin, C. *Cognitive control of mother-child interactions*. Washington, D.C.: U.S. Office of Education, 1970.

Baldwin, A., & Baldwin, C. Personality and social development of handicapped children. In C. Sherrick, J. Swets, & L. Elliott (Eds.), *Psychology and the handicapped child*. Washington, D.C.: U.S. Dept. of Health, Education and Welfare, 1974.

Biggs, D. A., Orcutt, J. B., & Bakkenist, N. Correlates of marijuana and alcohol use among college students. *Journal of College Student Personnel*, 1974, pp. 22-30.

Bronfenbrenner, U. Childhood: The roots of alienation. *National Elementary Principal*, 1972, 52(2), 22-29.

Bryan, J. H., & Bryan, T. H. *Exceptional children*. Sherman Oaks, Calif.: Alfred, 1979.

Bryan, T. H., & Bryan, J. H. *Understanding learning disabilities*. Sherman Oaks, Calif.: Alfred, 1978.

Burchinal, L. G. Characteristics of adolescents from unbroken, broken, and reconstituted families. *Journal of Marriage and the Family*, 1964, 26, 44-51.

Burgess, E. W. The family as a unity of interacting personalities. *Families*, 1926, 7, 3-9.

Carns, D. E. Talking about sex: Notes on first coitus and the double sexual standard. *Journal of Marriage and the Family*, 1973, 35(4).

Coleman, J. S. Athletics in high school. *Annals of the American Academy of Political and Social Science*, 1961, 338, 33-43.

Coleman, J. S. The adolescent subculture and academic achievement. In M. Powell and A. H. Frerichs (Eds.), *Readings in adolescent psychology*. Minneapolis: Burgess, 1971.

DeFrancis, V., & Lucht, C. *Child abuse legislation in the 1970's*. Denver: American Humane Association, 1974.

Dulling, F., Eddy, S., & Drisko, V. *Learning disabilities and juvenile delinquency*. Unpublished study, Robert F. Kennedy Youth Center, Morgantown, W. Va., 1970.

Elder, G. H. Structural variations in the child-rearing relationship. *Sociometry*, 1962, 25, 241-262.

Erickson, M. T. *Child psychopathology: Assessment, etiology, and treatment*. Englewood Cliffs, N.J.: Prentice-Hall, 1978.

Erikson, E. H. *Identity: Youth in crisis*. New York: Norton, 1968.

Farber, B. *Mental retardation: Its social context and social consequences*. Boston: Houghton Mifflin, 1968.

Foster, G. G., Schmidt, C. R., & Sabatino, D. Teacher

expectancies and the label "learning disabilities." *Journal of Learning Disabilities*, February 1976, 9:2, 58-61.

Friedman, R. Using the family school in the treatment of learning disabilities. *Journal of Learning Disabilities*, 1978, *11*(6), 378-382.

Garbarino, J., & Jacobson, N. Youth helping youth in cases of maltreatment of adolescents. *Child Welfare*, 1978, *62*(8), 505-509.

Gardner, W. *Children with learning and behavior problems: A behavior management approach.* Boston: Allyn & Bacon, 1974.

Gordon, J. S. Working with runaways and their families: How the SAJA community does it. *Family Process*, 1975, *14*(2), 235-262.

Gordon, S. Reversing a negative self-image. In L. E. Anderson (Ed.), *Helping the adolescent with the hidden handicap.* Los Angeles: California Association for Neurologically Handicapped Children, 1970.

Grant, W. V. Estimates of school dropouts. *American Education.* 1975, *51*, back cover.

Hammill, D. D., & Myers, P. *Methods for learning disorders.* New York: Wiley, 1969.

Havighurst, R. L. Unrealized potentials of adolescents. *National Association of Secondary School Principals' Bulletin*, 1966, *50*, 75-96.

Havighurst, R. L. The middle school child in contemporary society. *Theory into Practice*, 1968, *7*(3), 120-122.

Hicks, J. B. All's calm in the crow's nest. *American Education*, 1969, 5.

Howard, M. A. P., & Anderson, R. J. Early identification of potential school dropouts: A literature review. *Child Welfare*, 1978, *62*(4), 221-229.

Jacobson, F. Learning disabilities and juvenile delinquency: A demonstrated relationship. In R. E. Weber (Ed.), *Handbook on learning disabilities*, Englewood Cliffs, N.J.: Prentice-Hall, 1974.

Johnson, D., & Myklebust, H. *Learning disabilities: Educational principles and practices.* New York: Grune & Stratton, 1967.

Johnson, S. W., & Morasky, R. L. *Learning disabilities.* Boston: Allyn & Bacon, 1977.

Kaats, G. R., & Davis, K. E. The dynamics of sexual behavior of college students. *Journal of Marriage and the Family*, 1970, *32*, 390-399.

Keniston, K. A second look at the uncommitted. *Social Policy*, 1971, *2*(2), 6-19.

Landis, P. H. *The broken home in teenage adjustment* (Washington Agriculture Experiment Stations Bulletin No. 542). Washington, D.C.: U.S. Government Printing Office, 1953.

Lewis, M. *Shared meaning within a family seeking help and the role of the identified patient.* Unpublished doctoral dissertation, University of Nebraska, 1976.

Lourie, I. S., & Cohan, A. M. Abuse and neglect of adolescents. *Child Abuse Reports*, 1976, No. 1.

Mead, G. H. *Mind, self and society.* Chicago: University of Chicago Press, 1934.

Millman, R. B. Drug and alcohol abuse. In B. B. Wolman (Ed.), *Handbook of treatment of mental disorders in childhood and adolescence.* Englewood Cliffs, N.J.: Prentice-Hall, 1978.

Rosenstein, P. J. Family outreach: A program for the prevention of child neglect/abuse. *Child Welfare*, 1978, *62*(8), 519-525.

Shafer, R. P. *Marijuana: A signal of misunderstanding.* New York: Signet, 1972.

Sheppard, M., Oppenheim, A., & Mitchell, S. Childhood behavior disorders and the child guidance clinic. *Journal of Psychology and Psychiatry*, 1966, *7*, 39-52.

Smigel, E. D., & Seiden, R. The decline and fall of the double standard. In H. D. Thornburg (Ed.), *Contemporary adolescence: Readings.* Monterey, Calif.: Brooks/Cole, 1975.

Theisen, W. M. What next in child abuse policy? Improving the knowledge base. *Child Welfare*, 1978, *62*(7), 415-421.

Thornburg, H. D. Peers, three distinct groups. *Adolescence*, 1971, *6*(21), 59-76.

Thornburg, H. D. *Contemporary adolescence: Readings* (2nd ed.). Monterey, Calif.: Brooks/Cole, 1975.

Unger, R. A. The treatment of adolescent alcoholism. *Social Casework*, 1978, *59*(1), 27-35.

Walle, E. Learning disabilities. Unpublished paper presented at the International Conference of A.C.L.D., Atlantic City, 1972.

Warner, R. W., & Swisher, J. D. Alienation and drug abuse: Synonymous? In H. Thornburg (Ed.), *Contemporary adolescence: Readings.* Monterey, Calif.: Brooks/Cole, 1975.

Wender, P. *Minimal brain dysfunction in children.* New York: Wiley, 1971.

Wynne, E. A. Behind the discipline problem: Youth suicide as a measure of alienation. *Phi Delta Kappan*, 1978, *59*(5), 307-315.

Yancy, W. S., Nader, P. R., & Burnham, K. Drug use and attitudes of high school students. *Pediatrics*, 1972, *50*(5), 739-745.

# SECTION TWO

# THE SCHOOL

The ability to understand the school environment, its influences, and how it functions is critical to planning the secondary special education program. The field of special education has had limited interest in adolescents. With most of research and program development concentrated on elementary programs and younger children, the need to provide comprehensive services to handicapped adolescents has found many special educators ill prepared to meet the challenge. There has been a tendency to imitate the elementary school resource room and to restrict special education goals to those that can be easily circumscribed by a remedial program. The unique needs of the adolescent, the peer group, and the adolescent subculture, and handicapping conditions have been considered in the previous section. The importance of preparing appropriate programming for these students is such that the organization of the school, the curriculum and instructional practices of secondary education, and supportive services available to the special educator must be considered in some detail.

Emphasis in this section is placed on the most important features of school administration and functioning. The special educator must be aware that the sources of power, formal and informal, can have a very direct impact on the special education program and will determine its success or failure to a great extent. Understanding school policies, the pressures on principals and teachers, the attitudes of mainstream teachers toward handicapped students, and many other issues will enable the special educator to plan for contingencies and realistically develop program goals. Understanding the nature of secondary teaching, the learning environment of students, and the nature of subject matter will aid the specialist immeasurably in planning individualized educational programs. The ability to fully utilize the services of support personnel is essential for the maintenance of a viable program that will actually help students to achieve their educational goals. Special education is not simply the delivery of special services to a group of students in a classroom. Methodologies must include strategies for fitting special programming into the system, for eliciting support from other professionals, and for changing the system to the advantage of the program.

Chapter 4

# ORGANIZATION AND ADMINISTRATION OF THE SCHOOL

The theory and practice of school administration is a subject that is rarely covered in textbooks for teachers and finds only brief mention in preparatory classes. The special educator should have more than a nodding acquaintance with school administration because (1) the attitude of school administrators can, directly or indirectly, have a profound impact on special education, (2) many of the issues and problems in special education are also administrative problems, and (3) understanding the administrative structure and demands on administrators provides the specialist with knowledge that can be useful in maintaining an efficient program and averting complications.

One way to appreciate the importance of administration, and the personalities of administrators, is to envision the public school as a social system with separate parts, each specialized for a unique purpose (e.g., social science department) but each contributing to an ultimate, common purpose (the education of students). At the apex of the school organization is the principal who is vested with certain specific and discretionary powers to administer, supervise, establish policy, and otherwise conduct the affairs of students and teaching personnel. Within each subsystem (departments, classes, etc.) there is significant activity determined by the purposes for which each is established. There is much less contact across the boundaries of subsystems, that is, there is a natural tendency to be isolated and preoccupied. Significant changes in the structure, activities, goals, or methods of the entire system are not likely to occur from within. Change in a system results from influences at the top (the principal or other administrators in the hierarchy of the larger district) or from outside the system (demands of school patrons, state and federal laws, etc.). From this perspective, it is readily apparent that the principal is a key person in the establishment of a climate that promotes and supports a successful special education program.

Cahn and Nolan (1976) contend that many learning disabled students can be educated within the conventional secondary school setting if the school is blessed with a knowledgeable, sympathetic principal. This contention is underscored by the fact that special education has systemic needs that are greatly different from any other subsystem, needs that can only be met by effective leadership. In general, these needs are (1) to locate, identify, and develop services for handicapped students; and (2) to elicit cooperation from all other subsystems (departments, teachers) in the provision of appropriate services. In order to do this, change must occur; and, as we have said, change is more likely to occur as a result of influence from the top of the organizational hierarchy. Ideally, district-wide policies established by the board of education and superintendent to benefit students would have a major impact; but it is necessary, at a minimum, to have the support of the principal in effecting change. Curriculum modifications, accommodatory techniques, and shared educational responsibility between mainstream teachers and special educators will not occur or will be given mere lip service if the principal is unwilling to support the efforts. It is imperative that the special educator be acquainted with the administrative structure, formal and informal power, and how to influence policy in order to achieve the outcomes of special education for mildly handicapped adolescents.

## ORGANIZATION OF THE SCHOOL

In the strictest sense, education is the responsibility of the various states because the U.S. Constitution contains no references to education, leaving it within the purview of state governments. It is the state legislature that establishes schools, provides for their basic support, prescribes, to varying degrees, the nature and scope of the curriculum, creates authority for the administration of schools, and defines the roles of personnel. The U.S. Congress has demonstrated significant interest in the education of children by the establishment of numerous agencies concerned with educational matters and the infusion of billions of dollars into educational institutions. More recently, the rise of litigation over many issues in education has caused state and federal courts to exercise control over education by giving definition to practices of states, school boards, administrators, and teachers in their numerous relationships with each other and with students.

## Typical organizational arrangements

The resources, size, and philosophy of a school district are variables influencing the type of organizational arrangement. In effect, most schools are similar because of bureaucratic structure. Small districts will have a central office with a superintendent, who may also have teaching responsibilities or act as a principal, and large districts will have a superintendent with an enormous supporting cast consisting of assistant superintendents, coordinators, supervisors, directors, principals, and assistant principals. Fig. 4-1 is an organizational chart of a small school district. A chart of a large district would be enormous in size.

Most secondary schools are organized into subject areas or departments, which are based on discrete areas of the curriculum. This organizational arrangement dates back to the traditional importance placed on certain academic subjects in the Latin grammar school, the academy, and the first high schools. The prestige of academic subjects of the curriculum has remained relatively unchallenged throughout history. Typically, departments are organized around social studies, mathematics, science, and language arts.

Moderately sized and large schools have department heads who are practicing teachers in the school elected by the faculty or appointed by the principal. The department head may or may not receive extra compensation or a reduced teaching load in order to perform such duties as attending district-wide meetings, planning the curriculum, selecting materials and books, and, in some cases, assisting in the evaluation of fellow teachers. The department head may exert considerable influence in the school and may be the "turf protector" for the department, assuring that other departments and teachers do not duplicate departmental efforts. This

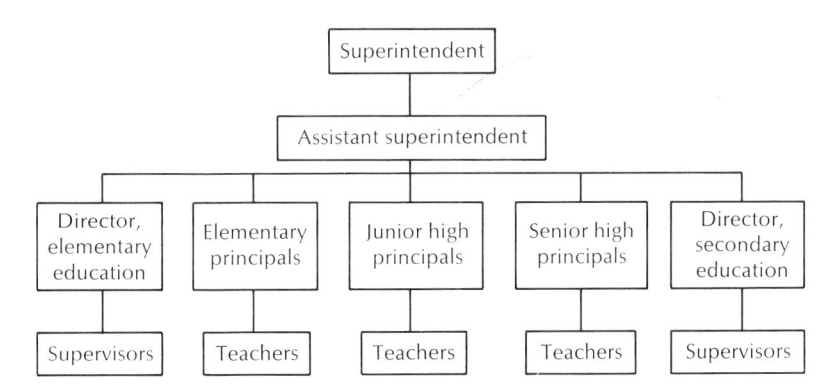

**Fig. 4-1.** Organizational chart of a small school district.

is particularly important to the special education teacher who, by assisting students with the various content areas of the curriculum, must deal with subject matter broadly defined as special education but which is certainly within the province of school departments. The following guiding principles are recommended in order to avoid conflict and enlist cooperation:

1. *Recognize administrative procedures such as going through channels. Adhere to protocol.* Keeping superiors informed, seeking advise and permission from them, and following their directives are important in the bureaucracy for efficient operation of the school. What may work successfully in one setting may not in another because key personnel in the bureaucracy have different personalities. A threatened, insecure, jealous, or petty individual may cause problems for no apparent or particular reason. Other will be magnanimous and cooperative. It is necessary to assess the formal and informal power structure, determine through experience and reputation those individuals who may be oppositional, and endeavor to use strategies to gain their confidence or at least not to invoke their ire.

Because the special education teacher will need to work closely with mainstream teachers concerning students and related services, the initial planning and groundwork for such contacts should be developed or approved by department heads. Although the principal may sanction certain activities or procedures, resistance may be forthcoming from aggrieved department heads who believe they were left out of the planning. It may be necessary to spend much time dealing with certain individuals, time that may seem to be wasted but that will pay dividends in the future.

2. *Communicate clearly to all administrative and supervisory personnel the objectives of your program.* So much emphasis in journals and textbooks on the topic of consulting with regular classroom teachers is naively considered without attention to administrators. As Arnold and Goodloe (1974, p. 64) succinctly state: "The road toward more effective schools is strewn with the wreckage of change attempts that failed because they lack sufficient understanding or sympathy from administrators. . . ."

Smith (1977) investigated the attitudes of administrators toward the handicapped and special programs for them at the secondary level; he concluded that (1) high school principals generally have a more positive attitude toward nonhandicapped students than toward the mentally retarded or the learning disabled, and (2) even minor negative attitudes affect educational programming, but (3) principals who had worked for a number of years in schools with effective secondary programs (work-study) tended to have more positive attitudes.

If the special education teacher is employed in a school that previously had a well-accepted program, continuing the predecessor's work and embellishing on it will probably be an easier task than in a setting where employment requires embarking on a new course of action where no program had existed or following a special teacher who alienated most of the staff. Clear attention to the matters of administration, lines of authority, and communication with administrators and department heads is essential.

3. *Avoid the "missionary complex" that sometimes infects special educators.* Missionaries have often been eaten. The fervor and zeal expressed by some special educators is a "turn off" with many secondary teachers partly because such behavior implies that regular educators do not really care about students. Special education teachers who set out to save the world will more likely end up frustrated, unsuccessful, and detrimental to the goals of special education. It is true

that there is injustice in the system, that some teachers do not seem to care, and many changes could be made, but working patiently within the system will enable the teacher to more closely approximate the ultimate hopes of programming.

4. *In contacts with departments and department heads, clearly written agreements about interaction with the special education program may lay the foundation for success.* Agreements with department heads might include:
   a. Agreements about curriculum responsibility
   b. Policies about use of materials and equipment
   c. Concurrence about modification of curriculum materials
   d. Consensus about examination of students with reading or writing disorders
   e. Agreements that the curriculum will not be "watered down" because students will be expected to achieve in subject areas, but modifications may be introduced
   f. Agreements about supervision and input from faculty about materials and curriculum modification

## Organizational patterns of special education

There are various arrangements of special education within the administrative organization of school systems affected by the variables of size, resources, philosophy, and intervening laws and regulations. There are very few districts that have special education *administrators;* most serve in a staff or consulting position. The following arrangements exist.

**Local educational agency (LEA).** In an arrangement based on an LEA, depending on the size, an assistant superintendent may have primary responsibility for all special education programs. More commonly, a staff-level assistant is employed to coordinate special education under the direction of an administrator, usually an assistant superintendent. In larger units there may be a director or coordinator of special services programs, which include special education as one element. There will be a number of subordinates with responsibility for various facets of special education.

**Intermediate educational unit (IEU).** The IEU exists in those states where legislation permits its development. It is a cooperative arrangement between political units (counties) or two or more school districts, which share in the expense of providing special education. Examples of cooperative programs are Coop's, Board of Cooperative Services (BOCES) in Colorado and New York, and Regional Education Service Agencies (RESA) in Iowa.

## Supervisory personnel in special education

Except in the case of a separate special school where a principal is in charge of special education programs, most persons who perform management roles in special education are responsible for one or more components of the special education program in an LEA or IEU. They are recognized by various titles in different states, for example, director, supervisor, or coordinator. The scope of duties and responsibilities for supervisory personnel will vary in accordance with the attitudes of superintendents; some may be restricted to routine, perfunctory matters such as data collection and completion of paperwork. Others will have wide latitude. Generally, the duties of the special education supervisor will include the following roles (Gearheart, 1974):
1. General administrative duties
2. Supervisory duties
3. Research and continued professional study

4. Public relations
5. In-service training

Additionally, duties include monitoring of IEPs, curriculum development and modification, management of due process procedures, placement of students, recommendations about budgets and allocations, selection and maintenance of materials and equipment, staff development activities with regular educators, and interaction with parents and examiners concerning referral, diagnosis, and placement.

## Qualifications of special education management personnel

The qualifications of management personnel (directors, coordinators, supervisors, etc.) are inconsistent from one state to another, in part because of the lack of clarity about what the role should be, what duties should be performed, and the relative recency of the need for extra leadership in administering special education programs. Consequently, some states do not have requirements for the position and those that do reflect wide differences in the need for administrative training. Some special education teachers complain about supervisors who do not have training and experience in special education, believing that successful performance of the job is predicated on understanding subtle diagnostic issues and specialized educational methodologies. To determine the necessary qualifications one should consult with the individual state department agency that certifies school personnel.

## External organizational structure

Although the special education program is controlled by the school superintendent and his or her subordinates, or by a cooperative agreement between two or more superintendents who participate in an IEU, most state governments exercise some control over the special education programs of the state. Typically, there is a state director or supervisor of special education who may have a number of subordinates. The responsibilities of the state director include preparing budgets and seeking funding from the legislature for special education, coordinating procedures for reimbursing school districts for special education programs (salaries, units, transportation, etc.), preparing and assisting in the preparation of legislation relating to special education, implementing regulations pertaining to the administration of special education (class size, qualifications of teachers, etc.), evaluating local school programs, coordinating federal programs, monitoring the districts for compliance with federal legislation and regulations (P.L. 94-142), and many other minor duties.

There are myriad regulations, and several agencies of the federal government have some control over aspects of education and provide federal monies to support special education and related services. Most notable, the Bureau of Education for the Handicapped (BEH) supports research and service and establishes regulations for federal interests in special education. Each state is assigned a project officer who determines that the state is in compliance with the regulations of P.L. 94-142. Generally, a close working relationship exists between the project officer and the state director of special education.

## Federal legislation

Increasingly since 1965, federal legislation has tightened its direct control of education at the local level by creating sources of funds available to the schools and demanding specific conditions of compliance. The Elementary and Secondary Education Act, P.L. 89-10, was the beginning of intense federal involvement in schooling, which, among other factors, complicated school administration by requiring reports and documentation of program activities. Subsequently, the burden on the state education agency (SEA) and the LEA has become manifold, necessitating the employment of numerous staff and clerical personnel to attend to the details of federal compliance. Examples include the Buckley Amendment regulating student records, compliance with civil rights regulations, and most significantly, the implementation of P.L. 94-142, which dramatically increases the responsibility of local schools to central control of the federal government.

**P.L. 94-142.** The major provisions of The Education for All Handicapped Children Act (P.L. 94-142) that affect local school administration may be summarized as follows:

1. *All handicapped children are entitled to a free, appropriate public education.* Extraordinary responsibility is placed on the school to identify handicapped children and to develop appropriate programs for them. Considering the fact that less than 10% of a school population will be handicapped, many administrators suddenly found themselves confronted with regulations, policies, and terminology foreign to their training and experience. The confusion and complexities surrounding these issues have caused some administrators to harbor hostility and resentment about the act, and there were some states at one time that reportedly considered cutting ties to federal monies and ignoring the act, primarily because of perceived administrative burdens that would follow and the centralization of federal control over education.

2. *The referral, assessment, and placement process is very elaborately designed around due process safeguards.* The school must institute policies to assure that:
   a. Parents have prior notification about a change in the child's program or status
   b. Parents have access to school records
   c. Parents attend and participate in referral and placement conferences
   d. Parents have an opportunity to secure an independent evaluation
   e. An impartial hearing be conducted in the event of disagreement about the child's status or program, with parents represented by counsel and with the right to appeal the decision of the hearing
   f. Handicapped children be educated in the least restrictive environment
   g. Referred students be assessed with multifactorial, nondiscriminatory tests

3. *Each handicapped child must have an individualized educational plan (IEP).* The IEP is a written statement of the present levels of educational performance, annual goals, anticipated duration of specific services, and methods of evaluating the plan to see that objectives are being achieved. The requirement of the IEP has caused significant administrative problems for principals because of the need for meetings between personnel and parents, active involvement of teaching personnel in the development and execution of the plan, and the demand for clerical assistance.

4. *Each school district must prepare detailed plans for state approval demonstrating how it will meet the conditions of the law pertaining to education of handicapped children.* The development of an annual plan for special education is another task that must be assumed by the school administration. The dollars and working hours invested in the development of procedures, utilization of school personnel, development of forms, and processing of forms to meet the requirements of the law represent a new level of activity required by federal regulation.

• • •

The powerful forces of legislation, actions of the courts, and social change have impinged on the schools, from without, to cause the necessary realization of a free, appropriate education for all handicapped children. Many administrators who were formally little concerned with a small segment of the school population are now confronted with the challenge of creating exemplary programs for them. It is understandable that many school administrators would be resistant to change, hesitating in acceptance of the premises of the new federal direction and suspicious of the centralization of authority. Some concerns that might be expressed by administrators are:

1. They do not understand the needs of handicapped students.
2. The services provided for less than 10% of the school population seem to be inordinately expensive.
3. The magnitude of the demand of special education on the administrator's time seems to be disproportionate.
4. Attention to special education causes some administrators to feel that they are more vulnerable to litigation.

Special education personnel who are sensitive to the pressures on administrators and who have some insight about their concerns (1) will be in a better position to provide assistance to them for the purpose of forwarding the cause of special education, (2) will be able to share the responsibility by their expertise in the fulfillment of regulatory mandates, and (3) will earn the respect of administrators. Specialists who find themselves assigned to buildings with unsympathetic administrators will be able to devise strategies for circumventing bureaucratic obstacles if they also know the role of the administration, its obligations and encumbrances, and methods of communicating with superiors about issues.

## CHARACTERISTICS OF ADMINISTRATORS

Knezevich (1975) characterizes secondary administrators in the following way:

The typical secondary principal is male, is in his 40s, and possesses a master's degree. There seems to be little distinction between the characteristics of junior and senior high school principals. The complexity of school administration has caused the increasing use of assistant principals, even in relatively small schools.

Administration has become so complex through its evolution that former roles have been rapidly disbanded. The modern principal is no longer expected to be a headmaster who exerts leadership as an instructional supervisor and who exemplifies excellent teaching by conducting one or more classes during the day; rather, the principal is concerned with scheduling and attending numerous meetings to represent the school; he or she also communicates between the superintendent and the teachers, directs and evaluates teaching, supervises nonprofessional personnel, and is the school disciplinarian and advisor to parents.

Assistant principals have highly variable duties, depending on what the principal delegates. Some are responsible for certain clerical duties, others inherit disciplinary matters and contacts with disgruntled parents. The assistant principal may be one of the most unsatisfied of school personnel, being partly responsible for many things but not really in charge of any aspect of school administration. It is not uncommon for the special education teacher to be subordinate to an assistant principal, especially because of the traditional attitude that many of the "special ed kids" are disciplinary problems.

## THE POWER STRUCTURE
### Formal power

The secondary school is controlled by the principal and his or her subordinates. Policies are determined by the board of education, the superintendent issues regulations, and principals adhere to them. The principal has considerable autonomy within his or her domain and can have a great effect on the morale of teachers. Theoretically, important decisions, policies, allocation of the budget, and many other matters of the school's operation are decided by the principal. It is certainly true that the principal can support or subvert innovations. However, the traditional power of principals to make decisions has been eroded by social and legal challenges.

The emergence of teachers' unions, organizations, and bargaining rights (permitted or required in 30 states) has resulted in power being transferred to teachers. Teachers can have a strong voice in working conditions, the design of the curriculum, duties, and many other decision-making areas traditionally controlled by administrators.

No less important is the definition of parental and student rights secured through litigation over a number of years. Since the middle 1960s there have been many challenges to the authority of schools to issue policies affecting the lives of students. The most comprehensive specification of rights is that found in P.L. 94-142, which was summarized earlier. This is most likely a prelude to major changes in the defined rights of all students, handicapped and nonhandicapped.

As noted above, the schools have lost power to the federal government (the Congress and the courts) since 1965 with the passage of the Elementary and Secondary Education Act and intervening court decisions on a host of topics. Even though the principal is still a powerful figure in the school, the job of administration must be tempered with patience and caution because of the contingencies and consequences of each decision and every act. Many representatives sit at the table to make policies about the education of children.

## Informal power

The special educator must recognize one fact of life that may not be illuminated in the training program—there are many sources of informal power in the secondary school that have a bearing on decisions of administrators. The informal contacts of personnel may lead to influence on key individuals as the following account will reveal:

A special class for severely physically handicapped and retarded children was housed in a facility jointly operated by two school districts. Another school program, an alternative school for male adolescents with a history of school failure and poor attendance, shared the facility. The administrator of the alternative program was a personal friend of one of the superintendents of a district involved in the cooperative program for physically handicapped children; and the administrator's wife was employed in the program as an aide with the responsibility of feeding, toileting, and lifting the children. She was never content with her job, complaining about the "vegetables" who were placed in the program, finding the chore of changing diapers to be personally aversive, and actively resisting the placement of children in the program who she thought would increase her burden of daily care giving.

On one occasion she refused to perform a duty required by the teacher, whereupon she was informed that she would perform her role or she would be reported to the administrator. She resigned her position as aide immediately and was granted a meeting with an assistant superintendent. She related a number of her criticisms of the program, made unsubstantiated incriminations about the personal lives of teachers in the program, and charged that various types of abuse had been inflicted on children in the program. Although there was no truth in her charges, and even though the administration did not accord much credibility to her remarks, her informal contact as a wife to a school administrator who was a personal friend of one of the superintendents of the cooperative vested her with considerable clout. The outcome was that she would be given her job again, if she wished, and she would be assisted by a certified teacher in the program who would function part of the time as an aide! Three certified teachers resigned in indignation and dismantled an excellent program and service.

There are many other examples that could be related, but the point is clear; those who have contacts with decision makers in the power structure have influence. This can be nurtured by persons outside the system as well. Husbands, wives, and friends of school administrators can wield influence and can express opinions about the curriculum, various departments, and personnel, opinions that might effect operation of the school. The teacher should assess the local setting, strive to identify those persons who have influence, avoid conflict with especially important persons who might undermine the special education program, and establish rapport with those persons, and, if necessary, take protective measures in the event that self-defense would be necessary in a public forum.

In view of these remarks, it would be important for the special education teacher to consider the following points:

1. Not all administrators and teachers will have positive attitudes toward handicapped students and special education.
2. Certain teachers, especially remedial reading teachers, may be frankly hostile because they often have the opinion that special education is not necessary and most cases could be handled in remedial reading classes.
3. Mainstream teachers may resent what they regard as extra duty, that is, any appeal for cooperation with the special education class.
4. Many of the students who are in the special program are likely to be viewed as discipline problems, and in fact they may be. With increasing concern about discipline in the schools, administrators and teachers may be unsympathetic to the needs of the students. (Duke [1976] discovered in a study of chronic discipline-problem students that most were poor in academic subjects dating from the early grades.)
5. The special education teacher is likely to have a concentration of problems and needs due to the nature of the students, which will tend to cause the principal to view the special education teacher as a complainer unless problems are handled efficiently and burdens are not dumped in the principal's office for resolution.
6. Administrators and teachers may be irritated by the many requirements of P.L. 94-142, which creates extra work and problems for them. This feeling of ill will may be transferred to the specialist.

The special educator may be vulnerable to criticism and attack on many fronts, maximizing the need for excellent personal-social skills and public relations in dealing with others. There are many sensitive areas that can produce problems: removing students from classes, a procedure that disrupts a mainstream teacher's routine; appeals for cooperation of mainstream teachers, which increase their duties; the view that the small class size of the special education room constitutes an easy job; conflict between students; and incurring the displeasure of influential parents.

## Pressure groups and power

Another area that may forebode problems for the special educator relates to contact with parents and professional organizations, which apply pressure to school boards and principals. Some principals, in fact most, deal with problems each day. There are discipline problems of students, conflicts and demands of teachers, complaining parents, and a variety of crises. The principal's role is not easy. Due to the oppositional nature of school administration, anything that appears to be a sign of disloyalty may strain relationships between the principal and the special education teacher. The reason that this might occur is that specialists are frequently in the role of advocating the rights of students and giving advice to parents. It is recommended that the teacher avoid being caught between the school and pressure groups of parents, a circumstance that frequently follows a misunderstanding.

The best practice is to develop a written handout explaining information about parental and student rights; information about the special education program may be included, and parents should be referred to the principal for a discussion of complaints that could lead to controversy or a due process hearing. In any event, the principal should be informed that a problem exists so that planning can be made to resolve it before the issue gets "out of hand" and surprises the administrator. A great deal of common sense in such matters, or the exercise of good judgment, will permit the teacher to perform his or her job and still be an advocate without jeopardizing the program or his or her employment status. One preparation is to consider all the possible consequences of an act or statement and to consider the issue from the principal's point of view.

## ADMINISTRATIVE ISSUES THAT CONCERN THE SPECIAL EDUCATOR

There are many issues that are of importance to any special educator in the working conditions of their employment and the conduct of daily activities, but some transcend others in importance at the secondary level. The following topics are of concern to any teacher or administrator at the secondary level, but they may be of particular interest to the secondary specialist.

### Discipline

Schools have the right to regulate the conduct of pupils and to establish rules for that purpose. Discipline has become a topic of particular importance and sensitivity to school administrators as reports of violence, vandalism, beatings of teachers, fighting, and drug abuse have reached the public through magazines, newspapers, and sensational television documentaries. Although this is a critical issue, complex and difficult to assess, the blame for disciplinary problems seems to be placed on the schools. Numerous restrictions on students in various schools have been challenged in the courts. The *dress codes* of schools, which require a certain hair length, dress length, and grooming standards have been especially challenged. The courts have stricken them in some areas and supported them in others. Hence there is no uniformity of opinion in the courts about these matters. The rule of thumb, however, is that there should be some reasonable connection between a rule and the educational process.

As in all important matters, the special education teacher should acquire a clear, written set of regulations on discipline and policies about student conduct. The special educator may anticipate more disciplinary problems than other teachers; thus he or she should be thoroughly prepared to handle the range of problems. One reason is that this is an effective way to gain the confidence of other teachers, while assisting students, and will curry the favor of the principal.

It is interesting that teachers and administrators see disciplinary problems differently, as indicated by Duke (1978); teachers are most concerned with discourtesy whereas principals regard skipping class, truancy, and tardiness as their most pressing problems. Aside from psychologists or counselors at the secondary level, the special education teacher is likely to be the only professional who is trained in effective methods of coping with discipline problems through a variety of techniques.

Actions of the school to discipline students fall generally into these categories:
1. Detention
2. Corporal punishment
3. Suspension
4. Expulsion

The school may impose reasonable punishment on students for infractions, but care must be taken to review policies frequently because the courts tend to hold that changing mores of the culture and the increased sophistication of students cause "sins" of yesterday to be permissible in contemporary society. Profanity and smoking are examples of conduct that are much more tolerated; some schools even provide smoking areas for students.

More serious punishments must follow due process procedures such as expulsion because these deprive the student of the right to an education. Corporal punishment has been upheld as an acceptable measure to be used for control and punishment of students, but we would argue strenuously against its use. It is not an effective measure, and attempting to paddle adolescents into being better behaved invites anger and retaliation.

### Suspension and expulsion

States permit schools a great deal of latitude in the suspension and expulsion of students. In most cases, suspension is fixed for a specific period of time but some schools have the authority to suspend students indefinitely. Suspension or expulsion of a student is a serious consideration and must follow due process procedures. The special education teacher should advise students about the rules of the schools and the possible consequences of their acts; some students may simply not know the rules. Troubleshooting on the part of the specialist may restrain some students who are pushing the limits, thus protecting their interests.

### Searching students and lockers

Students are protected from shakedowns and frisking in schools. Administrators in some inner-city schools have developed elaborate means of control of students, including identification cards and paid policemen to monitor the hallways because of weapons and drug traffic. If a student is suspected of having drugs or a dangerous weapon, the student may voluntarily open a locker for inspection but the evidence may not be permissible if charges are to be filed with the authorities. The student may be sent home and a search warrant secured. In the area of search, citizens are protected by the Constitution and it is necessary that due process procedures be followed.

### Records of students

The Buckley Amendment (Family Educational Rights and Privacy Act of 1974) requires schools to have a written policy about privacy and access to records of students. Parents, and students of the age of majority, have the right to view all test scores (including IQ tests), evaluations of teachers about student progress, grades, counselors' records, and any information recorded about the family and the student's behavior. Parents may request that irrelevant or inaccurate information be changed or removed. Although it is presently not a requirement that notes of a teacher about a student that are used in making educational decisions be included in the written policy, it would be advisable for the special educator, who is dealing with atypical students, to be deliberate and cautious about any written record.

### Tort liability

Because the teacher stands *in loco parentis* (in the place of the parent), the parent has a right to expect that the school will take reasonable care to assure the safety of the child. If a student is injured because of negligence the parent may sue the teacher and, in some states, the school as well. The greatest concern would be negligence or failure to supervise students, although claims of parents for compensation because of death and property damage sometimes occur. Teachers who send students on errands must be particularly careful, especially if the teacher is aware that a request may be dangerous. Asking students to stand on a precarious platform to decorate a room or fix a light may result in injury and subsequent liability of the teacher who should have recognized the danger. Other areas in which bodily injury and negligence may occur are:

1. Sending students off campus for the purpose of an errand or sending the student home for disciplinary reasons. If the student is harmed or does not return and is subsequently injured, or otherwise incurs harm, the person who sent the student from school may be liable.
2. Transporting students in a privately owned vehicle on field trips is rife with danger. Written permission of parents is required for field trips, and the statement signed by the parents should include the information about the destination, purpose, time of departure, and estimated time of arrival.
3. First aid is occasionally administered to students in schools. Fortunately, most injuries are superficial, but care must be taken that the treatment is necessary. If a medical condition is aggravated by the first aid treatment or if a condition does not constitute an emergency, the teacher may be vulnerable.

## Tenure

Teachers are generally employed under three types of contracts: term contracts for the period of a school year, continuing contracts that are renewable each year unless one or the other party chooses to terminate the contract, and tenure contracts that secure the teacher's employment, unless he or she is dismissed for valid reasons or unless teaching positions are no longer necessary and a cutback in personnel ensues.

## Dismissal

Teachers may be removed and their contracts terminated for incompetence, cruelty, negligence, insubordination, and immorality. It is generally not easy to prove any of these charges without scrupulous attention to the activities of the teacher and comprehensive records.

In all matters wherein the teacher may be vulnerable to litigation, violation of school policy, and conflict, the best protection is to know the laws and rules of the state and the policies of the school. It is possible to acquire liability insurance from professional organizations at a nominal cost and some schools provide it; but the best informed are the best equipped to deal with the complexities of the secondary school and will thus reduce the chances of adversity.

## SUMMARY

Understanding and working with school administrators is essential to the success of special education programs. Administrators are decision makers; hence they have power in the school. Although it is a necessary and admirable goal to consult with mainstream teachers and enlist their support, administrators must not be ignored because they have considerable power to make policies and decisions.

This review of the rudiments of administration in the public school has included an overview of the organization, the formal and informal power structure, discussion of the status of special education in school administration, and selected administrative issues that concern the special educator. The purpose of presenting an uncommon topic in a volume of this type was apparent with the illuminating facts concerning the responsibility of administrators in the implementation of P.L. 94-142, the effects of administrators' attitudes on special education, and the complications of programs caused by inattention to political realities. The best-trained specialists will encounter problems in program development and implementation that are not anticipated because most teacher-training programs do not dwell on facts and issues stemming from school administration, the bureaucracy, and role conflict.

**REFERENCES AND READINGS**

Arnold, D. S., & Goodloe, A. How to innovate successfully. *Today's Education*, 1974, 63, 62-66.

Cahn, L. S., & Nolan, C. E. Learning disabled adolescents: Creating a climate for learning. *NASSP Bulletin*, October 1976, 60, (402), 16-20.

Duke, D. L. Who misbehaves? A high school studies its discipline problems. *Educational Administration Quarterly*, Fall 1976, pp. 66-85.

Duke, D. L. How administrators view the crisis in school discipline. *Phi Delta Kappan*, 1978, 59(5), 325-330.

Gearheart, B. R. *Organization and administration of educational programs for exceptional children.* Springfield, Ill.: Thomas, 1974.

Knezevich, S. J. *Administration of public education* (3rd ed.). New York: Harper & Row, 1975.

Smith, T. E. C. Principals' attitudes toward the handicapped and workstudy. Unpublished doctoral dissertation, Texas Tech University, 1977.

Chapter 5

# CURRICULUM AND INSTRUCTION IN THE SECONDARY SCHOOL

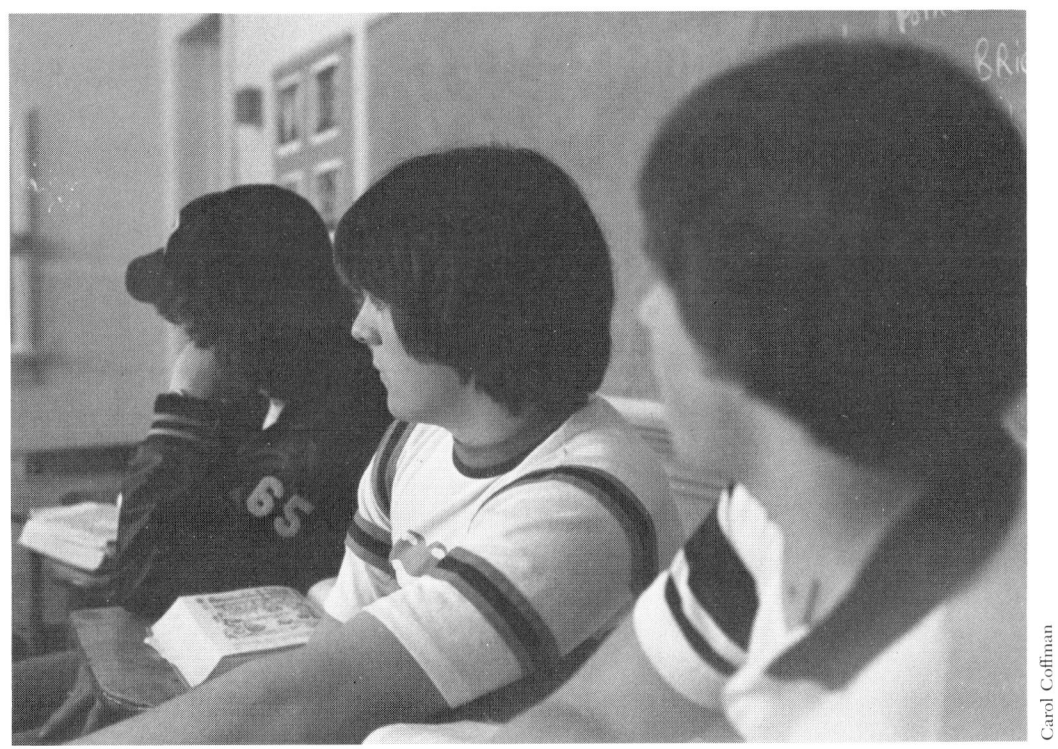

Although the basic administrative organization of the secondary school is relatively constant from one setting to the next, there are numerous organizational patterns for grouping students and for arrangement of the curriculum. The secondary school includes the high school, the junior high school, and the middle school. Many educators became dissatisfied with the junior high school. It had originally been designed as a transitional state between elementary school and the high school, but gradually it mirrored the high school in every aspect. Consequently, the middle school is spreading rapidly across the nation and many educators share the hope that it will succeed where the junior high school has failed.

Although curricular patterns and instructional approaches in many elementary schools have centered on individualized or small group instruction, organization of the secondary school has been remarkably similar to that of the college. Many curricular variations exist in secondary schools, but the most common pattern is the traditional subject-centered curriculum. The predominant instructional approach of the secondary teacher is the lecture, and students are typically expected to memorize facts and recall them upon examination. Although more effective methods of instruction and learning can be used, the fact that they are not means that traditional practices pose significant problems for the mildly handicapped student who attempts to participate in the mainstream.

Primarily as a result of an emphasis in special education on younger children and certification procedures reflecting that emphasis, the growth of secondary programming for mildly handicapped students has been unimpressive until the recent surge of activity stimulated by P.L. 94-142. There have been a minority of school districts scattered throughout the nation that have long had highly developed vocational programs for mildly handicapped students, especially for the segment who are classified as the educable mentally retarded. However, programs for students who have the ability to benefit from the general school curriculum have been extremely limited.

For the entire population of mildly handicapped students it is essential to stress survival in the school, to emphasize teaching strategies that will assist each student toward the goal of graduation, and to support them with approaches that are not far removed from their daily needs. The use of any special education model, compensatory, remedial, or vocational, will interact at some point with the regular curriculum. Interaction will be greatest in compensatory models and in categorical programs for learning disabled and emotionally disturbed students who may be expected to participate more fully in mainstream classes.

## CURRICULUM OF THE SECONDARY SCHOOLS
### Curricular patterns

The curriculum is greatly influenced by the organization of the school. It is not free to vary much from the way the school is organized to teach students. The more traditional the pattern of grouping, the more traditional the curriculum will be.

The most common curricular pattern is the *subject-centered* curriculum. In essence, there is a *general* curriculum consisting of the traditional liberal arts courses in one cluster and traditional vocational courses in another. The most able students and those who are college bound may progress through the liberal arts curriculum and may select some vocationally oriented courses in the process. Less academically oriented students may be able to take *basic* courses that are actually watered down general courses with simplified materials and less complex instruction but essentially the same basic goals as general courses. In most schools a pecking order has existed that values the liberal arts curriculum and accords much less status to vocational coursework. This has been reinforced by the practice of relegating less academically talented students to vocational courses.

## The nature of subject matter

In spite of a variety of experiments and trends, most schools are organized around subject-centered content areas. School subject matter has traditionally been restricted to the content of organized disciplines and developed in the curricula of specific school subjects. The common core is comprised of courses in *social studies*, *science*, *language arts*, and *mathematics*. Typically, schools are organized into departments with teachers assigned to them according to their areas of specialized training.

The subject matter of most secondary courses can be classified by Bloom's (1956) taxonomy as being in the *cognitive domain*. It will be recalled that these processes include knowing, comprehending, applying, analyzing, synthesizing, and evaluating, in ascending order of difficulty. Many courses stress the lowest level of cognitive activity; namely, *knowing*—recalling facts, words and other symbols, classifications, events, trends, principles, ways of working, and theories.

The instructional challenge to any teacher is to try to make subject matter, or the content of specific units, as relevant to students as possible. One of the tasks of special educators, especially resource room teachers, is to assist mainstream teachers to organize information, to present it to students, and to illuminate important concepts for retention. Another is to encourage teachers to consider the individual needs of the learner. The specialist can assist the teacher with understanding learning styles, how to assist students to develop mental programs for learning content, how to organize input, and how to store and retrieve information. Although these activities are divorced from the usual concept of remediation per se, they are quite properly within the realm of an expert in special education.

## SUBJECT AREAS

The common subject areas of the secondary school are social studies, science, language arts, mathematics, fine arts, business subjects, foreign languages, vocational subjects, and physical education. Emphasis here is on the common core of subject areas. Vocational subjects will be considered later.

## Social studies

Social studies commonly includes the following courses at specific grade levels:

| Grade | Subject |
|---|---|
| 7 | Geography |
| 8 | U.S. history |
| 9 | Citizenship |
| 10 | World history |
| 11 | U.S. history |
| 12 | Problems of the American government |

The National Assessment of Educational Progress (NAEP), a project of the Education Commission of the States, has established objectives for social studies (1974) and for citizenship (1974-75). The social studies objectives are as follows:

1. Develops a knowledge base for understanding the relationships between human beings and their social and physical environment.
2. Develops an understanding of the origins and interrelationships of beliefs, values, and behavior patterns.
3. Develops the competencies to acquire, organize, and evaluate information for purposes of solving problems and clarifying issues.

4. Develops the human relation skills necessary to communicate and work with others.
5. Develops a positive self-concept, builds self-esteem, and moves toward self-actualization.
6. Develops and demonstrates a commitment to the right of self-determination for all human beings and a willingness to take rational action in support of means for securing and preserving human rights.

Shaver and Larkins (1973) have reviewed research in the area of social studies and concluded that very few serious attempts to investigate teaching in this area have been made because practitioners and professors seem to have little commitment to research. Therefore there is no body of research to indicate if social studies education is contributing to the goals and objectives proposed in the field.

The most activity in the field has been in the rearrangement of offerings and consolidation of courses, apparently without any rational basis to make such changes. Due to the requirements of state laws and regulatory agencies in education, history units are required; the former courses of citizenship, civics, and problems of government have disappeared in most schools. Some schools have experimented with seminars, minicourses, and short courses, with students able to freely select a number of electives to be ultimately equivalent to a total number of required units for graduation. Minicourses have been criticized by some because students may not independently acquire a balanced collection of units. In some schools, especially with a large group of college-bound students, elective courses in psychology, sociology, anthropology, and political science are available. Although any of these courses might be available to mildly handicapped students, especially college-bound LD students, major concern for most students will be with geography and history courses.

## Science

The traditional design of the science curriculum has been as follows:

| Grade | Subject |
| --- | --- |
| 9 | General science |
| 10 | Biology |
| 11 | Chemistry |
| 12 | Physics |

This pattern was established for college-bound students, but all students were required to take one general science class after which they could manage to avoid further involvement with the science curriculum. In many schools this pattern is still fixed because science courses are designed for students intent on postsecondary training. In some schools the general science course is pushed down to the eighth grade to permit electives later. In districts with a high concentration of college-preparatory coursework, a variety of advanced science subjects may be available and, in some instances, students can receive college credit for honors classes. Minicourses and short courses are uncommon in science.

The NAEP (1972-73) has listed the following objectives for science:

1. Know the fundamental aspects of science
2. Understand and apply the fundamental aspects of science in a wide range of problem situations
3. Appreciate the knowledge and processes of science, the consequences and limitations of science, and the personal and social relevance of science and technology in our society

If there has been little change in the course offerings of the sciences, there has been a wave of activity in the development of curricula, materials, textbooks, and modes of presentation. Much of the activity has crested since the space race, but a significant amount of loosely connected research about teaching has been conducted, principally by doctoral students completing dissertations (Shulman & Tamir, 1973). There are excellent science programs available, most notably the Biological Sciences Curriculum Study (BSCS) programs, which are suitable for students with learning problems because they are primarily hands-on, activity-oriented instructional units punctuated liberally with audiovisual materials.

The major concern of the specialist will probably be the general or applied science classes required of all students. The curriculum for these courses is so general and predictable that there should be little reason for the most reluctant specialist to despair about the content. The revolution in science instruction with clearly delineated tasks and behavioral objectives should make this area rather easy to convert into manageable units for mastery by students who have limited reading ability in a tutorial or compensatory approach.

## Mathematics

The traditional mathematics program has followed this sequence:

| Grade | Subject |
| --- | --- |
| 9 | General math or algebra |
| 10 | Geometry |
| 11 | Advanced algebra |
| 12 | Trigonometry |

The NAEP (1978) has listed objectives in mathematics in a 4 × 5 matrix as follows:

1. Mathematical knowledge
2. Mathematical skill
3. Mathematical understanding
4. Mathematical application

a. Numbers and numeration
b. Variables and relationships
c. Size, shape, and position
d. Measurement
e. Other topics

The major change in the mathematics curriculum has been the introduction of new math concepts and electronic calculators. Otherwise, the curriculum has been rearranged more logically with introductory and advanced algebra following in sequence, and more electives available for students who wish them. The curriculum is essentially for students who wish to enter college. The courses of interest to many mildly handicapped students will be general mathematics or a more simplified course, basic mathematics, each of which will usually be sufficient to satisfy graduation requirements. Either course should be of such simplicity that any teacher can easily conceive strategies for assisting students and can work cooperatively with mainstream teachers in designing support systems.

Dessart and Frandsen (1973) indicate that the field of secondary mathematics will undergo considerable curriculum revision in the future and will accommodate itself to the impact of technological innovations that have not yet been fully embraced by educators. Because of the abilities of some LD and ED students to achieve in mathematics, and with the added support of electronic technology, some talented handicapped students should be encouraged to enroll in higher level classes.

## Language arts

The typical language arts (English) requirements have been for students to take English each year. The twelfth grade was reserved for the college-bound student and would usually emphasize literature, critical reading, and theme writing.

The NAEP (1972, 1974, 1975) goals for reading, writing, and literature are:

I. Reading
   A. Demonstrate behavior conducive to reading.
   B. Demonstrate word identification skills.

C. Possess skills for reading comprehension.
D. Use a variety of approaches in gathering information.
II. Writing
A. Demonstrate ability in writing to reveal personal feelings and ideas.
B. Demonstrate ability to write in response to a wide range of social demands and obligations. Ability is defined to include correctness in usage, punctuation, spelling, and form or convention as appropriate to particular serving tasks, for example, manuscripts, letters.
C. Indicate the importance attached to writing skills.
III. Literature
A. Experiences literature—is aware that literary qualities exist in a variety of forms; seeks experiences with literature in any form, from any culture.
B. Responds to literature—responds to literature in any form, from any culture, in a variety of ways—emotionally, reflectively, and shares responses with others.
C. Values literature—recognizes that literature plays a significant continuing role in the experience of the individual society.

Blount (1973) has reviewed research in this area, and it would appear that very little research has occurred as contrasted with other areas of the curriculum. It is also apparent that the curriculum of language arts has been the most resistant to change, having a protracted emphasis on grammar. Although reading is expressed as a major concern of teachers in language arts, very few are prepared to teach developmental or remedial reading. In recent years, some schools have offered a variety of minicourses but there has been little distinction in the course content at successive grade levels and no evidence that repetition has been of any value to students. Because this area has been regarded as the backbone of education, students are ordinarily required to have several units for graduation.

## THE SPECIAL EDUCATOR AND MAINSTREAMING

Professional isolationism of the resource teacher, that is, restricting services to remediation in a resource room, is justified by some writers for the following reasons:

1. Special teachers do not know anything about subject areas.
2. Assisting students with their courses may result in passing grades but a lack of reading skills.
3. The focus of the secondary program should be only on remediation.

A priori statements such as these should be considered more carefully to examine their underlying assumptions, the possible effect on students, and the impact on programming. Each premise is considered as follows:

1. *Special teachers do not know anything about subject areas.* As a group, it is probably true that special teachers know very little about such subject areas as social studies, science, English, and mathematics. But the question is, what do they need to know in order to help *students* in subject areas? To apply the principles of learning theory, to design individualized instructional programs, and to improve the learning environment through consultation and cooperation with mainstream teachers requires specialized training in teaching individuals, not subject matter. The specialist would engineer new teaching systems to account for individual differences. The specialist would not be a tutor but would orchestrate IEPs for mildly handicapped students, as well as provide an important link between developments in learning research and practice. The specialist will not need to be an expert in subject matter anymore than a mainstream teacher will be expected to be an expert in special education. There is a common ground for shared responsibility.

2. *Assisting students in their courses may*

result in passing grades but no reading skills. Considering the low probabilities of successful remediation with older students, the obverse might also be true—assisting students with reading may result in illiteracy and ignorance. Time may be wasted if students are prodded to read but fail to achieve functional literacy or a diploma. Remediation for many students is employed long beyond its usefulness. However, there is no reason to prevent students from learning in subject areas simply because they cannot read. Some success in subject-area classes, through compensatory approaches, may thwart the effects of the failure syndrome and give a student a sense of renewal, an improved self-concept, and a transformed sense of motivation to attempt achievement in reading. In any event, completing school should be a major priority, with or without reading abilities, because occupational adjustment is more highly correlated with years in school than with reading levels.

3. *The focus of the secondary program should be on remediation.* A narrow focus on remediation inevitably narrows other goals to the extent that, under the guise of sound educational principles, a constellation of "educational truths" becomes accepted, which might have the effect of undermining the fundamental purposes of education. It becomes easy to believe that being able to read is a total prerequisite for learning, that instructors cannot teach students who cannot read, and that the goals of the general school curriculum are not very important. One consequence of this attitude may be a narrowing of programmatic options for a segment of the school population that needs diversified opportunities. Links between the special education programs and mainstream classes should facilitate shared responsibility and teaching that provides a broad spectrum of learning experiences, namely, remediation *and* learning in subject areas.

## Instructional techniques

A rather bleak picture has been painted about the nature of secondary school instruction. The subject-centered curriculum and the tradition of the lecture have been indicted for insensitivity to individual needs. The special educator can adopt instructional techniques for use in the special education program and can communicate them through example and consulting efforts to mainstream teachers. A key concern is compatibility between content to be learned and the learner.

Students develop information into an organized system. Throughout infancy and early childhood, learning entails perceptual testing, classifying, and categorizing the concrete world. This process is random and subjective and is accomplished, as some learning theorists explain, as children program their own brains. As a program is learned it becomes continuously useful and available to speedily and efficiently serve its purpose, as in common patterns of thinking and motor acts. Driving a car, typing a letter, and solving a variety of problems are acts based on previous experience and learning that eliminates the need to concentrate on the mechanics of a process. Much of learning can be characterized as detecting meaningful patterns from the environment. However, the learner must be motivated to find patterns, perceive relationships, discover principles, and so forth, because learning is a personal experience. A poorly motivated student presented with complex material that neither relates to his or her previous level of learning nor to his or her motivational state will result in failure.

A variety of sources (Ellis, 1963; Kolstoe, 1972; Mercer & Snell, 1977; Robinson & Robinson, 1976; Scott & Scott, 1968; Spitz, 1963; Zeaman & House, 1963) provide us with a wealth of information about learning among one segment of the mildly handicapped, which might have wider application for the general group of students classified in this category.

**Memory**

At the foundation of classroom learning is the memory process, which consists of three parts: encoding, storage, and retrieval. Memory deficits are considered to be indicative of learning disabled and mentally retarded students, but most research has centered on short-term memory, which is usually examined by use of an auditory digit span. It is true that many mildly handicapped students have deficient ability to recall digits, but the average normal adult is only able to remember about seven digits, an unspectacular achievement of limited usefulness. Normal adults have limited ability to encode short-term stores of information without resorting to note-taking or otherwise recording information for later reference.

More important is the long-term store of information. There have been relatively few studies with LD and ED subjects, but a number have been completed with mentally retarded subjects, a group generally regarded to be much more handicapped in the school environment. Kolstoe (1972, p. 98) has concluded that retarded youngsters "waste more time in random, trial and error efforts than do normal children in the initial states of learning, but once they find out what to do they learn at the same rate as their peers." Once long-term memory storage has been achieved, recall and forgetting seem to be similar to that of normal peers.

**Input organization**

Primarily from the work of Spitz (1963), we find that initial learning is deficient, and this is confirmed by the work of Zeaman and House (1963). The explanation may be one of improper attention to the learning task requirement, confusion by an array of irrelevant stimuli, and simply, poor short-term memory; but Spitz postulates that greater attention by the teacher to organization and isolation of the information to be learned will result in improved learning. Streamlining initial input for the learner, that is, focusing on what is to be actually learned, and avoidance of shifts to other learning tasks are important. The clustering of information, "chunking" of material to be learned, and sufficient repetition can improve learning.

Simultaneous input (visual and auditory) results in better recall than one-channel input. Much of secondary school classroom learning involves verbal presentation of material in the lecture. External cuing, such as underlining or fading techniques, will aid in the learning of sequential tasks. Lengthy strings of verbal material and unorganized material will be defeating to the learner.

**Verbal learning**

As noted above, serial learning should be avoided or minimized because it is an extremely difficult form of learning for any student. Learning activities should avoid strict auditory input for the same reason. Learning should be relational, built on previous experience by the learner and expressed in terms familiar to him or her. To establish compatibility between content to be learned and the learning characteristics of the learner, many of the suggestions made in this text will be helpful, such as the use of outlines, advance organizers, external cuing, study guides, and other types of learning aids. The emphasis is on isolating what is to be learned, organizing the content for the learner in a meaningful relationship, and avoidance of the random, subjective organization permitted for most students.

One technique that may be applied with anticipated success is the use of modeling in the classroom. Usually conceptualized as a procedure for imitating motor acts and social behavior, the ability of mildly handicapped students to observe and interact with competent peers in the learning environment may lead to learning in such nonbehavioral content as subject areas of the curriculum. Learning in the academic setting is enhanced by a model (teacher, peer, etc.) who is competent and who is accorded some social prestige in the learning environment. Application of this technique would seem to have certain advantages in vocational courses where a substantial part of what is to be learned can be demonstrated. Teaching subject matter should be presented with the following points in mind:

1. Material should be presented at a level that the student understands.
2. Concrete, real-life experiences should be used when possible.
3. Material should build on what the learner already knows.
4. Material should be presented with a few strongly contrasted points and proceed to many points in gradually increasing differentiation.
5. Sufficient probes should be made to determine that the student is progressing in learning material.

Many programs will attempt to serve ED, LD, and some EMR students capable of benefiting from accommodation and compensatory education in the regular school curriculum. The key to appropriate planning is in the process of enabling students to function in the regular class. It is within this setting that the student must succeed, and the specialist must assume responsibility to assure that success.

## REGULAR CLASSROOM TEACHERS

Regular teachers of the junior and senior high schools are the most important allies of the specialist and the key figures determining the success or failure of students who participate in mainstream classes. However, regular teachers may not offer their support voluntarily, may have negative attitudes toward handicapped students and special education, and may not know what they have to offer or how they can help. Some will be frankly hostile, rejecting, and uncooperative. It is imperative that the resource teacher understand the abilities and limitations of the regular faculty and the relationship of special education to the predominant curriculum.

### Instructional interface

Fig. 5-1 is a schematic representation of the interface between the secondary resource room and the regular class as they embrace the student; this example is common in compensatory and remedial models. When considering this relationship, it should be remembered that academic success or survival in the secondary school is determined by competition in regular classes, meeting the evaluative criteria of each instructor, and accumulating an acceptable grade point average. Although the ability to compete for grades is, in part, determined by ability in reading, written and oral expression, or mathematics skills, grades are not specifically awarded for these skills and abilities.

The resource room is a supportive service *to the student* and not necessarily a service to regular class instructors unless they want it. The resource room is set apart, and, unlike the elementary school resource room, is not a natural extension of the regular class because of the differences in the nature of activities, the basic goals, and the orientation of teachers.

It should be obvious that if the resource room teacher neglects to assist the mildly handicapped student with course work or is denied the opportunity to fulfill this function, the student's academic survival will be in jeopardy. Even belated dramatic achievement through remediation of basic academic skills in the resource room will not assure success in the regular class wherein learning

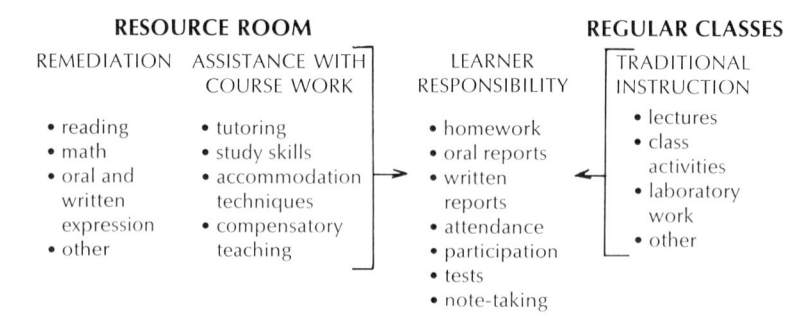

```
                    RESOURCE ROOM                                          REGULAR CLASSES
        REMEDIATION      ASSISTANCE WITH         LEARNER              TRADITIONAL
                         COURSE WORK             RESPONSIBILITY       INSTRUCTION
                                                                       • lectures
        • reading        • tutoring              • homework            • class
        • math           • study skills          • oral reports          activities
        • oral and       • accommodation    →    • written          ←  • laboratory
          written          techniques              reports                work
          expression     • compensatory          • attendance          • other
        • other            teaching              • participation
                                                 • tests
                                                 • note-taking
```

**Fig. 5-1.** Interface of instruction.

entails extensive reading, note-taking, homework, written assignments, and performance on examinations. Provision of services to regular classroom teachers in the form of consultation is not a right of the resource teacher but, rather, an outgrowth of mutual trust and respect. For many resource teachers, the first line of attack in delivery of relevant services will be to students by means of assisting them to succeed in regular classes.

## Behavior of regular teachers

Much of the research about teaching in regular and special education concerns an examination of student outcomes (products) rather than the interactions of the various classroom actors (process). Most product findings are reported as *pupil achievement* determined by standardized tests. It is interesting that standardized tests are primarily measures of low-level knowledge rather than the thinking process of students or the integration and application of knowledge.

We are limited by the narrow kinds of information and facts that we know about teaching if we must rely on designs that report student achievement data and leave us to speculate about how students learn. Very few studies, especially at the secondary level, have been devoted to the examination of teacher-student(s) interactions through direct observation.

Currently, there is a trend in special education to include ecological assessment in collecting data about students. In fact, classroom observation of students is required in the diagnosis of learning disabilities by federal guidelines for assessment. However, there is no mention of *what* we are to observe or what to do with observations after they have been completed.

Ecological assessment should be used to systematically collect data in the *study of teaching* and not only in the study of student behavior. Knowing what happens in a classroom, interaction between the teacher and students, and interactions between peers will yield more meaningful information about teaching handicapped students in regular settings and special settings than concentrating on a narrow range of student products (achievement).

Some insight about the instructional practices and other behaviors of secondary teachers and their interactions with students is available from research utilizing the observational technique (Adams & Biddle, 1970; Hughes, 1973; Perkins, 1964; Smith & Meux, 1962).

**Verbal behavior.** Teachers at the secondary level talk a great deal of the time. Teacher talking may consume about 25% of the time in the early grades but may increase to 50% or more of the time in secondary school.

Teachers emit about 60% of all verbal activity in the classroom in the form of either questions or dissemination of information. Male teachers tend to talk more and longer than females. Younger and inexperienced teachers tend to wander off the topic, but older teachers stay on target. Teachers spend very little time in individualizing or helping students (as resource, evaluating, or socializing), acting more as managers leading discussions and lectures.

## Student behavior and interaction

Teachers tend to stand in the front and center of the classroom and move very little. This varies in some courses, such as science, where the nature of activities makes the traditional arrangement impractical. There is little or no interaction between students because is is not usually permitted or encouraged. It has been demonstrated that efficient learning can occur when small subgroups of students work together on relevant topics and are supervised and occasionally supported by the teacher. This is a rare occurrence. Verbal interactions between the teacher and students are limited to infrequent exchanges, usually a question and answer sequence. Interestingly, the amount of pupil responding in class is unrelated to pupil achievement, but underachieving pupils spend time in withdrawal, nonacademic work, or studying work for another academic class while they wait out the class period.

Many secondary teachers are out of social contact with students; that is, teachers are not aware of subculture rituals, slang, and nonverbal interactions. This becomes more distinct if the teacher is older.

## Subject matter influences

The nature of the subject matter can shape the mode of response for students. All upper-grade-level lessons entail dissemination of information with considerable intellectualization about relevant subject matter. Most classroom learning involves relatively low-level or concrete cognitive processes rather than abstract learning; and standardized measures reflect concrete learning. Specific subject-matter areas tend to affect teaching style and what is expected of students in classroom interactions. For example, in English class students will be required to state and evaluate information. In science they are more likely to be required to define and describe. Mathematics demands statements of facts, while much of the social studies curriculum is based on recall and statement of opinions.

Teachers require students to respond to questions using the lower cognitive processes. It may be that this is necessary at the junior high school level because one would not ordinarily expect students of this general age to have the cognitive ability to make analogies, to evaluate, and extrapolate from a basis of personal experience. However, the striking revelation of research is that teachers at the secondary level spend a lot of instructional time explaining and describing and requiring their students to state facts, repeat descriptions, and make definitions. Similarly, written work, such as tests and assigned papers, requires the same kinds of responses.

In summation, the classroom environment of the secondary school is highly structured, teacher directed, and dominated by teacher talk. As an apparently preferred style, the teaching lecture requires students to attend to the teacher for long periods of time to acquire information. Teachers do not ordinarily employ teaching strategies that encourage the development or utilization of high-level cognitive processes. However, the sheer weight of content covered, the unique terminology of each subject area, and the complexity of associated textbooks can be taxing of pupil attention, understanding, and stamina. The written work of students is likely to be criticized more severely by teachers than are the oral responses. Written tests and papers may be marked down for lack of abstract quality, a quality not often used by teachers in class nor demanded of students in verbal interactions. There are few rewards for the student who manages to sit through lectures each day, but he or she is expected to be docile, unmoving, and passively attentive. This is a general prerequisite to success.

**Attitudes of teachers**

With the advent of P.L. 94-142 there has been a spate of published surveys concerning the attitudes of regular teachers toward the handicapped. Bryan and Bryan (1979) indicate that teachers may be more accepting of LD students than of EMR or ED students. This must be because of the perceptions of the labels more than because of actual attitudes. The believability of such research is questionable because it is one thing to express an opinion and quite another to behave in accordance with professed beliefs. The best proof of teacher attitudes would be teachers' treatment of the handicapped in the regular classroom, which ideally is determined by observational techniques. We have no such data, but there are some presumptions that can be made in view of the pressures on teachers, their training and experience, their goals, and the challenge of a handicapped pupil.

Most teachers are very busy, having four or five classes each day with 30 or more *different* students in each class. They are trained to impart knowledge about content of a subject area, not to teach reading or collect baseline charts on ED students, and they are expected to cover predetermined amounts of information in a specified period of time to coincide with a syllabus or state curriculum. They expect students to arrive in their classes with the necessary skills to cope with their demands, and they may not have much sympathy or tolerance for those who do not. Many secondary teachers are not willing to assume responsibility for instruction in areas outside their area of training. They do not understand how or why they should individualize their instruction. The predominant style of teaching, the lecture, does not yield easily to innovation. The special teacher will have to devise strategies that fit into the patterns and habits of secondary teachers, that do not seem to cause more work for them, and that do not threaten them. Their attitudes toward the mildly handicapped will be generally negative and variable in accordance with their perceptions of the three labels, namely, LD, EMR, and ED.

**Influence of unions and teachers' organizations**

As the power struggle for control of schools has increased in recent years, the authority of the school administration has been diminished. Federal legislation has weakened local autonomy. Parents have demanded a stronger voice in local issues, and courts have clearly defined student rights, which limit and prescribe, to a great extent, the role of administrators.

Another sphere of control has been achieved, gradually, by the rise of strong teachers' unions and organizations that bargain for salaries, working conditions, and work responsibilities. The latter aspect is of importance here because as a *work norm* is established, the faculty in a district are going to become more rigid in their activities and less tractable in experimenting with innovations or assuming responsibilities not defined in a contract. In those districts where there are intense "labor and management" sentiments, cooperation on behalf of mildly handicapped pupils may be difficult to obtain in the vacuum created by the adverse relations. It is essential that the specialist appreciate the work load of fellow teachers, recognize their natural antipathy toward efforts that make more work for them, and try to sell the program by providing as much assistance to other teachers as possible as the cooperative elements of the secondary special program are installed.

## COURSE REQUIREMENTS

The following discussion concerns the basic ingredients of the secondary instructional program as they affect the learner. The curriculum of a school encompasses the written courses of study, the precise courses offered, the subject matter to be taught, and the experiences of the learner, which are partly determined by the curriculum and partly by the discretion of the individual teacher. The learning activities determined by secondary teachers are most important to the adolescent because they lead to success or failure in school. Fortunately, they can be altered to improve the chances for success with adequate planning and cooperation.

### Attending to lectures

As noted above, the student's primary task in the traditional classroom is to sit in a desk, look at the teacher, and remain passively attentive. As students get older they seem to be able to do this more skillfully. Although elementary teachers talk a lot, they cannot successfully hold the attention of all pupils for long periods of time. A lot of group activities and seat work are used to good measure. However, at the secondary level the expectations of teachers are that students will endure several hours of lecture-type instruction and most can do it rather well. Those who cannot conform to expectation will be easily noticed. Such factors as the tolerance of teachers and the norm for classroom disruption in the building determine whether students who have problems attending will or will not be punished or reprimanded for certain unacceptable behaviors as long as they fall within the bounds of established propriety as determined by the environment. Students who exceed the limits willfully or who appear to be disrespectful, uninterested, or flippant will attract the attention of students and teachers. The underachiever, upon observation, is known to spend time in withdrawal or nonacademic pursuits during the lecture; this may be acceptable as long as there is the appearance of conformity with the basic expectations, that is, to sit still, remain quiet, and be passively attentive.

One of the ways to incur the wrath of a teacher is to subvert the lecture and control of the class. If the behavior of mildly handicapped students is perceived as disruptive, abrasive, or bizarre by peers and teachers, it is important to enlighten them about the rules of classroom behavior and appropriate "stroking" of the teacher as a minimum requirement for academic achievement. Simply stated, a student who displays aversive behavior may be greatly aided by social skills development.

From a more instructional point of view, listening to the lecture, if not participating at brief intervals when student responses are requested, can reap important benefits when examinations are given. Teaching students how to listen, how to record information, and how to use it to discover the teacher's emphases and biases is important to academic survival.

### Note-taking

Ordinarily, students will be expected to maintain notes on classroom activities although very little effort is taken to teach students *how* and *why* notes are taken. A clear record of salient points of classroom lectures can be very useful to the student in understanding the content of subject matter and in preparing for examinations. Many mildly handicapped students will not be able to take notes because of a variety of problems (dysgraphia, illegibility, slow motor speed, inattention, etc.); alternatives may be used, however, by enlisting the support of other students or by making tape recordings. Both of these techniques are unsatisfactory due to the unreliability of students who take notes and the discomfort teachers may feel about being recorded. These matters will be discussed more fully in another section.

### Homework

Many classes will require students to accomplish a considerable amount of out-of-class work. Traditionally known as homework, these activities are extensions of in-class activities and are related to planned experiences thought to lead students to mastery of subject matter. Such assignments may be classified in the following manner.

**Daily problems.** Daily problems are usually ones in math or science classes that are to be reported the following day in class. The amount and importance of such problems depends on the teacher who makes such assignments. As a form of independent learning activity, successful completion of these out-of-class assignments can be important to satisfactory completion of the course.

**Reading assignments.** Courses that are comprised mainly of discussing printed matter rely heavily on the student's ability to keep abreast of subject matter in textbooks and other related sources. English and social studies classes typically have extensive readings, and these increase with each successive year in secondary school. Traditionally, all major courses have considerable reading associated with meeting course objectives. Poor readers are seriously penalized because of the massive reading chore.

**Special assignments.** Some teachers require book reports, papers, oral reports, and experiments as special projects.

• • •

Depending on the course and the teacher, considerable emphasis is placed on homework as a part of the course grade. Homework definitely has an effect on the teacher's attitude toward the student, and it figures prominently in the course grade, if not in learning.

## GRADING PRACTICES

In most secondary schools conventional letter grades are used. An estimated 82% of junior high schools and 84% of senior high schools use a letter grading system to evaluate the performance of students (National Education Association, 1974). Letter grades are thought to be a good predictor of performance in college, the grade point average (GPA) ranks students for many purposes such as the awarding of scholarships, grades are thought to be motivating to students, and they reflect the American system of competition. Although the grading system is firmly entrenched, it has not been without its critics. Grades have been blamed for causing students to cheat, for viewing the teacher as a manipulable object, and for preventing teachers from individualizing instruction (Evans, 1976). If the grading system is rigid and adheres to the principles of variance and dispersal of scores, someone must fail.

### The curve

Endemic to the letter grading system is the use of the normal curve (Gaussian curve) in determination and assignation of grades. Although it is unlikely that many teachers actually employ a strict curve in making decisions, many will arrange the scores of students on tests and all assigned work into a rank ordering of class scores. By eyeballing the scores for natural breaks or by employing more scientific procedures such as the use of Z scores, cutoff points are determined to separate the scores that will be given the letter grades (A, B, C, D, F). The underachieving students are frequently doomed to fall at the lower end of the grading curve under these procedures. Other procedures require students to meet expected levels of accuracy on tests and assignments in order to earn a letter grade (80% = B, for example).

## Test scores

There are generally two major kinds of tests to which students will be subjected. One is the standardized achievement test used by local districts as part of a required assessment schedule. The other, more numerous type of testing is associated with course requirements. Depending on the class, it is not uncommon for students to have weekly quizzes, unit examinations, quarterly evaluations, and semester examinations, all of which are aimed at the assessment of information and skills learned in subject-matter areas. The familiar essay and objective tests are very popular with teachers for most courses, especially English and social studies. Science and mathematics are likely to have practical problems that require the application of knowledge in the solution. Test scores weigh heavily in the determination of final letter grades. Most tests require students to state, describe, or relate information (facts) about subject matter. Occasionally, teachers will require students to compare, evaluate, or critique some work or position. This can be extremely difficult because it involves higher level cognitive processing, something that many students are not able to do easily, and very little instructional time is used to enhance this ability.

It should be noted that tests permeate vocational course instruction also. Tests about automobile mechanics or small engine repair are no less difficult than those in a traditional subject area. Unfortunately, some vocational teachers in trade classes have less formal preparation and may develop the most unreliable examinations for students. Although mildly handicapped students may be channeled into vocational courses in the belief that they are unsuited to the rigors of the liberal arts courses, many such courses are actually very complicated.

## Attendance

Attendance is important to the school because state financial entitlements are based on the average daily attendance. Thus teachers take roll each day and some schools have procedures to check the attendance of students throughout the day. Truancy and tardiness are particularly detrimental to the success of some students because the accumulation of absences prevents promotion, even if course objectives are otherwise met by the student, and many teachers resent the student who demonstrates lack of interest by truancy.

# EXTRACURRICULAR ACTIVITIES

As previously stressed, peer acceptance and interpersonal relationships are of paramount importance to the adolescent. It is imperative that all students have an opportunity to participate in the full range of extracurricular activities because of the pleasant side effects of socialization and indirect influence gained by a sense of belonging, esprit de corps, and loyalty to an institution. The more a student feels a part of the school and its functions, the greater the involvement in related social activities. In turn, this can have the additional benefit of motivating students to achieve in their academic courses and can reduce the students' tendency to become alienated from the school setting. For this purpose, it should be a major concern of the specialist to involve students in appropriate activities and social functions of the school.

In any high school or junior high, there are numerous clubs, groups, and activities that would be suitable for students to join. Aside from the inclination of some students to avoid such participation, there are frequently barriers to joining extracurricular activities. The primary obstacle in many places is that school organizations require a specific grade point average for participation. The social prestige of athletics is so significant that any student who can succeed in this endeavor will virtually be assured of status and respect among peers. The value of this aspect of extracurricular activity was considered and investigated by D'Alonzo (1976) as a possible right for handicapped students. It appears that participation is a privilege. Students must meet a variety of criteria for eligibility. Although a student may participate in physical education as a part of the general school curriculum, playing varsity football may only be a remote possibility. First of all, the student would have to be able to make the team, which means a need for adequate physical potential for the sport. In this matter, most students of the school would be excluded. However, the requirement for a specific grade point average may be punitive to handicapped students in varsity sports as in other organizations and activities of the school. Needless to say, the united efforts of school patrons, special interest groups, and parents should be brought to bear on eligibility requirements, which in effect prevent a segment of the school population from enjoying equal status and opportunity.

## GRADUATION REQUIREMENTS

Successful completion of a specific number of units of study in various areas of the curriculum is necessary for promotion from junior high school and for graduation from high school. Students are not required to have a C average for a diploma but may not fail classes to be counted toward graduation credit.

## Competency examinations

Several states have enacted legislation requiring minimal competency examinations of students, many state boards have adopted regulations to the same effect, and many more states and local districts are debating the issues. Students must satisfactorily meet the criteria of examinations before being promoted and/or being issued a diploma on graduation. The minimal competency examination is the only visible manifestation of the back-to-basics movement fueled by the belief that there is a massive lowering of basic student achievement, although there is little proof of this belief (Farr & Tone, 1978). Actually many factors have contributed to the conservative backlash in education, including costs of repairing vandalized school buildings, violence in schools, and suspicions of adults about the morality of the present generation of teenagers. The force and hope behind the back-to-basics movement seem to be the desire to have students who respect their teachers and other adults, students who have mastered the basic skills, and schools that are accountable for their expenditures in education.

It is an irony that the trend to minimal competency testing and the requirement of a free appropriate education for handicapped students should converge at the same point in time—a time when the use of intelligence tests and other standardized measures has been eliminated or restricted. Minimum competency may become a universal standard, thwarting individualization and ignoring individual differences while reasonably well-developed standardized tests will be supplanted by competency exams that are invalid and unreliable.

The possible problems created by competency testing programs, no matter how benignly conceived, include (1) poor and minority students will be labeled, as they have been with conventional intelligence testing programs; (2) millions of dollars will be requested to remediate the "incompetent" so he or she can pass the tests; and (3) new cases of "learning disabled" students will be identified, willy-nilly, after students fail the examinations.

For those students who are currently classified as mildly handicapped there are some hidden jeopardies in the competency testing program. Although the future may bring about competency tests in subject areas, as well as real life simulations such as balancing a checkbook, basic skills are the first priority. If a student cannot read at a certain grade level commensurate with the competency, he or she will not be passed to the next grade level. The individual abilities, inabilities, and disabilities of students may not be considered. The criterion will be grade level equivalency for *all* students of the same chronological age in spite of the fact that they are all different in capacity to learn. The unfortunate consequence may be that more secondary students will simply leave school defeated, that is, the incompetent.

The following questions should be asked of those who would design the testing program (Brickell, 1978, p. 551):
1. What competencies will you require?
2. How will you measure them?
3. When will you measure them?
4. How many minimums will you set?
5. How high will you set the minimums?
6. Will they be for schools or for students?
7. What will you do about the incompetent?

Many mildly handicapped students can learn in the subject areas although they may not have the basic skills necessary for learning in the traditional sense. But, the use of accommodation, compensatory teaching, and other ecological manipulations can promote learning and prevent failure. If minimal competencies are established, the mildly handicapped student should be accorded special consideration and, at all costs, the new label "incompetent" should be avoided.

## SUMMARY

In this chapter we have presented the reader with a broad overview of the secondary curriculum, instructional practices, requirements of students, and related issues. Understanding the educational environment is essential to planning for students. Schooling, it was noted, is governed by very traditional concepts about education. The major purpose of teachers is to train students in content of a fractionated curriculum by means of lectures. Progress is documented by attendance, completion of assignments, and acceptable performance on tests.

The subject areas of the curriculum were described, with a discussion of traditional requirements, contemporary trends, and problems of instruction. Specific practices for grading and promotion were included. The point was made that special education is related to the total curriculum and mildly handicapped students must function in the system. The ability of the special educator to understand the practices, conventions, and traditions of the secondary school will provide the basis for effective planning for special programs and individual students.

## REFERENCES AND READINGS

Adams, R. S., & Biddle, B. J. *Realities of teaching: Explorations with video tape.* New York: Holt, Rinehart & Winston, 1970.

Bloom, B. (Ed.) *Taxonomy of education objectives: The classification of educational goals* (Handbook 1: Cognitive domain). New York: McKay, 1956.

Blount, N. Research on teaching literature, language, and composition. In M. W. Travers (Ed.), *Second* handbook of research on teaching. Chicago: Rand McNally, 1973, pp. 1072-1098.

Brickell, H. M. Seven key notes on minimal competency testing. *Educational Leadership*, 1978, 35(7), 551-557.

Bryan, J. H., & Bryan, T. H. *Exceptional children.* Sherman Oaks, Calif.: Alfred, 1979.

D'Alonzo, B. J. Rights of exceptional children to participate in interscholastic athletics. *Exceptional Children*, 1976, 43(2), 86-94.

Dessart, D., & Frandsen, H. Research on teaching secondary school mathematics. In M. W. Travers (Ed.), *Second handbook of research on teaching.* Chicago: Rand McNally, 1973, pp. 1177-1195.

Ellis, N. R. (Ed.) *Handbook of mental deficiency.* New York: McGraw-Hill, 1963.

Evans, F. B. What research says about grading. In S. Simon & J. Bellanca (Eds.), *Degrading the grading myths: A primer of alternatives to grades and marks.* Washington, D.C.: Association for Supervision and Curriculum Development, 1976.

Farr, R., & Tone, B. What does research show? *Today's Education*, 1978, 67(4), 33-35.

Hughes, D. C. An experimental investigation of the effects of pupil responding and teaching reacting on pupil achievement. *American Educational Research Journal*, 1973, 10(1), 21-37.

Kolstoe, O. P. *Mental retardation.* New York: Holt, Rinehart and Winston, 1972.

Mercer, C. D., & Snell, M. E. *Learning theory research in mental retardation.* Columbus, Ohio: Merrill, 1977.

National Assessment of Educational Progress. *Writing objectives.* Denver, 1972.

National Assessment of Educational Progress. *Science objectives.* Denver, 1972-73.

National Assessment of Educational Progress. *Social studies objectives.* Denver, 1972, 1974.

National Assessment of Educational Progress. *Reading objectives.* Denver, 1974.

National Assessment of Educational Progress. *Citizenship objectives.* Denver, 1974-75.

National Assessment of Educational Progress. *Literature objectives.* Denver, 1975.

National Assessment of Educational Progress. *Mathematics objectives.* Denver, 1978.

National Education Association. *What research says to the teacher: Evaluation and reporting of student achievement.* Washington, D.C.: The Association, 1974.

Perkins, H. V. A procedure for assessing the classroom behavior of students and teachers. *American Educational Research Journal*, 1964, 1(4), 249-260.

Robinson, N. M., & Robinson, H. B. *The mentally retarded child* (2nd ed.). New York: McGraw-Hill, 1976.

Scott, K. G., & Scott, M. S. Research and theory in short-term memory. In N. R. Ellis (Ed.), *International review of research in mental retardation* (Vol. 3). New York: Academic Press, 1968.

Scranton, T., & Downs, M. Elementary and secondary learning disabilities programs in the U.S.: A survey. *Journal of Learning Disabilities*, 1975, 8(6), 394-399.

Shaver, J., & Larkins, A. G. Research on teaching social studies. In M. W. Travers (Ed.), *Second handbook of research on teaching.* Chicago: Rand McNally, 1973, pp. 1243-1262.

Shulman, L. S., & Tamir, P. Research on teaching in the natural sciences. In M. W. Travers (Ed.), *Second handbook of research on teaching.* Chicago: Rand McNally, 1973, pp. 1098-1148.

Smith, B. O., & Meux, M. O. *A study of the logic of teaching.* Urbana, Ill.: University of Illinois Press, 1962.

Spitz, H. H. Field theory in mental deficiency. In N. R. Ellis (Ed.), *Handbook of mental deficiency.* New York: McGraw-Hill, 1963.

Zeaman, P., & House, B. J. The role of attention in retardate discrimination learning. In N. R. Ellis (Ed.), *Handbook of mental deficiency.* New York: McGraw-Hill, 1963.

Chapter 6

# SUPPORT SERVICES

A successful special education program will be encompassed by the total school program, but it will maintain its separate identity. Its vitality will be determined by the ability of professionals to integrate special services with the total school program, an interdependence of dynamic interacting parts. This relationship must be carefully designed and nurtured so that the special education program can stand alone to serve its basic function to students, yet be meaningfully related to the mainstream. Success depends on interdependence, which must be achieved and maintained by the special educator. As society has historically rejected its handicapped, so have schools rejected classes for the handicapped—a microcosm of manifested social values. The greatest weakness of the traditional self-contained classroom was its nearly total isolation from the mainstream. Not only were the students segregated, but so also were the curriculum and the special teacher. The special education program will have little significance if it does not support each student in his or her *daily* needs and if it does not have the active involvement of mainstream teachers. Activities of the special program must be directly related to those of the regular program, the specialist must know what is required of students in those classes, and the vigor and quality of the program must be evaluated by its functional relationship with the system.

Fig. 6-1 depicts the interdependence of the special and mainstream programs and the support personnel who are responsible for assisting the special educator to achieve program goals. This schema includes the relationships with various professionals and agencies outside the system that have intermittent but significant interactions with the system.

In its most basic sense, the special education program, regardless of its approach to services, will have two major functions: (1) primary service to students enrolled in the program and (2) secondary service to teachers who share responsibility for educating mildly handicapped students. In the zeal to provide *primary* services there is the ever-present danger that the program will become fractionated, that activities across the boun-

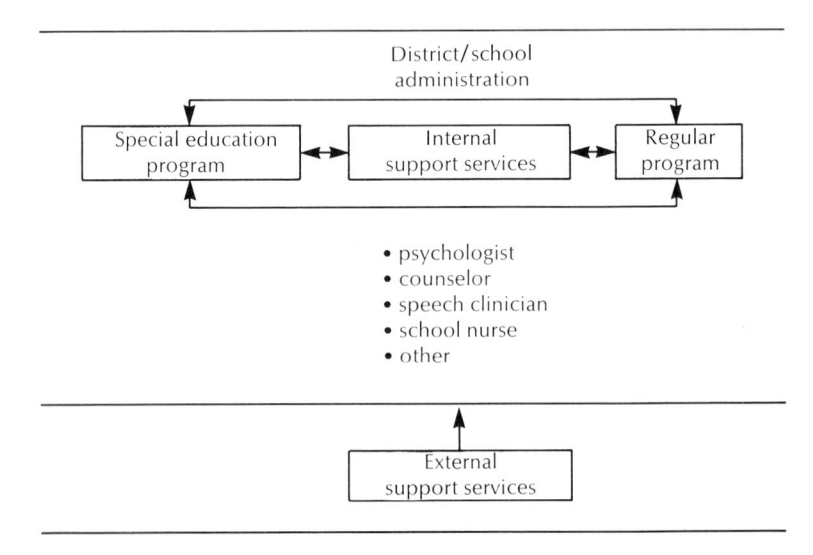

**Fig. 6-1.** Relationships of school programs to internal and external support services.

daries of the special education room will not occur or will diminish in intensity. Active involvement with the school curriculum, departments, teachers, special personnel, and extracurricular functions is critical if the program is to ultimately meet the needs of students. The propensity to define a narrow focus in the isolation of the special education classroom must be averted.

In order to function properly, the program must have support from a variety of internal and external professionals who will assist in referral, assessment, development of the IEP, arrangement for external services, linkage between the school and home, intercession with other school personnel, program evaluation, and dismissal of students from the program. Special services personnel in the school or district comprise the first line of support necessary for program vitality and accountability. External services are also of great value to the program, especially in the event of a need for medical intervention or information. It was deemed necessary to include this chapter on support personnel for the following reasons:

1. Many special educators do not fully utilize support personnel.
2. Some professionals do not have a conceptualization of a method for assisting the special program or the students in the program.
3. A more detailed analysis of the functions of key personnel is important to the purposes of a special education program.
4. Legal requirements are involving support personnel, but regulations define only a superficial relationship.

Although there are many supportive services that might be provided, the most basic need of the special education program on a continuous basis seems to be in the referral/assessment process, at least as judged by the amount and frequency of contacts. To a lesser extent, direct services to students in the form of counseling and other contacts are provided. A more complete utilization of support personnel can be effected by defining the roles and functions of key personnel who are available and suggesting ways in which their services may be articulated with those of the special education program.

This chapter has been organized around assessment and the roles of three types of personnel in the school system. The reason is that assessment tends to be the one *major* activity commanding the attentions and energies of a variety of school personnel (administrators, regular teachers, special services personnel, etc.). Depending on the resources available or committed in some districts, some schools will have a variety of highly specialized personnel, possibly including a social worker, a school psychologist, an audiologist, and medical personnel. Most school systems do not ordinarily employ such personnel. Their services, if required, are obtained by contact with external agencies. Most school districts, from the smallest to the most comprehensive, commonly employ the services of a counselor, speech clinician, and school nurse. Hence these professional roles are highlighted in this chapter.

The roles of external support personnel should be understood by professionals in special education because the field is gravitating increasingly toward involvement with the fields of medicine, social work, psychology, and others. Historically, teacher training programs have prepared their graduates within a very narrow scope. Many teachers have not understood the roles, functions, and language of specialists in other professions. If special educators are to communicate with persons of other professional disciplines and to benefit from association with them, something must be known about their professions and how to utilize their services.

## ASSESSMENT

At no other point in the process of special education will the attention and energy of support personnel be so intensely involved and directed for a common purpose as in the activities of assessment. Most of the contact between special educators and support personnel is related to assessment or to matters determined by decisions made during assessment; namely, classification of students, placement, instructional strategies, and appropriateness of programming. Many of the independent professional activities of each support staff member are stimulated and shaped by a need for information and services to be provided for regular teachers, parents, and, of course, students involved with the special education program of the school. Although it would be desirable to have the unique contributions of a variety of professionals of the various disciplines devoted to daily instructional activities, the limitations of time and resources dictate that most of the attention of support personnel will be directed to the assessment process.

### Learning disabilities: assessment issues

As the demand for special education services has been so suddenly and dramatically expanded at the secondary level, the need to resolve assessment practices with the legal definition has created predictable controversy and confusion in the diagnosis of adolescents. The lack of specificity in the definition, identifying characteristics, and assessment practices, as well as the turmoil over these issues, becomes compounded at the secondary level. There has been a clear trend for secondary schools to diagnose and label students as learning disabled on the basis of poor academic skills. The greatest concern has been with reading deficiency. It is not likely that the trend will be abated, in spite of the alarm expressed by some (e.g., Deshler, 1979, p. 4) because leaders in the field have been unable to develop an acceptable (i.e., precise and restrictive) definition of learning disabilities, to develop instrumentation suitable for prescribed diagnostic tasks, and to support claims about specialized treatment approaches and other remedial notions. School personnel, many of whom do not claim to have special knowledge about learning disabilities, are required by law and prodded by local pressures to identify and serve students who are thought to be learning disabled. Understandably, the most obvious indices of learning disabilities are measures of academic achievement that are clearly related to school tasks and that can be used to classify students more conventionally than by measures of such vague, ill-defined constructs as "thinking disorders."

A great deal of research by learning disabilities authorities concerns reading, which indicates that the field shares a major concern with school personnel. The so-called back-to-basics movement only heightens anxiety about poor achievement, especially in reading, and causes school personnel to seek learning disabilities programming as an answer to their problems, an expectation that they have certainly been encouraged to believe. It is therefore not surprising that most teachers and administrators consider students to be learning disabled if they do not perform well in reading tasks. Although some authorities may describe and discuss learning disabilities in sophisticated terminology, practitioners are unable to secure much beyond the application of an underachievement model in diagnosis. The problems of the definition and the diagnostic process are interrelated, leading to confusion and the assertion that we have applied a label to behaviors that we cannot accurately define, describe, or change.

A critical aspect of the learning disabilities movement has been the presumption that some underlying psychological process has been faulty; identification of such a disorder has been important in the diagnosis as well as in generating treatment strategies to either strengthen or circumvent the disorder. Much of the debate about learning disabilities pertains to process disorders. There are those who contend that it is not possible to measure process disorders (either because they are erroneous constructs or because tests are not rigorous enough to identify them); and it is believed that very little benefit can be realized from remediation of process disorders. This issue becomes increasingly important in the diagnosis and assessment of adolescents because of the extreme lack of research with this population, the lack of agreement about adolescent characteristics, the fact that application of concepts used with younger children is not necessarily appropriate with older counterparts, and the questionability of applying process-training procedures to adolescents.

It may be true that unless we attend to this aspect of the definition we will only have an underachievement model (Goodman & Price, 1979), but there are those who contend that this is all we have *ever* had. In the most scathing criticism of the field to date, Coles (1978), in the *Harvard Educational Review*, invokes arguments, which cannot be easily refuted or ignored, to discredit the assessment practices of learning disabilities. After an extensive review of validation studies on the most frequently used tests in learning disabilities, he charges that authorities in the field of learning disabilities do not have special knowledge claims about learning disorders, that there is no compelling reason to believe that learning disabled students can be discerned from among the general population of underachieving students, and that the diagnostic judgments of specialists are unscientific, being ". . . caught up in evidential and logical weaknesses from which they cannot be extricated without considerable qualification" (p. 329).

Although our science is weak, our instruments are ineffective, and some of our concepts are primitive, there is hope in the future that a more precise definition and methods of assessment will emerge to clarify the cloudy issues and extricate us from our "evidential and logical weaknesses." Currently, the assessment process is so riddled with error that a wide range of children with various emotional, neurological, and environmental characteristics are embraced by the catchall term "learning disabilities." In spite of the criticisms, there is hope of a better clarification; the question is, "What are the parameters of learning disabilities?"

Evidence of this may be cautiously accepted from the early work of psychobiologists who have used neurometrics, a blending of electroencephalography and advanced computer science, in the examination of brain response to patterns of stimuli (John, 1976, 1977; Restak, 1979). Not only do the results confirm clear differences between learning disabled children and normal students, but specific dysfunctions are revealed by evoked-potential recordings, which indicate that subgroups can be delineated according to the type of hemispheric involvement. This approach to assessment will need to be further validated before it can be put into widespread use.

This application of technology is certain to meet resistance in the field for a variety of reasons. One is the social/ethical problems surrounding the use of technology in probing the human psyche. Another is the assault that electrophysiology would cause on firmly entrenched behaviorism in education because it is increasingly apparent that the human brain reacts to patterns by continuously generating hypotheses about the environment, the antithesis of some current professional beliefs.

For the time being the status of assessment in learning disabilities is much less precise than what may be anticipated in the future. Given the current state of affairs, there are no clear directions in assessment at the secondary level and the federal regulations seem to add to the confusion. Additionally, the imprecise definition, the questionable validity of popular test instruments, the differences of opinion about assessment among authorities, and the increasing criticism of the field complicate assessment decisions.

**Significant discrepancy.** According to the regulations, it may be determined that a specific learning disability exists if the student does not achieve commensurate with his or her age and ability levels in oral expression, listening comprehension, written expression, basic reading skill, reading comprehension, mathematics calculation, or mathematics reasoning. The following points summarize problems of assessment as they pertain to the adolescent:

1. *Statistical significance between scores should be determined as the evidence of a significant discrepancy.* Regardless of the tedious nature of such determinations and the limitations of the procedure, the best evidence of a significant discrepancy is based on confidence levels for single scores and difference scores. This procedure is clearly explained by Salvia and Ysseldyke (1978, pp. 88-91). The major drawback is that *if two tests are correlated*, the discrepancy score *may* be less reliable than either score. In any event, to determine the reliability of differences between scores on two tests it is necessary, among other factors, to have the correlation between the two tests. Unfortunately, most of the tests in common use have not been correlated, so that comparisons cannot be accurately made.

2. *The use of a criterion measure is questionable because of the inability to distinguish between groups of underachievers.* Some schools have adopted the practice of admitting students to LD programs providing they fall below some arbitrary level of academic achievement (e.g., a sixth grade reading competency). The weakness of this procedure is obvious when one considers the fact that a sizable portion of the secondary school population may not read above a sixth grade level. Depending on the demographic characteristics of the school (some schools will have many more poor achievers than others as a function of socioeconomic status), students with low IQ scores, underachievers, and unmotivated students will have equal chance of being selected for LD classes based only on a criterion measure. Kirk and Elkins (1975) found that 35% of 3000 children classified as learning disabled had IQ scores below 90. Not only is this practice in violation of the eligibility standards of the required assessment procedures, but it is likely that many of these students actually perform well within the range of their ability levels. Obviously, their scores on academic achievement would be low by comparison with their normal peers but not unexpected in accordance with their abilities. Students who generally have IQ scores within the range of 70 to 85 are able to perform between a fourth to sixth grade reading level by the end of the twelfth grade of school. By definition we know that half the student population will fall below the median on reading tests but this does not qualify them for learning disabilities placement! Another danger inherent in the use of a criterion measure is that learning disabled students who need services will be excluded from programming unless they fall below the criterion or will be promoted into the mainstream as a reward for reaching the competency. Mastery of all the basic reading skills will not assure success and cannot be used to justify curtailment of services to students who continue to have problems in the acquisition and retrieval of information and the handling of verbal and mathematical concepts.

3. *Significant discrepancies between ability and some performance areas are of little consequence at the secondary level.* There

are sufficient tests of basic reading skill, reading comprehension, mathematics calculation, and mathematics reasoning. However, there are no standardized tests of oral expression, listening comprehension, and written expression. For the most part, students who are significantly deficient in oral expression are likely to be classified in other diagnostic categories. Written expressive deficits are likely to be developmentally related to the inability to read, although some cases of dysgraphia exist with reading development and other language skills intact. There is little reason to believe that students with significant problems in listening comprehension, as presently conceived, would be classified as learning disabled.

**Test instruments.** In a previous attempt to ascertain the instruments used in assessment of LD adolescents, an analysis of the tests used in Child Service Demonstration Centers was made (Marsh et al., 1978). A total of 41 tests were used in seven demonstration centers. Only one (WISC-R) was uniformly employed in each center. It was interesting to note that many of the tests in use were inappropriate for the age group in question and very little interest in vocational assessment was indicated.

The most important consideration in the selection of test instruments should be the statistical properties of validity and reliability. It is surprising how many tests have no reliability data reported in the manuals; in the strictest sense they should not be considered tests without evidence that they measure purported traits reliably. Without reliability data the test is a guess that is no better than any subjective opinion. Many states and school districts have developed required assessment procedures which specify tests that must be used or which make recommendations. The examiner should read each manual carefully to determine the necessary statistical information and secure recent reviews about test instruments from the *Mental Measurements Yearbook* and other sources. For a more complete discussion of assessment of adolescents the reader is referred to Marsh et al. (1978) and to Salvia and Ysseldyke (1978).

**Observation.** The requirement for observation of the student in the classroom is perplexing to most school personnel because the reasons for the observation, the nature of the observational process, and the uses of information are not clear in the guidelines. We have been conducting research with the *Coping Analysis Schedule for Educational Settings* (CASES), developed by Dr. Robert Spaulding, currently of the College of Education, San Jose State University, in San Jose, California. We have found the instrument to be one of the most useful and efficient methods of observation in that it enables the observer to gather highly reliable information in a short period of time. Moreover, an accurate picture of the student's behavior and response to the academic environment can be depicted and treatment strategies can be applied to the patterns that emerge. The observation is unobtrusive, does not cause attention or embarrassment to the student, contributes significantly to understanding the student, and aids greatly in assessment.

### Mental retardation: assessment issues

Assessment of students who are mentally retarded has become a very sensitive and controversial process since the growing body of case law began over litigation concerning the misclassification of minority students. As noted earlier, the major immediate response was to lower the cutoff point for classification on the basis of an IQ score and to include measures of adaptive behavior. Of course, the reason for this is clear, in that it is not desirable to be regarded clinically as mentally retarded nor is it acceptable in our culture to be regarded as stupid. Due to the social stigma and the unacceptability of any label that may be used to classify people, no matter how good the intention or the possible benefits, it is possible that the identification of a child as mentally retarded and the provision of special education may result in harm to the child (Robinson & Robinson, 1976).

As a consequence, there has been a distinct trend to eliminate or change labels or to refuse to label students. The term "noncategorical" usually refers to the three groups included in the mildly handicapped population, and little distinction is made between the LD, EMR, and ED subgroups because of the overlap of characteristics. Actually, with the increasing tendency to recognize the AAMD definition of significant subaverage intellectual functioning there will probably be more disparity of the EMR group because LD and ED students will generally have IQ scores near 100 while the EMR subgroup will be near 70. Although behaviors may be similar, the cognitive processes will be divergent and more obvious at the secondary level.

However, the use of an IQ score is insufficient, singly, to diagnose mental retardation. A low IQ score and deficient adaptive behavior must be found concurrently. If the use of intelligence tests is disputed, unfortunately so are measures of adaptive behavior. The construct of adaptive behavior has been criticized, and there are no well-standardized measures of such behavior. A further complication of the process is that a person may be considered to be retarded at one point in life but at other times and ages he or she may not because adaptive behavior and environmental influences will alter. From a humanitarian point of view this is desirable because the condition has promise for improvement; however, conceptually it may mean that the construct of mental retardation is faulty or that identification procedures are lacking in scrutiny.

Shifting to a different mode for assessment of mental retardation presents a different set of advantages and disadvantages, as in the qualitative evaluation of subjects rather than the quantitative. If traditional intelligence tests are displaced by Piagetian tasks, a logical culmination of the definition proposed by Kolstoe (1972), then it permits the practitioner to focus on what the individual *can* do rather than on deviations from the norm. Education and training would be keyed to levels of ability rather than attempts to close the gap between functional levels and normality. However, in this view the retardate (mildly retarded) will not surpass the concrete levels of functioning and may not develop formal operational thought. This portends a more unfortunate prognosis than many would accept under prevailing philosophies about mental retardation.

It is unlikely that many students will be initially classified as mentally retarded in secondary school. Most will have been in special education programs for several years prior to junior or senior high school. Moreover, there is a rather general procedure used in most settings for assessment, which includes a variety of measurements such as intelligence and adaptive behavior.

## Emotional disturbance: assessment issues

Much of what has been said about assessment in learning disabilities and mental retardation could be applied to the area of emotional disturbance/behavior disorders. The label ED or BD tends to be more mysterious to educators than the others, which cannot be explained as specific inability to achieve in basic skills or as overall deficient intelligence. There may be many causes of emotional disturbance, none of which is easily explained or understood within the educational context. Such terminology as neurosis, psychosis, and schizophrenia are totally foreign to the public school sector and frightening to teachers who may attach many misconceptions to the general label emotional disturbance. Bryan and Bryan (1979) have discussed three broad categories of emotionally disturbed children: conduct problems, withdrawal, and inadequacy and immaturity. Of the three, students who have conduct problems are the most likely candidates for placement in public schools because they are aggressive or hyperactive or both. The obvious overlap of these characteristics with the EMR and LD categories reveals the reason why many authorities are content to simply lump the three together for programmatic purposes. The characteristics are similar, the identification and assessment approaches are not very different, and remediation and behavior modification techniques can be equally applied with each group. Children with more serious emotional disorders are of little concern in the noncategorical approach because they are so disturbed that they will be in a segregated special class or special facility.

Special educators have adopted behavioral techniques for use in the educational setting so that objectives for this population involve extinguishing conduct problems while stimulating growth in academic subjects. This is not much different from the approach that would be used with a learning disabled student with superimposed or secondary emotional problems. The distinction is in the label, not the approach. There is a reluctance of some educational practitioners and school-based diagnosticians to diagnose students as emotionally disturbed because of the psychiatric connotation of the term. Many writers in the field of special education have expressed intense dissatisfaction with the classification system of the American Psychiatric Association, which bases its categories on clinical impressions rather than observable, measurable behavior. The most noteworthy classification system for use in education is that proposed by Quay (1975), which recognizes three broad categories: conduct problems, personality problems, and immaturity.

Due to the training and certification of teachers, the unavailability of highly trained psychiatric personnel for the school setting, the disaffection with psychoanalytic interpretations of emotional problems, and the need to meet *educational* objectives, programming for mildly handicapped emotionally disturbed students pivots on behavioral techniques to improve behavior and remediation of learning problems if necessary. In essence, this is the learning disabilities approach, and the practice, if not the theory, behind distinctions between subgroups of mildly handicapped students leads some authorities to conclude that there are no diagnostic differences.

The pattern that runs through all assessment considerations with the three traditional categories within the mildly handicapped population is that there are dramatic similarities in the characteristics and assessment practices. Differentiating between an emotionally disturbed child and one who is learning disabled may hinge more on the composition of the total behavioral pattern that is presented to the examining team— local tolerance in the school environment for conduct disorders, and the relative discrepancy of academic achievement. The greater the magnitude of one dimension over the other, the greater the chances that one or another label will be applied, although educational efforts may not be much different in either event. The inclusion of EMR students may vary considerably, depending on the tendency of the examining team to use IQ scores either at one or two standard deviations below the mean. The lower the average IQ of the EMR subgroup the more divergence there will be in terms of peer-group disunity and ability to benefit from mainstream courses that require higher cognitive processes in learning. Of course, if local special education arrangements are categorically based, the assessment process will be directed by more traditional criteria. Nonetheless, as a group comprised of "mildly handicapped students" in the noncategorical approach, or as discrete categories in the traditional approach, the individual characteristics and unique pattern of abilities and disabilities of each student dictate that the best educational decisions will be made on a student-by-student basis. The most significant contribution that could be made in this effort would be the addition of observational techniques and expanded ecological assessment.

## General procedures in assessment

The following general points are made about required assessment procedures:
1. Federal regulations have been adopted that dictate the general assessment procedures for all handicapped students.
2. Additional assessment procedures include (a) assurances of the inclusion of specific professionals on the multidisciplinary team, (b) criteria for determination of learning disabilities, (c) required observation of referred students, and (d) culmination of assessment activities in a written report.

All students suspected of being handicapped, including the learning disabled, are to be evaluated in accordance with the following general procedures (*Federal Register*, 1977, *43*(163), 42496-42497):

State and local educational agencies shall ensure, at a minimum, that (1) tests and other evaluation materials are provided and administered in the child's native language or other mode of communication, unless it is clearly not feasible to do so, have been validated for the specific purpose for which they are used, and are administered by trained personnel in conformance with the instructions provided by their producer; (2) tests and other evaluation materials include those tailored to assess specific areas of educational need and not merely those which are designed to provide a single general intelligence quotient; (3) tests are selected and administered so as best to ensure that when a test is administered to a child with impaired sensory, manual, or speaking skills, the test results accurately reflect the child's aptitude or achievement level or whatever other factors the test purports to measure, rather than reflecting the child's impaired sensory, manual, or speaking skills (except where those skills are the factors which the test purports to measure); (4) no single procedure is used as the sole criterion for determining an appropriate educational program for a child; (5) the evaluation is made by a multidisciplinary team or group of persons, including at least one teacher or other specialist with knowledge in the area of suspected disability; and (6) the child is assessed in all areas related to the suspected disability, including, where appropriate, health, vision, hearing, social and emotional status, general intelligence, academic performance, communicative status, and motor abilities.

These procedures are imposed on school districts for all students with handicapping conditions that are included in the federal definitions and that are eligible for entitlements under P.L. 94-142. There are additional procedures for pupils who are suspected of having learning disabilities. A synopsis of these regulations is found in the following section.

## Additional assessment procedures in learning disabilities

In December 1977 the Office of Education announced final regulations to direct the states in the identification of children who might have learning disabilities. These regulations expand the general procedures; they are as given below (*Federal Register*, 1977, *42*(250), 65082-65085).

**Evaluation team.** In the process of evaluating a child who is suspected of having a specific learning disability, each public agency shall include the following professional persons on the multidisciplinary team:
1. The student's regular teacher or, in the event the student has no regular teacher, a regular classroom teacher qualified to teach a student of the age of the referred student.
2. A child of less than school age will be represented by a person who is qualified by the state to teach children of that age.
3. At least one person qualified to conduct individual diagnostic examinations, such as a school psychologist, speech therapist, or remedial reading teacher.

Although it is curious that the professional list in no. 3 above does not specifically include the designation of a learning disabilities specialist, and although some professionals have expressed concern about the exclusion, it would seem that, in accordance with state regulations pertaining to the certification and/or licensure of examiners, that many learning disabilities specialists are, in fact, qualified "to conduct individual diagnostic examinations" because of their training. Nonetheless, it is obvious that learning disabilities specialists are not excluded from serving on the multidisciplinary team in any event.

**Criteria for determination of learning disabilities.** The team may determine that a child has a specific learning disability if the child does not achieve commensurate with his or her age and ability when provided with appropriate learning experiences, and if the team determines that a child has a severe discrepancy between achievement and ability in one or more of these areas:
1. Oral expression
2. Listening comprehension
3. Written expression
4. Basic reading skill
5. Reading comprehension
6. Mathematics calculation or reasoning

The team may not identify a child as having a learning disability if the severe discrepancy may be attributed to a visual, hearing, or motor handicap, mental retardation, emotional disturbance, or environmental, cultural, or economic disadvantage.

**Observation.** At least one team member other than the child's regular teacher shall observe the child's academic performance in the regular setting and, in the case of a child of less than school age, a team member shall observe the child in an environment appropriate for a child of that age.

**Written report.** The team shall prepare a written report of the results of the evaluation, which must include:
1. Whether or not the child has a learning disability
2. The basis for determination of the learning disability
3. Relevant behavior noted during observation
4. Relationship of observed behavior to academic functioning
5. Educationally relevant medical findings
6. Whether or not there is a severe discrepancy between achievement and ability that is not correctable with special services
7. Determination of the team concerning the effects of environmental, cultural, or economic disadvantage

Each team member is required to stipulate that the written report either does or does not reflect his or her opinion. Dissenting members of the team are to submit a separate statement presenting a minority view of the data and interpretation of information.

**Implications of the additional assessment procedures.** There are two striking features evident in the additional procedures for assessment: (1) the absence of a requirement to provide assessment data relating to process disorders (basic psychological processes incorporated in the definition); (2) the inclusion of a requirement to determine a significant discrepancy between ability and performance in one of the specified performance areas.

Although the presumption has been that some form of neurological deficit or disorder of one or more of the basic psychological processes is responsible for learning disabilities, the present assessment procedures ignore evaluation of processes. Emphasis is to be placed on achievement discrepancies. Many practitioners and examiners will undoubtedly object to the exclusion of process-assessment measures. It should be recognized, however, that there are very few tests that have the validity or the reliability to adequately provide examiners with useful information about process functioning with adolescents, there is little empirical evidence to determine the relationship between process disorders and academic performance, and there is no reason to believe that remedial efforts directed at process functions will benefit the student. It is apparent that the examining team may determine that a student is learning disabled without providing measures of basic process functioning; and, any use of such measures must be defended in the written report to demonstrate how they contribute to the diagnosis. It can be assumed that this dilemma will remain unresolved for some time and will continue to be a source of debate. Clinical assessment based on measures of process deficits must be carefully considered and justified by the examiner.

## Conclusion

Without question, the assessment of adolescents who may be mildly handicapped is muddled. The difficulty in discerning students from among the general group of underachievers is perplexing. Many students, however, will be carried over from elementary programs so that initial identification will probably not be a serious problem. The difficulty has been that a continuum of services has not existed for adolescents. Assessment of intelligence is fairly well established; the Wechsler scales seem to be a predominant choice of examiners. Beyond this, however, there is very little agreement about what instruments should be used. The most valid, reliable instruments should be selected for use in the specified areas of reading and mathematics. Although the regulations about assessment ignore process measures, many examiners will continue to use tests in these areas. Additional assessment to account for social, cognitive, and other developmental differences of adolescents should adhere to the same test of reasonableness as other instruments. If possible, adherence to the guidelines to determine significant differences should be made. Use of a criterion measure for admission and dismissal from special programs should be used with the greatest caution because of the potential harm to students.

In spite of the criticism of some writers, the lack of agreement among authorities about assessment and the educational needs of adolescents, and difficulties in establishing more defensible assessment procedures, schools will continue to identify students and will be increasingly expected to widen services at the secondary level. Theoretical and practical spheres of activity in special education will likely travel divergent, independent paths for the present. This creates problems that must ultimately be addressed in regulations of governmental agencies, and school personnel must deal with them. Theoretical concerns aside, the real problem confronting the school practitioner is a practical approach to assessment. It is certain that whatever position is assumed by a particular school system, one or another critic will emerge to attack it; but the practitioner must develop procedures that conform with regulations and not necessarily with the particular viewpoint of an academic authority, one who will have no administrative or supervisory authority.

## SUPPORT PERSONNEL
### School counselor

**Qualifications.** Counselors employed in public schools must acquire certification through state departments of education. Shertzer and Stone (1974) discuss the *Standards for the Preparation of Secondary School Counselors*, which reflect input from professional organizations; namely, the American Personnel and Guidance Association (APGA), the American School Counselors Association (ASCA), and the Association for Counselor Education and Supervision (ACES). A minimum of 2 years of graduate study or completion of a master's degree is required. Training programs equivalent to 60 semester hours of graduate work are being encouraged by the APGA (Forster, 1978). The training programs include extensive practicums and internships.

Assessment of the student's environment and identification of coping techniques required for survival are stressed in counselor preparation, and methods are emphasized that build on existing strengths of the student's personality. Career education is becoming more prominent in the role of today's counselor because of both legislation and public interest ("Interview with Kenneth Hoyt," 1978). As a result, graduate programs are offering more training in career development.

**Role of the counselor within the school.** The school counselor has traditionally provided two primary types of service for students: personal-social adjustment counseling and guidance. The vocational concerns of the counseling profession are still evident in most secondary schools as are the psychological models of the 1940s and 1950s. The role of the counselor is diverse because of the different student outcomes expected by the school administration. Principals determine, to a major degree, the distribution of the counselor's time and counseling priorities (Warnath, 1974).

The types of intervention typically used in counseling are *individual* or *group* therapy sessions and the provision of information. In both instances, the interventions emphasize therapy instead of prevention, are performed in an environment separate from the rest of the school, and appear to be somewhat disassociated from the goals of the school (Wellington, 1974). All of these factors have isolated the counselor and may explain why counseling has been regarded as ineffective by many teachers, a circumstance that should be heeded by special educators.

The recent trend toward accountability has resulted in an additional component for the counselor, namely, consulting. The emphasis placed on student outcomes requires the counselor to attend to the environment within which the student must function and to interact directly or indirectly with that environment. Consultative and coordinating functions have emerged as equally important aspects of the job of the counselor. Hoyt ("Interview with Kenneth Hoyt," 1978) emphasizes that the counselor must assume a facilitative/participatory/leadership function, which we describe as an *extended counseling model* (ECM). Arbuckle (1968) acknowledged this trend by noting that the counselor should have expertise and training in diagnosis, work adjustment, postsecondary programming, behavior, and communication. The implications include changes in counselor education, a broader range of interventions, and a more aggressive, active role.

This expanded view of counseling has opened up avenues of communication be-

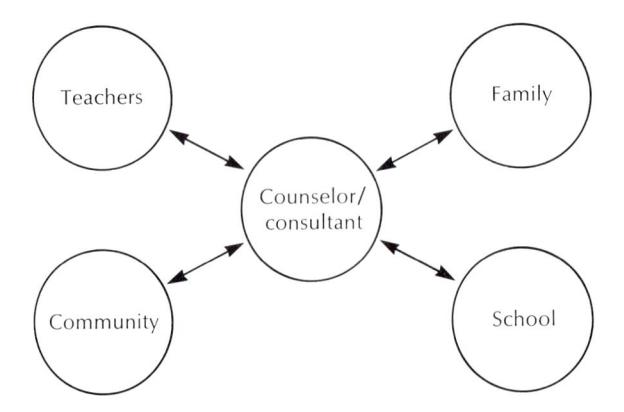

**Fig. 6-2.** Interactions of the counselor-consultant.

tween the counselor and other individuals and institutions within the student's environment. Fig. 6-2 illustrates the additional interactions of the counselor-consultant. Increased communication and contact with *parents* reflect acknowledgment by school counselors of the influence of parents in vocational and educational planning. Sharing information and responsibility with *teachers* can have a multiplier effect in terms of students affected (Keefe, 1975; Sweet, 1972). This more contemporary view of counseling includes interaction within the *school as an institution*. The total counseling program must be expanded within the institution to gain input and support and to develop a team approach (Feltham, 1972). The environment of the student includes the *community*, and a more interactive approach may call for the counselor to become a change agent (Dwyer, 1974) or a social reconstructionist (Riccio, 1970). Involvement with city leaders, employers, and community groups may be necessary to affect policy within the student's environment (Bradley, 1978).

### Expanded role in programming for mildly handicapped students

*Assessment.* The school district's compliance plan includes a designation of responsibility for handling referrals and placements. The counselor may be the designee in many instances, in which case the role is as described in the general discussion of assessment earlier in this chapter. Contributions made by the counselor can include taking the required social history and collecting behavioral data.

*Services.* The *extended counseling model* (ECM) is a conceptual model central to providing appropriate educational programming for mildly handicapped students, especially in the secondary school. We believe this model provides services beneficial to *all* secondary students as it is based on the tasks of adolescence, but it could be vital to the success of handicapped adolescents.

The components of the ECM are listed below. It should be stressed that the counselor, special educators, regular teachers, and peers or volunteers may serve as counseling agents to provide a wide range of services to mildly handicapped students. The components listed here are not necessarily under the absolute control of the counselor, especially those that relate to educational programming per se. However, the counselor may be a logical choice to exert the necessary leadership and organization to improve services for this group of students in need.

The general components of an extended counseling model are:
1. Parent counseling
2. Consulting
3. Environmental assessment and change
4. Career education
5. Study skills
6. Goal setting
7. Personal counseling
8. Decision making
9. Training in social skills

*Parenting systems/information.* There will be limited opportunity for the counselor to actually involve the parents of secondary school students in parenting classes, such as Parent Effectiveness Training (PET). However, the secondary school counselor should be familiar with such parenting programs so that information can be provided to interested parents. Parents can be trained to assist their child in social and academic development (Shearer & Shearer, 1972); and, although most of such efforts have been directed at parents of younger students, parental training must not be discounted at the secondary level. Parents of mildly handicapped students may approach the counselor for information about parenting programs in a desperate effort to alter strategies they believe are ineffective. More frequently, parents may inquire about such programs for assistance in dealing with younger siblings of the atypical student in an effort to prevent the recurrence of a learning problem.

Parent education programs are available and are offered through various church and community organizations. Counselors should keep an active file of such programs and their sponsoring organizations for quick reference. Particular note should be taken of any programs slanted specifically toward the problems of parents and adolescents.

*Management systems/information.* Concern over behavior problems or disciplinary actions may result in direct contact between the counselor and parents. Cooperation between the school and home can often hasten solutions to behavioral problems, but such cooperation requires that all parties understand the nature of the problem and agree on an intervention strategy. Behavior modification interventions have been utilized effectively with adolescents and may be selected as appropriate strategies for use at home and at school.

Behavioral intervention requires counselors to coordinate activities of teachers and parents using specific management techniques. Counselors should have training in behavior management systems and be able to relate these to home situations. Parents can be trained in basic behavior modification strategies and can contribute to the solution of problems (Hall et al., 1972; Patterson & Gullion, 1968). The purpose of this is not to make parents experts in behavior modification nor to imply that this approach is appropriate for all situations. However, parents of adolescents can synthesize the basic aspects of behavior modification and positive reinforcement techniques into an alternative method of viewing behavior of adolescents with problems and responding to that behavior.

The counselor may find it helpful to maintain a file for parent reference on the topic of behavior modification. Below is a list of possible items for inclusion in such a file.

1. Handout of basic vocabulary from the field of behavior management.
2. List of books on the subject written in a less technical format. A library of such books should be kept on hand for parent or teacher loan.
3. Resource list of films and filmstrips on the subject appropriate for parent viewing. If these are available through inservice programs within the school, they should be shown to interested groups.

4. Summary forms to communicate to parents the nature of management systems being utilized with their child.

Knowledge of the principles of positive reinforcement and assessment of reinforcement systems of adolescents will prove valuable to parents and can be conveyed in general terms through a personal conference between parents and the counselor. The suggested reading list included in the parent file can supplement such a conference but typically can not replace a direct meeting. In fact, several work sessions may be necessary before the parents have a grasp of the principles and can begin to see home applications. The counselor's training and experience with behavior management, as well as the ability and receptiveness of the parents, will determine the extent of utilization possible and the amount of training needed to reach maximum effectiveness.

A summary form provides a means for informing the parents of the management systems being used at school, even in those cases in which parent participation is not achieved. Knowing that certain behaviors are being reinforced may spur parents to join the effort or, at least, to understand what the school is attempting to do. If parents agree to participate, the management plan should be developed cooperatively to ensure consistency in approach. Consistent responses of adults to certain behaviors of the student can greatly facilitate behavioral change. *The form should not be sent home without some prior explanation to the parents.* The counselor should be certain that the parents understand the plan and its purpose. The use of this form is optional, and professional discretion by the counselor will dictate when its use will facilitate programming for the atypical student. There may be a school policy concerning the use of management strategies of which the counselor should be aware because it may specify the level of parental involvement.

*Parent conferences.* Counselors and resource teachers conduct parent conferences for a variety of purposes, including referral, assessment, IEP development, program evaluation, and parent counseling. Academic difficulties and correlates of the handicapping condition are of mutual concern to parents, counselors, and special education teachers, which may result in a conference being called by the school personnel or by the parents. The leadership role in these conferences appears to be an issue of some concern to both teachers and counselors: who calls such meetings and who chairs them? This need not be a territorial battle for power or a responsibility each wishes to "give" to the other. In the ECM, the counselor assumes a leadership role but the special education teacher must cooperate with the counselor to deliver total programming to the handicapped adolescent. Achieving this type of cooperative effort will result in improved services to special students and a reduced need to squabble over specific job responsibilities for each position.

The purpose of the parent conference will determine who assumes primary responsibility. Parents of elementary school children can approach a teacher and ask how their child is performing. At the secondary level, this is much more difficult to do because of the number of teachers involved and the impersonal structure of the school. The parents of atypical students concerned with academic progress or a specific problem will probably make inquiries or requests for conferences directly to the special education teacher, perhaps requesting the presence of additional professionals. However, depending on the involvement of the counselor and the nature of parental concern, the first contact or request for a conference may be made with the counselor.

*Parent counseling* falls clearly within the domain of the school counselor. Parents of handicapped students have some special

| Special needs of parents of handicapped students | Possible strategies | |
|---|---|---|
| | Direct services | Referral |
| Need to communicate about problem | Individual counseling | Local parent groups |
| Explanation of the etiology | Providing factual information on condition | Medical specialists |
| | | Private counseling firm |
| Help with correlates of handicapping condition | Conducting parent group sessions | Specialized professionals |
| Help in maintaining normal family life | Providing vocational information | Agencies providing support services |
| Assistance in planning student's future | | |

needs of which the teacher and counselor must be aware (Chinn et al., 1978):
1. The need to communicate about a problem
2. An explanation of the etiology
3. Help with correlates of the handicapping condition
4. Help in maintaining a normal family life
5. Assistance in planning the student's future

These needs may be directly addressed through parent counseling conducted by the school counselor or through referral to outside individuals or agencies as detailed above.

The amount of parent counseling conducted by the school counselor will vary as determined by the school administration, community setting, and other factors. The demand for parent counseling will probably be less at the secondary level than in elementary schools. However, the high school counselor should be knowledgeable about the handicapping conditions, types of problems encountered by families of such students, and life options available to mildly handicapped adolescents. Armed with accurate, factual information and counseling tools of the profession, counselors can assist parents with their problems. Even though extensive parent counseling may not comprise a major part of school-counseling services, parental interaction and assistance are important.

*Management consulting with teachers.*
Secondary teachers are trained primarily in content areas with little or no training in classroom management. Ironically most of the problems experienced by secondary teachers center on discipline or management difficulties. In the case of atypical secondary students, academic assistance must be accompanied by social-emotional adjustment. The ECM calls for the counselor to interact with the special education teacher and the regular teacher to facilitate a more positive handling of special students. Chapter 3 described the interpersonal relationships of mildly handicapped adolescents, and from that it should be evident that there is great potential for management problems in the regular class. The regular teacher may be reluctant to open up his or her classroom to scrutiny. However, the counselor may be in a position to offer suggestions to alter the atmosphere of the classroom or, at least, the management of the special needs student. A regular classroom teacher can request assistance from the special education teacher and counselor in identifying strategies that can reduce stress between the student and the regular teacher (Fig. 6-3).

Management suggestions from the counselor or the special education teacher might include training in behavior modification, reorganization of the daily instructional period, and/or rearranging the room itself. If the teacher is willing, an analysis can be made of the manner in which the teacher directs the

## THE SCHOOL

```
                    SERVICE ASSISTANCE REQUEST FORM

Teacher_____ Room no._____ Subject_____
Counselor_____ Special Education Teacher_____
_____

1.  Does the request involve a specific student?_____ Yes _(X)_ No
    If yes, student's name:_____
2.  Brief description of the problem with which assistance is needed:
    (•Failure of handicapped students to complete homework_____
    •Difficulty keeping students' attention during lecture_____
    •Students cannot complete assignments)
3.  Period:___(3rd period American history, room no. 410)_____
4.  Problem-solving strategies I am willing to try:
    _(X)___ conference with counselor or resource teacher
    _____ observation by counselor or resource teacher
    _____ read materials provided in problem area
    _____ other:_____
5.  My schedule of time available for consulting:
    1st period (workroom)_____
    Noon by appointment (12:30-1:15)_____
```

**Fig. 6-3.** Request for assistance in management problems in classroom.

class and in which feedback is provided. Admittedly, few teachers probably will allow this, making this aspect of the ECM extremely unlikely. However, the handicapped student and other students might benefit from examination of teacher behaviors. This consultative effort conducted jointly by the special educator and the counselor can serve to achieve the goal of serving mildly handicapped students in regular classrooms.

*Liaison between academic programming and adjustment training.* The total program of handicapped adolescents will include direct services in the area of social-emotional adjustment. These services may include participation in social skills training, goal setting, and other components of the counseling model. The special education teacher and the counselor will be involved in delivering these direct services, but the regular teacher may be unaware of these programs or the students involved. The fragmented nature of most secondary schools is not conducive to such communication, making the liaison role an important one for the counselor.

There are several methods of communication that can occur; an obvious one is a conference or meeting with regular teachers. Teachers may not be predisposed to participate in more meetings, making this an unpopular method in most school settings. However, the counselor should consider inservice training for the entire staff at the beginning of the term during which all components of the program are explained. The teachers' handbook should include brief descriptions of the program components and how they relate to other special and regular services within the school. A description and a sample of all forms, such as referral forms, should be included in a handbook in an attempt to increase teacher understanding and participation.

*Environmental assessment and change.* Secondary students are on the verge of adulthood and are beginning to interact with the adult society. Vocational planning is one obvious area requiring knowledge of the world outside of school. Many services pertaining to vocational planning are not utilized simply because other professionals, including school personnel, and families are not aware of their existence. The counselor should be informed and perhaps maintain a file on such community services. A directory of community services is usually available to the counselor, which may assist him or her in developing awareness about services to handicapped students.

*Career education.* Career education consists of two subcomponents: information/definition and vocational planning; these will be fully described in Chapter 12. The role of the counselor in vocational preparation and career planning has a long-standing history recognized by most educators.

*Study skills.* The subcomponents of study skills are:

1. Note-taking: critical listening, shorthand, outlining
2. Library use: reference, card catalog, periodicals
3. Organization: daily time schedule, teacher interaction, organization of materials
4. Test-taking: types of tests, memory development, test vocabulary
5. Writing: idea organization, technical aids
6. Audiovisual aids: tapes, films

Structured class sessions serve groups of handicapped students and are conducted by special education teachers or counselors as part of the regular schedule. Interaction with the counselor in developing this area of training can be beneficial and, in some instances, the counselor will assume responsibility for directing such sessions for mildly handicapped students and other pupils.

*Goal statement/strategy planning.* This

facet of ECM assists students to state realistic goals and select coping strategies to achieve goals. It is important because systematic goal setting is difficult (Harway & Robbins, 1977). Limited school involvement and personal accomplishments contribute to students dropping out of school (Howard & Anderson, 1978). It appears that efforts to involve the student through planning might prevent dropping out of school or withdrawal from activities. The overall purpose of planning is to aid atypical students in identifying small goals that can be realized and that can contribute to a sense of self-direction, self-worth, and accomplishment. A by-product of goal training may be positive responses from teachers and peers, which can generally contribute to the student's self-concept and perception of school. As small goals are met, a foundation is laid for addressing major life goals realistically. Mildly handicapped students may not be equipped to make vocational or life plans because of a lack of expertise in setting their own goals and perceiving the future. Parents and schools have dictated "the next step" and accompanying behaviors so that the adolescent is unprepared to make plans for the future.

This first phase begins with talking about concerns and exploration of ideas about one's self. Big ideas about the future should be encouraged, and sharing should be reinforced. Eventually, some goal should be identified for each group member and specifically stated in terms of the student's behavior. Students can be taught to use and write behavioral objectives using any of the programmed texts available or through class instruction and practice. Specifying the behavior the student hopes to accomplish eases the process of selecting strategies and aids in recognition that a goal has been reached (Mager, 1972; Popham & Baker, 1970).

Once a goal has been behaviorally stated, a plan should be developed for achieving it and a date anticipated. Feedback is important during the statement of the goal, and development of strategies should be emphasized in training. Fig. 6-4 shows a sample plan that can be completed individually or collectively.

The example shown (Fig. 6-4) may appear to be insignificant; but as we pointed out in Chapter 3, involvement in school may not automatically occur for some handicapped students, and membership in formal/informal groups may need to be encouraged. Goals need not be limited to school situations, but such goals make an easier starting point. However, goals must be selected by the student in order to make planning successful.

*Evaluation.* Student forms include a column labeled "evaluation," which encompasses action, evaluation, and comments. This part of evaluation allows the student to examine the action to see if it was appropriate. If the goal is not achieved, it may be discovered that the student failed to accurately follow the plan or that the plan was faulty. Group sessions should include an examination of the student plan in the evaluation column.

Group evaluation sessions also provide opportunity to reinforce student behavior, a very useful tool in training for goals (Harway & Robbins, 1977). Positive reinforcement for accomplishment of small goals can be provided by the group leader, group members, and other teachers.

*Affective first aid.* Crisis situations may arise with regularity in the lives of handicapped students. The counselor and special education teacher must be able to react to such crises and be able to aid students in dealing with transient situations so that consequences are not intensified by illogical actions. Problems might include conflict with parents and teachers, disputes with friends, and strained relations with a love interest.

```
                        MAKING APPROPRIATE PLANS

Date   (9/15)
                                         Special
Student   (Tommy Smith)   Counselor  (L. Spark)  Education Teacher  (A. McFadden)


    Goal              Plan                       Evaluation

(I will join      (• Play two games of      Action              Comments
the chess club.)  chess per day for a       (• Played with Jim.
                  period of 5 days to
                  practice skills.
                  • Contact club presi-     • Tried twice 9/19:
                  dent to ask require-      reached him by phone
                  ments of membership.      9/20: requirements:  pay
                  • Go to next meeting.     $2.00 dues, attend
                  • Pay dues.               weekly practices,
                  • Fulfill membership      play in 1 meet monthly,
                  requirements.)            have picture taken for
                                            yearbook, take turns on
                                            cleanup after practice.
                                            • Joined 10/1.)
```

**Fig. 6-4.** Sample student form.

*Individual and group counseling.* Mildly handicapped students should have access to the same professional counseling services provided to other students in the secondary school, including individual and group counseling. The nature of these services is within the professional domain of the counselor. A significant reduction in the dropout rate was accomplished by training regular secondary teachers to conduct counseling sessions in a secondary school (Krivatsy-O'Hara et al., 1978), and handicapped students can certainly benefit from such counseling efforts.

*Decision-making model.* Training in decision making must be structured so that the student can generalize the procedure to other situations in life. Decision making does not mean counselors or special education teachers tell students how to make decisions but rather enable them to make them independently (Krumboltz & Thoresen, 1976; Shertzer & Stone, 1974). Counselor training includes experience with decision-making models, which can be modified for use in secondary schools. Generally, a decision-making model includes sequential steps such as the following:

1. Definition of the problem
2. Identification of correlates (e.g., values, goals)
3. Specification of alternatives (brainstorming/data collection)
4. Selection of tentative decision
5. Action
6. Evaluation

Counselors can select a model or synthesize a series of steps from the literature. Groups of students can be introduced to the model and acquainted with the process.

Making decisions requires information gathering and processing (Janis & Mann, 1977; Shertzer & Stone, 1974; Stewart et al., 1978). This is a critical point because it requires *accurate* information about one's self, the environment, and feedback (Krumboltz, 1966; Stewart et al., 1978). Some mildly handicapped students have difficulty monitoring their own behavior and performance (Deshler et al., 1978) and interacting or understanding their social environment (Gardner, 1974). The implication is that some atypical students could benefit from training in information gathering prior to making decisions. Systematic training in examining one's self in relation to normative data can aid the student in identifying his or her values, interests, and abilities as well as in changing them (Stewart et al., 1978).

Feedback training in this component is geared to assisting a student to observe reactions of others to his or her behavior and interpreting that information. This results in greater utilization of environmental information in making decisions and determining behavior. Students obtain information through direct experience, self-observation, standardized tests, and constructive confrontation.

*Decision-making practice groups.* Once the model and sources of input have been identified, application becomes essential for generalization. Counselors can anticipate some critical decisions that must be made by adolescents, such as postsecondary plans or selection of a marriage partner. Anticipating these major decisions can reduce some of the anxiety associated with decision making and provide training in information gathering (Stewart et al., 1978). Groups of five to ten students participate in sessions dealing with problems or concerns through case studies presented as videotaped vignettes, written descriptions, and oral descriptions, with the counselor leading the group through the decision-making model. Identification with the case problem increases the level of involvement of the adolescents and provides practice in solving problems.

Data collection is conducted in relation to the case example just as if the problem belonged to members of the group. People outside the group are interviewed, books examined, and situations considered as information is collected about the correlates of the problem. Discussions reflecting values and goals lead to clarification for group members as alternative decisions are offered to the group. A decision-making balance sheet may even be used (Janis & Mann, 1977). Sessions should be held on a regular basis, be informal in nature, and be highly relevant to group members. The counselor's contribution to special education in this area could be significant.

*Social skills training.* The social skills training component aims at assisting mildly handicapped adolescents to improve their self-concepts and interactions with peers and adults. Interpersonal conflict is a recognized characteristic of emotionally disturbed students, and a corollary of learning disabilities. Social incompetence has long been regarded as a pervasive corollary of mental retardation. Although here, as in other aspects of counseling activities, the curriculum may include elements dealing with social skills, a significant contribution of the counselor to augment social skills objectives would enhance this area as a major aspect in secondary programming.

*Self-awareness.* A generally accepted goal of counseling is helping clients to better understand themselves (Krumboltz, 1966; Mortensen & Schmuller, 1978; Shertzer & Stone, 1974). We believe that this is also an appropriate educational goal, especially for mildly handicapped students. An accurate perception of one's self is not easily accomplished, and the process may be even more complicated by a learning problem. Comparison with normative data may point out that the handicapped student is different, and this may be difficult to accept (Kronick, 1976). However, through therapeutic programming in social skills training, students can be helped to view their abilities in a more positive light and deal with feelings about deficits (Bonham, 1975; Browne, 1974; West et al., 1978).

Training can be tailored to the individual student population comprising the groups and can include a number of topics: personal grooming, hygiene, language patterns, attitudes/opinions, abilities, talents, and interests. The amount of emphasis placed on the various topics will differ with the needs of each group and the nature of the handicap.

Activities suggested for increasing self-awareness include role playing, simulations, questionnaires, discussion groups, and open-ended films and games (Bailey, 1975; Sherry & Franzen, 1977). Unfortunately, some professionals fail to remember that adolescents are not elementary school children. These activities, if used, must be presented as an option or must be open to modification so that adolescents are not "turned off" by games. The teacher or counselor must use straightforward discussion with them. Listening is a valuable approach (Erickson, 1978), and once rapport has been established, feedback can be provided by group members or the facilitator (Stewart et al., 1978).

Values clarification is treated in a number of materials such as *Values Clarification* (Simon et al., 1972), *Person to Person* (Galvin & Book, 1974), and the *ZING Curriculum* (Sherry & Franzen, 1977). The *ZING Cur-*

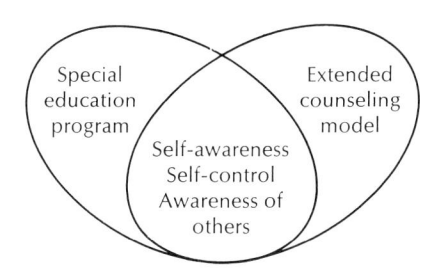

**Fig. 6-5.** Training model for social skills.

[Diagram: Two overlapping circles labeled "Special education program" and "Extended counseling model"; intersection contains "Self-awareness / Self-control / Awareness of others"] *riculum* was developed in the Madison, Wisconsin schools as a guide to assist teachers to incorporate specific coping techniques into the support program for ED and LD students. The counselor or special education teacher can draw on such materials on the market or their own experiences and those of their students.

*Self-control.* Self-control is a process through which an individual charts and manages his or her own behavior (Goldfried & Merbaum, 1973). This is important for atypical adolescents but may be difficult to achieve due to their suggestibility, peer dependence, and self-doubts.

Self-control training appears to be beneficial to handicapped students (Broden et al., 1971; Meichenbaum & Cameron, 1974). College students have been trained to increase their self-control in the area of study habits using self-reinforcement (Jackson & Van Zoost, 1972). Investigations suggest that self-observation as a self-control strategy can increase classroom participation (Gottman & McFall, 1972). Instructional programs intended to assist LD students in developing more self-control appear to be appropriate and useful (Kurtz & Neisworth, 1976).

*Awareness of others.* Some handicapped students may misinterpret the actions and reactions of others, and this causes them great difficulty in social interactions. They frequently never know what went wrong or even that something went wrong. They may perceive that they are not popular but may not realize that they have "asked for it." Research indicates, for instance, that LD students have less empathy for the feelings of others (McGlannan, 1977). This contributes to the miscommunications that seem to plague interpersonal relationships of LD and other mildly handicapped adolescents. Studies of verbal interactions indicate that more rejecting and competitive statements mark the language patterns of LD students. All of this adds up to ineffectual social interaction.

Training in social skills addresses the need of the special student to more accurately read the behavior of others. This phase of training consists of objective observation, body language, and active listening. As in the self-awareness component, simulations and other activities can be used. Students can greatly profit from such social skills training (Bonham, 1975; Browne, 1974), and such attention to the environment can be most fruitful.

## Speech and hearing clinicians

**Qualifications.** There is traditionally a close relationship between audiologists and speech pathologists. The American Speech and Hearing Association (ASHA) dictates certification standards for both specialists, which include academic coursework and practicum experiences. The preparation of both disciplines centers on the basic tasks for which they are responsible:

1. *Prevention* of communication and hearing disorders
2. *Assessment* of the nature and severity of a communication or hearing problem
3. *Direct services* to students with mild problems
4. *Support* of other professionals providing intensive therapy to students with severe disorders

The respective training programs reflect a clinical orientation and individual treatment. Clinicians are trained within a medical model in which the symptoms are identified and a treatment plan is designed based on those symptoms. Training in assessment and diagnosis comprises a major part of the professional preparation of speech and language pathologists and audiologists.

**Role within the school.** Audiologists are utilized by public schools in assessment and perhaps on a consultant basis. The speech clinician or school nurse may perform the initial auditory screening. Children failing this screening are usually given a more intensive examination, which in turn may lead to referral to a physician.

Speech and language pathologists are usually part of the regular school staff or part of a cooperatively shared staff of specialists who provide regular, full-time services to students. A major responsibility of public school speech clinicians is screening to locate students with defective speech. Clinicians use informal and formal techniques to elicit samples of a child's speech in order to ascertain whether or not there is a possible speech problem (Lundeen, 1972). If there is some question following this informal screening a more in-depth analysis of the child's speech is recommended in order to decide if a speech problem does exist. The following questions are of concern to the clinician:

1. What caused this problem?
2. What defects are associated with it?
3. What is the most appropriate treatment procedure?
4. What is the prognosis?

Individual and group therapy have traditionally been the primary modes of intervention in public school speech and language programs. The student receives services from the specialist outside the classroom two or three times per week for 20 to 30 minutes. Classroom interventions are usually directed at the kindergarten or primary grades and take the form of brief game activities. The caseload for the public school clinician usually is between 65 and 95 students per week.

General speech and language objectives are as follows: (1) to assist the student in learning language patterns; (2) to improve voice quality, syntax, semantic usage, rhythm, and articulation; (3) to develop alternative means of communication (Falck, 1978). A student's therapy plan may include one or more of these objectives depending on the assessment data collected by the clinician. The major types of speech disorders, including causative factors, symptoms, and therapeutic interventions, are well known to most special educators. The most salient points for a teacher to remember are made by Van Riper (1972): speech is defective when (1) it brings negative attention to the speaker, (2) it interferes with communication, and (3) it causes the speaker to be maladjusted.

**Expanded role in programming for mildly handicapped students: assessment.** The initial point of involvement of the speech and language clinician is in the screening portion of the referral process. The speech clinician or school nurse may complete hearing screening to ascertain if a hearing acuity problem is present and contributing to learning problems. States require this, and it is usually one of the very first diagnostic steps in assessment. Speech screening for the atypical adolescent will probably not be necessary other than as compliance with the guidelines for assessment. However, there may be rare instances in which the student has not been receiving services in the previous educational setting or a recent emotional or health problem has precipitated a speech disorder.

Speech and language clinicians may have a limited number of clients at the secondary school level, but these clients usually exhibit severe problems that require intensive effort. Involvement with mildly handicapped students may result from temporary, situational problems or from continued efforts to improve speech and language. Such specialists in the secondary schools may additionally be involved in cooperative efforts with the school counselor and resource teacher to facilitate the adjustment of atypical adolescents.

The point should be made that speech clinicians are *not* trained to provide *total programming* for handicapped students. These professionals may be trained in the area of language, but they are not adequately prepared to function in the role of special education teacher without further training in other aspects including classroom management, curricula areas such as reading and language arts, child development, psychology of exceptional children, and nature and needs of exceptional students. Practicums, internships, and student teaching are certainly necessary for preparation as special education teacher, and the laboratory experiences of speech clinicians do not fulfill these requirements. Speech clinicians are being hired to organize and direct special education programs for some mildly handicapped students, and this concerns many special educators because speech clinicians are not trained to provide appropriate educational services in a special education room.

### School nurse

**Qualifications.** The public school nurse is typically a registered nurse (RN) with specific training and experience in direct health services and indirect consultation. The nurse should be part of an allied health services team within the community whose purpose is to provide comprehensive services to all students. The nature of the position requires the nurse to communicate with others in the medical profession, with parents, teachers, and students. In-service education in the nursing field is usually required for continued service and certainly recommended for the school nurse because of the vast number of advances in medication, prevention, and knowledge of common conditions that can be relayed to others serving public school students.

**Role within the school.** School health services vary greatly among schools because of budgetary constraints and philosophical differences in communities. However, the general components include the following:

1. Maintenance of health records on each student
2. Health education for students (nutrition, sex education, life adjustment)
3. Consultations with teachers concerning health topics of specific cases
4. Vision and/or hearing screening
5. Nutrition screening
6. Parent consulting on health-related topics or specific cases
7. Liaison with other medical professionals and school personnel
8. Aministration/monitoring of medication

The American School Health Association (ASHA) is an important determiner of the services provided within public schools and represents a major source of information in various areas of concern to the school nurse.

School health examinations should include a medical history, physical examination, laboratory procedures, and hearing screening ("The doctor and school health today," September 20, 1976). Results of examinations are usually reported on school forms and are maintained by the school nurse. Confidentiality procedures necessitate that the nurse understand the educational implications of some conditions, discuss these with parents, and, with parental permission, relay these implications to the teacher. Health examination for school sports programs are extremely important and are required in all high school athletic programs. The nurse will need to cooperate with coaches in securing these examinations and utilizing information that is gained. Student interactions may increase in secondary schools if the students view the nurse as someone to be trusted and as someone who has accurate information concerning various health problems and concerns ranging from pregnancy and venereal disease to acne and allergies. Professional ethics will dictate the actions taken by the nurse in such cases, but the channels of communication with students should be kept open and encouraged.

**Expanded role of the nurse in programming for mildly handicapped students**

*Assessment.* A medical history is required on each student referred for special services. The school nurse should have a medical history on file and should be able to assist in the use of information for educational programming. The nurse should follow up any medical questions raised by teachers and other school professionals. The emphasis here should not be placed on causative factors so much as on educational implications. The nurse may need to contact neurologists and other specialists to assist in securing services, but all efforts must be coordinated through the person responsible for the assessment process. This ensures that legal guidelines are followed and parental involvement has been secured. The nurse may even be given specific questions, which will require investigation on his or her part, by the special education supervisor, special education teacher, or other person responsible for coordination of the data collection. Regardless of the nature of the involvement in assessment of mildly handicapped students, the nurse performs a *support* role.

*Services.* The school nurse may have increased contact with LD and behaviorally disordered adolescents as a result of psychosomatic illnesses or phobic conditions. We could find no objective evidence that such adolescents have a greater number of health problems that would require attention from the school nurse. Direct contact with the parents may also be precipitated by the psychosomatic tendencies of some behaviorally disordered and LD adolescents. In some cases the school nurse may be approached by the parents to discuss such concerns as neurological examinations, electroencephalograms (EEGs), and medication. However, more frequently such topics are dealt with by the family physician. The school nurse may be in contact with the physician at the request of the parents or at least with the permission of the parents.

Medication of students usually requires interaction between the family physician, the parents, and the school nurse. Drug therapy in conjunction with educational intervention has been found to be useful in some cases. Medication is not often used with LD students beyond the age of about 12 years because hyperactive behavior is not as common (or it becomes less visible) and the neurological signs become more subtle (Millchap, 1973). However, some mildly handicapped adolescents do seem to benefit from drug therapy (Solomon, 1978). In such cases the school nurse as well as the special education teacher should have some specific information about the student and the nature of the drug being used in the treatment.

The two major types of drugs are dextroamphetamines (e.g., Dexedrine) and methylphenidate hydrochloride (Ritalin). Both have rapid onset (about 1 hour) and disappear in 4 to 6 hours. Methylphenidate hydrochloride appears to be the preferred drug (Millchap, 1973). Side effects of both drugs may include insomnia, anorexia, and gastrointestinal problems. The length of such drug treatment usually is 6 months to 4 or 5 years. Other types of drugs are used occasionally with students; these include chlordiazepoxide (Librium) and diazepam (Valium), both of which may have a calming effect. Thioridazine (Mellaril) may be used, but it frequently produces extreme drowsiness as a side effect.

Concerns frequently voiced in connection with drug therapy include its effect on growth in younger children. Some studies indicate that growth is suppressed during the period of medication (Safer & Allen, 1975; Safer et al., 1972), while others found that

## STUDENT MEDICATION REPORT

Student's name _____ Date _____

Birth date _____ Teacher _____

Physician _____ Office phone _____

Name of drug _____ Dosage _____

Description of how medication works:

Possible undesirable side effects:

Expected changes in student behavior:

Motoric or behavioral indicators of toxic reactions or inadequate dosage:

Length of time student has been on this medication: _____

Date when medication will be reviewed: _____

**Fig. 6-6.** Sample form for recording pertinent drug therapy information.

```
                    ADMINISTRATION OF MEDICATION

Student's name_____ Date_____
Teacher_____ Room no._____



    ┌─────────┐
    │         │  Attached copy of prescription and recommended dosage
    │         │
    └─────────┘

(To be completed by the student's physician)

1.  Medication prescribed:                    Dosage:


2.  Method of administration:


3.  Frequency of administration:


4.  Anticipated reactions of child to medication:



   _____         _____
      (Physician's signature)                       (Date)

PARENT STATEMENT:

    I approve the administration by school personnel of the above medication
in the manner described.


   _____         _____
      (Parent's signature)                          (Date)
```

**Fig. 6-7.** Sample form for administration of medication.

medicated youth develop normally while under medication (Gross, 1976).

Another concern associated with drug therapy is the increased possibility of drug addiction later. A higher incidence of drug addiction has not been found in the population treated with medication. Students treated with medication seem to have a reduced likelihood for drug addiction because of an increase in ego strength, lessened curiosity about drug experimentation, and absences of feelings of elation (Solomon, 1978).

Parents and teachers may make inquiries of the school nurse about medication and its effects on the student. With written permission from the parents, the nurse should contact the physician to obtain specific information about the medication if the physician does not make arrangements to do this otherwise. The sample form in Fig. 6-6 might be used by the nurse to systematically record information about the student's medication program. Parental permission allows this to be shared with teachers.

The school should have specific written policies concerning the administration of prescribed medication by school personnel during school hours. Storage of medication should be included in the written policy. Medication should be kept in a locked, limited access space in either the office of a full-time registered school nurse or in the building administrator's office.

The Council for Exceptional Children recommends that a record of medication administration be kept on file for each student receiving medication. Fig. 6-7 shows a sample form the school might use for this purpose. It should be completed by the student's physician and returned to the building administrator's office prior to the administration of medication by school personnel. This form must be completed each year and when the prescription is changed by the physician. A copy should be kept by the building administrator in the student's file. An additional copy should be kept by the nurse or the personnel designated to administer the medication. The professional should be warned in writing of personal liability in the administration of medication. The professional has the right to refuse to administer medication if the school does not have clearly stated written policies that include the administration form and storage provisions, or if these policies are not strictly followed.

## Other support personnel

The contextual factors that may contribute to the need for greater internal or external support personnel are the wealth of a district, its proximity to urban areas, and the incidence of such social maladies as delinquency, poverty, drug use, pregnancy, and so forth. Some school districts, because they have the resources, employ a large staff of special support personnel such as police officers to patrol buildings, social workers to manage a school-based caseload, psychiatrists, psychologists, and physical therapists. Other districts, with more limited resources, may rely on external support personnel for the provision of special services. In any event, the problems of students and their families may cause professionals or legal agencies to become involved with school authorities for a variety of reasons. The focus of this text has been on the factors that impinge directly on the role of the special teacher. Although the special teacher may not need to interact frequently or intensely with many professionals who provide additional support, it is likely that occasional problems of students will detract from class time and will require the teacher's attention to some matter arising from community contacts.

When considering the range of services, one must not overlook such internal services as transportation, maintenance, dietary services, and the clerical staff of a school. Functions of these services must be apparent, but one important consideration is that mildly handicapped students, especially those who have conflict with authority or who have a tendency to engage in passive aggressive or aggressive acts, may experience difficulty in noninstructional environments. Hence, unacceptable behavior on a bus, throwing food in the cafeteria, defacing a toilet wall, or evidencing disrespect in the presence of a noninstructional employee may create serious problems.

It is also true that secretaries, bus drivers, custodians, and others are in a position to support, ignore, or abuse students. Staff members may react in various ways to behaviors of students. Out of this mix, a number of fortunate and unfortunate experiences may develop. The special educator and/or the counselor should note that students will interact with noninstructional staff in two general and important ways: (1) as benefactors of indirect services and (2) as benefactors of direct services. Aside from being transported, fed, and cleaned up after, it is also possible that students may need to be placed in simulated work situations with staff members. The specialist should recognize that a custodian or other staff member may have considerable informal influence on the administration and with members of the faculty. A custodian is privy to the happenings of many classrooms and can carry tales throughout the building. To this extent, courtesy of the teachers and students to the custodian will help garner support for the program in the building and will lay the foundation for other endeavors, such as simulated work experience where the support of personnel is necessary. In-service programs should include the noninstructional staff to foster an understanding of handicapped children among these persons who are important to the institution. It is apparent to any principal that the smooth functioning of a school is greatly dependent on the secretary, the custodian, the bus driver, and food service personnel. These people must not be taken for granted, they should be respected for their contribution, and they should be encouraged to interact with handicapped students on a basis of sound rapport.

Professional noninstructional staff, who may be employed as full-time or part-time personnel or who are representatives of community agencies, may be broadly classified into two general categories: (1) law enforcement/judicial services and (2) human services. These personnel will be referred to by many titles and will be employed in various organizations.

**Law enforcement/judicial services.** The reputed connection between learning disabilities and delinquency (Keilitz et al. [1979] report that 32% of delinquents are learning disabled), the expected antisocial behavior of many emotionally disturbed students, and the intentional or unwitting involvement of retarded youths in crime assures that school personnel will have some contact with law enforcement personnel who will have responsibility for truancy, apprehension, investigation, probation, prevention, reeducation, or protection.

At times, the special education teacher may find it necessary to interact with a truancy officer or school guards who are employed to patrol the building and grounds during and after school hours. The alarming increase in assaults against teachers and students and acts of vandalism and drug trafficking have caused schools to resort to extreme measures to secure the building, students, and faculty.

The special educator may share as much common interest in the protection afforded faculty by police patrols as any other teacher but *may* have more reason to anticipate rule violations and other troublesome behavior from his or her charges because of the many factors that relate to alienation of handicapped students from the school and non-handicapped peers, their general level of immature social behavior, and the real possibility that they may tend to engage in violent acts more than others. We suspect that the incidence of this behavior will vary with the norms of communities and settings of schools, but it is apparent that some students will have the potential for violence and vandalism. It can also be expected that, in some settings, the conduct of special education students will be more closely scrutinized than others. If the special education class has a reputation for incidents it may cause authorities to be more watchful. It is important that the special educator protect students from harassment and teach them the rules and consequences of unacceptable behavior. They should not be duped by peers or faculty into violating rules.

It is also more likely, based on the expectations that handicapped students in this general category are more prone to status and criminal offense, that police and probation officers will contact the school or interview students in the school on occasion. Although the special educator may not be directly involved, interrogation of students at school will undoubtedly have an unsettling effect on all students who are aware of the presence of legal authorities. In the unlikely event that a student is to be interviewed without the knowledge of the principal, the teacher should inform the principal or his or her agent and should remain with the student at all times. An official of the school should be present during the interrogation to assure that the student's rights are protected.

The special education teacher is not protected by the doctrine of confidentiality, as are priests, physicians, and counselors in some states, so that information learned from and about students may be subject to exposure in a legal proceeding. This places the teacher in a dangerous and tenuous position with students. There are many examples that might be used. One that is rather common is the use of marijuana by students. The practice is so commonplace that a teacher may actually witness students smoking near or on the grounds. The teacher is placed in a dilemma: to report the incident as an official of the school or to ignore it in the interest of maintaining rapport. Other acts of students may require direct and immediate intervention to protect students and property. In any event, the teacher should use self-appraisal to determine a course of action in many situations. A weak, frail person should never intercede physically to separate students if there is a likelihood during a scuffle that the teacher will be injured or become the object of aggression. Intimidation of a teacher by students cannot be tolerated if the teacher is to be able to function freely in the school environment. Unfortunately, these and other types of situations develop in some settings, which makes the practice of teaching more an act of coping and subsistence than a professional art.

As a representative of the adult world and a buffer between the adult world and that of the teenager, the special educator must be cognizant of the extreme pressure of the peer group on students and the immature but forceful dedication of students to the unwritten code of conduct that controls many students in their dealing with and reactions to legal authorities. The macho style of young men, especially predominant with some cultural groups, can be a detriment to youths who must prove themselves to their peers. There are many behaviors that might be identified. For example, it is unacceptable to report ("fink on," "rat on," and so forth) another student for violation of rules or even serious crimes. Aside from the fear of retaliation in some instances, it is a violation of a social rule to tell authorities about the acts of others. Group punishment should not be used to force a confession or an informant to supply information because this invokes the indignant wrath of all students. The teacher can lose status in the eyes of students that may be difficult to recover for many years. The teacher should, when possible, leave interrogation to the school disciplinarian who is paid to deal with such problems and who will naturally be resented by most students because of his or her role. The teacher should never feign identification with the peer group, patronize it, or insult it. All teenagers tacitly agree that someday they will grow up and they will respect an adult who plays by the rules in a consistent manner.

Therefore it is important that the teacher explain adult norms and rules, with all the associated hypocrisy and contradiction, in a manner that is clear and direct. Students may disagree with laws (e.g., a drinking age of 21), but they will understand the consequences of getting caught with alcohol by the police. They will take precautions to avoid apprehension, even though they may not forego drinking until the age of majority. Philosophical debates about the veracity of laws against smoking marijuana, shoplifting, and other issues may be fruitless exercises in logic, but students will understand the seriousness of conviction for committing a crime or misdemeanor, even if they question the premises of laws. The teacher cannot hope to impose his or her own morality on students and cannot expect students to refrain from sexual intercourse, drugs, alcohol, or violence because they are "not nice" or illegal; but the teacher can induce students to recognize that status rules and legal statutes are important to the adult world, which will not be very tolerant and which will inflict serious penalties for violations.

It should be pointed out to mildly handicapped students that they may be more likely to invoke the ire of legal authorities than other students because many of them will have histories of problems in the school and community. The authorities are more likely to mete out severe punishment for relatively insignificant acts because of the past record of behavior. If teachers can facilitate the adjustment of students through the teen years, many students will cease to have brushes with the law as they assume adult responsibilities.

Most laws, and the moral underpinnings, are rooted in abstract concepts that may elude the mental grasp of students. The teacher is in a constant battle with the naive interpretations of mores and laws by students and the consequences for them of their behavior. An example of a moral issue is that of a mildly retarded girl who permitted boys to touch her breasts. Although she knew that it was wrong to allow several of her male classmates to fondle her each day, it was not the act but discovery that concerned her. After this situation came to the attention of her teacher, a series of conferences with the nurse and parents brought the occurrence to an end. She said that she enjoyed the physical contact (a concrete experience) and the attention of the boys (social acceptance) but did not fully comprehend the disdain that the boys had for her. Knowing that she had been used by the boys was painful but, in terms of cultural imperatives, was a natural consequence in our society.

There are examples of students who steal to gain status or who commit more serious crimes such as arson, rape, and murder for the same end. The factors that precipitate such acts are complex and idiopathic, but it is certainly evident that much of the variance can be explained by the rejection they feel, the inability to achieve conventional status, academic failure, and limited options for future growth. Whether a student's violation is as innocuous as a traffic ticket or has the gravity of a serious criminal act, encounters with legal authorities will bring the school into contact with outside agencies. Here, as in other aspects of student relations, the teacher should be an advocate and a support. Knowing the rights of students, the consequences of illegal acts, and the roles of various professionals, such as the probation officer or the social worker, will enable the teacher to approach this distasteful part of the job with the best preparation. Some students will be convicted of crimes and sent to reformatories or prisons. Others will be able to avoid such dire consequences, and the teacher can provide the important link, in some instances, to a happier future.

**Human services.** Unhappy or tragic circumstances that contribute to the adjustment of many students also affect the lives and dynamics of entire families. In some settings, depending on the associated factors in the community, a number of students will come from families that require services or monitoring from agencies. Welfare, food stamps, unemployment compensation, and child-care casework are examples of services that may be provided by a variety of professionals who are not employed by the school but who may have some interaction with the school on behalf of students. Any professional service available in the school (psychology, counseling, and speech pathology) may be duplicated in the community, and a variety of other services (e.g., psychiatry and social work) may not be feasible in the school system but will be available through contractual agreement or as an extension of agencies.

As in other situations, dealings with human services personnel will be limited to contact with the family and school officials, but the special educator may have occasion to deal directly with these individuals or may have access to some of their information. In many instances, outside professionals will contact the teacher to gather information about students such as attendance, personal appearance, and general school adjustment.

The nature of such contacts should be carefully evaluated by the teacher in order to outline clear responsibilities so that the interests of the students are served and the teacher's role is clarified. Requests to supply information to external agencies must be governed by the Family Education and Privacy Act and school system policies about releasing information. The confidentiality of information from either source, the school or the agency, must be protected, especially from becoming teachers' lounge gossip, as sometimes happens.

The school can and should cooperate with external agencies in an effort to assist troubled youths. Mistakes and poor judgment during adolescence can pay off in long-term unfortunate consequences, and the attraction or seduction of the counterculture can damage or destroy young persons who may become physically and mentally abused, turned into prostitutes, encouraged to commit crimes, or victimized by alcoholism, drug abuse, or depression.

## SUMMARY

In this chapter we have described the roles of a few key support personnel who share responsibility for the educational adjustment of mildly handicapped students. Although some comprehensive school districts employ a variety of specialized professionals, most schools have a professional staff that at least includes a counselor, a speech clinician, and a nurse. Obviously, the most intensive need for the involvement of support personnel is created by assessment. We have described some of the significant issues in assessment of adolescents but have also recommended the utilization of professionals in support of instructional programs. The greatest emphasis has been placed on the expanded role of the counselor in assisting atypical students, a worthy endeavor for the counselor and a beneficial service to students who experience many complications in adjustment.

# REFERENCES AND READINGS

Arbuckle, D. S. A question of counselor function and responsibility. *Personnel and Guidance Journal*, 1968, 47, 341-345.

Bailey, E. J. *Academic activities for adolescents with LD*. Evergreen, Colo.: Learning Pathways, 1975.

Bonham, S. *Suggested procedures for designing instructional systems for secondary students with LD. An interim report on activities, 1975*. Washington, Ohio: Ohio Division of Special Education, 1975.

Bradley, M. K. Counseling, past and present: Is there a future? *Personnel and Guidance Journal*, 1978, 57(1), 42-45.

Broden, M., Hall, R. V., & Mitts, B. The effect of self-recording on the classroom behavior of two eighth grade students. *Journal of Applied Behavior Analysis*, 1971, 4, 191-199.

Browne, D. *A demonstration center for secondary learning disabled students*. Cushing, Okla.: Wilson School Child Service Demonstration Center, 1974.

Bryan, J. H., & Bryan, T. H. *Exceptional children*. Sherman Oaks, Calif.: Alfred, 1979.

Bryan, T. J. LD children's comprehension of nonverbal communication. *Journal of Learning Disabilities*, 1977, 10, 501-506.

Chinn, P. C., Winn, J., & Walters, R. H. *Two-way talking with parents of special children*. St. Louis: Mosby, 1978.

Coles, G. S. The learning disability test battery: Empirical and social issues. *Harvard Educational Review*, 1978, 48(3), 313-340.

Deshler, D. Issues related to the education of learning disabled adolescents. *Learning Disability Quarterly*, 1979, 1(4), 2-10.

Deshler, D., Ferrell, W. R., & Kass, C. Error monitoring of schoolwork by learning disabled adolescents. *Journal of Learning Disabilities*, 1978, 11(7), 401-414.

The doctor and school health today. *Medical World News*, September 20, 1976, 17(20).

Dwyer, C. E. Training for change agents: A guide to design of training programs in education and other fields. *Industrial and Labor Relations Review*, 1974, 27, 658-659.

Erickson, M. T. *Child psychopathology: Assessment, etiology, and treatment*. Englewood Cliffs, N.J.: Prentice-Hall, 1978.

Falck, V. T. Communication skills—translating theory into practice. *Teaching Exceptional Children*, 1978, 10(3), 74-77.

Feltham, D. W. *Teacher and administrator opinion survey of guidance services in the secondary school*. 1972. (ERIC Document Reproduction Service No. ED 084 485)

Forster, J. Counselor credentialing revisited. *Personnel and Guidance Journal*, 1978, 56(10), 593-598.

Galvin, K., & Book, C. *Person to person*. Skokie, Ill.: National Textbook Co., 1974.

Gardner, W. *Children with learning and behavior problems: A behavior management approach*. Boston: Allyn & Bacon, 1974.

Goldfried, M. R., & Merbaum, M. A. A perspective on self-control. In M. R. Goldfried & M. A. Merbaum (Eds.), *Behavior change through self-control*. New York: Holt, Rinehart & Winston, 1973.

Goodman, L., & Price, M. BEH final regulations for learning disabilities: Implications for the secondary school. *Learning Disability Quarterly*, 1978, 1(4), 73-79.

Gottman, J. M., & McFall, R. M. Self-monitoring effects in a program for potential high school dropouts: A time-series analysis. *Journal of Consulting and Clinical Psychology*, 1972, 39, 273-281.

Gross, M. D. Growth of hyperkinetic children taking methylphenidate, dextroamphetamine, or imipramine. *Pediatrics*, 1976, 58, 423-431.

Hall, R. V., Axelrod, S., Tyler, L., et al.: Modification of behavior problems in the home with a parent as an observer and experimenter. *Journal of Applied Behavior Analysis*, 1972, 5, 53-64.

Hallahan, D. P., & Kauffman, J. M. *Exceptional children*. Englewood Cliffs, N.J.: Prentice-Hall, 1978.

Harway, N., & Robbins, R. Goal setting and reactions to success and failure in children with learning disabilities. *Journal of Learning Disabilities*, 1977, 10(6), 356-362.

Howard, M. A. P., & Anderson, R. J. Early identification of potential school dropouts: A literature review. *Child Welfare*, 1978, 57(4), 221-229.

Interview with Kenneth Hoyt. *Guidepost*, December 21, 1978, Vol. 21.

Jackson, B., & Van Zoost, B. Changing study behaviors through reinforcement contingencies. *Journal of Counseling Psychology*, 1972, 19, 192-195.

Janis, I. L., & Mann, L. *Decision making: A psychological analysis of conflict, choice, and commitment*. New York: Free Press, 1977.

John, E. R. A model of consciousness. In G. Schwartz & D. Shapiro, (Eds.), *Consciousness and self regulation* (Vol. 1: *Advances in research*). New York: Plenum Press, 1976.

John, E. R. Neurometrics. *Science*, 1977, 1966(4297).

Keefe, J. *The role of the advisor and changing role of the counselor*. 1975. (ERIC Document Reproduction Service No. ED 101 470)

Keilitz, I., Zaremba, B. A., & Broder, P. K. The link between learning disabilities and juvenile delinquency: Some issues and answers. *Learning Disability Quarterly*, Spring 1979, 2(2), 2-11.

Kirk, S. A., & Elkins, J. Characteristics of children enrolled in the child service demonstration centers. *Journal of Learning Disabilities*, 1975, 8, 630-637.

Kolstoe, O. P. *Mental retardation.* New York: Holt, Rinehart and Winston, 1972.

Krivatsy-O'Hara, S., Reed, P., & Davenport, J. Group counseling with potential high school dropouts. *Personnel and Guidance Journal,* 1978, 56(8), 510-512.

Kronick, D. The importance of sociological perspective towards learning disabilities. *Journal of Learning Disabilities,* 1976, 9, 115-119.

Krumboltz, J. D. Behavioral goals for counseling. *Journal of Counseling Psychology,* 1966, 13, 153-159.

Krumboltz, J. D., & Thoresen, C. E. (Eds.). *Counseling methods.* New York: Holt, Rinehart and Winston, 1976.

Kurtz, P. D., & Neisworth, J. T. Self-control possibilities for exceptional children. *Exceptional Children,* 1976, 42, 212-216.

Lundeen, D. J. Speech disorders. In B. R. Gearheart (Ed.), *Education of the exceptional child.* New York: Crowell, 1972.

Mager, R. F. *Goal analysis.* Belmont, Calif.: Fearon Publishers, 1972.

Marsh, G. E., II, Gearheart, C. K., & Gearheart, B. R. *The learning disabled adolescent.* St. Louis: Mosby, 1978.

McGlannan, F. Empathy in learning disabled children. *Journal of Learning Disabilities,* 1977, 10(8).

Meichenbaum, D. H., & Cameron, R. The clinical potential and pitfalls of modifying what clients say to themselves. In M. J. Mahoney & C. E. Thorensen (Eds.), *Self-control: Power to the person.* Monterey, Calif.: Brooks/Cole, 1974, pp. 263-289.

Millchap, J. G. Drugs in management of minimal brain dysfunction. *Annals of the New York Academy of Sciences,* 1973, 205, 321-334.

Mortensen, D. G., & Schmuller, A. M. *Guidance in today's schools.* New York: Wiley, 1978.

Patterson, G. R., & Gullion, M. E. *Living with children: New methods for parents and teachers.* Champaign, Ill.: Research Press, 1968.

Popham, W. J., & Baker, E. L. *Establishing instructional goals.* Englewood Cliffs, N.J.: Prentice-Hall, 1970.

Quay, H. C. Classification in the treatment of delinquency and antisocial behavior. In H. Hobbs (Ed.) *Issues in the classification of children* (Vol. 1). San Francisco: Jossey-Bass, 1975.

Restak, R. M. *The brain: The last frontier.* New York: Doubleday, 1979.

Riccio, A. *Guidance for the NOW student.* Report of the 18th annual All-Ohio Guidance Conference. 1970. (ERIC Document Reproduction Service No. ED 046 022)

Robinson, H. B., & Robinson, N. M. *The mentally retarded child: A psychological approach.* New York: McGraw-Hill, 1976.

Safer, D. J., & Allen, R. P. Side effects from long-term use of stimulants in children. In R. Gittleman-Klein (Ed.), *Recent advances in child psychopharmacology.* In *International Journal of Mental Health,* 1975, 4, 105-118.

Safer, D. J., Allen, R. P., & Barr, E. Depression of growth in hyperactive children on stimulant drugs. *New England Journal of Medicine,* 1972, 287(5), 217.

Salvia, J., & Ysseldyke, J. E. *Assessment in special and remedial education.* Boston: Houghton Mifflin, 1978.

Schackenberg, R. C. Caffeine as a substitute for schedule II stimulants in hyperkinetic children. *American Journal of Psychiatry,* 1973, 130, 796-798.

Shearer, M. S., & Shearer, D. E. The Portage project: A model for early childhood education. *Exceptional Children,* 1972, 39, 210-217.

Sherry, M., & Franzen, M. Zapped by ZING. *Teaching Exceptional Children,* 1977, 9, 46-47.

Shertzer, B., & Stone, S. C. *Fundamentals of counseling.* Boston: Houghton Mifflin, 1974.

Simon, S. B., Kirschenbaum, H., & Howe, L. *Values clarification.* New York: Hart, 1972.

Solomon, G. E. Minimal brain dysfunction. In B. B. Wolman, J. Egan, & A. O. Ross (Eds.), *Handbook of treatment of mental disorders in childhood and adolescence.* Englewood Cliffs, N.J.: Prentice-Hall, 1978.

Stewart, N. R., Winborn, B. B., Burks, H. M., Jr., et al. *Systematic counseling.* Englewood Cliffs, N.J.: Prentice-Hall, 1978.

Sweet, G. *A role change strategy—decentralized counseling.* 1972. (ERIC Document Reproduction Service No. ED 070 009)

Van Riper, C. *Speech correction: Principles and methods* (5th ed.). Englewood Cliffs, N.J.: Prentice-Hall, 1972.

Warnath, C. F. *The school counselor as institutional structure.* 1974. (ERIC Document Reproduction Service No. ED 105 313)

Wellington, J. A. *Counselors—Where do you get your inner strength?* 1974. (ERIC Document Reproduction Service No. ED 095 467)

West, M., Carlin, J., Baserman, B., & Milstein, M. An intensive therapeutic program for learning disabled prepubertal children, *Journal of Learning Disabilities,* 1978, 11(8), 56-57.

Yoshida, R. K., Fenton, K., Kaufman, M. J., & Maxwell, J. P. Parental involvement in the special education pupil planning process: The school's perspective. *Exceptional Children,* 1978, 44, 531-534.

# SECTION THREE

# THE SPECIAL EDUCATION TEACHER

The roles of the special educator at the secondary level are still emerging in response to the increasing demands for educating handicapped students in junior and senior high schools. There are a variety of influences on secondary special education programs and a great deal of uncertainty. The traditions of the elementary resource room have had an initial impact on secondary programming, but teachers find that the value of remediation wanes. The daily needs of students in the school, interaction and conflict with peers and adults, the instability of the adolescent period, and the need to prepare students for responsible adult roles require new strategies and programs.

There are three general types of programs for mildly handicapped students, which are loosely described as compensatory, remedial, and vocational. The types of service delivery range from self-contained to consulting models and may be designed for categorical and noncategorical classifications. Hence, the role that a special educator may assume in a secondary school could be extremely different from the traditional concept of the special educator. Special educators may need to prepare themselves for programs in certain settings until such time that certification requirements and delivery systems are resolved. Self-preparation might entail the identification of roles performed by the special educator in a particular setting and the selection of appropriate training to adequately prepare to meet responsibilities in that setting.

In any event, it is certain that role functions in the secondary setting common to any school should be understood and mastered. These include the relationships with the administration, parents, aides and volunteers, support personnel, and mainstream teachers. Knowing how to handle responsibilities relating to students and colleagues, and how to facilitate role interactions are essential to effective programming.

In accordance with these premises, Chapter 7 identifies the training competencies of the special educator, personal-social skills necessary for performance of the role, and ways to relate to the students, faculty, and community. Chapter 8 extends this process with a more detailed analysis of roles and responsibilities.

Chapter 7

# ROLES OF THE SPECIAL EDUCATION TEACHER

Much of the history of special education in the public school has been characterized by segregated services—the self-contained classroom. Although other patterns have been in existence, most schools found it convenient to promote a separate curriculum under the direction of special educators. With the social and legal trends of the last decade, most programming for the mildly handicapped in elementary and secondary schools has been conceived within the *resource-room model* because the students are able to remain in the mainstream of education, regular teachers share responsibility for handicapped students, and more students can be managed by fewer numbers of special educators. Other options, such as *consulting* and *itinerant* models, have not been as widespread because they are expensive to operate, do not permit as much contact with the students, and are difficult to defend on the basis of educational benefit or impact on targeted students.

In spite of the popularity of the resource-room approach to special education, most experimentation with it has been at the elementary school level and relatively few efficacy studies have been conducted. There is no validated model for use at the secondary level with learning disabled students. Consequently, we have provided a comprehensive outline of the roles of the secondary resource teacher. Much of the chapter is based on available research evidence as well as practical experience with secondary programming.

## RESPONSIBILITIES OF THE SPECIAL EDUCATOR

The position of the special education teacher has been examined by some investigators in an effort to identify competencies associated with the teaching role (D'Alonzo & Wiseman, 1978; Newcomer, 1977; Weiderholdt et al., 1978). Efficacy studies of resource rooms have been conducted to explore the rationale, the nature of the curriculum, and the components of the teaching role. Research has resulted in suggestions for modification of the special education model and the responsibilities of the teacher. The rationale, curriculum, and teaching role(s) are interwoven; it is inevitable that continuous evaluation of the special education program and experimentation with it will effect the role of the teacher as it evolves and reflects new knowledge.

Current studies of teaching roles have resulted in a list of major responsibilities, which includes:
- Teaching
- Public relations
- Educational diagnosis
- Curriculum development
- Administration
- Behavior management
- Technical expertise
- Liaison between education and medicine
- Counseling
- Specialization in methodologies

The exact nature of the teaching role will vary in accordance with instructional approaches selected, administrative differences of principals, school variables, such as the size of the school and its proximity to other services, and the personal commitment of the teacher. Other aspects of the role will be discussed in other sections but emphasized here are selected roles that have been consistently identified in the literature. These are especially important in the practical experience of teaching: namely, direct pupil services, administration, teacher consultation, public relations, and child advocacy (Fig. 7-1).

### Direct pupil services

Teaching responsibility is the most obvious and important role. Although a detailed discussion of teaching will be found in various parts of this text, the emphasis here is on

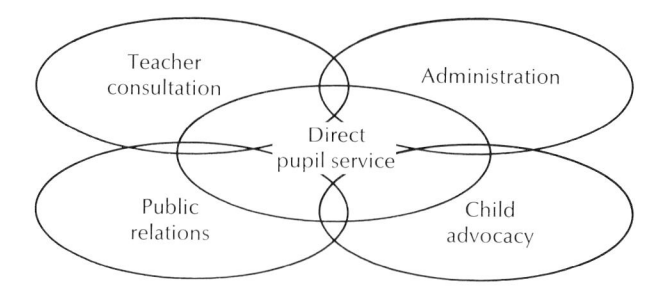

**Fig. 7-1.** Selected teaching roles within the resource model.

general considerations about direct services in special education approaches.

**Compensatory or accommodation model.** There are some unique characteristics in this approach that may not be found in any other teaching position. *All* teachers, regardless of their fields of specialization and levels of assignment, share common tasks of instruction. Only in the accommodative (resource) model, however, is a teacher responsible for direct instruction of students that is subordinate to other classes, for direct support to other teachers in addition to primary teaching responsibilities, and for multifarious professional relationships with numerous agencies, organizations, and professional disciplines.

Skills, tasks, and curricula in which students are instructed may vary from one school district to another, although a certain uniformity exists because of common goals and standards. The unique task of each resource teacher is to provide instruction in a subordinate, supportive manner that permits students to succeed in the mainstream with regular teachers and peers. Unless the resource teacher elects to provide only remediation, a focus that is too narrow to adequately serve most students, it is incumbent on him or her to invoke nonteaching strategies that assist the student toward achievement on many fronts, not only remediation.

The kinds of performance necessary to succeed in the regular classroom are relative to the tasks, the handicaps of students, the personality variables of students, and the styles of teachers (Jenkins & Mayhall, 1976). The teacher using a compensatory approach should attempt to isolate facts and information to understand the following areas:

1. Knowledge of the curricula of the school
2. Personality characteristics/teaching styles of teachers
3. The general code of social demeanor exhibited by mainstream students
4. Limits of social and behavioral acceptability in classes
5. The types of environmental controls used by teachers (e.g., teacher-directed methods, interactional methods)
6. Specific core tasks expected of learners (generally and in specific classes)

Each IEP should center on specific core tasks required for acceptable performance in the regular class, not just isolated remedial goals that will have little meaning or significance to mainstream teachers. The key to effective programming is not inherent in a particular methodology; it is relevant, direct service to the student in the mainstream class. Isolated marginal gains in reading will be of little comfort to a seriously disabled reader who is failing in all of his or her subjects.

The resource teacher's awareness and knowledge of the regular program is essential to all instruction and student success.

**150** THE SPECIAL EDUCATION TEACHER

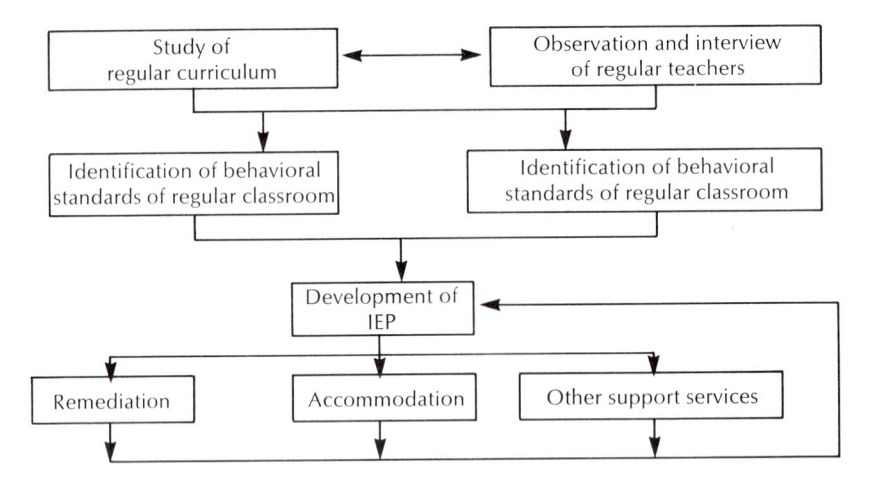

**Fig. 7-2.** Preliminary steps in making instructional decisions in the preparation for direct services: compensatory model.

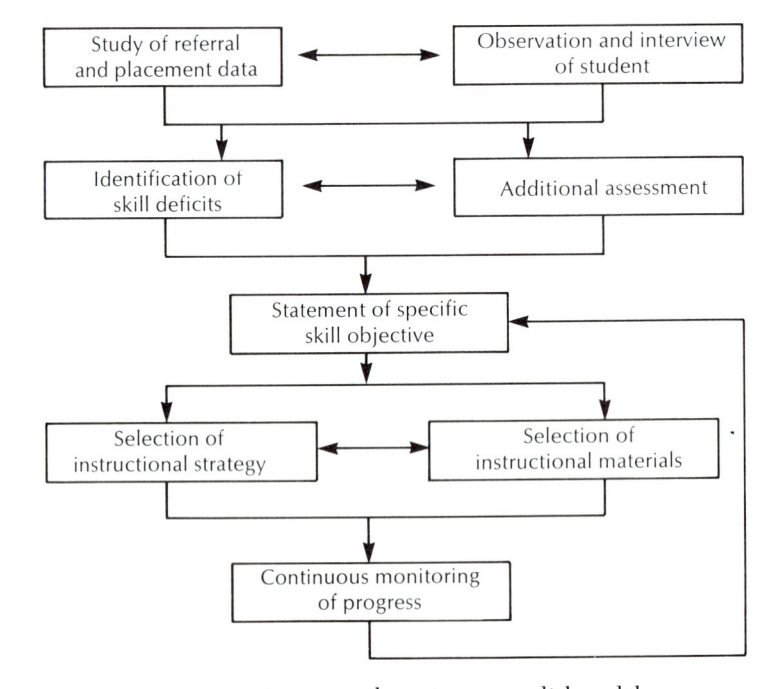

**Fig. 7-3.** Direct pupil services: remedial model.

Integrating a compensatory program with other programs should be considered the first step in delivery of direct instructional services (Fig. 7-2).

**Remedial model.** Direct pupil services subsumed under the remedial model are probably the most familiar aspects of the teaching role. These services are centered on the individual student's strengths and weaknesses and directed toward the goal of improving performance in the basic skill areas. The traditional teaching responsibilities of skill assessment, instructional design, and evaluation usually associated with the term "teaching" are the core of the pupil services of the remedial model.

The teacher who implements a remedial model for direct instruction must have competencies in assessment and task analysis, as this model requires specific identification of skill deficits and the development of sequential instruction (Fig. 7-3). Continuous monitoring of student progress is central to this model. The instructional design must continually be modified to reflect progression to a new skill or a need to change strategies.

There are general areas of knowledge and expertise required by the remedial specialist delivering direct instruction to mildly handicapped students:

1. Knowledge of a wide variety of assessment tools, their uses and limitations
2. Knowledge of the basic skill progression in reading, mathematics, and other instructional areas
3. Understanding of motivational aspects of learning
4. Awareness of commercially available materials
5. Creativity in designing teacher-made remedial materials

Obviously, these are aspects of teaching that are important regardless of the model used in the program. However, these take on increased importance in the remedial model because of the singleness of purpose: skill acquisition. The IEP implemented in

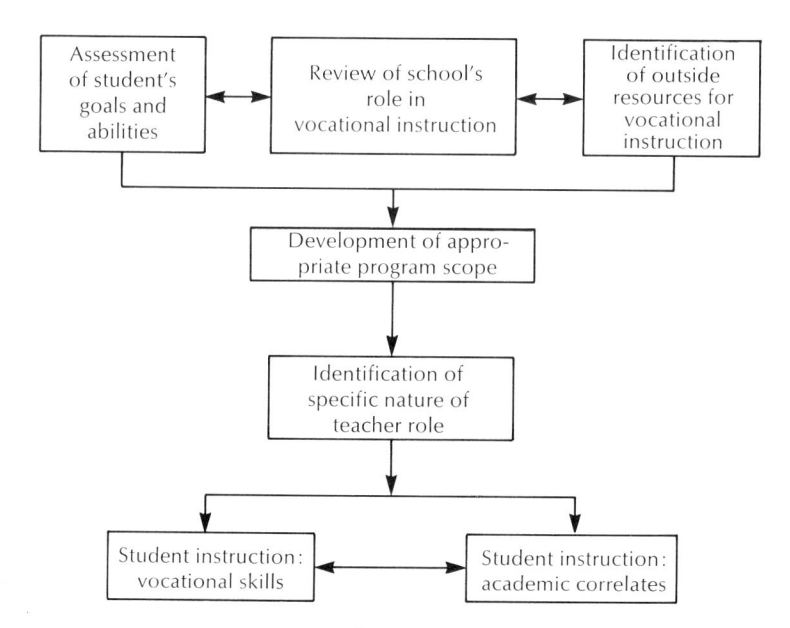

**Fig. 7-4.** Direct pupil services: vocational model.

this model centers on stated skill objectives of each student, dictating that direct pupil services be strictly remedial and in isolation of the mainstream program.

**Vocational model.** Direct pupil services to mildly handicapped students by special educators in a vocational model may be wide ranging and will be different at the junior and senior high school levels. Although the teacher may need to make contacts with other educators in the school, the tasks will be much more self-contained and the curricula will be increasingly separated from the regular curriculum as the program extends into the high school. Typically, a prevocational program, traditionally for EMR students, may be offered at the junior high level with a heavy emphasis on work orientation, work attitudes, and skills of personal grooming and communication. A great deal of attention to consumer mathematics and functional reading may be a part of the teacher's responsibility.

At the senior high level a variety of direct pupil services may be provided by a teacher, depending on the nature of the vocational program and the type of delivery model that is used (Fig. 7-4). Some teachers will be required to provide on-the-job training or work experience, others will be employed in a sheltered workshop or skills center, and others will be subordinate to a more comprehensive vocational program. Under this latter arrangement, the special educator may provide direct instruction in material related to specific job clusters in which students are preparing for employment.

## Administration

The special educator is often expected to assume administrative functions as related teaching tasks (D'Alonzo & Wiseman, 1978). The amount of administrative responsibility is determined by the effectiveness of the special education supervisor and the degree of involvement of the building principal. Some administrative functions include:

- Supervising volunteers, tutors, and aides
- Handling a variety of forms
- Making decisions about the use of resources
- Coordinating the efforts of other professionals
- Preparing accountability data on program effectiveness
- Maintaining a file of important records
- Collecting data on the cost-benefit ratio of programs
- Providing input for the overall school system
- Making community and parental contacts

Many of these functions will be performed cooperatively with other administrative officers within the system but will consume some of the teacher's time.

The unique nature of the special education program requires that the teacher operate somewhat as an independent manager. More control can be exerted over various aspects of the program than in a typical classroom, making administrative decisions a part of the daily routine of the specialist. Extra latitude may be given the special education teacher in making decisions about the budget, outfitting the room, structuring the program, and utilizing outside assistance. The special educator is expected to have accurate information concerning the placement process, legal implications, funding restrictions and guidelines, and program development. Knight (1976) suggests providing quarterly reports for administrative officers to aid them in gaining an accurate overview of the program's goals, progress, and problems. These reports might include some of the following subjects:

1. Tests used in the program
2. A current roster of students receiving

services including age, grade level, and dates/times of special help
3. Suggestions and plans for in-service workshops to facilitate teacher consultation
4. Special problems requiring administrative attention
5. Future scope of the program

A final, cumulative report is more easily prepared if such quarterly information is maintained. The final report should also include placement recommendations, an evaluation of the total program, and additional resources needed for the coming year (Knight, 1976). These administrative demands should be viewed *positively* by the teacher and eagerly accepted because of their obvious relationship to the success of the overall program. However, the teacher must avoid becoming totally immersed in administrative tasks, which should be performed by a special education supervisor or other administrator.

The fact that the special education teacher may assume more administrative responsibility lays the foundation for potential conflict. The teacher should be cautious not to exceed the bounds of the loosely defined administrative role nor to assume responsibility for accountability in areas that clearly belong under the supervision of an administrator. Role conflict can jeopardize the program, if not the teacher's employment. Great care must be taken to clearly establish lines of authority and to protect one's self from fault-finding and blame in the event that errors are made or conflict arises.

## Teacher consultation

The role of the teacher as a consultant has become a widely accepted part of the concept of shared responsibility for serving handicapped students (Reynolds, 1978). An entire chapter (Chapter 8) describes the relationship of the special education program to other programs of the secondary school and the responsibility of the special educator to other professionals. Consultation can have a tremendous multiplier effect (Montgomery, 1978) because of the broadened scope of impact. The advantages of implementing a teacher-consultant model as part of the special education program include:

1. Increased cost and time effectiveness (Montgomery, 1978)
2. More comprehensive services to handicapped (Reynolds, 1978)
3. Prevention (Cantrell & Cantrell, 1976)
4. Help for students without the need to label them (Newcomer, 1977)
5. Sharing of benefits of special techniques with more students (Beery, 1974; Newcomer, 1977; Swift & Spivack, 1975).

The goals of consultation are viewed somewhat differently among educators, but generally they are (1) to increase the competence and confidence of the regular teacher in serving atypical students (Ozer & Dworkin, 1974) and (2) to see that services to a particular student are coordinated. Regardless of which goal is elevated, there are some *difficulties* involved and a number of underlying *assumptions*.

1. *Consultation takes place between peers.* This circumstance requires rapport between the regular teacher and the special educator while the latter is, at the same time, viewed as an expert. The special educator must tactfully and effectively wear both hats: peer and expert. The perception of an expert prevalent in teachers' lounges is not necessarily complimentary! The special education teacher is in a unique position to work with other professionals (Montgomery, 1978) because the program overlaps and blends with the regular curriculum and special services. Special education should be viewed as an arm or extension of regular education with the potential to provide extra instructional support

to all children (Beery, 1974; Cantrell & Cantrell, 1976). Therefore it is logical that the special education teacher serve as a consultant. However, in order for the role to be developed to its full potential the emphasis must be on mutual exchange of information and be a collaborative endeavor (Dinkmeyer & Carlson, 1973).

2. *Consultation requires the regular educator to not view problem students as the sole responsibility of special education* (Newcomer, 1977). This requires a drastic change in attitude for many teachers in public schools. Traditionally, special education has been responsible for problem students with many regular teachers regarding regular placement as inappropriate. The trend toward mainstreaming has the appearance of admitting failure. Regular teachers may not believe that specialists have any worthwhile advice to offer, that handicapped students cannot be remediated, and that consultation is a waste of time. An investigation into the effects of a crisis-resource program produced results that underscore negative attitudinal development of regular teachers (Kerlin & Latham, 1977). Three methods of service (crisis-room placement, crisis-room and regular class placement, and regular placement) were compared. Regular teachers were asked to rate the effectiveness of two approaches: the placement requiring 30-minute meetings *between* teachers and the crisis teacher and the method *without* teacher contact. Results indicated that regular teachers had a more positive attitude toward the program in which they did not meet with the crisis teacher! Such attitudes will be slow to disappear, and until they do, the resource consultant can expect resentment and resistance.

3. *Consultation for integrating mildly handicapped students into the regular curriculum assumes specific competencies on the part of the regular educator.* Extensive money and effort have been invested in in-service education of regular teachers in an attempt to increase their awareness of handicapping conditions and to promote the integration of handicapped students into the regular classrooms. The success of such projects is difficult to assess, based on attitudes that are complex and hard to measure, but in-service projects have succeeded in the isolation of mainstream teacher competencies, which were identified in one study as follows (Redden & Blackhurst, 1978):

   a. Develop orientation strategies for mainstream entry.
   b. Assess needs and set goals.
   c. Plan teaching strategies and use of resources.
   d. Implement teaching strategies and use resources.
   e. Facilitate learning. (This competency includes behavior management techniques and management of psychological climate of the classroom.)
   f. Evaluate learning.

These competencies appear to be extremely difficult to implement in the typical *secondary* school. The nature of the secondary school and the manner in which content is taught make it unlikely that individual needs are assessed and goals set. Management techniques used by teachers are limited, reducing the likelihood that special efforts will be made on behalf of the atypical adolescent. The specialist may discover that, even though the regular teacher is willing to consult and work cooperatively, there are many gaps in the areas of behavioral management strategies, task analysis, and individualization techniques with which the regular teacher needs specific assistance.

4. *Consultation should be viewed as more than a "one shot" experience.* Consultation seems to have better results when it is part of a continuing long-term relationship rather than infrequently scheduled brief meetings (Moed & Muhick, 1972). The relationship

needs to be open, trusting, and professional, qualities of interaction that will take time to establish (Knight, 1976). The special educator cannot expect that securing a regularly scheduled meeting is the essence of consultation. Counselors and therapists will attest to the fact that consultation is based more on the spirit of the interaction between participants than on a schedule or agenda. The specialist must genuinely wish to consult and be willing to let the relationship grow before the full potential of the role can be realized. Several techniques are suggested for facilitating the consultation role, including after-school coffees, regular brief meetings, demonstrations of materials, and exchange visits between rooms (Knight, 1976). All of these may be of benefit but will not bring the role of consultant to fruition. Only consistent, positive interaction that results in obvious, tangible help to the regular teacher will ensure the utilization of the special educator as a consultant. Some teachers' unions will limit such meetings in frequency and scope of action, and a few teachers will refuse to cooperate.

Some basic information and suggestions to consider for the consulting role are:

1. Clarify for yourself your role as special educator.
2. Examine your own training and experiences for areas of expertise you can share.
3. Expect some resistance and criticism in the beginning but do not become defensive.
4. Expect the regular teacher to question whether you know the problems of the classroom teacher.
5. Remember that consultation takes place between peers!

Below is a list of some questions that can be anticipated and some tips that will facilitate the relationship of the special education program and the regular instructional program.

**Initiating the teacher-consultant role.** Questions to anticipate from regular educators include the following:

1. How much experience have you had?
2. Have you ever been a regular classroom teacher?
3. What is a special education teacher supposed to do?
4. How many students do you serve?
5. Are you paid on a different salary schedule?
6. Do you have duties similar to other faculty members (club sponsor, etc.)?
7. Why do I have to help this student?

Possible concerns of regular educators include:

1. Will the specialist really listen to my problem?
2. If I ask for assistance will it appear that I am incompetent?
3. Will the administration hear about my classroom from the special education teacher (Is that person a "spy"?)?
4. Will my request for help only result in extra work for me?
5. Is there really anything that can be done to help this student?
6. Does this person really know anything that will make any difference?

Some tips to aid the teacher-consultant are as follows:

1. Be professional and personable.
2. Make known the types of services included in the special education program. You can do this with pamphlets, posters in the lounge, and meetings. Your program should be described in detail in the faculty handbook complete with samples of all forms used. You might consider a separate handbook with complete instructions for referral, consultation, and conferences. If there is a series of meetings at the beginning of the year, schedule a time block to describe the program.

3. Get to know the other faculty members.
4. When you get a request for service of any type, *speed* of response is crucial! If for some reason (which better be good) there is a delay, an honest explanation to the teacher helps. Remember they have no idea of the constraints within which you work. They want results fast, and this one factor alone can influence a program.
5. Schedule services with input from the teacher to avoid conflicts. It is more difficult for them to criticize the schedule if they have helped develop it.
6. Make reports that are problem related, clearly stated, and brief.
7. Conferences should be open to all parties with participation encouraged and reinforced.
8. Invite exchange visits between the teachers and the special education room.
9. Remember you must be a public relations specialist.
10. Be patient and positive.

## Public relations

Public relations as a competency for the special education teacher is a concept that has gradually emerged as it has become necessary for specialists to intervene with regular educators on behalf of handicapped students. As a marketing concept it means that the special educator has a product to sell to consumers and efficient sales techniques require good interpersonal skills and a product image. As with so many roles emerging with the evolution of the resource teaching position, this aspect is not one that has been formally introduced in a typical college training program; rather, it is a role created by exigencies of the daily demands of the mainstream setting. Lately, public relations has received formal recognition by some writers in the field (D'Alonzo & Wiseman, 1978; Marsh et al., 1978; McNutt & Heller, 1978). The successful special education teacher must not only provide services but also information about services to teachers and the public, must communicate within the system as an important part of providing direct and indirect pupil services, and must relate with the administration to maintain support for the program.

An important part of communicating the role of the teacher and information about mild handicapping conditions may occur in contact with clubs and organizations in the community. There is interest in the field as evidenced by the great number of articles appearing in popular magazines and general television coverage. The special educator may be invited to speak to groups or to prepare television and radio spots about handicapped populations. A frequent emphasis is on prevention or information for parents. There are advantages and possible pitfalls from such exposure. Below is a list of suggestions for preparing such presentations and avoiding embarrassment and mistakes.

### General guidelines for group presentations

1. Make a "textbook" presentation with good eye contact, appropriate gestures, and liberal use of audiovisual aids.
2. Most presentations will range between 15 and 45 minutes in length so it is necessary to make a few good points (two or three in an average presentation).
3. Remember that most audiences can only process general information and will be confused by complicated terminology and jargon.
4. Avoid brief discussions of diagnosis that may panic parents, and do not do long-distance diagnoses based on information supplied by parents.

5. Avoid the use of real names and locations.
6. Stress the positive aspects of the population rather than dwelling on atypical characteristics.
7. Be able to provide referral information about community services and have printed handouts.
8. Be sure to avoid the presentation of information about medical aspects such as opinions about the need for medication. Refer questions about medical issues to appropriate medical authorities.
9. Try to schedule your presentation *before* the business meeting of a group because the audience will be more receptive.
10. Be prepared to receive numerous phone calls to inquire about services.
11. Be prepared to hear complaints about teachers and administrators. Judge your response carefully and say exactly what you mean.
12. Be prepared to deal with an occasional heckler who will attack your position.
13. Be prepared to respond to controversies that exist between various groups such as the learning disabilities movement and the International Reading Association (IRA).
14. Clear donations from clubs and groups through your appropriate school administrator.

The special education teacher may receive many requests for appearances at meetings of clubs, organizations, P.T.A. meetings, and professional conferences. The sheer magnitude can become burdensome for those who make excellent presentations. It may be necessary to learn how to say "no" to a group if too much time becomes involved with the speaking circuit. It is always easier to refuse if you can supply the caller with a suitable substitute. A great deal of time can be saved if a record of each presentation is maintained. You do not want to say the same thing to the same group at a later date, and a file will make presentations easier. Modifications and revisions can be made over time, and this can reduce time and effort in preparation. The teacher should maintain a file that includes the following information:

- A list of films (sources and cost)
- A list of resource persons in the community
- Sample handouts appropriate for the general public
- Outlines of all previous presentations
- A compilation of anecdotes and jokes
- A bibliography appropriate for the general public
- Audiovisual supports

These materials can be accumulated gradually and evolve into a very useful resource to aid the teacher in fulfilling this aspect of the public relations role.

## Advocacy

Advocacy is the assumption of an active stand on the acquisition of rights for handicapped students. Many special education teachers are committed to child advocacy and believe in the value of every individual. As an advocate in the school and the community, zeal must be tempered with reality and emotional reactions must be supplanted by rationality. The cause of special education cannot be advanced by antagonists. The special educator can effectively blend teaching responsibilities with advocacy postures and attitudes and can facilitate the growth of advocacy in colleagues by patient endeavor. To be an advocate it is necessary to know the laws, the regulations, and the limits. A list of key personnel and resources should also be maintained. The teacher should have at least general knowledge in the following areas:

- State laws pertaining to rights, education, and training

- State procedures and regulations
- Specific federal legislation and regulations
- Particular groups and individuals that can be helpful

The teacher should have specific knowledge about:
- Education
- Employment
- Parental rights
- Student rights
- Institutional rights
- Transportation
- Other services

Advocacy groups are being formed in each state as part of a national network, and there are many local groups. The special education teacher should become familiar with such groups and maintain a list of contact individuals and phone numbers. These groups can provide support and information to parents and other interested parties. Although the teacher may be actively involved in the advocacy cause, this should be done with the full knowledge of the school administration. Contacts with parents to explain their rights should be recorded for self-protection because recollections of interactions can become distorted. The lines between advocacy, loyalty to the district, and duty may not always be clearly distinguishable, hence a possible source of conflict.

Groups providing advice and legal assistance to parents may offer the following services:
1. Explanation of rights and provisions of legislation
2. Legal assistance
3. Contact with attorneys and surrogate parents
4. Referral (a) to agencies for special services and evaluations and (b) to volunteers for tutoring, etc.

An advocate will attempt to provide appropriate, accurate information to assist parents in making decisions about their children in the educational setting. The role of the advocate is not to incite parents. Care should be taken in communications with them to assure that they understand what has been said to them. Misunderstandings, misinterpretations, or unreliable information cause antagonism and frustration, which can be spread to all the parties involved in an examination of a student's program. Concerns that might be expressed by parents include:

1. Does the school have to provide services for my child?
2. How do I find out if my child is eligible for services?
3. How would my child benefit from your program?
4. Will placement in special education services interfere with other classes?
5. What is the purpose of assessment, and do I have to accept what the school examiners say?
6. What is an Individualized Educational Plan?
7. What can I do if I do not agree with what the school proposes to do/is doing with my child's educational program?
8. Where can I get a lawyer?
9. Will special education be a blackmark on the records and keep my child from attending college?
10. Will my child be able to graduate?

This does not encompass the entire range of questions that might be asked, but it includes some typical examples that may be fielded by a special educator or other advocate. Obviously, unless very specific, accurate information is given to parents, it will be possible for many problems to develop. Parents should be referred to other professionals in the school and community for answers to questions beyond one's capabilities or expertise. The advocate should attempt to resolve as many issues as possible to prevent them from developing into major conflicts between parents and the school authorities because resolution would be in the best interest of the student.

## Other role functions

Five major roles of the specialist were emphasized in the preceding section because they are unique in education and critical for programming. The unique aspects of consultation, administrative responsibilities, public relations, advocacy, and pupil services are evident to the observer as the dynamics of the roles are revealed in practice. The special education teacher, unlike most other educators, must direct considerable energy and planning into professional relationships with other teachers and the administration, must work as a champion for the rights of students and direct public relations efforts to different groups in the school and community, and must provide a multitude of direct services to students. These roles are not just different in degree; they are qualitatively different from common teaching duties expected of mainstream educators. Many of the more commonly known roles of special educators have been addressed at different points in this volume, but mention of the categories should be included here for continuity in the description of comprehensive services.

**Educational diagnosis.** Although educational diagnosis or assessment is typically regarded as an important function of the special educator, the term is somewhat misleading. Special educators actually provide observational, formal, and informal test data to assist in placement decisions, to determine the adequacy of instruction, measurement of changes in students, and to meet requirements of the school or state. Educational measurement can therefore be classified by kind: *instructional, administrative,* and *assessment.*

The special education teacher will need to have a command of a variety of assessment tools and put them to good use in a number of prescribed ways to either improve instruction for students or to meet administrative requirements. Assessment per se may not be a major part of the teacher's role in the secondary setting, depending on the extent of support services. There will be a demand for the use of assessment tools in planning educational programs for students, assisting mainstream teachers to understand the needs of students, and assisting mainstream teachers to develop reliable classroom tests for content areas. It should be remembered that many secondary teachers have absolutely *no* training in test theory, development, or use. Some of the teacher-made tests constructed in an English or history class are very poorly made. There may be occasion to help teachers develop better tests that will benefit all students.

The special education teacher should understand the uses of tests and be able to use them in accordance with the following purposes:

1. *Standardized evaluation of pupils.* The specialist should know the major standardized tests used in the school for measurement of group achievement in basic skills and content areas. Although the special education teacher will not ordinarily administer such tests (e.g., Metropolitan Achievement Tests), they will be required in schools and the teacher may be able to assist students, parents, and mainstream teachers in the interpretation of results. It will be necessary to understand basic principles and statistical properties of measurement such as reliability, validity, norms, types of scores, and profiles.

2. *Individual and diagnostic measurement of pupils.* This area includes assessment approaches familiar to special educators. Individual measurement in basic skills and other

abilities will be a substantial part of the assessment effort in placement decisions and progress of students.

3. *Criterion-referenced measures of progress.* The ability to identify criteria in content areas and construct tests for use with mildly handicapped students will be invaluable.

4. *Teacher-made evaluations.* Students and mainstream teachers may be greatly assisted if the special education teacher aids in the process of establishing behavioral objectives and the creation of essay and objective tests.

**Curriculum development.** The special educator should be able to identify appropriate curriculum materials to be used with mildly handicapped students in reaching goals of remediation in the special education program and in altering instruction for students in the regular curriculum. Chapter 5 is provided to acquaint the special teacher with the various curricula of the secondary school.

**Behavior management.** One of the most effective ways of securing the cooperation and respect of teachers is to be able to introduce management systems that improve the teacher's control over the learning environment and increase the interest and achievement of students. The variety of operant techniques known by many special educators will be of utmost importance in the secondary setting because, as in other areas of teaching skills, most secondary instructors are not trained in behavior management.

**Counseling.** In this text we have suggested the use of a model, which we call the *extended counseling model,* to be coordinated by the school counselor. The special education teacher, mainstream teachers, and peer counselors could be used to *extend* counseling beyond the limitations of resources and a small staff of certified counselors. It has been demonstrated in research that teachers who were able to provide group counseling under the supervision of a counselor were able to reduce the dropout rate significantly. It is also known that peer counseling is very effective; even the ability of classroom teachers to engage in private discussions with students, as opposed to persistent group conversations, can dramatically influence and motivate students. The special education teacher should be able to share in this important activity.

## PERSONALITY VARIABLES AND THE SPECIAL EDUCATOR
### Tolerance for frustration

Schools have been indicted as joyless, oppressive, and overly concerned with structure and control (Silberman, 1971). The high school curriculum has been described as irrelevant to real life (Clark et al., 1972; Siegel, 1974). Although this may not be true of all schools, it is a factor that must be considered when planning the secondary special education program. Morale of teachers and students is related to institutional bureaucracy and as power is distributed more evenly between teachers and administrators, change will occur. In-service education is making inroads in changing attitudes and practices within modern secondary schools, but the specialist may be impatient with the slow rate of change.

It is unrealistic to expect secondary schools to make drastic changes and improvements within the immediate future. It is naive for new teachers to anticipate that significant, immediate strides will be made overnight in any school. However, the teacher must be convinced that the special educator can have great impact on the school program as a whole, as has been shown in various studies. A positive attitude about the impact potential, coupled with a high tolerance for frustration, can serve to bring the teacher and the special education program to the forefront in services to handicapped adolescents. There will be obstacles and constraints inherent in the system, which the teacher must circumvent in some clever manner or systematically attempt to change.

Tolerance for frustration is also associated with direct pupil services. Handicapped students, like all learners, will have uneven rates of progress and periods of regression. They will be subject to personal adjustment problems that will interfere greatly with their progress. They may be unpleasant or overtly obnoxious. Knowledge of adolescent behavior and awareness of special problems associated with being an adolescent with a learning handicap will be of great benefit to the teacher and help reduce frustration. The teacher should not accept personal blame every time a student "blows up." Special education teachers can expect to have frustration, greater on some days than others, and should acknowledge such feelings. The difference between the successful teacher and the one who may ultimately resign may well be the ability to cope with frustration. Some suggested personal coping strategies include the following:

1. Admit it when things become too much to handle!
2. Find a fellow professional (preferably another special education teacher) with whom you can "suffer" and share remedies.
3. Identify the *exact* "straw that broke the camel's back" and decide to:
   a. Ignore it because you can't change it
   b. Circumvent it
   c. Change it
4. *Don't* continue to harp about it or "beat" yourself.

Remember that you are human. As a matter of fact, that is probably the greatest asset a special educator has. Being human and understanding other human beings and their shortcomings can be invaluable.

## Temperament and attitude

The approach the special education teacher uses with the students and other teachers is greatly colored by his or her individual disposition. A personality that might be described as positive, easygoing, and personable can be a great asset. Anticipating resistance from parents, teachers, administrators, and students is realistic. Role reversal, looking at the student's situation from the perspective of the regular teacher, can contribute to flexibility and understanding for the special teacher (Knight, 1976). Understanding the natural reactions of teachers to special education and to students is extremely important. The teachers' temperament can remain relatively constant with the awareness and understanding of why the teachers may be resistant and hostile to entreaties for change and cooperation.

Willingness to acknowledge efforts of regular teachers rather than assuming "it is just their job" to cooperate is also important. Reinforcing and rewarding such behavior will benefit the program immeasurably. This is true in dealing with students. Communicating the attitude that they are in the class to learn, as a form of imposed regimentation, will make the program difficult to manage. An honestly cheery disposition combined with the attitude that initiative will be rewarded will culminate in rich benefits to all.

Realistic expectations and a willingness to accept individual students and teachers on the basis of their merits will earn for the special teacher the same privilege. Feelings must be accurately monitored and care taken to develop and sustain rapport with others. It should be remembered that most problems will have solutions but not all students nor teachers or parents will be pleased with the program. A certain amount of worry about keeping everyone happy is natural, but dwelling on setbacks and criticism becomes detrimental to the program and relationships with students and teachers. The time and effort would be most productively spent identifying the exact nature of a problem and selecting a course of action from among possible strategies.

## TRAINING AND PROFESSIONAL GROWTH OF THE SPECIAL EDUCATOR

The selection and training of teachers have always been difficult tasks for universities for a variety of reasons. One continuous problem has been that teaching has been defined more as an art than as any specified science or technology. Consequently, most of the personnel who enter the teaching field are not really expected to do more than pass certain courses and succeed in a student teaching experience. The core of teaching competency rests mainly on course work that is recognized by a state certifying agency. Although there are no easy answers to the development and evaluation of teacher training, there are specific factors involved in the teaching role, which can be used in selection of candidates and for teaching experience in the training process. "Soft" characteristics considered important are the attitude and temperament of teachers. Early field experiences of students may give them an opportunity to determine if they really want to teach in a high school setting, if they can contend with the demands, and if supervisory personnel feel that they have promise for the profession. The ability to relate to students and colleagues is important to the role of the teacher, although it may be presently difficult to select students with appropriate personalities.

### Course work

The course work required of the special educator may reflect great differences in accordance with the variability of certification requirements and emphasis of colleges and universities. Many have been so preoccupied with the needs of elementary programs that very little attention has been devoted to secondary programming.

It has not been clearly established that course work necessarily leads to competency, so it would be ludicrous to list specific courses that should be taken by candidates for the special educator role. We also have some hesitancy about listing specific competencies at this point in time as the field is still emerging and finding direction. Some authorities, it will be recalled, would staff the secondary program with a traditionally trained specialist who would provide only remediation. We recommend a more comprehensive training program that encompasses a broader range of skills and competencies, which reflect the unique aspects of the adolescent and the secondary setting. We would suggest that, in addition to other requirements of states and universities, emphasis in the training program should be placed on these general areas:

- Legislation
- History of the development of the field
- Characteristics of the population
- Issues and trends in definition and services
- Assessment techniques (formal and informal)
- Instructional sequence development
- Remedial techniques
- Accommodation
- Learning theory
- Adolescent psychology
- Vocational education
- Selected secondary course work
- Relationships with parents and teachers
- Career education
- Curriculum development
- Behavior management
- Management of materials and equipment
- Utilization of personnel and volunteers

Internships and practicums are essential to the development of skills because of the opportunity for modeling and the use of evaluative feedback from experienced teachers and university training personnel. Field-based experiences are probably the most critical in the training of special education teachers and serve as the points at which previously learned information is synthesized into a philosophy and an integrated approach to programming.

## Additional training experiences

Training should also emphasize organizational skills required to perform the job professionally because this appears to be a major area of difficulty for new teachers. Establishing priorities in the face of an overwhelming need or deciding what to do first may prove to be a major hurdle for beginning teachers. The most common tactic employed in such situations is to try to do it all, resulting in a lot of frantic activity directed at solving all problems and serving *all* aspects of the students' needs at once! Obviously this is not only counterproductive but also results in increased frustration on the part of the teacher and may cause the teacher to "burn out" early. Internships and practicums should provide experience in making such priority decisions.

Awareness of co-lateral fields with which the teacher may interact should be incorporated into the training program. Survey courses may include components on the health professions, psychology, child development, and administration. Understanding how to interact with other disciplines is absolutely necessary because services to the many mildly handicapped students, such as LD adolescents, require a multidisciplinary approach (Lerner, 1976). As we have stated before, the practicums are the most appropriate points to emphasize such interaction.

## Professional organizations

No description of the role of the special educator would be complete without a discussion of the contribution of professional organizations. The list included here is certainly not exhaustive since the interests, training emphasis, and professional needs of individual teachers may vary as do the groups in which they have membership. Included here are only a few of the major organizations. Special education teachers are urged to consider membership in these and/or other organizations because of the personal and professional rewards and professional growth.

- Council for Exceptional Children (CEC) and its appropriate divisions
- American Association for Mental Deficiencies (AAMD)
- Association for Children with Learning Disabilities (ACLD)
- National Association for Retarded Citizens (ARC)
- International Reading Association (IRA)
- Orton Society

These organizations provide benefits to the membership, which include professional journals, professional workshops and meetings, liability insurance, access to listings of materials, correspondence with other professionals, group health/life insurance, group travel plans, and discounts on professional books.

Teachers should belong to professional organizations because of the dynamic nature of the field of special education and the evolution of knowledge. Research continues to reveal new information concerning the definition of the populations and the evaluation of learning strategies employed by mildly handicapped students. Special education teachers must keep abreast of the developments in the field in order to properly serve students.

Among the many aspects of the special

education teacher's role, five role functions that seem to be paramount in the complex of teaching responsibilities have been emphasized. The special education teacher must view direct teaching efforts in the context of the program goals, must provide direct support to other teachers, and must manage numerous contacts with agencies, organizations, and professional disciplines not expected of other teachers. The role of the special educator is very demanding and still evolving. At the secondary level it presents one of the real challenges in modern education.

## CONCERNS AND ISSUES RELATED TO ROLES

The following concerns and issues may surface as the special education teacher implements a secondary program for junior high or high school students. For some problems, there are not clear answers; for others, courses of action seem rather evident if contingencies can be anticipated. There is no attempt to order these topics because they defy logical classification, although each could be easily subsumed under various topics in this text.

*Are the majority of teachers in school able to clearly identify what the special educator does and what are the purposes of the program?* Teachers will not utilize a service if they do not know it exists or if they do not understand how it can help. Internal public relations is a necessity and can only be conducted by the teacher.

*Does the special teacher attempt to make contacts with all the teachers in the building, can he or she address each teacher personally, and can he or she identify what subjects each teacher has responsibility for in the curriculum?* Although a teacher may develop a circle of friends in a building, it is imperative that the special educator extend contact to *all* teachers and attempt to become personally acquainted with each. As in all relationships, there will be some conflicts between personalities but services depend on the ability to relate to other professionals.

*How does the special education teacher monitor the progress of students in content areas?* The level of this responsibility depends on the service model selected. If it is a responsibility of the teacher, any of a number of systems may be employed to determine that a student is progressing in content subjects. Some could be as sophisticated as using a school-based computer terminal (available in some comprehensive schools) or as simple as making personal contacts with a checklist. Monitoring is important to determine that the student is attending classes, completing assignments, and making progress. Finding out that a student failed science at the end of the quarter is too late to salvage the course or do anything about the deterioration of rapport between student and mainstream teacher.

*Does the special education teacher keep mainstream teachers informed of students' progress in the special education activities?* Simple communications in a written form and verbal communications with mainstream teachers about student progress can be reinforcing to the attitudes and efforts on behalf of students. Knowing that a student is really trying to succeed is encouraging news.

*Do the special teacher and mainstream teachers share materials?* The programs of students cannot be integrated unless there is cross-utilization of materials. Agreements should be established between the special education program and departments about sharing materials and equipment. Planning is necessary to avoid disagreements and complications.

*Should the special educator be responsible for teaching regular classes?* There is no clear answer to this question. It is a primary concern of many specialists. In practice, some special education teachers provide only remediation or vocational training. Others tend to provide tutoring. There are very few programs, to our knowledge, that attempt to use a comprehensive approach in which remediation and support in the mainstream are provided simultaneously. If this approach is adopted then a lot of problems will clear up in the process. As it is, a teacher who provides only remediation will find that students will come to the special education room with assignments or questions about work in mainstream classes that are likely to be of more interest to the student than remedial drills. The teacher can refuse to assist the student or can attempt to get mainstream teachers to provide teaching of reading in content areas, something that is not very successful.

It would appear that when there is overlap, as in a comprehensive or tutorial approach, the student's work can interact with supportive activities in the special education program. The teacher must be able to extend his or her skills by means of paid or volunteer tutors, peer tutors, aides, and teaching equipment in order to provide the substantial parts of teaching to a diverse group of students. Therefore paragraph writing, handwriting skills, graph reading, grammar, or literature may or may not be included in the program. This depends entirely on the individual needs of students and the scope of the program.

*Should the special educator instruct students in reading and mathematics in the special program if remediation will be the only focus?* This is similar to the question listed above. In reality, if a teacher is willing to assume only the responsibility for remediation in the basis skills—usually regarded as reading, arithmetic, and written expression—then involvement with the curricula of the mathematics and English departments has already occurred. There can be conflict with remedial reading and remedial mathematics instructors in the school. In fact, in those schools where both the remedial reading instructor and the remedial special education teacher coexist, tremendous conflict occurs and generally the faculty tends to support the remedial reading teacher because they understand what remedial reading is and do not understand the role of the special educator. We recently observed a secondary school faculty meeting during which time the staff discussed the need for assisting students who were having difficulty making it in the various classes. The faculty was presented with the task of voting on a recommendation to secure the services of either a remedial reading teacher or a special education teacher. They chose the remedial reading teacher. In either event, remedial teachers or special educators who act like remedial teachers are not likely to help students very much if the school is content to isolate poor achievers in a room for reading instruction but not impact the environment through accommodation. Judging from what can be expected of tertiary efforts at remedial reading during senior high school, most students will probably not make significant reading gains, those who do will have difficulty applying these gains to the reading tasks of the classes, and many will continue to fail in their subjects and end their school careers unpleasantly.

If the intent of remediation is to assist students to complete reading skills through the sixth grade level and to teach addition, subtraction, multiplication, and division before severing relationships with the student, there will probably be very little conflict with mainstream teachers. We would question the value of the other daily school experiences of the student, however. The training and interests of many specialists far exceed the limitations imposed by the remedial-classroom paradigm. To truly tackle the problems of the mildly handicapped students in the mainstream, that is, to provide services directly related to their immediate and long-range daily needs, it is necessary to plan, organize, manage, and monitor a comprehensive program that utilizes a tremendous support system consisting of personnel and resources.

*Should the mathematics curriculum in the special education room be related to that of the mainstream?* If a student is functioning very far below grade-level expectation in the mainstream mathematics class, most of the basic skills will be seriously deficient so that it will be impossible for the student to be able to perform ably in the class. The question arises, what should be done to assist the student? The most obvious approach seems to be to provide remediation into the mainstream, which usually consists of drill. There are some commercial programs being developed ostensibly for the handicapped, although they have yet to be validated. Programs especially designed for this population must be viewed suspiciously if the teacher expects special significance to be associated with the materials because of the title. In order to use them it may be necessary to supplant the mathematics curriculum or to risk confusing the student because the mathematics curricula may be competing, inconsistent, and covering different skills, or dealing with the same skills but at different rates. This will be a more serious problem in the junior high program than in the senior high.

In senior high, students are not required to have as many credits in mathematics as they are in other subjects; consequently, they will tend to avoid mathematics. If a student has acquired functional competency, or survival skills, in mathematics by the time of senior high and the student expresses no continued interest or aptitude, the decision may be made to discontinue remediation in this area. If services are to be continued it would be advisable to seek as much assistance from the mathematics department as possible, even though the student may not be enrolled in any mathematics class.

*Should a student who reaches seventh grade competency in reading achievement be discharged from the program without further support or services?* This question may be asked by a teacher in a program influenced by the use of clear-cut criteria. If the rule is that a student who acquires basic reading skill should be discharged, then the operating procedures make the decision rather than professionals utilizing a variety of probing analyses to make the determination.

Reading at the seventh grade level does not mean much without having knowledge of the tests that are used to affix the grade-level score and some knowledge of the qualitative aspects of reading behavior. Two students who read at the same grade level will probably have very different reading abilities in reality because the score does not convey much but the crudest of information. A student who performs well on measures of word meaning and word analysis (phonetic and structural analysis) but who lags in comprehension and study skills may have a sixth to seventh grade competency on a test but may be ill prepared to succeed in the demands of course work. If a sixth to seventh grade competency causes the student to be dismissed from the program without further assistance by the specialist, the continued reading problems of the student, regression of skills without maintenance support, and the challenge of the textbooks with seventh to twelfth grade reading levels will be defeating. The reasoning implicit in the criterion-dismissal concept is that a sixth grade reading level is tantamount to reading survival in our society; if one assumes this, it cannot also be assumed that a student's knowledge of phonics and ability to decode will be sufficient to compete in the mainstream with printed matter requiring an ever-increasing level of comprehension, application of reading to abstract concepts, and interpretive reading skill. It is predictable that most students who remain in reading instruction would not be able to acquire such skills anyway, but without reading instruction, it is absolutely necessary that accommodatory approaches and other forms of support be used to relate to the daily demands of learning. The inability to read, as we have described, does not mean that students cannot learn the knowledge of the various subject areas.

*Can the special education teacher manage several students at different grade levels in many different subject areas?* It is curious that special educators tend to talk about special students being *regrouped* for services while at the same time they talk of *individualization*. The ability to work with several students with varying abilities and subject areas has been successfully accomplished in modern interactional models of teaching, in the mastery learning approach, and in the one-room schoolhouse. The key is that teachers who succeed are able to orchestrate the program after careful planning and organization of program direction. The need to work with a group or entire class while everyone does the same thing is convenient only for the teacher, who, in effect, makes preparation for one student—the "class." If the special teacher cannot individualize then he or she has no right to expect it of mainstream teachers. This subject will be discussed in greater detail in Chapters 9 and 10.

*Should the special educator give course grades to students in such subjects as English or mathematics?* Because students are required to amass specific, earned credits in order to graduate, their time must be accounted for in some manner. If they spend time in the special education room for remediation in reading and mathematics, then courses are sometimes designed that will generally relate to the subjects being taught. The typical approach is for reading instruction to translate into some kind of English or language arts credit and mathematics can become vocational mathematics or consumer mathematics. This is a necessity if a student is enrolled for a full load of courses and attends a special program for support and tutoring; then teachers may cooperate on the assignation of grades. Typically, grades are not awarded for reading per se in the secondary program. Different circumstances and procedures will dictate grading in each state. Careful examination of the grading practices is recommended to assure that students are not provided inferior education in the midst of confusion about roles and responsibilities of teachers.

Grades awarded in the special education program can be a topic of great concern to the administration and teachers. There is a concern about what the course should be called, how the special program will be listed, what should be designated on the report card, and if a letter grade will give parents and future teachers an unrealistic picture of the student's ability and potential. Concern is not with what the student learns but how the student ranks. This may be an area deserving of attention in order to resolve many complex issues.

*Should the program include the enrollment of students labeled emotionally disturbed, mentally retarded, and learning disabled?* The answer to this question depends on a number of variables affecting programs at the local level. In that it has not been empirically determined that services should be differentially designed by label, it becomes difficult to find a definite direction that can be supported by research or authority. There has been a clear trend in many schools to group three categories (ED, EMR, and LD) together for instruction in elementary programs. The thinking behind this is that the labels do not clearly distinguish between the three groups, there is overlap in characteristics and needs, and the fundamental teaching and management techniques that are applied with each group are essentially identical. There are certainly differences in the styles of behavior and learning of learning disabled and mentally retarded elementary children (May, 1979), which may dictate different instructional modes, even though remedial techniques and other instructional components may be similar.

Many of these issues are transcended at the secondary level by extremely divergent cognitive processes and abilities of learning disabled adolescents (Marsh et al., 1978). The abilities of learning disabled and behaviorally disordered students to engage in hypothetical-deductive reasoning and to use thinking processes that deal with abstractions (formal operational thinking) enable them to achieve in subject matter of content classes equivalent to their nonhandicapped peers, with proper and appropriate accommodation. Many mentally retarded students will not be generally capable of similar performance.

These issues are further complicated by the type of program that is developed, based on local determination or state requirements. If a vocational track is established for nonacademic students, it is simple to rationalize the exclusion of learning disabled and behaviorally disordered students from participation in most of the mainstream classes because they will be occupied with a program leading to job placement. The fact that many of them could benefit from enrollment in liberal arts and regular vocational course work is not considered. If a tutoring program is developed, students of any diagnostic category may be enrolled in the special education program; as in elementary models, the focus will be on tutoring and remediation of basic skills for all students.

It is possible to deemphasize the artificial significance of labels, categories, and program tracks and truly individualize for each student. Those who can succeed in mainstream classes would be permitted to, and those who would benefit most from vocational course work or special vocational programs designed for the handicapped should be enrolled. This should be done on a student-by-student basis with a variety of options available to each student. Programs should be made to fit students' needs rather than forcing students through tracks based on presumptions about the needs of categories of handicapped students.

## SUMMARY

A popular conceptualization of the teaching role among special education teachers is that a competent professional is one who is fully trained in the special techniques necessary to educate handicapped children and who merely needs the appropriate materials to effectively employ such educational techniques. It is apparent, however, that there are many important roles of the specialist that cannot be ignored in the training program of teaching candidates if they are to function adequately in the school setting. The roles of special educators are many and complex, far exceeding the limited roles of the clinical model used in many institutions of higher education to prepare future teachers.

Teaching methods and procedures of a specialist in a secondary setting include many other skills than that of possessing special knowledge and educational techniques. Specifically, the well-prepared specialist will also be able to perform roles of consultation, administrative responsibilities, public relations, advocacy, educational diagnosis, curriculum development, and counseling. It was emphasized that these roles are not just different in degree from roles of regular teachers, but are qualitatively different from common teaching duties expected of mainstream teachers. This chapter included specific recommendations for performing the various roles associated with teaching in a comprehensive secondary special education program.

## REFERENCES AND READINGS

Beery, K. Mainstreaming: A problem and an opportunity for general education. *Focus on Exceptional Children*, 1974, 6, 1-7.

Bersoff, D., Kabler, M., Fiscus, E., & Ankney, R. Effectiveness of special class placement for children labeled neurologically handicapped. *Journal of School Psychology*, 1972, 10, 157-163.

Cantrell, R. P., & Cantrell, M. L. Preventive mainstreaming: Impact of a supportive services program on pupils. *Exceptional Children*, 1976, 42, 381-386.

Clark, L. H., Klein, R. L., & Burks, J. B. *The American secondary school curriculum*. New York: Macmillan, 1972.

D'Alonzo, B. J., & Wiseman, D. E. Actual and desired roles of the high school LD resource teacher. *Journal of Learning Disabilities*, 1978, 11, 390-397.

Deno, E. (Ed.) *Instructional alternatives for exceptional children*. Reston, Va.: The Council for Exceptional Children, 1973.

Dinkmeyer, D., & Carlson, J. *Consulting: Facilitating human potential and change processes*. Columbus, Ohio: Merrill, 1973.

Edwards, J. L. In loco parentis: Definition, application, implication. *South Carolina Law Review*, 1971, 23, 114-126.

Glavin, J., Quay, J., Annesly, F., & Werry, J. An experimental resource room for behavior problem children. *Exceptional Children*, 1971, 38, 131-137.

Hammill, D., & Weiderholdt, J. *The resource room: Rationale and implementation*. Fort Washington, Pa.: Journal of Special Education Press, 1972.

Jenkins, J. R., & Mayhall, W. F. Development and evaluation of a resource teacher program. *Exceptional Children*, 1976, 43, 21-29.

Kerlin, M., & Latham, W. L. Intervention effects of a crisis-resource program. *Exceptional Children*, 1977, 44, 32-34.

Knight, N. Working relationships that work. *Teaching Exceptional Children*, 1976, 8(3), 113-115.

Lerner, J. *Children with learning disabilities*. Boston: Houghton Mifflin, 1976.

Marsh, G. E., Gearheart, C. K., & Gearheart, B. R. *The learning disabled adolescent: Program alternatives in the secondary school*. St. Louis: Mosby, 1978.

May, B. J. *An assessment of classroom behavior patterns with learning disabled, mentally retarded, and normally achieving students utilizing a specific observational instrument*. Unpublished doctoral dissertation, University of Arkansas, 1979.

McNutt, G., & Heller, G. Services for learning disabled adolescents: A survey. *Learning Disability Quarterly*, 1978, 1, 101-102.

Moed, G., & Muhich, D. E. Some problems and parameters of mental health consultation. *Community Mental Health Journal*, 1972, 8, 232-239.

Montgomery, M. D. The special educator as a consultant. Some strategies. *Teaching Exceptional Children*, 1978, 10, 110-112.

Newcomer, P. L. Special educational services for the mildly handicapped: Beyond a diagnostic and remedial model. *Journal of Special Education*, 1977, 11.

Ozer, M. N., & Dworkin, N. E. The assessment of children with learning problems: An inservice teacher training program. *Journal of Learning Disabilities*, 1974, 7, 539-544.

Redden, M. R., & Blackhurst, A. E. Mainstreaming competency specifications for elementary teachers. *Exceptional Children*, 1978, 44, 615-617.

Reynolds, M. C. Staying out of jail. *Teaching Exceptional Children*, 1978, 10, 60-62.

Sabatino, D. An evaluation of resource rooms for children with learning disabilities. *Journal of Learning Disabilities*, 1971, 4, 84-93.

Siegel, E. *The Exceptional child grows up*. New York: Dutton, 1974.

Silberman, C. E. *Crisis in the classroom*. New York: Random House, 1971.

Swift, M. S., and Spivack, G. *Alternative teaching strategies*. Champaign, Ill.: Research Press, 1975.

Trahms, C., Affleck, J. Q., Lowenbraun, S., & Scranton, T. R. The special educator's role on the health service team. *Exceptional Children*, 1977, 43, 344-349.

Turnbull, H. R., & Turnbull, A. P. Deinstitutionalization and the law. *Mental Retardation*, 1975, 13, 14-20.

Weiderholdt, J. L., Hammill, D., & Brown, V. *The resource teacher*. Boston: Allyn & Bacon, 1978.

Chapter 8

# ROLE RELATIONSHIPS AND INTERACTIONS OF THE SPECIAL EDUCATOR

As we have noted in Chapter 7, a distinctive characteristic of the special educator's role is that of his or her professional relationship with other personnel, a primary relationship on which much of the success of the special education program is to be predicated. Other teaching personnel, for the most part, are primarily concerned with the direct instruction of students with only minimal contact with other teachers or other responsibilities. Most regular teaching duties occur within the confines of the classroom. The special educator, however, may endeavor to become involved with many teachers in the mainstream and attempt to have a direct impact on the nature of their attitudes, the type of instruction, and the adjustment of students in other classes.

Role functions and interrelationships with others are critical to the achievement of goals in the special education program. This chapter includes a listing of some of the most important role functions and practical suggestions for conducting duties associated with each role relationship. The relationships of the special teacher with the administration, parents, paraprofessionals, counselors, psychologists, speech therapists, school nurses, regular teachers, and the community have been stressed.

## RELATIONSHIP WITH ADMINISTRATION

The special education teacher will have frequent contact with special education supervisors (who may often function with administrative authority although technically they hold staff positions), with assistant principals, and with principals. There are three areas of responsibility to the administration; namely, the referral process, programming, and program evaluation. An inordinate amount of paperwork will be required to comply with internal administrative needs and state and federal regulations governing special education. The special education teacher should recognize certain general facts about the administration that might make the job more palatable:

1. Many administrators have only the most basic understanding of special education, have had very little actual experience with handicapped students, and may resent the amount of time that is demanded by special education concerns, a part of the program that involves little more than 10% of the student body.

2. Services to the handicapped have changed dramatically and rapidly in recent years, and the general confusion about assessment practices and programming, the fear about litigation, and the pressures of parents, advocacy groups, and other organizations cause special education to be an area of worry to administrators.

3. The mandated involvement of parents (referral, placement, and the IEP) complicates administrative procedures.

4. Major decisions have to be made at the local level concerning such aspects as the allocation of the budget, the scheduling of students, assignments of teachers, and modification of the curriculum because of special education. These are perceived as additional complications and problems for the administration.

Because of these facts, the relationship of the special educator with administrators may be more involved. Administrators may rely on special educators for advice and unusual assistance in making policy decisions, school organization, and curriculum development. Some may totally ignore special educators.

The essential administrative responsibilities of the school administration in the area of special education can be summarized in the following categories:

1. Establishment and assurance of due process procedures
2. Understanding of and compliance with

state and federal legislation and regulations
3. Maintenance of records to assure compliance with due process procedures
4. Assurance of confidentiality of student records
5. General record keeping
6. Compliance with regulations for unbiased assessment
7. Provision of transportation and barrier-free buildings
8. Collection and use of evaluation data

In addition, state and federal agencies are likely to visit local schools to monitor compliance with regulations. This places burdens on administrators who must make special arrangements for such visitations, take time out from other duties to be available to visiting officials, and react to deficiencies by submitting reports and implementing remedies. As a consequence, it is likely that the special education teacher will be called on to assume extraordinary responsibility in administratively related activities. This places an extra burden on these teachers because of the duties involved and it is possible that mistakes or errors in the administration of special education may, in part, be blamed on the special education teacher. This is most probable in schools where the administrative lines of authority are loosely defined and where record-keeping functions are poorly organized. The special education teacher should share in the responsibility of maintaining accurate records and meeting other requirements of the regulations in special education; but the special educator is not an administrator, does not receive extra compensation for administrative activities, and should not be held accountable for errors clearly beyond the purview of the special education classroom. A special education teacher should assess the administrative climate and take any actions necessary for self-protection and should make every effort to expeditiously complete clearly assigned tasks.

The special education teacher can be of great assistance to the administrator in the interpretation of special education terminology and accompanying guidelines. Administrators may not know the meanings of diagnostic terms, diagnostic labels, the names and uses of assessment instruments, and the abilities of students. Misinformation, negative attitudes, and misperceptions of special education lead quite naturally to a lack of leadership and support. Not only may the special education teacher assist the administration in a variety of ways when opportunities arise, but secondary benefits to the program may accrue as administrators develop a greater level of awareness and better attitudes about handicapped students. It should be remembered that the principal is the key individual in the school for the development and implementation of policies. The location of the classroom, size of the budget, and policies that affect handicapped students may well depend on the attitude of the principal. Hence, this part of the special education teacher's role is not inconsequential. To provide a succinct view of the interaction of the special teacher's role with the administration, Table 9 lists the areas of administrative responsibility and the types of assistance required by the special educator.

Most of the activities listed as actions of special education teachers may be regarded as normal expectations for job performance although they may be taxing. The importance lies in the fact that they must be done and efficiency can strengthen ties between administrator and teacher. Each role can greatly facilitate the other and lead to improved programming and services.

Special education supervisors are being employed by many school districts and cooperatives to formally provide the administra-

**Table 9.** Administrative responsibilities in services to mildly handicapped students and types of supportive input needed from the special educator

| Area of administrative responsibility | Types of assistance from special educator |
|---|---|
| **Referral/diagnosis** | |
| Implementation of referral process | Parent liaison |
| Student assessment | Assistance in securing services of other professionals in diagnostic process |
| Implementation of diagnostic process | Record keeping |
| Parent participation | Setting up meetings/staffings |
| **Programming** | |
| Personnel development | Leadership in IEP development |
| Enrollment | Input in school policy affecting handicapped students |
| Pupil progress | |
| Physical provisions for program | Providing direct student services |
| Parent reporting | Aid in materials/equipment decisions |
| Curricular variations | Parent liaison |
| | Input in staff development/in-service |
| | Providing teacher consultation |
| **Program evaluation** | |
| Pupil progress | Maintaining student progress data |
| Cost-benefit analysis | Record keeping on parent contact |
| | Keeping inventories on materials/equipment |
| | Collecting summary data on mainstreaming support activities |
| | IEP review |

tive support required for total special education services. Supervisors *must* have training and/or experience in special education in order to fulfill the responsibilities of the position. Supervisors with the proper qualifications and personal-social skills can facilitate the development of an outstanding program. Unfortunately, some supervisors do not have adequate qualifications and cannot provide the leadership needed by teachers. They cannot speak for the program with upper level administrators, do not have the background to understand subtle issues and problems, cannot support the special educator, and are unable to effectively influence policies. The special education teacher may find the job complicated in schools where leadership is weak or nonexistent.

## ROLE TO PARENTS

Parent involvement should be solicited. At certain points it is required by legislative guidelines, an involvement that presents opportunities to the special educator. Parent participation in referral and assessment conferences has been positively received by school planning teams (Yoshida et al., 1978). Parents can provide relevant information such as behavioral observations, perceptions of strengths or weaknesses, educational concerns, and management ideas (Escovar, 1976). Special education teachers should encourage parent participation and open channels of communication because of the benefit to students. The interactive roles of the special educator and parents are outlined in Table 10.

### Parent conferences

Some parents of secondary handicapped students may not participate or may exhibit negative attitudes about conferences because, over the years, such conferences may have ended fruitlessly or with parents assum-

**Table 10.** Interactive roles of the special educator and parents

| General area of input from parents | Possible actions by special educator | General area of input from parents | Possible actions by special educator |
|---|---|---|---|
| **Referral/diagnosis** | | **Programming—cont'd** | |
| Provide observational data | Make parents aware of their rights and provide clear, precise information | Read parents' literature | Share samples of activities/materials as well as strategies to be used |
| Cooperate with school and members of team | Arrange conferences at times/places convenient for parents | Attend conferences | |
| Attend conferences | | Observe student's behavior | Identify concrete and specific ways in which parents can assist student |
| Share relevant information from other evaluations | Notify parents well in advance of meetings | Cooperate in placement decision | |
| | Share reports and information | Participate in parent organizations | Provide information on parent groups |
| | Provide samples of student's work | Support the program/model a positive attitude | Provide reading materials and sources for those parents interested but do not force these on parents |
| | Explain the purpose of conferences in advance | Reinforce child's positive behavior and efforts | |
| | *Listen to parents* | | *Listen to parents* |
| **Programming** | | **Program evaluation** | |
| | | Observe student's behavior | Encourage continuous contact between parents and school |
| Share concerns about educational goals desired for student | Clearly explain program curriculum | Provide feedback to school | Provide feedback to parents |
| | Facilitate classroom visits | Be realistic and open | |
| Study placement options, including visiting programs | Point out similarities and differences in the various placements considered | Participate in parent groups | Support parent groups |
| | | Keep in touch with overall program | Provide anecdotal information in addition to grade reports |

ing blame or guilt. The communication skills of the teacher may initially be taxed in the effort to overcome such previous experiences or to get parents to attend. In some cases, parents may request a conference to discuss concerns or problems, but contacts are more likely to be requested by teachers. Most teacher-initiated conferences may be held to comply with legislative mandates for parental involvement. Regardless of who initiated the conference or the reasons for it, the conference may represent the only parent contact and so it should be conducted in a manner to be mutually beneficial to school personnel and parents.

Careful *advance planning* for the parent conference can ensure that it accomplishes its purpose. Using a systematic format to reduce the anxiety of all participants and clarify the purpose of the meeting has been recommended (McAleer, 1978). Fig. 8-1 illustrates a conference format outline. The special education teacher should approach the conference to share and learn from the parents by listening (Kroth, 1975). The key to being able to approach the conference in this manner is careful preparation (Long, 1976). Careful advance preparation should include the following:

1. Selecting a site for the conference

2. Sending adequate advance notice to all participants, including time, location, date, purpose, and length of conference
3. Studying the school file of the student
4. Taking note of previous teachers' comments, pertinent test data, relevant health data, and other factors
5. Developing a clear understanding of the purpose of the conference
6. Listing any information specifically to be included, such as anecdotes, test scores, and comments
7. Having work samples available if they would contribute to the conference
8. Listing positive aspects of the student's performance/behavior to prevent a totally negative focus

Conducting the conference is a skill the teacher must develop, and there are some general suggestions to assist in the process:

1. *Conference site.* Select a private location for the conference (Kroth, 1978; Long, 1976). Be sure the temperature is comfortable. An informal seating arrangement, preferably *not* with teacher and parents on opposite sides of a table, can facilitate communication (Kroth & Simpson, 1977).

2. *Materials.* Have relevant materials organized but set aside at the beginning of the conference. Huge stacks of disorganized materials can appear overwhelming to the parents and detract from the interaction of the participants. Shuffling through a sheaf of papers can also have negative connotations.

3. *Handling the conference.* Be as relaxed as possible. Talk in everyday language but do not talk down to parents (Long, 1976). Begin with a friendly remark or some indication of a positive attitude. Informal conversation about some neutral topic will aid in relieving anxiety on the part of all participants. The tendency is to begin discussing the problem immediately, but this may get the conference off to a difficult start. Clear, straightforward handling of the conference, explaining the process itself, and requesting and using parent information can enhance the role of parents (McLoughlin et al., 1978). Listening is a vital conference skill for the teacher (Kroth & Simpson, 1977). Parents generally realize when a teacher genuinely wishes their input and will respond more eagerly and openly. Taking notes during the conference is in some instances warranted. The teacher should "read" each situation to see that note-taking is not making the parents uncomfortable or distracting participants. Parents should be told that notes are being taken in order not to miss any of the information they are contributing and can be read back to the parents to ensure clarity. If note-taking is not possible, notes should be made immediately following the conference. These can be recorded and shared with the parents and others. Follow the conference format planned in advance to avoid sidetracking *unless* an emergency or otherwise urgent problem or event presents itself.

4. *Terminating the conference.* Setting a definite time limit for the conference can be very helpful to all concerned and can enhance effectiveness (Barten & Barten, 1973). Following the planned conference format and attending to the behavior of the parents will aid the teacher in gauging conference pace. Overdiscussion of issues will be counterproductive. Summarize the conference proceedings to see that all participants have the same perception of its outcomes: Sincere gratitude for parental participation should be expressed and the doors left open to future interaction. If a follow-up conference is needed, schedule it while participants are present to ensure their convenience and attendance.

The effects of the parent conference do not end with termination of the conference. Some time should be spent reflecting on the conference itself and reexamining it for implications and information overlooked at the time. Conference follow-up activities may be as varied as the conferences themselves. A sequence of steps for follow-up might be conducted as listed below*:

1. A conference report should be completed and filed (Fig. 8-1).
2. A conference summary should be completed and sent to parents and other participants (Fig. 8-2).
3. The teacher *must follow through* on additional tasks identified during the conference such as testing, arranging another conference, securing other information, and interviewing other professionals.
4. If additional tasks were identified, conference participants and parents should be notified that the extra steps have been accomplished.

Referral, diagnosis, IEP planning, and evaluation include parental participation; also, the required conferences are defined in each state and local special education plan. The special educator will be particularly interested in parent input in developing and evaluating educational plans for handicapped adolescents because of the social-emotional emphasis. Planning or assessment teams are more receptive of parental involvement in the referral process than in instructional planning (Yoshida et al., 1978); however, this need not be the case in secondary schools. Admittedly parents may not be knowledgeable of course content and requirements, but they can contribute to discussions of life plans and goals of their children. Parental support can be elicited for social-skills goals and other affective components of the program that directly relate to school and postschool success. Parents can provide valuable feedback on the student's attitude and social behavior indicating generalization of adjustment skills being taught in the extended counseling model (ECM) and the special education program (McLoughlin et al., 1978).

Another point often overlooked by special educators is the fact that they have skills and strategies from which the parents may benefit (Kroth, 1978). Mutual sharing of information fosters a trusting atmosphere and results in a more positive attitude and relationship (Heffernan & Todd, 1969). Parents may gain new ideas from the conference as well as reinforcement for some aspects of interaction with their adolescent. At the very least, they should leave with a sense of being better acquainted with the special education teacher and the program.

## Other types of parent communication

The conference summary form (Fig. 8-2) is an example of *written communication* between parent and teacher. The purpose of the form is to ensure that the parents understand the reason for the conference and its outcomes. Fig. 8-3, a summary of a management plan, is another example of written communication with parents. The form outlines strategies being implemented as part of the special education program and the extended counseling model. It would be sent to the parents to inform them of plans and to elicit support within the home setting. There are some admonitions that must be kept in mind when communicating in writing:

1. Communications should be done with full knowledge of the school administration. There may even be specific school policies concerning parental communications.
2. A *personal communication* should precede any form such as the management plan in Fig. 8-3 because the form may not be self-explanatory and may only confuse the parents.
3. It is generally recommended that sec-

---
*Official forms for due process procedures may be found in Appendix 2.

```
                        CONFERENCE REPORT

Conference date_____ Special Education Teacher_____
Student_____ Parents_____
Address_____ Phone_____
_____

Purpose of the conference:


Specific relevant information:


Information gained or modified during conference:


Conference outcomes:


Conference participants:


Is additional action needed:  Yes_____  No_____
If yes, specify action and time deadline:


_____ Action completed  _____ Date


_____          _____
  (Teacher's signature)                        (Date)
```

**Fig. 8-1.** Sample conference report form.

```
                          CONFERENCE SUMMARY


Special Education Teacher_____  Room no._____


Conference date_____  Student's name_____
_____


Purpose of conference:


Conference outcomes:


Conference participants:


Comments:
```

**Fig. 8-2.** Sample conference summary form.

```
                        MANAGEMENT PLAN


Date    (9/15)                  Anticipated review date   (10/30)

Student's name      (Meredith May)                        Age    (15)

Class(es) in which plan is being utilized     (resource room,

    American history, and biology)

Counselor    (Lena Spark)                                 Phone  (846-2261)

Teachers cooperating in plan      (resource room:. Ms. Anna McFadden;

     American history: Mr. Bill Hess:  biology: Ms. Barbara Berry)
```

| Target behavior(s) | Management plan summary |
|---|---|
| (Appropriate question asking during classroom instruction or lecture) | (1. Meredith will be reinforced with praise for asking for assistance or explanations from the teacher[s].<br>2. Questions asked concerning topics or situations unrelated to the purpose of the lesson will be ignored.<br>3. Questions asked at appropriate times during the instructional period will be immediately answered and Meredith will be reinforced for selecting the appropriate time.<br>4. Questions asked at inappropriate times during the instructional period will be ignored.) |

```
Reinforcers being used    (personal praise, positive responses from teachers,

privileges such as free time in the media center)

    ✓    The student is aware of the management plan being utilized and assisted

         in its development.

    _____ The student is NOT aware of the management plan being utilized.
```

**Fig. 8-3.** Parent communication form for management plans.

ondary students be shown the communications or at least informed about them.
4. Have a professional colleague check the correspondence for clarity and appropriateness.
5. Use clear, concise language.
6. Keep a copy for your own files.
7. Another caution . . . because of the Buckley amendment some older students may wish to bar parental access to records and data.

In addition to conferences and written communications, phone conversations represent a frequently used means of exchanging information. Phone conversations should be recorded in a log or perhaps on a form similar to the conference summary form. Regardless of the method, the teacher should make note of such communications.

**Parent organizations.** School personnel should encourage parents to participate in parent organizations (Cain, 1976). Unfortunately, the importance of such organizations is sometimes overlooked. These groups provide information to parents, become a medium for sharing ideas and problems, encourage involvement, organize valuable activities, and lay a foundation for parent training (Kroth, 1975).

Parent organizations can also provide support and evaluative feedback to the school. Advisory boards of parent organizations can be utilized to review various aspects of the school's program and contribute ideas as well as to offer constructive criticism. This feedback can be used to good advantage by the administrators and teachers willing to do so. Cooperatively, school and parent groups can identify program strengths and weaknesses and combine resources to secure better services. However, many parents of teenagers will not have much interest in such organizations.

Parent groups are often affiliates or chapters of national organizations such as Association for Children with Learning Disabilities (ACLD), Council for Exceptional Children (CEC), or Association for Retarded Citizens (ARC). Local groups may develop that do not have national ties, but parents should also be encouraged to participate in these major organizations.

## RELATIONSHIPS WITH PARAPROFESSIONALS

A number of problems are reported by teachers who use aides or volunteers: "They are more trouble than they are worth," "They soon try to take over the class," and "They are just in the way." These problems can be avoided if care is given to setting up and managing volunteer or aide programs. Paraprofessionals can play integral roles in an individualized classroom structure (Bijou, 1977) if properly *selected*, *trained*, and *supervised* (Mayhall et al., 1975).

### Selection

Selection begins with the identification of possible sources of aides, volunteers, and tutors such as parents, paid aides, school organizations, and community groups. Parents are used as paraprofessionals for clerical tasks and even for academic tutoring of students other than their own (McLoughlin et al., 1978; Poper, 1976). Some school districts employ full-time, paid aides to assist in instructional support activities and limited teaching. School organizations, such as Future Teachers of America (FTA), Youth for Handicapped (YH), and other service organizations may have members interested in being involved in paraprofessional services in classrooms. The special education program fortunate enough to be located near a college or university may find that many classes require students to volunteer a specified number of hours in a nearby school. These college students can be valuable to the special education teacher and at the same time can learn through the experience. Community service groups may become involved in supporting special education efforts, volunteering several hours of assistance. Groups of retired teachers in some areas contribute endless hours to school programs.

Once sources of aides have been identified the next step is actual selection. This may be a difficult process requiring a great deal of tact on the part of the teacher. Some of the most willing volunteers may not be well suited to the job or the situation. The following factors should be considered in selecting paraprofessionals:

1. Number of hours available per week and the exact time periods available
2. Experiences or talents that can be utilized
3. Personality and disposition of applicant
4. Relationship to any students in the program
5. Reasons for volunteering
6. Expectations concerning the experience

One of the primary keys to success in utilizing paraprofessionals is the attitude of the teacher toward those individuals. *A good rule of thumb is for teachers to select persons with whom they feel rapport and in whose presence they feel comfortable.*

## Training

Training of aides, volunteers, and tutors should be carefully planned to ensure that all parties understand what the job entails and to prevent the development of most of the problems commonly associated with the use of paraprofessionals in the classroom. The following aspects of training should be considered.

**Manual.** A training manual should be prepared in advance by the teacher for the aides' personal reference. It should include pertinent information such as school schedule, calendar, and daily schedule; phone number to call if unable to come; program philosophy emphasizing *confidentiality*, *commitment*, and *cooperation*; a map of the school building indicating important locations such as principal's office, workroom, library, media center, nurse's office, and restrooms; a list of equipment that aides are expected to be able to operate such as duplicator, copier, film projector, tape recorder, and earphones; a list of the students' names by period; and a brief summary of major behavioral expectations or rules of the classroom.

**Training sequence.** Participation in a brief training program should be required of all paraprofessionals. This will entail some work on the part of the teacher initially but will reduce the amount of individual orientation and training required throughout the program. The training should include a tour of the building; an explanation of the nature of the special education program and a brief orientation to the types of students served; a discussion of *confidentiality*; a discussion of the importance of dependability with instructions given about reporting when absences are necessary; identification of a designated place for the paraprofessional to store his or her materials, receive messages, and pick up assigned work (this relieves the teacher of having to stop and give instructions on the aide's arrival); orientation to equipment that the aide is expected to operate, including demonstration and practice; a review of the rules of the classroom; and an introduction to the location and care of materials they will be using such as scissors, glue, pencils, roll book, paper cutters, workbook, teachers' guides, blank tapes, and books.

All of the above training can be accomplished at one meeting if the teacher has planned properly. Those individuals unwilling to make the commitment to this one hour or so of training are probably not going to contribute much as aides and should be excluded from the paraprofessional program!

**Supervision and utilization**

Supervision and utilization of paraprofessionals need not detract from the amount of time the teacher has for individual pupil instruction. The amount of time required for supervision varies inversely with the structure provided through preplanning and orientation of the aides. There are some strategies, discussed below, that can improve utilization and reduce the supervision required.

**Tasks.** Select tasks for the aides that are appropriate; then make certain they understand each task. There really are no clear limits as to the nature of the tasks other than the teacher's ability to structure and the aide's ability to understand what is expected. However, there are two general categories of tasks:

- Clerical—making bulletin boards, duplicating work sheets, making graphs, checking out library resources, and taking roll
- Instructional support—making tapes, conducting drill sessions, leading discussion groups following a basic outline of major points, showing films and doing follow-up activities, doing individual tutoring following a teaching script developed by the teacher, and monitoring learning centers

**Communication.** The teacher should not have to stop each time an aide comes into the classroom and give instructions as to what needs to be done. Following are several ways to avoid this.

An individual mailbox for each aide can be used. As the teacher thinks of things to be done the next day or next week, instructions can be outlined and left for the aide. Examples include:

Date: 1/8

Prepare a taped reading of *Silas Marner*.
1. Secure a copy of the story from Ms. Duncan, librarian.
2. Read into tape (during the paraprofessional training sequence the teacher has shown the aides where the tapes are located, how to operate the recorder, and taping locations).
3. Review the tape once completed.
4. Label tape: title, length of time, reader's name.
5. Place in teacher's in-box.
6. Needed by: 1/12.

Date 1/8

Conduct a 15-minute discussion group on photosynthesis.
1. Study attached outline from text.
2. Review additional resources on subject available from media center and library.
3. Prepare any charts or graphs needed.
4. Be ready to conduct group with three students by 1/14.

Date 1/8

Prepare list of support materials available on our banking system.
1. Examine attached economics outline of objectives on banking.
2. Survey library and media center for books, films, charts, etc. on the topic.
3. Preview each of those.
4. Prepare complete list of those available and list preview comments concerning interest level, attractiveness, and appropriateness.
5. Return list to teacher: 1/13.

A group mailbox may be used if all aides are equally capable of performing all tasks. In this situation the above communications would be left and individual aides would select their own tasks.

Communication should also include feedback to paraprofessionals concerning their performance. Reinforcement in the form of a little note or a word of thanks should never be underestimated.

A bulletin board for aide communication is useful in some classrooms.

The important point to remember in supervision of paraprofessionals is that the ultimate responsibility for the program rests with the teacher but a cooperative spirit can make that responsibility more a pleasure than a burden.

## PEER TUTORS

Special mention should be made of the potential use of peer tutors in the secondary special education program. There has been considerable support for the use of 1:1 cross-age peer tutors over small group teacher instruction (Jenkins et al., 1974). This also can have benefits consistent with the affective goals of the special education program, including increased peer contact and peer understanding. Using peer tutors requires extremely careful selection and planning. The same procedures outlined above for other paraprofessionals should be followed, with additional emphasis placed on selection and structure.

Secondary handicapped students should be involved in the planning for use of peer tutors to ensure their cooperation and understanding of the process. Peer tutoring must be handled tactfully to prevent students from feeling inferior. Factors to be taken into consideration in avoiding such feelings include the age of tutors and students, the site of tutoring, the attitudes of both students, the maturity of the students, and the respect the student has for his or her tutor's ability.

The regular classroom teacher and handicapped students can be of great assistance in identifying possible peer tutors in the various subject areas. Each potential tutor should be interviewed by the special educator to determine willingness to participate, schedule of classes, subjects of interest, and relationships with students in the special education program.

Once peer tutors have been identified for the various subject areas and matched to mildly handicapped students, meeting times, activities, and locations can be decided by the students. Weekly reports should be given to the special education teacher concerning progress. The use of any volunteer should be handled in the same manner as a paid staff member. Volunteers who do not keep appointments or follow supervisory requirements should be dismissed because of the harm they can do to the program. Fig. 8-4 indicates some aspects of the peer tutoring to be monitored by the teacher.

## ROLE TO SUPPORT PERSONNEL
### Counselors

Responsibilities of the special education teacher and counselor obviously overlap because of the emphasis on affective education and the implementation of the extended counseling model (ECM). Chapter 5 includes a description of the role of the counselor and the components of the ECM as well as the relationship between the special education program and counseling services. A comfortable working relationship must be established between the two aspects of the secondary program and between the individuals directing those programs if the mildly handicapped student is to receive total benefit. Both professionals will have contact with handicapped students, regular teachers, and parents and therefore should coordinate their efforts.

Points of common interest to counselors and special education teachers include:
- Student progress data
- Parent interaction
- Personal-social development of students
- Teacher consultation
- Vocational choices of students

Greater results can be gained from time and energy expended cooperatively than in competition. The special education teacher should seek out the counselor at the begin-

PEER TUTORING REPORT

Tutor_____ Student_____ Date_____

Subject_____ Teacher_____

Special Education Teacher_____ Room no._____

Tutoring sessions conducted during the week:

Topics covered:

Tasks/problem areas unresolved:

Tasks completed:

Are the tutoring sessions proceeding without complication?

If not, what is the problem?

_____              _____
    (Tutor's signature)                          (Student's signature)

**Fig. 8-4.** Peer tutor report.

ning of the school year and set up an appointment to describe the program, learn about counseling services, and set the stage for interaction.

## Educational or pyschological examiners

Educational or psychological examiners are professionals responsible for data collection in the assessment/diagnostic process. The teacher can greatly facilitate the process by providing observational data on student behavior, pupil achievement data, and insight into social-emotional development. Examiners may not be housed in the building or even exclusively in the district and therefore may rely on the special education teacher to help coordinate student review.

The special educator is likely to use the services of the examiner more than other educators because of the IEP process itself and an increased orientation to using test data. The teacher should be acquainted with the various test instruments available, their purposes, limitations, and relationship to school performance. The time of the examiner can be more fully utilized if the special education teacher adheres to the following suggestions:

1. Be specific about the test desired or the exact question about the student's performance so that the examiner can identify an appropriate test.
2. Clearly state the reason for requesting an examination.
3. Provide data about the student, such as age, class placement, special sensory problems, daily schedule, birthdate, types/results of previous tests, and other demographic data.
4. Provide schedule of times available for posttesting conference with examiner.

## Speech therapist

Mildly handicapped students involved in speech therapy at the secondary school level will probably exhibit uncommon problems such as stuttering or voice disorders. There will be very few cases at the secondary level, as a rule. Contact between the therapist and the teacher may be limited but a vital ingredient in cases such as stuttering. The teacher may be able to assist the speech therapist by communicating on his or her behalf to mainstream teachers.

## School nurse

The relationship between the nurse and the special education teacher should be close because of the active role of the nurse. The nurse should be kept informed about students on medication because of the drug monitoring function. Sex and health information should be made available to handicapped secondary students through the school nursing program, although local and state laws will vary in this respect.

The special educator can aid the nurse in serving handicapped students through the following efforts:

1. Assisting in securing proper information about medication effects
2. Observing student behavior for signs of drug overdoses of prescribed drugs and street drugs
3. Informing students of nursing services available
4. Encouraging students to utilize health services
5. Informing nurse of health-related problems of students

## Role to regular teachers

The special education teacher's role to the regular secondary teacher does not lend itself to simple description. It is a multifaceted role affected by a number of variables such as the type of special education services in the program, training of the regular teaching staff, personalities of all involved, size of the school, nature of the student population, orientation of the administration, and luck! In Chapter 6 we described the training of the special educator, personality factors, and some responsibilities of the job. All of these contribute to the amount of interaction of the special education teacher and regular educators. The special educator is considered to be in a unique position to work with others (Dinkmeyer & Carlson, 1973), but concerted effort may be necessary for this to come to fruition.

*Establishing rapport* would be the obvious first step in initiating a cooperative relationship. Initial overtures on the part of the special education teacher may be met with resentment from the regular teaching staff (Newcomer, 1977). Younger special education teachers may be victimized by negative attitudes of veteran teachers. Developing rapport may entail considerable patience, which is based on a good track record rather than on promises. The special education teacher should understand some of the reasons for the resentment:

1. The ratio of students to teacher in the special education room may be a stark contrast to the ratio in most secondary classes, in spite of the fact that the actual work load is qualitatively similar.

2. The training of secondary teachers does not include courses in education of exceptional children, and most teachers lack knowledge of the special education program.

3. There is much misunderstanding about the purpose of special education, and many teachers expect the special educator to "cure these students."

4. Individualized instruction is a foreign concept to secondary teachers.

5. Interdisciplinary work is also a foreign concept within the segregated framework of the secondary school staffed with departmentalized specialists.

6. Most teachers already feel overburdened with their regular responsibilities.

7. The special education teacher is viewed as unrealistic and overzealous in attempting to "save the world"; a manifestation of another governmental fad that will pass once funding ceases to be available!

8. Money would be better spent on "bright" students and programs and salaries.

*Communicating* with the regular faculty is the avenue to cooperation. Communicating about specific efforts undertaken in the special education room can be extremely helpful. An example of a cooperative effort between the special education teacher, counselor, and teacher is depicted in Fig. 8-5. Awareness of the kind of students served, types of services provided, and areas of interaction between the special education program and the regular program can facilitate understanding. Achieving this level of awareness may require the special educator to do the following:

1. Prepare a brief manual outlining the various components of the special education program
2. Spend unscheduled time meeting other teachers informally
3. Conduct in-service programs
4. Distribute a brief newsletter describing special education services
5. Select specific teachers to cultivate as allies of the program

Serving the mildly handicapped adolescent requires that the special educator identify possible allies, potential problems, and areas of interaction. Knowing what is happening in the regular program is vital to maintaining a viable, responsive special education program. The component of the resource room identified as *mainstreaming support* in Chapter 6 is an example of this interaction; mainstreaming support activities of the special education teacher are given in the outline below. It includes teacher consultation, and this requires knowledge of the regular school curriculum and staff.

ADJUSTMENT TRAINING

TEACHER INFORMATION FORM

Student __(Kama Cooper)__  Counselor __(L. Spark)__  Date __(10/18)__

Special Education Teacher __(A. McFadden)__  Room no. __(103P)__

| Adjustment problem | Student coping plan | Suggested teacher support |
|---|---|---|
| (Self-control in lecture situations) | (1. Sit in a location conducive to eye contact with the teacher. <br> 2. Take outline notes that require active listening. <br> 3. Chart attending time to show progress.) | (1. Provide extensive eye contact with student. <br> 2. Encourage attention of student through positive body language. <br> 3. Rearrange seating or allow student to choose. <br> 4. Watch for signs of attention loss and change lecture position or approach to regain attention. <br> 5. Reward/reinforce attending behavior with praise or privileges.) |

**Fig. 8-5.** Sample form for liaison communication of adjustment training plan to regular teacher.

I. Interpretation of student data
   A. Explanation of test data
   B. Implications for instruction
   C. Realistic expectations for student progress
II. Content development
   A. Examining course content for major concepts
   B. Task analysis applied to course content
   C. Use of compensatory teaching techniques
   D. Suggest parallel curricula and materials
III. Classroom structure
   A. Suggest physical changes
   B. Outline alternative methods of instruction other than lecture
   C. Identify practical means of individualizing the course
IV. Classroom management
   A. Provide information on types of management strategies such as token economies/contracting
   B. Suggest possible reinforcement techniques

**In-service programs.** Many school districts have initiated in-service education programs for regular educators to acquaint them with P.L. 94-142 and its implications. Inservice training programs usually consist of some combination of three levels of training: awareness, instructional adjustments, and instructional technique development. The special education teacher may be called on to conduct such training sessions or to arrange for an outside consultant to conduct them.

Our admonitions concerning in-service efforts include the following:
1. If attendance is required expect some resistance.
2. Consider the in-service consumers' needs.
3. Avoid too many generalities.
4. Tie the session to practical considerations encountered by the regular staff.
5. Make certain that concrete suggestions/materials are available.
6. Attempt to get regular teachers to participate by demonstrating their techniques.

## SPECIALIZED ROLES OF SPECIAL EDUCATORS

Due to the nature of specific types of secondary programs, some special educators may be employed to perform services to students in a unique or uncommon manner. The following types of responsibilities may be required in some settings but with different titles than used here.

### Vocational adjustment coordinator

In some states, a special educator with additional training in vocational education and vocational rehabilitation may be used as a supervisor of students placed in the community. The role of the coordinator would be to establish relationships with the business community, assist in the evaluation of potential jobs in the community, provide information to the school about the needs of students in the field, and to generally coordinate the off-campus training of students. In many cases, this professional would not have specific teaching responsibilities although weekly seminars with trainees on the campus would be a reasonable instructional activity. The need to relate to business managers and employers, to follow up student progress, and to coordinate services between vocational rehabilitation services and the school preclude teaching responsibility.

Some sheltered workshops employ a person with training and knowledge in the area of handicapped adults and vocational training for the purpose of establishing relationships with businesses and industries of the community so that contracts for work may be secured.

### Facilitator

In some cooperative arrangements, special educators are employed in vocational training programs to deliver direct instructional services to students who are primarily in need of job- or task-specific reading and mathematics. A student may be working in auto body repair but be unable to read the required manual. The special educator, sometimes called a facilitator, provides the link between the instructional program of the vocational class and remedial or tutorial assistance.

## Vocational rehabilitation counselor

In many vocational programs of secondary schools that deal with handicapped students, a vocational rehabilitation counselor will have contact with the school. The rehabilitation counselor is employed by the state and located in a regional office. The many services that may be provided to handicapped students include covering the costs of psychological and medical examinations and of specialized training as well as purchase of prosthetic devices or specialized tools to make a handicapped person employable. Under some arrangements, financial support to the program and to employers for training handicapped students may be provided.

## Resource-consultant

The resource teacher as a consultant to the regular teacher is consistent with the intent to integrate mildly handicapped students into the regular program. The implication is that special education teachers be viewed as a support resource of general education in serving all students (Beery, 1974). We recognize that many of the strategies identified in Chapters 5 and 10 as instructional and support activities actually represent sound pedagogy for all students. Consultation, an indirect service, can have a long-lasting ripple effect on educational practices (Montgomery, 1978; Ozer & Dworkin, 1974). However, there are some difficulties associated with the teacher-consultant role:

1. It requires the regular teacher to change the view that the special student is the private domain of the special education teacher (Newcomer, 1977).
2. Regular education must acknowledge that large numbers of students not identified as special are experiencing some kind of difficulty in school (Swift & Spivack, 1975).
3. Recognition of the fact that properly trained resource personnel can affect significant gains in achievement for pupils at all ability levels (Cantrell & Cantrell, 1976).

## RELATIONSHIPS IN THE COMMUNITY

As noted previously, part of the professional role of the special educator will be that of providing programs for community clubs and organizations. Some recommendations for group presentations were presented under the heading of "Public Relations" in Chapter 5.

There are other professional demands that may require or invite community or state participation of the special education teacher. These may be varied, infrequent, and time consuming, but important nonetheless. Youth groups, advisory boards, advocacy groups, club memberships, and many other activities tangentially related to the professional status of the teacher may prevail as out-of-school role functions. Community activities can be professionally and personally rewarding. The teacher should, however, be careful to avoid overcommitments. Rest and relaxation are important to mental health and effective teaching.

Because of the problems of some mildly handicapped students, there may be occasion for the special education teacher to have contact with various juvenile officers, police, courts, and community agencies. It is strongly recommended that before the teacher respond to requests for information or other actions, that the nature of the request be understood, that implications are clear, and that the administration be fully apprised. Rights of students, parents, and the teacher should be respected and protected.

## SUMMARY

This chapter was presented to specify the duties and responsibilities of a specialist in performance of professional roles associated with relationships in the educational setting. These included the relationships of the special teacher with the administration, parents, paraprofessionals, counselors, regular classroom teachers, and others. The means of identifying role expectations were explained, concrete responsibilities were indicated, and a variety of methodologies and forms were listed to assist the teacher in carrying out responsibilities associated with the teaching roles. Unlike other teaching roles, the specialist is expected to support teachers, parents, and administrators to a much greater extent. The success of the program is greatly determined by other activities than direct pupil services. The more the teacher addresses these related issues, the more likely the major effort of direct pupil service will be enhanced. Included in this chapter were specific recommendations for handling administrative responsibilties, communicating with parents, conducting conferences, training paraprofessionals, supervision of aides, and conducting in-service programs. The importance attached to these issues in this volume underscores the increasing significance of emerging factors in the teaching role that are not directly related to specific teaching methodologies.

### REFERENCES AND READINGS

Barten, H. H., & Barten, S. S. *Children and their parents in brief therapy*. New York: Behavioral Publications, 1973.

Beery, K. Mainstreaming: A problem and an opportunity for general education. *Focus on Exceptional Children*, 1974, 6, 1-7.

Bijou, S. Practical implications of an interactional model of child development. *Exceptional Children*, 1977, 44, 6-14.

Cain, L. F. Parent groups: Their role in a better life for the handicapped. *Exceptional Children*, 1976, 42, 432-437.

Cantrell, R. P., & Cantrell, M. L. Preventive mainstreaming: Impact of a supportive services program on pupils. *Exceptional Children*, 1976, 42, 381-386.

Dinkmeyer, D., & Carlson, J. *Consulting: Facilitating human potential and change processes*. Columbus, Ohio: Merrill, 1973.

Escovar, P. L. Another change for learning—the assessment class. *Teaching Exceptional Children*, 1976, 9, 2-3.

Heffernan, H., & Todd, V. E. *Elementary teachers' guide to working with parents*. Englewood Cliffs, N.J.: Parker, 1969.

Jenkins, J., Mayhall, W., Peschka, C., & Jenkins, L. Comparing small group and tutorial instruction in resource rooms. *Exceptional Children*, 1974, 40, 245-250.

Kroth, R.: *Communicating with parents of exceptional children*. Denver: Love, 1975.

Kroth, R. Parents—powerful and necessary allies, *Teaching Exceptional Children*, 1978, 10, 88-90.

Kroth, R. L., & Simpson, R. *Parent conferences as a teaching strategy*. Denver: Love, 1977.

Long, A. Easing the stress of parent-teacher conferences. *Today's Education*, 1976, 65, 84-85.

Mayhall, W., Jenkins, J., Chestnut, N., et al. Supervision and site of instruction as factors in tutorial programs. *Exceptional Children*, 1975, 42, 151-154.

McAleer, I. M. The parent, teacher, and child as conference partners. *Teaching Exceptional Children*, 1978, 10, 103-105.

McLoughlin, J. A., Edge, D., & Strenecky, B. Perspective on parental involvement in the diagnosis and treatment of learning disabled children. *Journal of Learning Disabilities*, 1978, 11(5), 291-296.

Montgomery, M. D. The special educator as a consultant: Some strategies. *Teaching Exceptional Children*, 1978, 10, 110-112.

Newcomer, P. Special educational services for the mildly handicapped: Beyond a diagnostic and remedial model. *Journal of Special Education*, 1977, 11.

Ozer, M. N., & Dworkin, N. E. The assessment of children with learning problems: An inservice teacher training program. *Journal of Learning Disabilities*, 1974, 7, 539-544.

Poper, L. *A handbook for tutorial programs*. Brooklyn, N.Y.: Lab, Inc., 1976.

Swift, M. S., & Spivack, G. *Alternative teaching strategies*. Champaign, Ill.: Research Press, 1975.

Yoshida, R. K., Fenton, D., Kaufman, M. J., & Maxwell, J. P. Parental involvement in the special education pupil planning process: The school's perspective. *Exceptional Child*, 1978, 44, 531-534.

# SECTION FOUR

# THE PROGRAM

The final section of this text centers on the mechanics of program development at the secondary level. Common elements for coordination of the program are elucidated for the practitioner who needs a comprehensive plan for the use of physical space, the selection and use of materials, record keeping, and other management strategies. These topics are included in Chapter 9 and precede the discussion of program models.

Chapter 10 is presented as an effort to acquaint practitioners with a new concept in the education of handicapped students at the secondary level. The major emphasis is placed on accommodation, a term used to describe a variety of ways to make the secondary curriculum and general environment more conducive to the learning needs of mildly handicapped adolescents, especially those who are able to maximally benefit from the general school curriculum. Much of the focus of special education has been on remediation, but the ability of students to succeed in many classes of the secondary curriculum requires the cooperation of mainstream teachers in a planned response.

The nature of remedial programming is considered in Chapter 11. This of course is a rather traditional approach. However, the concept of functional literacy is regarded as an important consideration in secondary programming. This is generally regarded as a full sixth-grade competency in reading. Chapter 11 includes criteria for determining academic functioning in reading and arithmetic through the sixth-grade level. Also included are discussions of remedial techniques that might be used with mildly handicapped adolescents and consideration of important issues about remediation in secondary school.

Chapter 12 concludes the text with a presentation of a discussion of career education and vocational preparation of mildly handicapped students. The options in vocational programming are plentiful, but the discouraging fact is that many students will not find vocational adjustment easily obtainable, in spite of careful training, because of inevitable economic and technological trends. The schools cannot restructure society or correct the inequities of the work force, but they can continuously change to shift training emphases to match the demands of the society and to enhance the opportunities of mildly handicapped persons who have all too frequently been trained for dead-end jobs and lives of maladjustment.

Chapter 9

# COORDINATION OF THE PROGRAM

The philosophies of the special teacher and the administration dictate how the program is related to the total high school curriculum. It may be viewed as integrated with the other classes, isolated and directed toward skill remediation or vocational instruction, substituting for regular courses, or combining all of these purposes. The expectations for the special program and the student outcomes desired determine how services are structured and managed. State regulations concerning the operation of the special education room may encompass such aspects as the amount of time students spend in the program, the space required, and the relationship of instruction to graduation credit, grading, curriculum, and materials. There is some variance in the individual state plans in regard to these issues, so the teacher should be acquainted with the state regulations and guidelines affecting the program.

The special education supervisor should provide assistance in initiating the program so that it is consistent with other special education services offered in the district. Criteria by which the program effectiveness will be evaluated should be acknowledged in organizing services. For instance, if the number of students served is considered indicative of efficiency of operation, coordinating the program should be handled differently than if grades earned by students in regular classes is a major concern.

After these administrative determinants have been identified, the next step in designing the program includes these considerations:

- Organization and scheduling
- Daily planning
- Monitoring and record keeping
- Classroom management strategies
- Budget

| Day | Period | Grade/Students | Activity |
| --- | --- | --- | --- |
| Monday | 1 | 9: Kevin<br>Beth<br>Susan<br>Rebecca<br>Sam | Tutoring/instruction: general math<br><br><br>Tutoring/instruction: science<br>Remedial instruction: handwriting |
|  | 2 | 11: Robert<br>Marc<br>Sally<br>Mike<br>Graham | Remedial reading: decoding<br><br><br>Tutoring/instruction: American history |
| Tuesday | 1 | 9: Beth<br>Leslie<br>Tom<br>Sam<br>Kevin | Remedial reading: suffixes<br><br>Tutoring/instruction: English<br>Tutoring/instruction: science<br>Tutoring/instruction: general math |
|  | 2 | 11: Marc<br>Mike<br>Ben<br>Sue<br>Lee | Tutoring/instruction: American history<br><br>Remedial reading: decoding<br>Remedial reading: decoding<br>Tutoring/instruction: general math |

## ORGANIZATION AND SCHEDULING

The organizational pattern affects how students are served and how the daily program is planned. Self-contained classrooms are organized to serve a particular population and a specific age range. EMR classrooms may be established for each grade level or to serve all high school grades, depending on the size of the school and administrative policy. Even though some students are served in a self-contained classroom, they may be integrated into physical education, art, and other school-wide activities, requiring the organization of the classroom to accommodate such outside class schedules. In the case of the resource room model, the organization has to fit overall school policy requiring the resource teacher to use a particular structure, such as serving all sophomore students or all students with problems in reading at one period, or scheduling all seniors in the morning periods. Programs operate within a variety of organizational frameworks, which are included here for consideration.

**Grade or age level grouping.** In grade or age level grouping all LD or behaviorally disordered students of the same age or grade are scheduled into the resource room during a certain period or periods. This is usually done to conform to a fixed schedule dictated by the total school plan. A daily lesson plan for the resource teacher might look like the example shown on p. 194.

**Subject area grouping.** Students are scheduled into the resource program based on the area of the curriculum in which instructional assistance is needed. An example is given below.

| Day | Period | Grade/Students | Activity |
|---|---|---|---|
| Monday | 1 | 9: Tom<br>10: Bill<br>9: Sue<br>11: Allen | Language arts |

**Remedial area grouping.** Remedial area grouping works in much the same manner as the two plans just described, but students are assigned by specific skill areas requiring remediation. For instances, students needing remedial instruction in handwriting would be scheduled during the same period. This structure is usually utilized in those programs emphasizing remedial reading skills. To group students in this fashion requires that the desired skills be task analyzed so that instructional groups can, in fact, benefit from instruction. Chapter 11 is devoted to the remedial aspects of programming.

**Comprehensive programming.** Comprehensive programming calls for placement based on individual needs and individual student schedules. Groups may evolve but need not be forced in order to complete a schedule. A resource room coordinated via a comprehensive plan makes scheduling an individual matter; students come to the resource room for either accommodatory or remedial assistance in any area. The scheduled time fits into an open slot in the student's schedule who is assigned to the resource room. Another alternative is to assign students to the resource room for the regular class period being supplanted by the resource program. This permits the resource teacher to operate the program to provide appropriate individual instruction.

A description of the comprehensive approach is found in Chapter 10 designated as an *interactional model*, but a brief outline is in order here. This model utilizes learning centers for each curricular area, remedial instruction, reinforcement, tutoring, direct instruction, and modified materials. It provides the framework through which the resource teacher can provide *individualized* and *individual* instruction without forced grouping. It also provides a method of maximizing the instructional impact of the teacher.

**Scheduling.** As a major aspect of successful programming, scheduling is obviously tied to the organizational system selected. It is important to the teacher because of the development of daily lesson plans. However, it is equally important to regular teachers with whom the students are assigned and to the students themselves. Scheduling to serve students at a convenient time should be given important consideration. Its importance in the successful resource program is even greater because of the higher frequency of student integration found in such programs. Scheduling in the resource program, a complex process, may be accomplished in one or more of the following ways.

*Study hall time.* Some secondary students spend their study hall periods in the resource room receiving compensatory or remedial instruction or both. Teachers using this approach emphasize that it eliminates the problem of conflicting periods but also results in bunching of students at certain periods of the day. Also, one period per day may not be sufficient for all students. It would appear that study hall periods are probably more productively spent in the resource room and should be considered an additional instructional time.

*Release time.* Students may attend the resource room during the periods when content courses related to their instructional needs are being taught in the regular program. Attendance in this scheduling approach allows for *course supplantation* or *shared instruction*. In course supplantation the students would attend the resource room for special instruction in a subject area because they are unable to function in the regular class. Shared instruction means that the student attends American history part of the time in the regular classroom while receiving special outside assistance from the resource room. This can also mean that some days the student comes to the resource room during the history period to take tests, listen to taped assignments, or receive other instruction.

*Assigned period.* Resource-room programs may be given a time period within the regular school day just as English, history, or P.E. LD and behaviorally disordered students are scheduled into the resource room through the same process as they are assigned to their other classes.

*Reduced load.* One administrative option is for students to extend, by one year or so, the period of time required to complete high school. If this option is selected, a reduced course load is carried each semester by the student. Reducing the load allows additional time for supportive interventions in the resource room. Taking fewer courses reduces the fragmentation of effort for the student and the resource teacher, a strategy that may seldom be used but one that can have great results.

*Extra-time arrangement.* Noon periods and before or after school can add up to a substantial amount of time for the highly motivated adolescent. However, motivated students may also be few, especially at the beginning of the program. High school students also have jobs that may interfere with such scheduling. Teachers reporting the use of these blocks of time also report the extensive use of reinforcement and management systems as well as specifically selected populations of students. Making the resource room available during such time periods should be considered, but the resource program cannot realistically be expected to function with *only* these periods.

**Interactional model.** Scheduling in connection with this approach can be accomplished through any combination of the above techniques, depending on the individual student. Learning centers provide a means to individualized instruction during any time period. The resource teacher can serve students on a flexible schedule that allows them maximum instruction as well as participation in the mainstream.

## DAILY PLANNING

Regardless of the organizational pattern or the service delivery model, the special education teacher must develop daily lesson plans for each period. Although the self-contained room serves the same students throughout the day, the special teacher must plan to serve all students in all instructional areas, as well as providing support in those instances when students are integrated into regular classes. In the case of the resource model, daily planning can become extremely difficult as 5 to 15 students are served each period, all having a wide variety of needs. Subject-area or remedial-area assignment in the resource room appears to be the structure permitting the easiest daily planning. However, this is a misconception. In reality, if the special education program serves individual needs, it is very unlikely that much grouping can be accomplished in either of the service delivery models. Within any group of special students a wide variety of problems and abilities exists. The variance in conceptual and social-emotional development would also make grouping ineffective, necessitating individual instruction. The basic message for daily planning is obvious: *instruction must be provided for the individual student.*

It is necessary to make a distinction between *individual instruction* and *individualized instruction*. Many teachers provide individualized instruction but cannot manage to provide individual instruction. *Individualized instruction is instruction specifically planned for a particular student*. The teacher matches instructional materials to the learning objectives of the student. This could mean assigning the student to work in a group or selecting the appropriate workbook page. The student who is taught in a history discussion group may be said to be receiving individualized instruction if the student's needs were examined and it was determined by the teacher that this group would provide the required instruction. However, if the same student is placed in the group merely to simplify scheduling, then it is *not* individualized instruction. *Individual instruction is teaching that is delivered on a one-to-one basis.* Individual instruction can be provided through tutors, aides, and technological supports, as well as by the teacher personally. Thus if a teacher instructs a group of ten students in a particular concept or skill that each student needs, individualized instruction is taking place. If each of the ten students is taught separately, individual instruction has been used.

This may appear to be a matter of semantics and unrelated to the actual coordination of a program. However, when the outcomes expected of programs are examined, it becomes apparent that this is not an artificial distinction. Two of the outcomes generally expected are that individual students will exhibit increases in academic achievement and that a certain number will be served each day in the program. Few, if any, programs can afford the luxury of having only one student in the room at any given time. More typically, there are 1 to 15 pupils served each period of the day. Therefore the teacher must structure the program in such a manner as to provide both individualized and individual instruction to meet expected outcomes. It is the same problem regular teachers have always had: what do you do with the others while providing individual instruction?

Teachers can and do provide individualized instruction. Training programs and college textbooks are packed with information concerning assessment of individual needs and development of instructional strategies.

As one new teacher said, "I know how to provide individualized instruction, but my professors forgot to show me how to do it for 35 students at one time." What is reflected in this statement is that teachers are trained in matching instructional strategies and materials to test profiles and learning objectives, but they are not taught how to plan and organize to do so with more than one pupil at a time. If teachers could function in a clinical setting, individualized and individual instruction would be synonymous because there would be one student at a time for whom instruction would be personally designed and delivered. Such is not the case even in the resource room. Teachers must serve several students during the same period.

Comprehensive programming is an effective and practical way to furnish appropriate instruction and provides a solution to the problem of group versus individual instruction. Learning centers, aides, tutors, technical supports, and modified materials facilitate flexible scheduling and free the teacher for one-to-one instruction. Planning addresses the need for individual and individualized instruction through management of physical space, resources, time, and student behavior (Fig. 9-1). It provides the means for converting the special education room into a total service delivery model and prevents it from becoming simply a room in which the instructional groups are smaller than those in the regular classroom.

## Considerations in comprehensive planning

Fig. 9-1 depicts the variables involved in planning a comprehensive program:
- Resources
- Space
- Time
- Student behaviors

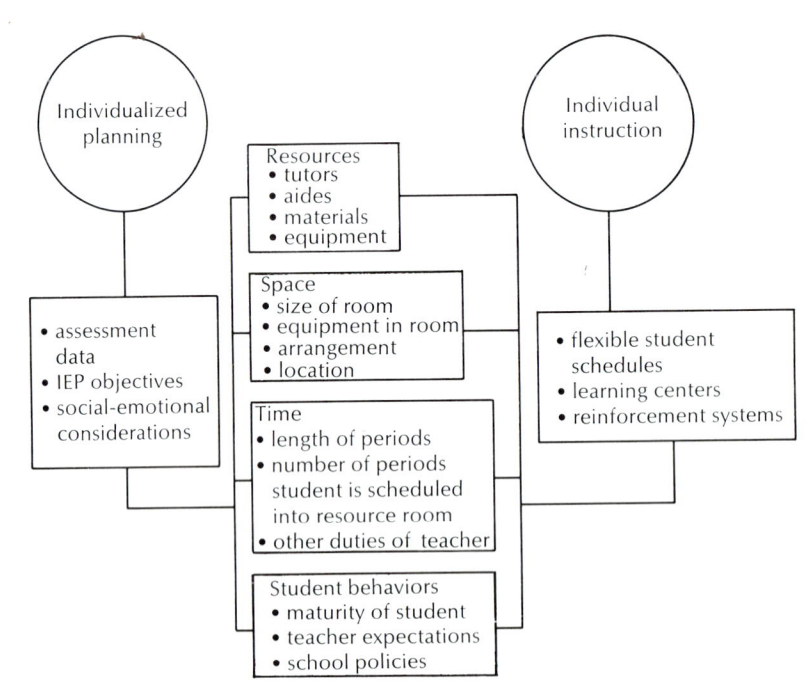

**Fig. 9-1.** Comprehensive programming plan.

Good planning provides a means for examining the variables that can affect the amount and quality of individual instruction rather than specifying a common program. Teachers using this model will find differences in the variables and will therefore design different programs. The model itself is designed to facilitate just such program planning and development. No two programs will be identical.

**Resources.** In order to develop any service plan, available resources within the system must be identified and additional resources may need to be secured. *Materials* are important resources for the teacher, and their selection and care should receive serious consideration. The use of an evaluation model can aid the teacher in making decisions concerning selection of materials.

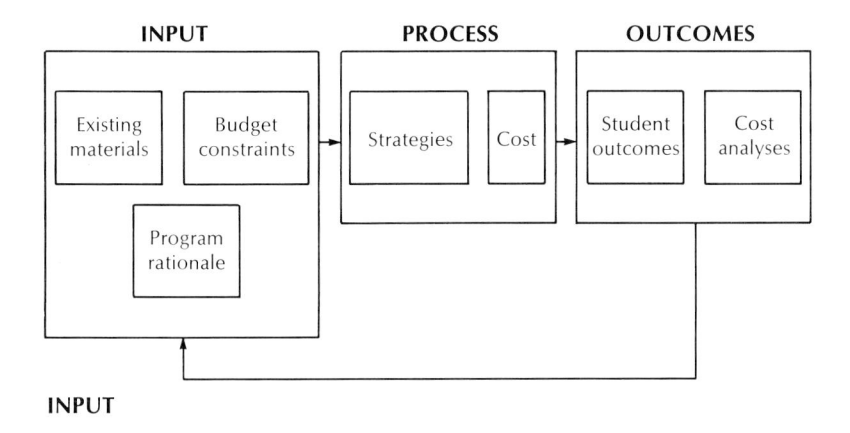

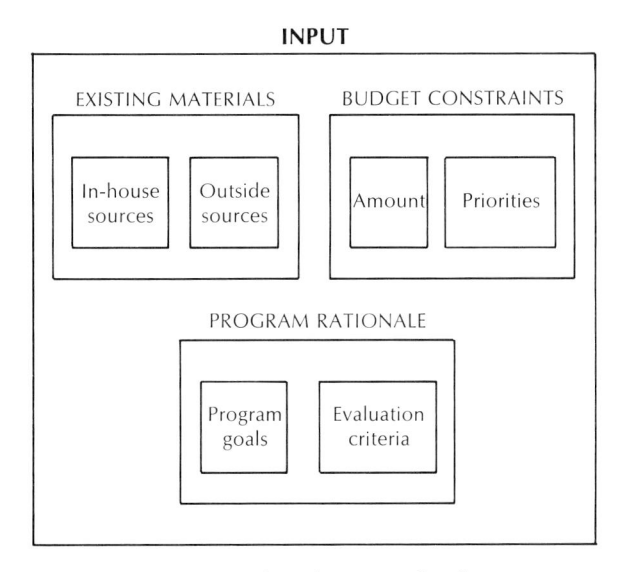

**Fig. 9-2.** Materials: selection and utilization.

*Existing materials*

*In-house sources.* Many teachers overlook materials available to them, concentrating on new purchases. Materials provided to the special program should be carefully examined for alternative uses or possible modifications. Materials available to regular classes should also be examined for possible use in the program. Listed below are some general steps in evaluating the availability of materials:

1. Inventory those materials provided in the resource room.
2. Examine the basic supplies provided by the school such as paper, staples, ditto masters and other copying supplies, as well as other consumables.
3. Find out the allotments of consumables, if such limits exist.
4. Obtain a list of materials and supplies such as workbooks, laboratory manuals, and tests required in each subject-area class.
5. Examine the building inventory, listing instructional supports such as maps, models, and charts housed in regular classrooms.
6. Secure a list of instructional support materials available through the school media center or library or both.
7. Survey regular classroom teachers to locate any teacher-made instructional aids available on loan.
8. Examine the basic texts and instructional supports such as filmstrips used or workbooks assigned in regular classes.

*Outside sources.* Frequently, materials are available at little or no cost if teachers are aware of their existence and are willing to scrutinize community sources. Some suggested actions include:

1. Request a list of free films available through the state education department, nearby universities, or other agencies.
2. Check local public libraries and professional organizations for materials or funds that could be utilized.
3. Explore local stores and industries for possible materials used as displays or for purchase (such purchases are tax deductible as professional deductions).
4. Peruse sources of free materials such as:
   a. *Free and Inexpensive Learning Materials*
      Norman R. Moore, Editor
      Division of Survey and Field Services
      George Peabody College for Teachers
      Nashville, Tennessee 37203
   b. Educators Progress Service Inc.
      Randolph, Wisconsin 53956
5. Contact local or national instructional materials center. A national network of Special Education Instructional Materials Centers and Regional Materials Centers (SEIMC/RMC) acquire, catalogue, and loan materials to educators free or at minimal costs. Table 11 lists the regional centers and the areas served.

**Budget constraints**

*Amount.* Typically, each classroom teacher is given a specified amount to spend on materials. The special education teacher may or may not have a line item in the budget. Even if there is it may be difficult to get administrators to reveal the amount, but this is information needed by the teacher before definite purchasing decisions can be made. If an amount is allotted to the program, the teacher may have control of its use but this may have to be approved by several superiors. Some teachers have also found that, in the event the amount is insufficient, good documentation of need can result in additional

**Table 11.** Special Education Instructional Materials Centers and Regional Materials Centers (SEIMC/RMC)

| Region | Areas | Addresses of centers |
|---|---|---|
| 1 | Alaska<br>Hawaii<br>Idaho<br>Montana<br>Oregon<br>Washington<br>Wyoming<br>Guam<br>Samoa<br>Trust territory | Northwest ALRC*<br>University of Oregon<br>Clinical Services Building, third floor<br>Eugene, Oregon 97403<br>503-686-3591 |
| 2 | California | California ALRC<br>600 Commonwealth Avenue, Suite 1304<br>Los Angeles, California 90005<br>213-381-2104 |
| 3 | Arizona<br>Colorado<br>Nevada<br>New Mexico<br>Utah<br>Bureau of Indian Affairs | Southwest ALRC<br>New Mexico State University<br>Box 3 AW<br>Las Cruces, New Mexico 88003<br>505-646-1017 |
| 4 | Arkansas<br>Iowa<br>Kansas<br>Missouri<br>Nebraska<br>North Dakota<br>Oklahoma<br>South Dakota | Midwest ALRC<br>Drake University<br>1336 26th St.<br>Des Moines, Iowa 50311<br>515-217-3951 |
| 5 | Texas | Texas ALRC<br>University of Texas at Austin<br>College of Education Building<br>1912 Speedway<br>Austin, Texas 78712<br>512-471-3145 |
| 6 | Indiana<br>Michigan<br>Minnesota<br>Wisconsin | Great Lakes ALRC<br>Michigan Dept. of Education<br>P.O. Box 3008<br>Lansing, Michigan 48909<br>517-373-9443 |

*Area Learning Resource Center.

*Continued.*

**Table 11.** Special Education Instructional Materials Centers and Regional Materials Centers (SEIMC/RMC)—cont'd

| Region | Areas | Addresses of centers |
|---|---|---|
| 7 | Illinois | ALRC<br>Materials Development and Dissemination<br>Specialized Educational Services<br>Illinois Office of Education<br>100 North First Street<br>Springfield, Illinois 62777<br>217-782-2436 |
| 8 | Ohio | Ohio ALRC<br>933 High Street<br>Worthington, Ohio 43085<br>614-466-2650 |
| 9 | Connecticut<br>Maine<br>Massachusetts<br>New Hampshire<br>New Jersey<br>Rhode Island<br>Vermont | Northeast ALRC<br>168 Bank Street<br>Highstown, New Jersey 08520<br>609-448-4775 |
| 10 | New York | New York State ALRC<br>55 Elk Street, Room 117<br>Albany, New York 12234<br>518-474-2251 |
| 11 | Pennsylvania | Pennsylvania ALRC<br>573 North Main Street<br>Doylestown, Pennsylvania 18901<br>215-345-8080 |
| 12 | Delaware<br>District of Columbia<br>Kentucky<br>Maryland<br>North Carolina<br>Tennessee<br>Virginia<br>West Virginia<br>Virgin Islands | Mid-East ALRC<br>University of Kentucky<br>123 Porter Building<br>Lexington, Kentucky 40506 |
| 13 | Alabama<br>Florida<br>Georgia<br>Louisiana<br>Mississippi<br>South Carolina<br>Puerto Rico | Southwest ALRC<br>Auburn University at Montgomery<br>Highway 80 East<br>Montgomery, Alabama 36117<br>205-279-9110, Ext. 258 |

funding from the administration. This justification should include:
- Intended use of the materials
- Number of students to use materials
- Period of time of use
- Cost
- Life expectancy of item purchased

An organized justification based on facts will be more effective with administrators than emotional statements of opinion. A well–thought out presentation may even result in the realization that the item really is not necessary or worth the cost.

***Priorities.*** Identifying the importance of certain materials to the program can aid decision making. Some priorities may be set by school policy, which will also affect purchasing choices. For example, materials relating to reading instruction may be favored as an overall school priority and may therefore be generally available. In some instances vocational information materials may be given preference as part of an effort to infuse career education into programming. In any event, school and resource room priorities should be part of a long-term plan. The special teacher may wish to purchase expensive materials by saving a portion of the yearly amount to carry over to the following year, thus requiring a plan for the program.

**Program rationale**
***Program goals.*** The goals of the program affect all aspects, including the selection of materials. For instance, a program with the major emphasis on remedial instruction will require extensive remedial materials. Programs incorporating affective goals will need materials for developing social-emotional objectives. Keeping program goals in mind will aid the teacher in selecting materials.

***Evaluation criteria.*** The criteria and general bases for evaluation of the program should be clearly stated prior to initiation of the program. Programs based on the number of students served will necessitate somewhat different materials than those programs evaluated against individual student progress. Such evaluative criteria must be determined cooperatively by the school administration and special education personnel and must include state requirements.

**Process**

**Strategies**

***Target population.*** The population of mildly handicapped adolescents varies, exhibiting a broad spectrum of learning characteristics and instructional needs. The nature of the population served should be an important consideration in utilizing materials. Factors to consider include:

**PROCESS**

| STRATEGIES | | COST | |
|---|---|---|---|
| Target population | Format | Number of students | Proportion of budget |
| Difficulty level | Level of independence | Durability | |

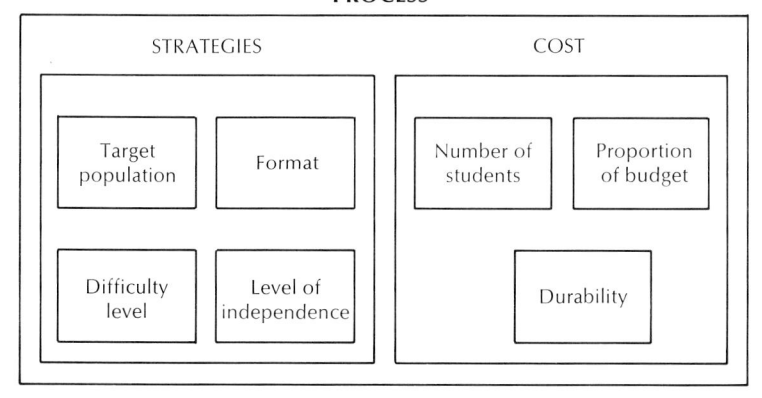

1. Age of students
2. Type of instructional program most frequently used
3. Presence of any additional handicapping conditions
4. Previous educational experiences (e.g., exposure to programming with a heavy workbook emphasis might lead the teacher to avoid any use of workbooks)
5. Reinforcement systems used effectively with this population
6. Special interests of the students

The consideration of additional materials should be delayed until there has been time to interact with the students served in the program. Purchases should always be made with the target population in mind.

*Format.* The format of the materials must be carefully examined for compatibility with programming approaches and student needs. Aspects to be considered include:
1. Size of print
2. Need for accompanying supplies (such as special pencils)
3. Clarity of information presented
4. Organization of materials
5. Appropriateness for age group
6. Presence of any grade level indication
7. Storage requirements
8. Hidden costs (updating, service, repair, etc.)

The learning characteristics discussed under "Target Population" above aid the teacher in evaluating the appropriateness of the format. Students exhibiting a high level of distractibility or poor initial learning require materials with reduced extraneous stimuli. In printed matter this means more use of white space on each page. Many considerations should be made to account for learning characteristics.

*Difficulty level.* Materials should be scrutinized carefully prior to purchase because the grade, subject matter, or ability level indicated by the manufacturer or publisher may not be accurate. Mildly handicapped students may not fit the exact grade specifications indicated and yet could benefit from instruction with the item. Also, inconsistencies have been noted among competing materials identified for a particular grade level, making it a somewhat unreliable clue to the use of the item. The teacher should note the grade or ability level but not make a definite decision based on that information alone.

Even so, examining materials at conventions and media fairs is time well spent on the part of the teacher. It is always a good practice to have the materials sent on approval prior to purchase. Free examination periods should be utilized, especially in the case of large purchases, because these allow trial periods with the actual student population. Be careful to read the fine print on examination trials. Some send a bill in ten days to two weeks and may require elaborate procedures for returning merchandise.

*Level of independence.* Some pieces of instructional equipment and types of materials, no matter how innovative or clever, may be inappropriate because they require a level of student independence not possible in the program. As mentioned earlier, numerous tape recorders, visual loops, and other equipment have been used with kindergarten and first-grade students with excellent success. Students can be instructed in the proper use and care of materials, but the teacher must be able to evaluate the likelihood that students will be responsible and must be prepared to spend the amount of time required to develop student responsibility for care and maintenance and to protect items from theft and vandalism.

The level of independent functioning required by the material and the characteristics of the population must be matched carefully. Manufacturer claims about ease of operation should be noted, but the teacher must evaluate materials to be sure.

### Cost

***Number of students.*** A major concern of the administration is how many students need a particular material. It is a cost-related factor that cannot be ignored, but, as will be demonstrated in the discussion of student outcomes, cost based on the number of students should not be the sole determinant in a purchase. Could the item be utilized on a sharing basis by other classes within the school? If so, this might increase the number of students benefiting from the expenditure.

***Proportion of budget.*** The cost of the materials should be considered as a proportion of the budget rather than in isolation. This will aid the teacher in scrutinizing the importance of a particular item. Is it worth spending 75% of the total available budget for the academic year? What other items *must* be purchased or are desired? What proportion of last year's budget was expended on similar items, on items in the same instructional area, or for this same type of instructional activity? These comparative calculations should be performed on all purchases to put costs into perspective.

***Durability.*** The initial cost of materials should only be considered as part of the expense of the item. Other cost factors include:
- Consumable items required with material
- Amount of maintenance expected
- Availability of separate components for replacement

The item should be examined for its general construction. For example, books should be evaluated for durability of the cover, quality of paper, and binding quality. Recordings might be examined to ascertain the durability of the storage cover. Kits or complete programs should have replacements available for items lost or destroyed. The storage case for a kit may prove to be the major protection from damage, thus prolonging the life of the materials.

### Outcomes

#### Student outcomes

***Relationship to total program.*** The overall goals for the program determine the nature of the materials used. Student outcomes are the direct result of the goals selected for the program. Student outcomes may vary from a strict emphasis on improving reading ability to occupational placement. The nature of these outcomes and the relationship of the special education program to the total secondary program are important considerations in selecting materials.

Budget constraints might indicate that a particular type of material would be too expensive, but examination of the desired student outcomes would reveal that these outcomes could not be realized without the item under consideration. If the regular

**OUTCOMES**

| STUDENT OUTCOMES | COST ANALYSIS |
|---|---|
| Relationship to total program / IEP | Cost efficiency / Cost benefits |

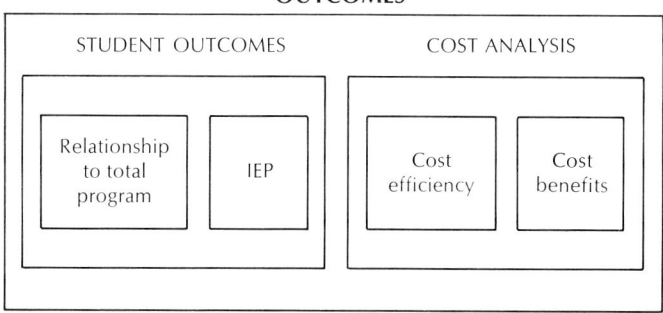

science program is so heavily scheduled that certain charts are not available for use in a resource room that provides tutoring, this might be sufficient justification for duplicate charts. It may mean that the science department could share the cost. Examination of overall programming and anticipated student outcomes may be the most important decision point in selection of materials.

*Individual educational plan (IEP).* An IEP must specify individual goals and instructional objectives to be used with the student. There may be instances in which a student requires highly specialized instructional materials to implement the IEP. The IEP, and teaching practices growing out of it, should be considered for such special circumstances.

Review of the IEPs for students in the program may also reveal some common goals that could be addressed by a type of material not currently offered in a program. Using the IEP as a point of reference in materials selection can result in more objective selections. Teachers should briefly review the IEPs, scanning for commonalities as well as for special or unusual needs.

**Cost analysis**

*Cost efficiency.* Administrators typically examine purchase requests made by teachers to ascertain cost efficiency. However, cost efficiency should not be used as the only variable in evaluating materials selection; as stated earlier, other aspects must be included in making the decision. The cheapest is not always the most appropriate choice!

Cost efficiency is usually measured by actual or real cost in proportion to the number of students served. The availability of the item through other sources might also be considered as part of cost efficiency. The teacher should be prepared to address cost efficiency by stating comparative costs with accompanying listings of advantages and disadvantages of the various materials under consideration. A sound, data-based choice may not be the most cost efficient.

*Cost benefits.* Benefits derived from a purchase should be a major factor in evaluating materials. As indicated throughout this discussion, the benefits obtained must be measured against individual needs, group needs, budget constraints, program goals, and costs. The greatest cost efficiency may not be consistent with cost benefits. When all data have been collected, an extremely expensive kit for use with only *one* student may be selected because the benefit in this case would outweigh the expense.

Teachers will constantly have to fight the cost benefit vs cost efficiency battle. Student benefits are often difficult to show quantitatively, but evidence of benefits will be necessary to justify purchases. This is the reason an evaluation model should be used to aid the teacher in weighing cost benefits to provide more objective and specific information to guide the decision-making process.

*Equipment* available to the special teacher is also a major determinant of the amount and quality of individual and individualized instruction. The equipment inventory should be matched against the following list:
- Record player
- Tape recorders*
- Earphone and listening posts*
- Overhead projector
- Blackboards, preferably portable on stands
- Worktables (rather than desks)
- Study carrels (folding screens are preferable)
- A filing cabinet
- Cassette storage units*
- Bulletin boards/pegboards
- Storage cabinets for large equipment/models
- Typewriters*
- Filmstrip projector

More than one tape recorder and ear-

---

*These items are essential.

phone-listening post will be necessary in order to operate learning centers effectively. There are a multitude of types of earphone setups, each with advantages and disadvantages that the teacher will have to evaluate. However, one of the most effective appears to be the type operating off a ceiling loop. The earphones are wireless, operating with batteries inside each headset and receiving transmission as long as the wearer is inside the overhead loop that is connected to the recorder or record player. It allows for increased pupil mobility and is particularly useful if the taped lesson deals with lengthy assignments. Literally hundreds of cassettes may be needed if a complete tape library is maintained. A basic-skills remedial program can require as many as 150 tapes. If the teacher has any flexibility in budgetary matters, money spent on tape recorders, tapes, and listening hookups should be a priority. Examples of taped instructional segments are included in this chapter.

Typewriters should also be considered necessary equipment for a special education room. The best model will depend on the particular circumstances, such as amount of money allotted, number and age of student typists, and frequency of use. The school administrators can probably identify a reputable sales company if a new machine has to be selected, or an approved list may exist.

The following is a list of equipment to which the special education teacher should have access within the school system:
- Duplicator
- Copier
- Opaque projector
- 16 mm Film projector
- Slide projector

Any specialized equipment used in a content course, such as science laboratory equipment, should be made available to the teacher and students. Some cooperative spirit may be required on the part of all parties in the use of laboratory or instructional equipment from regular classes. Equipment used in vocational programs may be industrial machines or other items needed for job clusters or work sample stations.

Other resources to be considered include tutors, volunteers, and aides. As discussed in Chapter 8, the selection of paraprofessionals is extremely important to a successful program. The following general suggestions, in addition to the information in Chapter 8, might prove beneficial:

1. Inquire of the administration if there are paid aides assigned to the program; if so, find out how they are selected and request inclusion in that process.
2. Check the student and faculty handbook to see if youth tutors or volunteer groups exist within the school.
3. Examine school policy for any specific guidelines connected with the use of volunteers as tutors.
4. Carefully design a plan for utilizing tutors, aides, or volunteers.
5. Secure administrative approval before implementing a tutoring or aide program.

These additional personnel can be used to monitor learning centers, provide skill tutoring, and prepare materials, as well as for numerous other instructionally related tasks.

**Other considerations**

*Space.* Space is an important consideration in coordinating a special education program and most state plans for special education specify the number of square feet per student required in the classroom. The room should have typical characteristics of other classrooms in the school building including general size, appearance, and proper electrical systems and ventilation. The lower number of students served per period should not be used as an excuse for putting the resource room into a converted closet. The nature of the program, rather than the number of students, should dictate space needs, especially in vocational programs. Listed below are some considerations that will affect the physical space requirements:

1. A broader scope of materials is necessary for the individualized instruction conducted in a special room, necessitating additional storage needs.

2. Even though only a few students may attend each period, the IEPs may be such that each student is working at a different learning center, thus requiring the same physical space for the center as for any classroom.

3. Vocational programs require space to safely accommodate special equipment.

4. If a reinforcement or contracting system is used, a reinforcement area and a time-out area may be required.

5. Study carrels or booths should be provided for those students requiring a less distracting work environment.

6. The room should be large enough to allow freedom for movement and free-flowing traffic patterns.

7. A certain degree of privacy should be provided to facilitate teacher-pupil communications and conferences.

8. Some provision should be made for office space, either in the classroom or in an adjacent area (D'Alonzo et al., 1979).

The special education room should be in a central *location* (Weiderholdt et al., 1978), close to other support services utilized in conjunction with the program. All efforts should be expended to avoid any stigma or to attract any negative attention to the room. One small survey of resource rooms indicated that (1) somewhat less than half of the resources rooms were located near heavy traffic, (2) most did not have work facilities, (3) most did not have space for a time-out area, and (4) over half were not located near the media center (D'Alonzo and Mauser, 1976). However, the same study revealed that most did have study carrels or booths.

Ventilation and lighting should meet the requirements outlined for other facilities in the building. The special education room may require additional electrical outlets for the extra equipment used as well as additional space to store equipment. Flexibility of the space should be increased through portable blackboards, portable walls, movable equipment, and adaptable lighting and electrical access.

*Floor plans* will vary greatly, but we have included a few examples to illustrate some possibilities. The teacher will have to examine educational strategies to be used, the equipment that will be required, the size of the room, the number of pupils to be served, the nature of the program (self-contained or resource), and the fixed physical characteristics such as doors, windows, and electrical outlets. After a plan is determined it should be evaluated for improvement and minor variations should occasionally be made simply to provide a change in atmosphere.

Fig. 9-3 shows a floor plan for a room designed to provide group instruction with some provisions made for individual study or tutoring or both. This might be used in self-contained classes.

Fig. 9-4 shows a model that would be more appropriate for a resource room in which learning centers and other instructional aids are used for maximum individualization and to permit flexible scheduling. It could be used for remediation, for compensatory models, and for support of the vocational programs. Interactional (program-directed student interaction) models could also be used. The key is the use of learning centers for any content: reading, mathematics, vocational skills, and subject-area content.

***Scheduling.*** There is probably no more disconcerting problem for the special educator than that of scheduling. As noted, the way in which students will be assigned to the program will depend on many factors; namely, if the program is self-contained or re-

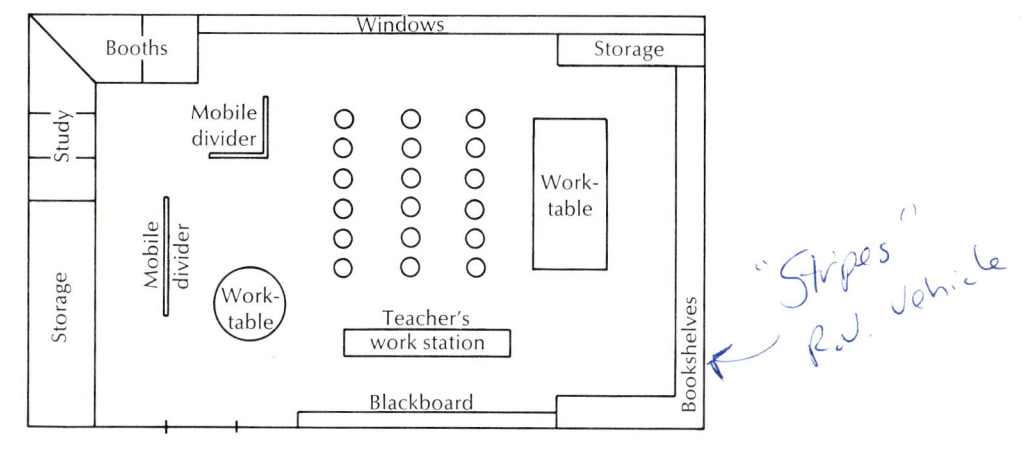

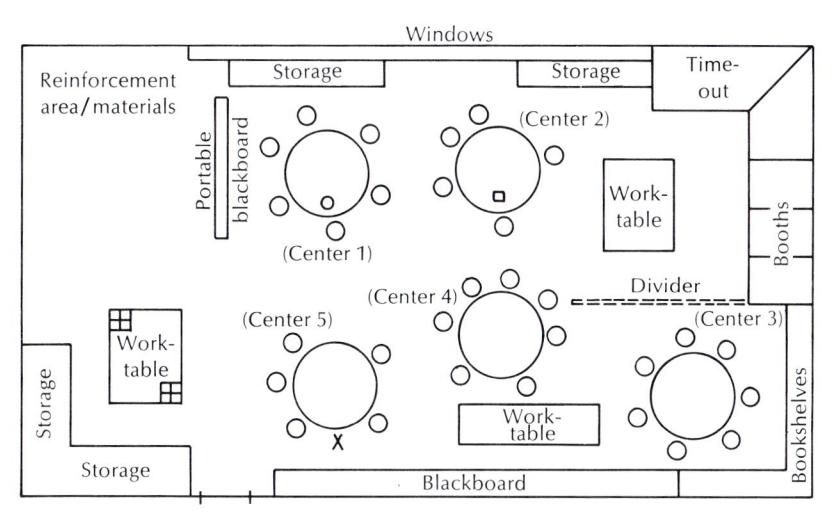

**Fig. 9-3.** Floor plan: example 1.

**Fig. 9-4.** Floor plan: example 2. X = Teacher. □ = AV equipment. ⊞ = Typewriter. ○ = Earphones/recorder or record player.

source, or concerned with compensatory, remedial, or vocational programming. There are also important distinctions if the services are provided at the junior high or senior high levels. Therefore any recommendations that are made here will have limited value for wide application due to the many factors cited above as well as the fact that some schools will have modular scheduling, others will be organized in 45- to 50-minute periods, and there will be variation in the number of class periods during the day. Moreover, if categorical programs are developed, there may be local policy about the amount of time and type of classes used for mainstreaming.

In general, schools will arrange schedules around periods, modules, blocks, or units.

The special education program will need to adhere to such a schedule, as a rule, because a student's time must be accounted for during the day. Some resource rooms have experimented with competency-based programs in which a student, after reaching a certain skill, need not return to the resource room until a new skill sequence is begun. This has caused some problems. Although it may be motivating to students and give them a concrete sense of achievement, they must be located somewhere in the building during the time originally set aside for the resource room activity. In more traditional, bureaucratic schools it will be necessary for some rather formal, supervised activity to replace the free time earned by achievement of competencies. In most cases, this seems to be arranged by means of a reinforcement area in the resource room or in proximity to it.

In traditional or innovative schools, scheduling will be set by a *specific time* or by *flexible time*, and the types of subjects or skills, whether they be in self-contained or resource rooms, will be generally *remediation*, *vocational* or *career preparation*, *tutoring* in *subject areas*, or a *comprehensive* approach that may emphasize elements of each, depending on the individual needs of particular students.

**Self-contained classes.** In categorical approaches, EMR and ED students are most likely to be grouped in a self-contained program for obvious reasons; however, there is a sentiment among some authorities that self-contained programs should be offered to LD students who are the most seriously deficient in achievement. The self-contained EMR program typically features career preparation at the junior and senior high levels; programs for ED students focus on behavioral change and progressive inclusion in mainstream classes; and the unusual self-contained class for LD students will, of course, be primarily concerned with remediation of basic skills and some type of compatible programming in vocational skills. For the most part, self-contained classes may be arranged by subject areas with appropriate breaks for recreation, physical education, and lunch. A typical prevocational or career awareness/exploration program of the junior high school will be blocked, especially in larger schools, so that students may attend the class as a group. In actuality, very few classes are truly self-contained because there is almost certainly placement in physical education, health, home economics, and selected courses outside the special class. Throughout junior high, a typical pattern may be as follows (the blocks may be switched if a different group of students attends in the morning):

| Period | Subject |
|---|---|
| 1 | Physical education/science/health |
| 2 | Mathematics |
| 3 | Language arts |
| 4 | Social studies |
| 5 | Lunch/break |
| 6 | Career awareness/exploration |
| 7 | Career awareness/exploration |

In the first two years of high school the schedule would be altered to include more aggressive vocational training, evaluation of work experiences, and concentrated training in occupationally related skills. During the final year, depending on a number of circumstances, the student would be placed in some vocational experience off campus for a part or all of the day with occasional follow-up visits and return to campus for seminars about experiences.

A well-known example of progressive inclusion, which is initially a self-contained model, is the engineered classroom for emotionally disturbed students designed by Hewett et al. (1969). There are four centers and eight stations through which students rotate each day to work on different topics. The progression of training (attention, response, order, exploratory, social, and mastery) leads ultimately to inclusion in the regular class. The system is highly structured, uses a reinforcement system, and is geared to educational tasks. Many programs have imitated this approach since its inception as the Santa Monica Project over a decade ago.

***Resource room with remedial emphasis.*** The resource room with a remedial emphasis is the easiest to describe because it is usually organized by periods with assignment to one or more periods for a student based either on administrative convenience or on the nature of the student's remedial needs. In some settings it may be observed that there are X number of LD students who have been labeled and placed in the resource room. The counselor, assistant principal, or the computer may assign students to the classes so that they are equally distributed throughout the day. In many schools, there seems to be a predominant pattern for students to be assigned to one period in the resource room during the day for remediation and to then be forced to fend for themselves in mainstream courses because remedial teachers refuse to provide assistance to students with their subject-area classes. We are aware (as of this writing) of two school districts where lawsuits are eminent due to this specific set of circumstances. The parents are disappointed with the special education services because the students are not making progress in remediation and are not passing their mainstream classes.

Remedial resource teachers may attempt to organize students into periods for small group instruction based on their commonalities. For example, students who share certain reading characteristics or deficits in mathematics are grouped together during the same periods. This is not very practical, however, so that it is not uncommon to find considerable individualization with students who attend the resource room during various periods. Therefore a small number of students will be permitted to attend at one time.

Implementing a comprehensive program within the high school special education room requires that the teacher design the program to be compatible with the time frame of the school. The number and length of periods into which the day is divided can affect the program as can the number of students to be served during each period. Typically, the periods are about 50 minutes, requiring that the teacher manage to serve several students during each period. In order to maximize effectiveness with limited time for each student we suggest the following procedure or some modification of it:

1. Once scheduling has been completed, prepare a timetable for each student.
2. Examine the IEP for each student, identifying priority goals for educational intervention.
3. Study the IEP for educational strategies related to objectives.
4. Make notes concerning any special considerations in planning for each student.

This initial organizational plan will aid in making daily plans. Some teachers use 5 × 8 in. cards or standardized forms to organize this planning information.

***Resource room.*** Fig. 9-5 outlines three days of resource room instruction for a student whose IEP includes assistance in American history, a course the student had previously failed. Student skills to be applied to all content classes and remedial instruction in specific reading skills such as decoding were included. The use of previously taped American history reading assignments and peer tutors allows the student to get individualized and individual instruction without receiving any direct instructional time from the teacher until Wednesday. The student has not engaged in busy work nor has he been inappropriately or unnecessarily

**212** THE PROGRAM

### LD STUDENT RESOURCE ROOM

Name _____ Regular homeroom _____ Teacher _____

Ages _____ Grade _____

| Day | Period | Area of instruction | Strategy | Notes |
|---|---|---|---|---|
| Monday: | 2 | AI: American history | Tape AH 13: (22 minutes) | Remember charts as he is in Mr. Jones' class and Mr. Jones uses charts in class. |
|  |  | AI: American history | Discussion with peer tutor (15 minutes) | Have tutor outline 5 major points. |
|  |  | AI: American history | Dictation of essay on _____ | Have blank tapes; to be completed prior to leaving school today and left in resource room for review. |
| Tuesday: | 2 | AI: American history | Review of essay with tutor (15 minutes) | Essay has been reviewed and transcribed by volunteer. Ready to turn in to Mr. Jones, who has approved this process for completing assignments. |
|  |  | AI: American history remedial reading | TI: Decoding skill practice using vocabulary from American history, tape AH 13. Major points outlined and written, then decoded. |  |
| Wednesday: | 2 |  | Study skills: summarizing | Tape AH 14 (16 minutes): TI: summarizes, using history as content. | Assignment: Type summary of tape AH 14 and have it reviewed by history tutor. |

**Fig. 9-5.** Daily plan for individual student. *AI*, accommodative instruction; *TI*, teacher instruction.

| Date (10/8) | | Period (2) | |
|---|---|---|---|
| Students | Area of instruction | Strategy | Notes |
| Steve | AI: history | Tape AH 13 (tutor) | |
| Robert | AI: science | Laboratory Lesson (tutor) | |
| Alice | Remedial reading: medial blends | TI: Taped Lesson MB 21 | |
| Bertha | AI: grammar | Worksheet (self-programmed) TI: taped lesson with objective quiz at end | |
| Mary | AI: science | Listening tape/graph completion to demonstrate principle | Graphic to be checked prior to leaving and turned in to science teacher |
| Mande | Remedial math: equivalents in fractions | Concrete instruction: Aide/follow-up worksheets | Graded in class |

**Fig. 9-6.** Sample daily plan: compensatory model.

grouped to fit a schedule. To appreciate the value of this for the teacher, an examination should be made of another sample plan. Fig. 9-6 shows the activities of five students in a resource room on Monday during period 2, one of the same periods included in the example in Fig. 9-5.

*Vocational programs.* Except in the case of a work-study program or other work experience controlled by a special educator, services for students in vocational preparation will vary greatly from one setting to another. Scheduling in these cases will be accomplished according to the type of program offered, which might be listed as follows:

1. Regular vocational courses (resource room support)
2. Segregated vocational program (self-contained)
3. Skill training or skill centers (resource support)
4. Vocational school or skill clusters (direct support of special teachers employed to work in setting)
5. Half-day vocational training/half-day regular placement (support may be afforded in each setting in a resource room)

Clearly, there are so many permutations possible in scheduling within these arrangements that it would be impractical to list a number of examples to typify enrollment and scheduling patterns. The suggestion should be made that the best approach to scheduling here, as in other approaches, is that which emphasizes the individual needs of the learner. The IEP, if properly considered and executed, can contribute immeasurably to the process of individualization by avoiding tracking of students into programs and grouping for the sake of convenience.

*Strategies* used by the special education teacher cover a broad spectrum of instructional approaches, unlike the traditional classroom, which relies on lecture, guided reading, and limited audiovisual instruction. The strategies include:

- Guided reading (through tapes, if needed)
- Discussion
- Demonstration
- Lecture (most likely one-to-one explanation)
- Audiovisual instruction
- Drill or guided practice

The realization that all instruction does not have to be lecture or require the presence of the teacher is not surprising. However, many instructional programs fail to utilize other instructional strategies, therefore losing the opportunity to increase (through other strategies) the impact of the teacher. A well-designed program with various other instructional strategies can, in fact, operate successfully without direct instruction from the teacher, which underscores the role of the teacher as an instructional manager.

*Teacher organizational skills.* Effective teaching relies heavily on the organizational and management skills of the teacher; this becomes obvious as daily lesson plans are developed. For instance, the plan listed in Fig. 9-6 for period 2 on Monday requires the resource teacher to accomplish the following:

1. Make arrangements for all of the American history assignments to be read onto tapes and categorized.
2. Set up laboratory equipment necessary for the week's science lessons.
3. Arrange to have science tapes made for all reading assignments.
4. Outline objectives to be covered by an aide for fractional equivalent instruction; prepare and store accompanying worksheets.
5. Prepare a series or purchase tapes of grammatical rules.
6. Prepare or purchase a series of tapes about phonics skills basic to remedial reading instruction.

7. Complete a peer tutor training program.

In this 50-minute period, six students have received individualized instruction and five of them have received individual instruction from a tutor, an aide, or the teacher. Self-instruction occurred in the case of the student who listened to the science tape and completed the graph as required by the taped lesson. This student will receive individual instruction in another period that day or on another day. Depending on the students and the goals of the program, each student may receive instructional time with the teacher several times per week with supplemental instruction through tutors, volunteers, aides or tapes, and other program-directed instruction.

The efficiency of using taped lessons may not be immediately apparent as the amount of time required to prepare them may seem to be forbidding. However, as pointed out earlier in the discussion of materials, *this is time expended only once.* For instance, explaining a basic grammatical rule or arithmetic principle might have to be repeated several times each week and numerous times each year. The lesson, permanently captured on tape, can be used for years with literally hundreds of students. It is an excellent means for multiplying teacher effectiveness. Also, these tapes can be made by volunteers or tutors, thus reducing labor of the teacher. Below is a sample tape format and some basic steps in using taped lessons.

**Suggested uniform format**

1. Identify general topic, tape number, specific skill: English, E-27, grammar (plurals).
2. List materials needed to complete the lesson: notebook paper, pencil, worksheet EG-27a, worksheet EG-27b.
3. Identify all parts of the lesson: this lesson will consist of a taped instructional segment reviewing worksheet EG-27a, examples of plural forms, and instructions for worksheet EG-27b.
4. Clearly specify instructions: put your name in the upper right-hand corner of a piece of notebook paper; under your name, list the date. List the tape number, E-27, on the third line. Along the left margin, number vertically from 1 to 10. Listen to the following sentences. If the sentence contains a plural, write an X; if the sentence does not contain a plural, write a 0. For example, "The boy is involved in a game of basketball." This would be marked with an 0 as it does not contain a plural.
5. Provide definite instructions when the taped segment has ended: complete worksheet E-27b independently; use the grading key to check your own work; record your score on your English graph on the wall; turn off the recorder and store earphones in proper place.

**Storage of taped lessons**

1. Label tape clearly, indicating general topic, tape number, specific skill, and length of tape.
2. List all materials required.
3. If tape is to be permanent, take precautions to ensure it is not accidentally erased.
4. Store tapes by instructional sequence and in order of use.

*Student behaviors.* A comprehensive program will make certain demands on students. The underlying assumptions are that (1) instruction keyed to ability reduces frustration, (2) individualized instruction facilitates learning, (3) instruction related to practical needs (passing classes) results in increased motivation, and (4) independent functioning accounts for individual rates of learning. The maturity of the students may often be underestimated because of the long-term effects of frustration and failure and the fact that many schools do not offer students the opportunity to assume responsibility. At the beginning of each term, behavioral expectations should be specified. These might include:

1. All equipment is community property and the responsibility of all "community" members.
2. Any special handling requirements of equipment should be clearly specified in orientation sessions and repeated frequently at the beginning of the year.
3. Behavioral limitations concerning inter-

rupting another student or the teacher should be clearly stated.
4. The policy concerning how assignments should be turned in for review should be posted and specifically outlined.

The use of a contracting system and some type of reinforcement system facilitates the process. Student behavior outcomes and expectations should be considered in the organization and coordination of a resource room.

*Potential problems.* Some of the most frequently encountered problems include cheating, mechanical problems with equipment, and the tendency for students to abuse independence. Cheating and most other problems can be handled with time and experience. Positive attention and rewards for appropriate behavior can be extremely effective in reducing the likelihood that such problems will exist. Handling problems rationally and putting them in proper perspective keeps the teacher from focusing attention on undesirable behavior.

Mechanical problems will happen infrequently, but the teacher should enlist the aid of a media specialist or a handy teacher for emergency help. Proper maintenance of equipment is essential and should be included in the time schedule of the teacher and the budget. Proper tape cataloging and storage will reduce the likelihood of tape mix-ups. These should be stored to allow student access, thus sharing the responsibility with students and saving a few valuable minutes per period of teacher time. In summary, a comprehensive program has much to offer the special education program, including:

1. More flexibility in scheduling
2. Increased opportunity for one-to-one instruction
3. More immediate feedback on performance
4. Reduced emphasis on interindividual performance and increased emphasis on individual needs
5. More time and opportunity for affective interventions
6. A broader scope of areas of instruction
7. Student evaluation more easily accomplished
8. Task analysis as part of daily planning
9. Resources more completely utilized

## MONITORING AND RECORD KEEPING

Monitoring the program and keeping appropriate records can consume great amounts of precious time. However, these are important administrative functions that must be performed to guarantee that the program meets stated goals. Monitoring includes student tracking, grading, program evaluation, faculty communications, and parental interactions. Monitoring functions can be accomplished through forms, interviews, conferences, tests, and observation. Computers may offer another monitoring capability.

### Student tracking

Secondary schools operate on a system of periods that requires the special education teacher and the regular teacher to cooperate not only in programming and scheduling but also in student tracking. Keeping up with individual students is usually handled with forms such as those used in any secondary guidance or scheduling program. In larger schools, without proper student tracking techniques, students may be "lost" between the special education room and the regular classroom. Monitoring may help prevent such problems as tardiness, truancy, and general mayhem in the halls. Suggested strategies for dealing with these problems include the establishment of rules and the use of reinforcement plans. Special programs structured to provide success experiences along with proper reinforcement approaches can prevent or greatly reduce the occurrence of common student mischief.

A variety of forms for student tracking may

be used for aspects of the program, including regular classes, counseling sessions, and the special program. Reporting from the regular teacher to the special teacher may be accomplished with a form that includes the grade assigned by the regular teacher, questions concerning the student's effort in class, and the status of homework completed by the student. Chapters 6 and 8 of this book included several forms for similar uses, such as reporting by the counselor to other teachers.

## Grading

The assignment of grades appears to fulfill two purposes: (1) to indicate achievement or relative performance and (2) to provide feedback to students about performance. The typical high school program uses letter grades for each subject, which raises a question about how grades should be assigned in the special education program and who should assign them. No clear-cut policy has evolved with regard to the issue of grading.

Accommodatory instruction for the LD or behaviorally disordered student enrolled in the regular classroom would seem to indicate that the grade be assigned by the regular teacher with input from the resource teacher. Learning disabled and behaviorally disordered students integrated into regular classrooms should be able to grasp the major concepts in the courses with appropriate assistance and be graded against the usual criteria. Compensating measures such as alternative tests, guided study, and assistance with assignments can be used to aid the student in reaching criterion.

If resource-room instruction supplants the regular course, the resource teacher will have to establish grading criteria and assign letter grades. In order to maintain credibility in such situations, the resource teacher must carefully outline instructional objectives and assess progress in accordance with them. The fear of cheapening grades through such a process can be reduced if it can be demonstrated that the *same major concepts* and *competencies* are being developed, the difference being in the strategies utilized to accomplish them.

Resource programs that emphasize remedial work with the students may need to report student progress through some other means than letter grades in regular courses, although many programs simply avoid a letter grade for the resource room class. Although such a grade would not ordinarily be related to graduation requirements, indications of progress in remedial areas must be reported. Use of a skill checklist or some other criterion-referenced instrument may be acceptable as an alternative.

Self-contained special education programs, such as those serving EMR students, may or may not provide most subject-area courses for students. In these cases, the grades are assigned by the special teacher based on the student's performance in the special class. The criteria are usually quite subjective with grading determined individually rather than by a norm. This is an issue of some concern in secondary programs, with the basic question being whether or not the grade report should really name content courses. Does an "A" in these special courses mean the same as an "A" in a regular class? If EMR students are graded against age and grade level expectancies, will it be possible for them to obtain passing grades? This may place the special education teacher in a dilemma. Mastery learning and other innovative concepts clearly demonstrate that an individual's rate of development is the important factor, not norms. Moreover, the IEP may clearly indicate what the criteria for grading shall be. The concern of most critics will be the relative standing of an individual, not his or her accomplishments.

The responsibility for designing a grading policy for secondary programs should be assumed by the administration with guidelines and policies established for special students (Hawisher & Calhoun, 1978). Many programs are caught in the debate over whether special students should receive diplomas or certificates of attendance. Concern over the validity of the high school diploma has caused some school districts to give certificates or special education diplomas to students. With additional time and resource assistance mildly handicapped students should be able to attain competency levels consistent with high school graduation requirements. If this is true, these students should also receive traditional diplomas.

Grading to provide feedback to students is not such a complex process. Continuous or daily feedback had been used to reflect task performance and classroom functioning (Hewett, 1968). Special education teachers can provide daily, immediate feedback on performance by grading assignments as they are completed. Students need information on their performance to guide them in their studies, and this information should be immediate and personal. Feedback can take the form of numerical or letter grades, charting of number of tasks completed, skill checklists indicating progress, conferences about performance, written evaluations, and test results. The important point is that students must know how they are performing in comparison with personal standards and objectives.

Using the IEP as a standard allows for individualized goals and contributes to the use of the IEP as an instructional tool rather than an administrative burden. Both short- and long-term goals are identified in the IEP; these can be used to measure student progress and provide evaluative information to the teacher and the student. Any type of feedback, written or spoken, is of great assistance to the student in guiding behavior. The value of feedback in the resource room should not be underestimated by the teacher.

### Program evaluation

Program evaluation can be a valuable tool in managing special services. Evaluation is usually regarded as a process initiated externally and conducted by an outside specialist. However, it should be viewed as a management tool useful in daily programming as well as for measurement of yearly outcomes. A useful approach is the Discrepancy Evaluation Model (DEM) refined by Dr. Robert Brinkerhoff of Western Michigan University. Factors to be considered in evaluation might include those shown in Fig. 9-7.

Monitoring the program for purposes of evaluation would require examination of the following factors.

### State and federal requirements

*Placement.* Has the program followed the specified guidelines for placement?

*Due process.* Have all procedures regarding due process been followed to guarantee rights?

*Parental role.* Have parents been involved as prescribed in legislation?

*IEP.* Has the IEP been developed to ensure appropriate educational services for the student?

### School policies

*Programming.* Are the procedures followed in the program consistent or at least compatible with school policy?

*Roles specified.* Have the teacher and the program fulfilled all of the roles or responsibilities expected by the school administration and/or dictated by school policy? How do other teachers view you/your program?

*Physical policy.* Has the room met specifications for physical environmental factors determined by school policy?

*Use of resources.* Have materials and other

```
STATE/FEDERAL REQUIREMENTS          SCHOOL POLICIES

   ┌─────────────┬─────────────┐    ┌─────────────┬─────────────┐
   │  Placement  │ Due process │    │ Programming │    Roles    │
   │             │             │    │             │  specified  │
   ├─────────────┼─────────────┤    ├─────────────┼─────────────┤
   │   Parental  │     IEP     │    │   Physical  │    Use of   │
   │    role     │             │    │    policy   │  resources  │
   └─────────────┴─────────────┘    └─────────────┴─────────────┘

                      STUDENT OUTCOMES
              ┌─────────────┬─────────────┐
              │     IEP     │Program goals│
              ├─────────────┼─────────────┤
              │   Student   │Postsecondary│
              │  attitudes  │  adjustment │
              └─────────────┴─────────────┘
```

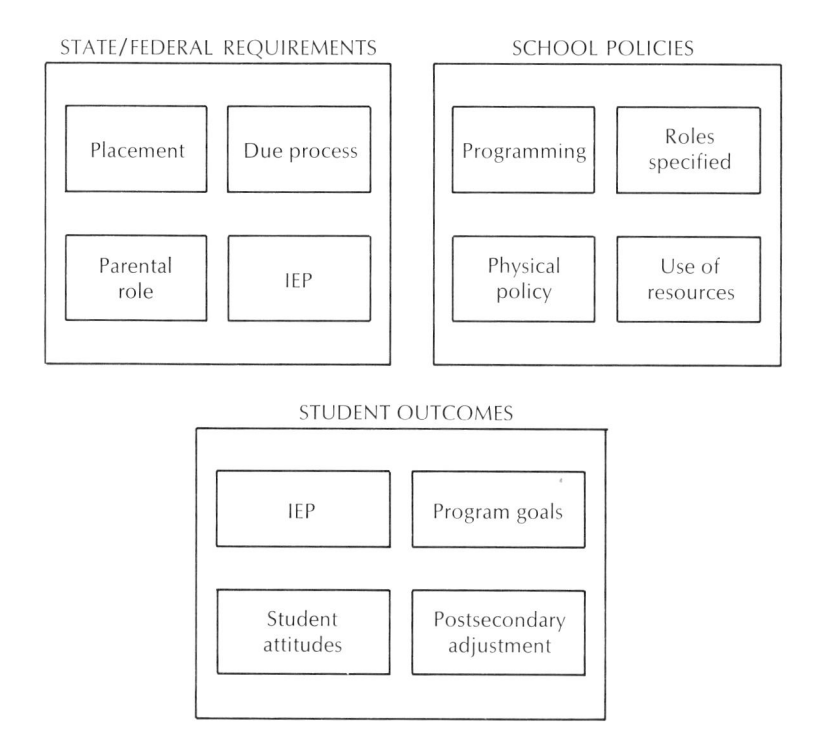

**Fig. 9-7.** Program evaluation. *AI*, accommodative instruction; *TI*, teacher instruction.

resources been used maximally and in accordance with school policy? Is the cost of the program in line with expectations?

## Student outcomes

*IEP.* Have the goals stated in the individual IEPs been achieved?

*Program goals.* Have program goals been achieved in terms of general student outcomes?

*Student attitudes.* Is the program successful and appealing to the consumers (students)?

*Postsecondary adjustments.* Does the program assist the students in functioning in the real world?

• • •

The teacher should design an evaluation model in which the above issues are more specifically stated and activities planned to guarantee that program objectives are achieved. The evaluation is based on a comparison between stated program objectives such as those listed above and actual accomplishments, thus creating a discrepancy model. The DEM is an approach to such evaluation that could be managed by the resource teacher, with training in the DEM. Administrators responsible for the program can provide guidance in designing such a model.

## Communications

**Faculty communications.** Interaction with the regular teaching staff is an integral part of the special education program, yet one that requires extensive record keeping if it is to be properly managed. As described in earlier chapters, personal interactions are

```
Conference report    (Special teacher's name)            Date_____
Contributors         (List other teachers/subject areas)
                     _____


Student_____ Grade_____ Homeroom no._____


Reason for conference:  (Succinctly state problem.)

Summary of discussion:  (Briefly outline points made in conference.)

Conference outcomes:    (List actions planned, other problems identified,
     solutions offered.)

Is there to be another conference?  If so, when?  (This reduces confusion
     as to the next meeting.)
```

**Fig. 9-8.** Faculty conference report.

necessary as part of the consulting role and as part of the direct-instructional role of the teacher. Conferences with faculty can be arranged on a regular basis as part of an in-service effort or as part of a case conference for an individual student. In either event, communications should be carefully planned to keep time to a minimum. A follow-up communication should be sent to the participating teacher(s) (Fig. 9-8). This will aid in maintaining clear communication.

In accommodatory instruction of mildly handicapped students it is imperative that the teacher communicate with regular instructors to maintain consistency in instruction and to monitor students. One possible means of accomplishing this is to use a report form carried by the student among teachers (Fig. 9-9).

Communications of this type keep regular teachers informed of efforts of the special educator to aid the student in acquiring major concepts in the regular course. The regular teacher can provide guidance to the resource teacher in the identification of priorities within the course content. This form, delivered weekly or daily, is an important part of the monitoring process.

Regular teachers can provide the resource teacher with weekly outlines or unit outlines. These outlines might follow the format shown in Fig. 9-10.

These are some examples of monitoring functions connected with faculty communications. Another approach is to survey the faculty to determine awareness of the special services program and satisfaction with the program as it relates to individual faculty members. Some questions to be asked might include:

1. Do you have a student in one of your classes who is being served in the special room?
2. Do you have a clear picture of how these services relate to your program?
3. Do you know how to refer a student for such services?
4. Have you received adequate information concerning special education services?
5. Can you offer suggestions to improve services?
6. What has been your greatest difficulty in interacting with the special education program?

Such information is not meant to measure popularity of the resource teacher, nor to gain status in the system, but it will provide insight about the effectiveness of the program as it relates to the regular teacher. If unsatisfactory responses are received, the special teacher has the opportunity to adjust the program or to explain it in more detail to teacher consumers.

**Parental communications.** Chapters 6 and 8 included descriptions of the role of the special teacher with regard to responsibilities to parents, including suggested outlines for conferences and other forms of communication. Part of the need for record keeping and specific monitoring is to assure that feedback can be provided to parents about student progress. Parental concerns include:

- Academic progress
- Behavioral patterns
- Specific or unusual problems
- Important accomplishments
- Materials/strategies utilized
- Student outcomes desired
- Social development
- Health factors

The well-organized teacher can manage the program to assure that such information is readily available to parents. This information can be provided through any one or a combination of the following mediums:

- Parent conferences
- Report cards or letters
- Phone conversations
- Program newsletter

**222** THE PROGRAM

```
                        RESOURCE REPORT

Name   (Steve)                    Grade  (11)    Homeroom no.  (B12)

Area of accommodation  (American history)     Regular Instructor  (Mr. Jones)

Resource period  (2)    Regular class period  (4)     Room no.  (224)

Resource plan for this week:  (List the student's daily plan here.)

     (Monday:  Review charts of governmental changes in colonies; outline major
               points of differences among governmental structures of the
               colonies; prepare an essay on tape.)

     (Tuesday: Review essay prior to turning in to Mr. Jones;
               vocabulary instruction in specific vocabulary from
               American history/this topic.)

         (Wednesday:  Summarize governmental changes of period;
                      summarize legacies from these governments we still have
                      today in our governmental structure.)
```

**Fig. 9-9.** Resource program report to regular course instructor.

```
Course  (American history)     Teacher  (P. Coonley)    Room no.  (134)
Period  (5)      Resource students enrolled    (T. Smith)
                                                (M. Price)
                                                (K. Cooper)

Outline for  (list time period)
```

| Topic | Major points | Text assignments | Homework assignments | Test date |
|---|---|---|---|---|
| Governmental legacies | • Colonies had variety of governmental patterns<br><br>• Identify those<br><br>• Specify differences<br><br>• Explain source of differences<br><br>• Explore effects<br><br>• Describe any effects of legacies in our government | Chap. 5 | Do study questions at the end of chapter for Friday.<br><br>Prepare time line (format attached) showing government changes during colonial period | Monday, 10/3 |

**Fig. 9-10.** Course outline provided to resource teacher by regular teacher.

## Computers

The monitoring function could be greatly improved and the role of the teacher eased with the use of computers. Computers are no longer incomprehensible machines owned by large corporations. Home computers are becoming the modern-day dream of business men of the Henry Ford visionary variety. Home computers are being used to control heating/cooling systems, balance budgets, and make the morning coffee. Computer billing is a reality for doctors, dentists, and lawn services, but education is lagging behind in utilizing the new technology that is now available at bargain-basement prices.

A computer complete with printer and visual printout (TV) can be purchased for as little as $2500, a small investment in contrast to $5000 to $10,000 weight sets for school gyms. Computers are beginning to be used by schools to more efficiently schedule transportation routes and classes and to monitor purchasing. However, this resource has not really been fully utilized for teaching, performance monitoring, and instructional development. The capacity of the computer-based instructional system to organize and supply comprehensive information is enormous (Dagnon & Spuck, 1977) and could reduce many mundane tasks.

One of the most innovative and important uses for the computer could be to assist in the development of the IEP as reported by developers of the computer-based system in Ohio known as HELPS (Lehrer & Daiker, 1978). The information explosion as well as the specificity of the requirements of the IEP place extreme demands on the ability of the teacher to diagnose and prescribe educational interventions. Knowledge of the population, objectives desired, materials and techniques, and assessment measures requires the teacher to continually weigh information and make decisions. Systematic handling of information in a computerized management system could greatly reduce the task of decision making.

Computers have had some role in instruction, and this appears to be on the increase (Stolurow, 1974). CMI (computer-managed instruction) and CAI (computer-assisted instruction) are two examples of computer application. Computer systems such as the Wisconsin System of Instructional Management and the State University College at Buffalo system have been used to handle data and provide instructional management assistance (Cross & Clayback, 1976; Dagnon & Spuck, 1977). Some training programs such as Computer Assisted Remedial Education (CARE) have used computers as a training medium for modifying existing teaching skills and developing new skills (Cartwright et al., 1972). As computers are increasingly utilized for instruction and planning, hopefully management and training functions will become greatly simplified for the teacher.

The day may come when schools and teachers have access to computers and canned programs that assist them in scheduling students into special programs, developing instructional plans, selecting materials, monitoring student progress, evaluating program effectiveness, and making management decisions. Many teachers are wary of the computerized age, thinking that it requires skills they do not possess. Present training programs are beginning to include such courses as Computers in Education, but teachers in the field can take advantage of computerized assistance with minimal training. Many of the functions can be performed through readily available programs such as those outlined in the Statistical Package for Social Sciences (SPSS) and other computer languages.

Farmers have begun to utilize the computer on a daily basis to make decisions concerning the need to spray for insects, application of fertilizers, and irrigation control.

Daily information is collected by the farmer on a data form, which is telephoned to a keypunch center. The computer program is designed to handle the information that is transmitted via punched data cards or other data-handling systems. A secretary or keypunch operator transmits the information, activates the program, and the computer does the rest. The output is a spray and treatment plan for the farm within 24 hours. The farmer has taken advantage of decision-making ability based on objective data rather than intuition, and the only personnel required at this stage are the farmer, a keypuncher, and someone to relay the results. Obviously the farmer has received prior information as to the type of results to be expected and the manner in which to collect data, and computer personnel have developed the appropriate program. If farmers can use this, why not educators?

## CLASSROOM MANAGEMENT STRATEGIES

Behavior management techniques should be developed as part of the special educator's professional training (Stewart et al., 1976). The amount of training needed to reach proficiency in utilization of behavioral management has not been clearly defined (Hall, 1971), but all special educators should have sufficient instruction and basic experience in application to implement a management system within the special classrroom. Behavioral management techniques can be used that reflect a teaching philosophy as well as aspects of a controlled science. Unless involved in research, the teacher may use behavioral management techniques without meticulous collection of base-rate data (Tomlinson, 1972). If the behavioral data are to be used for evaluative purposes such as program evaluation or completion of specific IEP objectives, the collection of base-rate data might be imperative in order to show change. The special educator should make this decision based on program goals and use of data.

The teacher who uses behavioral management in the classroom attends to the immediate antecedents and consequences of the student's behavior (Rosenfield, 1979). Focusing attention aids the teacher in analyzing the atmosphere of the classroom, the nature of the lesson, and the overall learning environment. Redirecting attention produces side effects such as anticipating, avoiding, or increasing the likelihood of events occurring. The teacher notices behaviors of students that would have otherwise gone unnoticed. Self-examination on the part of the teacher and the altered view of the student's behavior and performance are important benefits derived from the use of management strategies (Abidin, 1975; Rosenfield, 1979).

In classes with students having more disturbed behavior a complex system of behavioral management will be mandatory. With most mildly handicapped students, however, token economics and other less complex systems will be adequate. The use of one-to-one laboratory-based behavioral programs with sophisticated, expensive equipment will not be necessary nor appropriate. Social reinforcement, inexpensive tangible reinforcers, free time, and token economics or checkmark systems tied to contracts are extremely useful for most students and can be adopted for use in any model or delivery system. The more complex the system, the greater will be the amount of paperwork and a consequent reduction of planning and instructional time.

### Reinforcers

*Reinforcers* are anything considered valuable or important to the student. Reinforcers must be motivating to the students, not the teachers! The surest way to ensure the power of the reinforcers is to *ask the students* what they would like to see placed in the reinforcement area. Another helpful tool in selecting reinforcers is to observe student behavior. Polishing nails may not be particularly important to teachers but may be motivating for some students. Below is an outline of some reinforcers selected by secondary students.

I. Magazines
   A. *Mad*
   B. *Popular Mechanics*
   C. *Seventeen*
II. Games
   A. Playing cards
   B. Poker chips
   C. Chess
III. Beauty aids
   A. Nail polish
   B. Makeup
IV. Musical equipment
   A. Stereo or record player (with earphones)
   B. Earphones
   C. Tape players
V. Art equipment
   A. Oils/acrylics
   B. Sketch pads
   C. Art clay
VI. Books
   A. Automotive repair
   B. Beauty/body care
   C. Fashions
   D. Jokes

**Common systems utilized in classrooms**

**Token economics.** Token systems are based on earning tokens or tangible units that can later be exchanged for other reinforcers; such systems have been successfully used with groups of students (Neisworth & Smith, 1973). The tokens have no real value but can be exchanged for items or privileges in the same way money and trading stamps are examples of token systems in our culture. In such an economy students earn tokens for completing specified tasks, exhibiting desired behaviors, inhibiting targeted behaviors, or achieving some other goal.

Tokens can be points listed on a form, graph, or chart, poker chips, or other tangibles. However, the important point to be remembered is that the token selected must *not* be available outside of the classroom. The outside availability of the tokens obviously reduces the effectiveness of the token economy by permitting counterfeiting. The tokens can be redeemed each period, daily, weekly, or at whatever interval selected by the teacher and the students. They may be exchanged for reinforcers consisting of objects or privileges.

The special education teacher could, with input from the students, design an effective token economy to be used in any of the service models we have described. For instance, tokens could be earned for *properly* completing an assigned task at a learning center or for behaving appropriately in an instructional setting. The criteria for performance must be clearly stated so that the student will not be tempted to confuse speed with accuracy in completing an instructional assignment.

**Contracting.** Teachers who use a contracting system establish agreements with the students specifying the task or behavioral goal and the rewards earned on completion of the contract. Such contracts have the benefit of student input in the development, a factor contributing to student motivation to reach a goal. This reduces the likelihood of misunderstanding the goal or the criteria for acceptable performance. Following are examples of contracting systems used in special education classrooms:

*Example 1.* The resource teacher designed a contracting program using verbal contracts, all of which adhered to established criteria agreed on by the entire group of students served; the criteria for contracts were:

1. All aspects of task completed
2. Written tasks properly identified with name/date
3. Written tasks done on full-sized, lined

notebook paper, double spaced or typed with double spacing
4. Product tasks (other than written) properly identified with name/date labels (example: science charts)

Criteria were posted in the classroom and had been established by class members at the beginning of the program.

The rewards consisted of amounts of free time in the *reinforcement area* of the classroom or appropriate areas outside the room, such as the gym, canteen, or open hallway. The time allotments were 5-, 10-, or 15-minute periods of earned free time. The value of the contract in terms of amount of free time was negotiated between student and teacher when the contract was written. The reinforcement area contained items identified by the students as desirable, such as *Popular Mechanics* magazines, stereo with earphones, and card games. Passes for privileges included time in the following activities: gym, media center, courtyard, and library.

The contracting procedure consisted of seven steps through which each student progressed (Fig. 9-11). If a student was at step 4, performance, when the period ended, that was the point at which he or she would begin in the next session. The amount of time required for each student to complete a contract varied greatly. In this particular program, after a period of operation, it seemed that each student would be able to complete an average of three contracts per period. Fig. 9-12 shows the data sheet used to record the number and value of contracts. Daily and weekly review of the sheet by the teacher served as a means of program monitoring and student progress check. Failure to complete an average number of contracts was considered indicative of:

- Contracts too difficult for student
- Reinforcements unmotivating for student
- Necessary materials or equipment unavailable

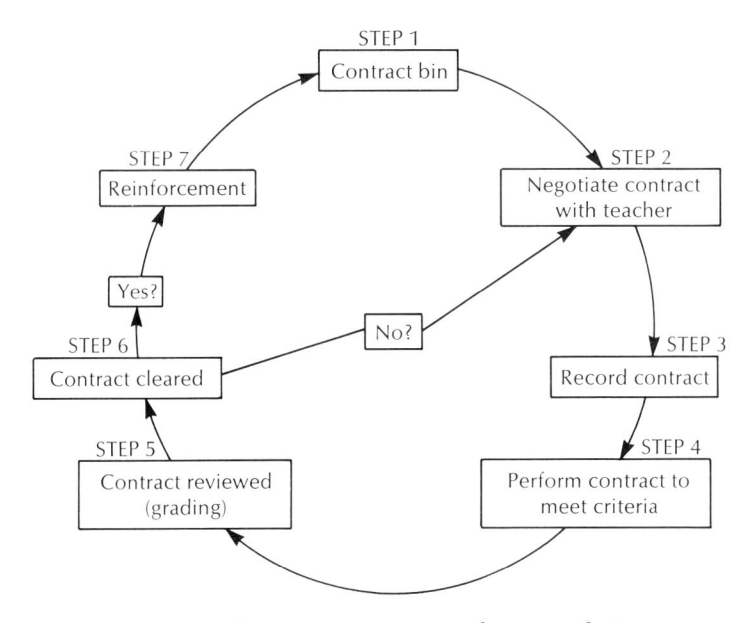

**Fig. 9-11.** Contracting process used in example 1.

| STUDENT | DATE 10/3 | | 10/4 | | 10/5 | | 10/6 |
|---|---|---|---|---|---|---|---|
| | CONTRACT (number indicates amount of free time) | | | | | | |
| Donald | ✓5 ✓10 ✓5 ✓5 | ✓15 ✓5 ✓10 ✓10 | ✓5 ✓5 ✓5 | | | | |
| Betty | ✓5 ✓5 ✓5 ✓10 | ✓10 ✓5 ✓10 ✓10 | ✓10 ✓5 ✓5 | | | | |
| Meredith | ✓5 ✓10 ✓10 ✓10 | ✓5 ✓5 ✓5 ✓10 | ✓15 ✓15 ✓10 | | | | |
| Kama | ✓10 ✓5 ✓5 ✓10 | ✓10 ✓10 ✓5 ✓15 | ✓5 ✓15 ✓5 | | | | |
| | DATE 10/3 | 10/4 | 10/5 | | | | |

✓ indicates completed

**Fig. 9-12.** Data sheet for recording contracts.

Paraprofessionals or volunteers were used at steps 3 (recording contract), 5 (contract review), and 6 (contract clearing) to relieve the teacher; however, this same contracting system was used in a self-contained classroom for EMR students. In that case the teacher used older students at steps 3 and 6, and in some cases when the contract was negotiated, indicated a specific older student authorized to review the contract (step 5).

Additional reinforcements included extensive use of social reinforcement from the teacher as well as from other students; this took the form of acknowledgement of number of contracts completed and frequency of visits to the reinforcement area. Speed in completing contracts was considered secondary to the other criteria established, but students were highly motivated to perform efficiently in order to gain time in the reinforcement area. The student completing enough 5-minute value contracts to earn, out of the 50-minute period, a total of 25 minutes in reinforcement obviously had applied good work habits!

The tasks were kept in *contract bins*. In reality these were shirt boxes, each bearing a student's name. Contracts were separated with heavy construction paper, so that each bin could contain a large number of contracts at any one time. These contracts consisted of worksheets, learning center assignments, and/or task assignments. Below is a list of some of the tasks. The student was *always* required to perform the contract on top; sifting through the bin to locate a task the student found pleasant was not allowed! This aided the teacher in establishing instructional sequencing in the contractual tasks, for example:

1. Complete the science chart and identify the specified parts of the plant; then listen to Sci tape no. 14 and check individual chart.

2. Listen to Amer Hist tape no. 8; complete the accompanying quiz.

3. Prepare English tape at English station. The assignment is to dictate an essay on the topic "Chaucer's Canterbury Tales." Review your work before submitting your tape for grading. Conform to essay guidelines established in English class.

4. Complete pages 35-41 in the Math workbook provided in your Math class.

Contracting can be the basis for establishing *individualized* instruction while also providing *individual* instruction. The teacher may design the learning tasks found in each student's bin based on the IEP and program objectives. Each student may also receive individual instruction from the teacher on a rotating basis. Thus the student might work with the teacher at the instructional center (the students named it the "hot spot") for a period of 15 minutes each day or every other day with individualized instruction while receiving individualized remedial or accommodative instruction through the contracts and learning centers. This application of the interactional model had the following effects on this particular special education room:

1. Situations requiring disciplinary action were reduced to infrequent instances.

2. A competitive spirit evolved around the number of contracts each student completed each period and the amount of free time earned.

3. Attendance problems and tardiness were nonexistent after 6 weeks.

4. Teacher planning was greatly facilitated/the amount of time required reduced. Contract bins were filled daily for the first month, then gradually as the teacher became more familiar with the students, tasks were developed and distributed to the bins monthly or even for a period of 6 weeks.

5. Teacher homework or grading each evening was eliminated as this was done at step 5, contract review.

6. Students received immediate feedback about their performance (step 5).

7. The teacher had continuous feedback on instructional strategies and student performance.

After seven months of operation, several of the students found completing the contracts to be more reinforcing than the free time and frequently skipped the earned reward time! Student progress and achievement reflected this heightened motivation.

*Example 2.* The special education teacher contracted with students individually to complete certain learning centers. For instance, the student would negotiate a blank contract to complete a particular learning center or set of learning center activities within a certain time frame and to meet established criteria. The teacher would agree to the compensation or reward to be given at the close of the contract, using amounts of free time, tokens, and other rewards. In this case the student and the teacher negotiated the contract from a "menu" of tasks the teacher expected the student to complete. This form of contracting was less individual than that in example 1 but served the same end: increased student motivation and achievement.

Introducing a contracting system requires organizational skills on the part of the special education teacher. Marsh et al. (1978) suggest the use of a contract checklist in initiating a contracting process. The teachers in examples 1 and 2 used such a checklist in the beginning of the program and posted it in the classroom for permanent reference. Both teachers also permanently posted the contracting-process flowchart describing their programs (Fig. 9-11).

**Cautions.** The teacher who implements a token economy or contracting system must not expect the tangible rewards to be reinforcing enough to maintain or eliminate behavior without social reinforcement as well. A smile or kind word of sincere praise may be appropriate for many teachers and students. The nature of the social praise varies with the individual personality of the teacher as well as the students. Some teachers have personal styles that utilize praise while others use humor or mild teasing. Regardless of the method with which each teacher feels comfortable, the message should be clearly given that the student has done well and that the teacher appreciates it!

Also the teacher must realize that there will be times when the difficulty of the task has been underestimated and the student has been asked to perform beyond capabilities. In these cases, exceptions should be made or assistance should be given in completing the contract or task. Success is the objective in these systems, and rigidity may not aid in achieving that objective.

The teacher who uses an interactional model and reinforcement techniques must have good organizational skills and a certain tolerance for frustration. When the program is begun there will be an expected amount of confusion. However, this will dissipate rapidly as the students and teacher become familiar with the system. The rewards to the teacher in terms of increased instructional time, reduced homework grading, and improved classroom atmosphere will make the wait worthwhile!

## SUMMARY

This chapter was presented to assist the teacher in the important process of managing the program. This process includes many aspects such as scheduling of students, comprehensive programming, individualization, assessment of instructional materials, purchases and storage of educational materials, utilization of classroom space, planning educational programming, monitoring pupil progress, and management strategies.

The point was made that the teacher can develop expanded effectiveness by means of careful planning and management strategies. The greatest detriment to effective programming is the unwise use of time and resources. Teachers who may expend energies in the development of comprehensive instructional and management systems are able to have an impact on many students and to provide the teacher with the appropriate systems to efficiently conduct a comprehensive secondary program.

### REFERENCES AND READINGS

Abidin, R. R. Negative effects of behavioral consultation: "I know I ought to, but it hurts too much!" *Journal of School Psychology*, 1975, 13, 51-57.

Cartwright, C. A., Cartwright, G. P., & Robine, G. G. CAI course in the early identification of handicapped children. *Exceptional Children*, 1972, 38, 453-459.

Cross, K. A., & Clayback, T. J. Learning resources data management systems. In F. B. Withrow & C. J. Nygren (Eds.), *Language, materials, and curriculum management for handicapped learners.* Columbus, Ohio: Merrill, 1976.

Dagnon, C., & Spuck, D. W. A role for computer in individualizing education—and it's not teaching. *Phi Delta Kappan*, 1977, 59, 460-462.

D'Alonzo, B. J., D'Alonzo, R. L., & Mauser, A. J. Developing resource rooms for the handicapped. *Teaching Exceptional Children*, 1979, 11, 91-96.

D'Alonzo, B. J., & Mauser, A. J. A survey of selected resource rooms in the state of Illinois. Unpublished report, Northern Illinois University, DeKalb, 1976.

Hall, R. V. Training teachers in classroom use of contingency management. *Educational Technology*, 1971, 11, 33-38.

Hawisher, M. F., & Calhoun, M. L. *The resource room: An educational asset for children with special needs.* Columbus, Ohio: Merrill, 1978.

Hewett, F. M. *The emotionally disturbed child in the classroom.* Boston: Allyn & Bacon, 1968.

Hewett, F. M., Taylor, F. D., & Artuso, A. A. The Santa Monica project. Evaluation of an engineered classroom design with emotionally disturbed children. *Exceptional Children*, 1969, 35, 523-529.

Kupyers, D. S., Becher, W. C., & O'Leary, K. D. How to make a token system fail. *Exceptional Children*, 1968, 35, 101-109.

Lehrer, B. E., & Daiker, J. F. Computer based information management for professionals serving handicapped learners. *Exceptional Children*, 1978, 44, 578-585.

Marsh, G. E., Gearheart, C. K., & Gearheart, B. R. *The learning disabled adolescent: Program alternatives in the secondary school.* St. Louis: Mosby, 1978.

Neisworth, J. T., & Smith, R. M. *Modifying retarded behavior.* Boston: Houghton Mifflin, 1973.

Rosenfield, S. Introducing behavior modification techniques to teachers. *Exceptional Children*, 1979, 45, 334-339.

Stewart, W. A., Goodman, G., & Hammond, B. Behavior modification: Teacher training and attitudes. *Exceptional Children*, 1976, 42, 402-403.

Stolurow, L. M. Suggestions for CAI curriculum development. *Viewpoints*, 1974, 50, 103-133.

Tomlinson, J. R. Implementing behavior modification programs with limited consultation time. *Journal of School Psychology*, 1972, 10, 379-386.

Weiderholdt, J. L., Hammill, D., & Brown, V. *The resource teacher: A guide to effective practices.* Boston: Allyn & Bacon, 1978.

Chapter 10

# COMPENSATORY PROGRAMMING AND ACCOMMODATION

The major purpose of secondary school is to teach students knowledge in a variety of content areas and practical competencies in vocational areas, not to teach basic skills. Very few secondary teachers have the training or interest to teach the skills of basic literacy. The academic survival of most mildly handicapped students depends on the advocacy of the secondary specialist who must encourage support for students who attend the mainstream classes of the school. Instructional practices of the secondary school will not yield easily to changes negotiated between the special educator and mainstream teachers because many teachers are unsympathetic, uncooperative, or bound by traditional attitudes.

The purpose of this chapter is to present major types of accommodatory approaches that may be used in compensatory models of special education for mildly handicapped adolescents. There are procedures that may be used in administration, the regular class, and the special class that will improve the opportunities for students to participate more completely in the mainstream. Although compensatory models are generally conceived for LD students, it is certain that many of the approaches would apply to emotionally disturbed or behaviorally disordered students as well as those classified as mildly mentally retarded. The method of delivery would be in a resource room, but consulting teachers could advocate the adoption of many of the approaches suggested in this chapter. However, the genesis for compensatory education in special education may be found primarily in the learning disabilities literature, where it is viewed as a responsibility of a resource room teacher. Hence, it is often regarded as a categorical approach for a segment of the mildly handicapped population that has the ability to benefit from the general school curriculum. Obviously, ED and many EMR students could also benefit, and compensatory techniques could be applied in remedial and vocational approaches that will be described in the following chapters. Much of the discussion that follows, however, will concentrate on programming for learning disabled students.

The dilemma for the secondary LD specialist, and the point of debate among authorities, is to determine the focus of the secondary program. Various notions have been expressed in the literature that advocate one or another specific approach. Decisions about what combination of remediation and compensatory teaching, or the extent of vocational preparation, should be determined on an *individual basis* rather than being preordained for all students who seem to fit a certain category because they share a label.

## CURRENT NOTIONS ABOUT SECONDARY LD PROGRAMS

Due to the importance of the issues about secondary programming for the learning disabled adolescent, it is necessary to consider the current notions expressed by various writers. What to teach or, more appropriately, what to emphasize for learning disabled students in a secondary program is the question on the minds of educational thinkers. The importance of these notions is underscored by the fact that (1) there is a general lack of agreement about the orientation of secondary programming, (2) the field is likely to devolve on one or more points of view, and (3) the welfare of students will depend on which decisions are made and in which direction the field goes.

Essentially, there are six major proposals about the nature and focus of the secondary LD program/curriculum (Brutten, 1967; Lehtinen-Rogan, 1971; Lerner, 1976; Maine, 1969; Mann et al., 1978; Marsh et al., 1978; Page, 1968; Reger et al., 1968; Siegel, 1974):

1. Students should be subjected to a cur-

riculum founded on perceptual training objectives.
2. Students should be subjected to intensive remediation of basic skills.
3. Students should have a separate, parallel curriculum.
4. Students should develop competencies in career education and functional survival skills.
5. Students should be trained in work skills leading to employment in specific job clusters.
6. Students should be accommodated to the maximum extent in the regular curriculum with a comprehensive support.

A number of factors probably shape the thinking of the various writers whose ideas are distilled into the six summary statements listed above. One can only infer from the writings what these factors might be, hence, why such diversity exists. Some writers are more closely associated with the contemporary problems of the educational system that impinge on the practitioners and students, while others propose broad, theoretical designs. Most of these approaches do not account for individualization but would group all students into a program with common group goals and processes. Each should be considered briefly:

1. *Perceptual training*. There is no evidence that many schools are actually adopting this approach with adolescents. It is difficult to defend in view of the dismal failure of remedial programs based on perceptual motor theories. Nonetheless, noted advocates contend that by the age of nine, most students will not benefit from corrective intervention (Wepman et al., 1975). There seem to be no compelling reasons to use perceptual motor training exercises with adolescents either because they cannot be expected to actually improve underlying processes or because adolescents have learned to compensate for deficits.

2. *Remediation*. Remedial programming will be considered as a major approach for general programming with mildly handicapped adolescents in Chapter 11, but it is considered here because of its popularity as a specific approach for LD students. Some professionals adopt the position that remediation of reading and mathematics disabilities is the *only* approach to be used with adolescents. This narrow view is supported by those who believe that achievement in basic skills is so essential that intensification of remedial efforts can be justified even if no support is provided to students with their mainstream classes.

3. *A parallel curriculum*. The need for a parallel curriculum provided in a self-contained program can only be justified if it can be determined that students are so atypical that there are no advantages to be gained from placement in the mainstream class and learning in the general curriculum. With respect to the social and legal changes of the last decade, especially P.L. 94-142, it would be most difficult to justify placement of otherwise intelligent students in a self-contained class. It seems that the most concern is with those adolescents who are nonreaders. There is little reason to believe, however, that persistent reading problems of disabled adolescents will improve much, even with massive remedial efforts extended over many years (Muehl & Forell, 1973-74). A parallel curriculum could only be defended if it could be demonstrated that the probabilities of dramatic success in achievement would be greatly enhanced by this approach.

4. *Career education and survival skills*. This denotation represents an approach that is a hybrid between remediation and vocational training. The danger is that a separate curriculum would develop similar to the work-study concept in which students would be encouraged to develop minimal competencies in reading and mathematics and be

trained for dead-end jobs. Common competencies for a diverse population would be established, although many students might benefit from other educational experiences in the school.

5. *Vocational preparation.* Placement of many adolescents in training of the various job clusters is certainly an acceptable approach because students may be able to develop work interests, attitudes, and skills to enter the labor force with a chance at vocational adjustment. Caution should be used to assure that students are not simply placed into vocational programming and that success in other parts of the general curriculum cannot be realized. Individual planning is the key to preventing tracking systems by considering the student rather than his or her label in making decisions about educational needs and training.

6. *Accommodation.* Accommodation may be considered as any of a variety of methods of adapting and adjusting school organization, curricula, or instructional methods to the learner; this would be part of a compensatory effort for students in liberal arts and vocational classes. As such, it is not a particular approach but a collection of strategies to help the learner cope in a setting where the major barrier to learning is institutionalized inflexibility of instructional procedures. Printed matter is one means of recording information, and reading is one medium of gaining access to it. The fact that printed matter may comprise as much as 75% of instructional activities of students does not mean that other means of learning, circumvention, and coping cannot be employed.

## ALTERNATIVE LEARNING MODELS IN THE REGULAR CLASS

The point has been made that secondary teachers generally make extensive reading assignments as the primary means of presenting information about subjects in the curriculum, that teacher talk (lectures) predominates as the characteristic instructional activity, and that students compete for grades by meeting teacher expectations on assignments and tests. This is a system survived by the most able students who have sufficient cultural orientation and motivation to prepare for long-range goals beyond the secondary school experience. It is less meaningful to the handicapped, low-achieving, unmotivated, and defiant.

The facts that 85% of high school course work is preparatory for college (Siegel, 1974) and that some high schools may be unpleasant and stultifying places to be (Silberman, 1971) do not alter the fact that this is the environment in which the students must learn, special educators must coexist, and advances must be made. Teachers cannot insulate handicapped students from the environment, as was once attempted with the mentally retarded, nor can they turn their backs on the secondary school and operate a self-contained class, like a haven. Teachers must assume a proactive role to bring about change, which may occur by the gradual assimilation of the best concepts, teaching strategies, and curricula of general and special education. Many excellent curricula and instructional strategies already exist.

The inquiry method of learning has been employed in the development of science materials by the Biological Sciences Curriculum Study Group (BSCS) of Boulder, Colorado. Not only has BSCS developed curricular and instructional systems that draw students into the methodologies of the disciplines they study, they have also developed very sophisticated approaches using this design for elementary and high school students, and for the educably mentally retarded. The *Me Now* and *Me and My Environment* curricula are excellent examples of methods that not only avoid the sterile, boring pedagogy of presenting lectures to students, but also utilize group processes in learning, emphasize the inquiry method of learning, and virtually eliminate the reading problem by circumventing reading as the means of gathering information.

Although there have been trends toward nongraded and cross-aged groups, most schools tend to continue in the pattern of grouping students by chronological age. Special education has been concerned with small groups and general education with larger ones, but rarely have groups been used as a medium for learning; rather, they have been viewed as the administrative manner by which students could be organized. There is good evidence that interaction between students in the classroom promotes more efficient learning. In order for this to happen, it is necessary for the teacher to stop talking as much and to become more of an interactor and facilitator. This has been accomplished in the BSCS approaches to the study of biological sciences and is a central concept in the interaction models of various curricular approaches: the T-group (Schein & Bennis, 1965), the social inquiry method (Massialis & Cox, 1966), the group investigation model (Thelen, 1960), and the classroom meeting model (Glasser, 1969).

In each of the interaction models for curriculum development, students assume active, rather than passive, learning roles: sharing in the learning experience, reducing the requirement to assume individual responsibility for gathering information, and utilizing the *group* as an educational *means* rather than an organizational pattern.

Innovations must become institutionalized in order for them to survive as viable strategies. For example, the problem with the inquiry method of teaching is that teachers tend to violate the rules of the paradigm on which the theory is based. Gradually, the process deteriorates into the familiar practice of students sitting passively as the teacher provides a straightforward lecture. One of the authors assisted in the development of an interaction model system for a senior high English class to accommodate mildly handicapped students who could not read well enough to manage the requirements of the school in the area of literature. By all accounts, the system was regarded as a success by the students and the teacher. The design is included in this chapter to serve as a model for extending the concept of individualization into the regular class.

However, special educators have much to learn from regular educators before they can presume to offer them advice about how to teach. In a sense this is part of the problem in gaining acceptance for inclusion of students in the mainstream class. Special educators are in the instructive (consultative) role with their colleagues and may not know what they are talking about. When special and regular educators approach one another on equal footing, freely admit their limitations, and share the responsibility of educating handicapped students, we will approach our goals more easily. For many special educators at the secondary level, it will be necessary to work in the system without the advantage of major efforts for change issuing from colleagues or the administration. For most special educators, the problems of assisting students in the mainstream will result from the information-processing, subject-centered curriculum that does not embrace the learner.

In reality, the typical classroom of the secondary school invites the learner to have a seat, to listen, to be passive, to read books and otherwise handle quantities of verbal material, and to take tests to demonstrate that knowledge has been acquired. There is a great deal of similarity between what happens in such a class and the theory of Ausubel (1963), who likens the information-processing system of academic disciplines to that of the human brain. The advance organizer model, as it is called by Ausubel, serves as an extremely efficient system of conceptualizing the organization of information, for developing lectures, covering predetermined amounts of expository information, and organizing the input of information to the learner. The purpose is to expeditiously reach levels of achievement: assimilation of factual information, development of concepts, and mastery of a body of knowledge. This is also the general purpose of the subject-centered curriculum.

The structuring of concepts and dependence on printed matter are the greatest obstacles to successful mainstreaming at the secondary level because they presuppose the need for students to read in order to learn. They are reinforced by the attitudes of some regular teachers that handicapped students have no place in regular classes. The challenge is to find ways to allow the student to participate in the mainstream class, to demonstrate competency in the subject matter of the class, and to do this without lowering the goals of education.

## INFORMATION FLOW AND INFORMATION PROCESSING

By suggesting the use of accommodatory techniques to complement instructional efforts on behalf of LD and other students, we are proposing a variety of ways to stimulate the flow of information to handicapped learners, information that is typically cut off because of the learner's deficits and instructional practices of the school. Clarification of the need for and uses of accommodation is included in the following points:

1. In keeping with the concept of the least restrictive environment, most mildly handicapped students will be expected to participate, as much as possible, in the regular curriculum of the school and will attend classes with their non–learning disabled peers. In those classes they will be expected to learn the content as prescribed by the curriculum and presented by various teachers.

2. Learning is the act of acquiring a *skill* or *knowledge*. Most secondary teachers are in the business of instructing students to *acquire knowledge* (factual information, concepts, etc.). Certainly, in the primary grades, and diminishing gradually throughout the middle grades, stress is placed on skill acquisition: reading, arithmetic, and writing. There is a major shift to acquisition of knowledge in the junior high as students develop the cognitive structures necessary to manage abstraction.

3. The major impediment to the acquisition of knowledge is the interruption of the information flow caused by (a) the student's lack of basic skills and (b) a lack of alternatives to reinstate the flow of information leading to the acquisition of knowledge.

Fig. 10-1 depicts the learning process involving students in the typical course of the secondary school. At least in this instance it can be seen that the medium (the medium of learning) is not the message.

Certain assumptions are made about the curriculum in most school districts for the purposes of this discussion. There are variations between school districts, but most predominant patterns invoke some type of specialization or centering on subject areas. In this section we are more interested in the organization of knowledge in curricula. Since the 1960s, curriculum planning has been based on knowledge as the element for design (Hass, 1977, p. 187). The relationships among a body of facts and concepts are organized sequentially and hierarchically; and all areas are conceived in this manner so that the curriculum can be thought of like a lattice. Knowledge is classified, categorized, and assigned to its particular discipline. Obviously, there are many criticisms of this approach, but there is a certain efficiency in this proce-

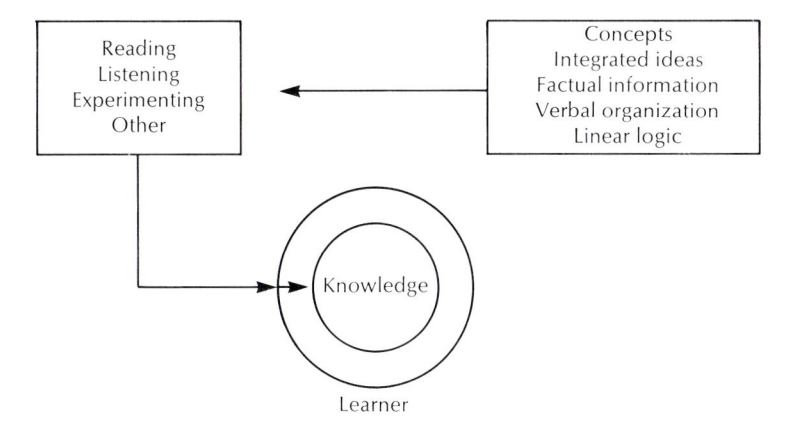

**Fig. 10-1.** Acquisition of knowledge as a product of information flow. NOTE: The learner must have the cognitive ability to assimilate abstract concepts that may result in reorganization of cognitive structures or accommodation to new structures.

dure because each discipline organizes its own knowledge and arranges it according to superordinate concepts, subordinate principles, and the structure of content around which learning activities may be designed.

A major task of the learner in the secondary school is to *acquire knowledge*. The ability to demonstrate that knowledge has been acquired is proved on examinations. Although it may appear to be an oversimplification, the greatest deficiency of most learning disabled and other handicapped adolescents is not an inability to develop concepts or acquire knowledge; rather, it is an inability to receive information necessary for learning and concept development in the disciplines. This inability (to receive information) may be thought of as an *individual* and an *ecological* variable. There will be differences in the disruption of information flow to individuals because of the severity of the reading disability, which varies with the individual, and differences in school settings because of variability in institutional flexibility to accommodate individuals.

If the cognitive structures of the learner are intact, if there is the ability to assimilate abstract concepts, then the learner is capable of acquiring knowledge. Most LD students have the capacity, theoretically, to attack any discipline or body of knowledge. The limiting factor in the educative process is that the learner may not be able to read efficiently, may not be able to perform mathematical calculations or to symbolize them, may not be able to produce acceptable written responses to class assignments, and may not be motivated. The learner is shut off from the information flow that leads to knowledge acquisition. In the same sense, blind students are shut off from the information flow but they are accommodated in a variety of ways to permit knowledge acquisition. Unfortunately, similar considerations have not been allowed for the learning disabled. The obstacles to learning created in and by the environment are institutionalized. These obstacles cannot be readily overcome unless remediation is totally, spectacularly effective. Accommodation is needed to open the learning process.

In summary, what must be done to bring many LD and ED students into the learning arena, to diminish their frustration and anxiety, and to permit them to succeed in many areas currently closed to them is to allow them to learn in classes in spite of their skill deficits. The following section deals with the specific approaches to accomplish this objective.

## TYPES OF ACCOMMODATIVE AND COMPENSATORY TECHNIQUES

Accommodation of the learning environment may be considered as any of a variety of methods of adapting the school organization, curriculum, or instructional methods to the learner. A number of techniques may be considered but not as a total programmatic approach for all students. Rather, they should be conceptualized as a series of possible strategies that might be applied to a specific student. Fig. 10-2 identifies the major components of accommodation.

### Administrative options in accommodation

The greatest amount of change in a system (organization, school, etc.) occurs as a direct result of major policy decisions at the pinnacle of the administration. Persons who have the power to make broad changes can affect the arrangement, goals, purposes, and conditions of all subsystems quickly and dramatically. Persons who hold positions with less power and influence at lower levels of the administration have a much more limited impact on the functions of the system. It seems clear that the mainstreaming movement has been most successful in those districts where school boards, superintendents, and principals were subjected to in-service training and assisted in making policy decisions about integrating the handicapped. Therefore, depending on the support of the building principal and other administrators in the school or district, the specialist can expect a wide range of variation in attitudes and concrete efforts to implement accommodatory policies. Some major administrative contributions are listed in Fig. 10-2: personnel development, enrollment, pupil progress, and curricular variations. Some states may have laws pertaining to some of these topics, which should be carefully considered before making recommendations about a particular course of action.

**Personnel development.** Included within this subcomponent are two important and

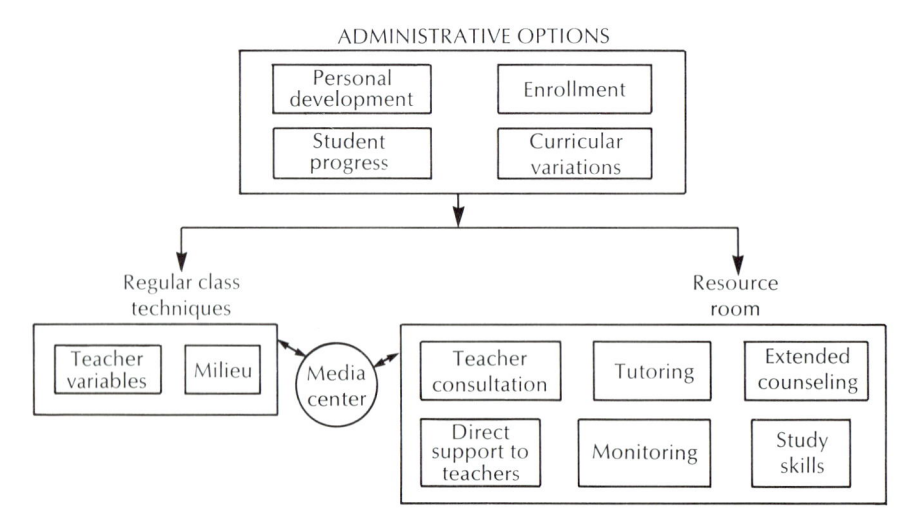

**Fig. 10-2.** Components of accommodation.

controversial issues: in-service training and release time. They are important because personnel development cannot occur without a formalized, concerted effort of the institution to bring about change in the attitudes and behaviors of teaching personnel and administrators. They are controversial because of the poor attitudes of teachers about in-service training, the emerging struggle for control of in-service programs (teachers vis-á-vis state departments vis-á-vis universities), and the fact that these issues are becoming bargaining points in deliberations between organized teachers and school boards.

The specialist can participate in active personnel development programs to communicate the general objectives of the special education effort and can attempt to affect the attitudes of the faculty and enlist their cooperation. In-service programming can be filled with "land mines" that can damage the effort.

Many secondary teachers have a period of time during the day that is variously called planning or preparation time. Whether the teacher uses this period to "smoke and joke" with friends or to actually prepare for classroom instruction, it is highly valued time and teachers will resent intrusions during that period. If provision can be made for the specialist to meet with regular teachers through release time or other arrangements, significant contacts can be made to benefit students. In any event, efforts should be made to avoid inconveniencing regular class teachers. There are a few agreeable teachers in most schools who will readily cooperate, and they provide a good beginning.

**Enrollment procedures.** The specialist should be thoroughly familiar with all facets of enrollment. Major concerns are:

1. The requirements for junior and senior high school students to be promoted/graduated—some states have very specific requirements (e.g., state history).
2. The options available for each required course—many schools have lower-level classes for many subjects designed for low-achieving students.
3. The names, personalities, attitudes, and characteristics of instructors should be known—this would include information about their attitudes toward students with learning disabilities, flexibility, willingness to provide assistance and to individualize, and other information important to placement.
4. Awareness of any policies that may pertain to such student-personnel issues as reduced loads, prolonged time periods for course credit, and delayed graduation.

Typically, the school guidance counselor, in league with parents and students, handles arrangements for scheduling. In some school districts the procedure is controlled by a management system, often computerized. Scheduling is an administrative function, and few classroom teachers have responsibility for it. For most students the procedure is quite routine and accomplished without much effort, but for LD and other mildly handicapped students this is no perfunctory matter. The wrong schedule, the impact of very difficult courses, the wrong teacher, and any of a number of other variables can be disastrous. For these reasons school survival is a dependent variable. The specialist should at least assume a *monitoring* role in this process. The specialist will be more familiar with each student's needs and can communicate these to the counselor or other persons administratively responsible for scheduling. Students and their parents should be actively involved in making decisions. The specialist must be equipped to give them appropriate information to make those decisions. Inappropriate enrollment can be a major cause of poor adjustment and failure.

**Curricular variations.** The administration has control over any policies that govern variations of curricular arrangements, credits, extensions or delays in course completion, and so on. Some types of curricular variation are described below.

***Exceptions to course credit and graduation policies.*** Under the regulations of Section 504, Rehabilitation Amendments of 1973, which primarily pertain to postsecondary schools, students are permitted to have prolonged time periods for course completion and meeting graduation requirements if they meet the criteria defining handicapping conditions. Moreover, they are entitled to exceptions in the conduct of course work, meeting specific requirements of instructors, and taking examinations. We would suggest that advocates attempt to have such policies adopted by state departments of education and local school boards because they are sensible, are in the spirit of equality, and would significantly reduce the number of students who would drop out of school, defeated by the system.

***Course equilibrium.*** A schedule, or course load, should reflect the needs of the student and be balanced between courses that are taxing and those that are less demanding. This, as in other determinations, must be based on the needs, abilities, and limitations of the individual student. A factor in this procedure is *which* teachers are assigned to certain courses under consideration. Cooperative teachers can be counted on to ease the burden on the student by providing support through accommodation.

Equilibrium is obtained when courses are balanced between those that are easier and those that are expected to be more difficult for a student. Courses can be *clustered* so that content in one is reinforcing to another. Scheduling should be individualized to account for different interests, rates of learning, specific learning disabilities, personality characteristics, and other individual factors that would impinge on learning. These might include such easily overlooked factors as when the student should have lunch, the best time for physical education, and what class should be arranged after lunch. For example, some students seem to be fatigued, inattentive, or aggressive at certain times during the day. An active class for a student who tires after lunch, rather than American history, or avoidance of a particular teacher who seems to be able to elicit anger from vulnerable students, would evidence wise decision making.

In order to have sufficient information the specialist should maintain a complete file of all existing courses as well as the associated requirements of particular teachers. The file would include, but not be limited to, the following information:

1. Course title
2. Prerequisites
3. Objectives
4. Description of content
5. Syllabus
6. Samples of lesson plans
7. Evaluative criteria
8. Extra assignments: reports, experiments, and so forth
9. Compatibility with other courses
10. Sources of related materials, films, tapes, and so on
11. Tutors available
12. Instructors

***Course substitution.*** Some school districts provide lower-level courses (practical English, basic math, etc.) that are far less demanding than the regular required courses taken by most students. Although these courses may be used to satisfy the required credit for students, we would suggest that decisions be selectively made for each student rather than tracking all LD students through these courses. The content of practical courses is designed for intellectually marginal students; thus there is a lower level of cognitive processing required and more concrete examples, in addition to lowered reading demands. Sometimes instructors in these classes "get stuck with the lower kids" because of assignments made by the department head. They may resent it and be hostile to students. The *skill* deficit should not be taken to mean that a student has low intellectual ability and should not be used to justify such placement. The experience could be stultifying. If proper accommodations and compensatory teaching techniques are used there should be infrequent reason for a student to have to be relegated to some low-track course.

There are, of course, situations and circumstances that would lead to the decision to select a substitute course. If it meets a need and suits the characteristics of the learner, then it might be feasible.

**Course supplantation.** We define supplantation as a course credit for a student earned under the supervision of a special education teacher in the resource room. In some states we are aware that special teachers at the secondary level can provide instruction for students that results in a course credit equal in value to courses taught by regular instructors. We are also aware that this has been abused. Some teachers without any background or training in a subject area involve students in inadequate activities purported to be similar to regular course content. There can be little justification for this. It is perfectly acceptable to assist students in the content of any course but inappropriate to assume major responsibility for the course work. If this method (supplantation) is attempted, it should be done only if the specialist also has certification in the content area and *only* with the full cooperation of an instructor of that subject. Under a cooperative arrangement, the regular class instructor and the specialist may be able to develop materials, adopt strategies, devise examinations that reduce reading, and accumulate materials and guides to make such a course maximally meaningful. With some experimentation and refinement and continued support, the regular teacher may elect to introduce the approaches into the regular setting for the benefit of all students.

*Alternative/modified curricula.* There are a few commercially available curricula, particularly in mathematics and science, that might be useful for students in a resource room. A note of caution about alternative or parallel curricula should be made. Before expending sizeable amounts of the school budget for materials, an effort should be made to assure that the materials are suitable and that they would not interfere with other instructional activities. With the exception of self-paced, programmable materials, most available programs will require considerable time and attention of the teacher because they are developed for group classroom use. One would not want to purchase materials if they supplant what can be readily accomplished in a regular class nor laboriously organize instruction that, in effect, becomes a course.

Modification of existing curricula to meet teaching objectives or the development of curriculum materials that are compatible with the goals of regular courses are time-consuming efforts worthy of the endeavor. Essentially, the procedure involves the identification of clear and stable concepts and principles in an organized body of knowledge to facilitate the acquisition of knowledge by reducing frustration on the part of the learner and using circumventive strategies to obviate the reading deficiency. Much of the work is actually done for the teacher because the curriculum (in this day of behavioral objectives) lists the most inclusive and subsequent concepts in the instructors' guide. These are the targets of all the learning activities in a course. In the process of developing modifications, efforts are made to reduce readability or eliminate it by use of tapes and audiovisual aids, and to simplify the process of acquiring the outcomes. The culmination of modification is clarification of content, simplification of materials, and development of criteria for mastery of materials that are known to the students and teachers. The concept of mastery learning is certainly germane for these purposes.

**Pupil progress.** Although the school guidance counselor and the specialist will assume some responsibility for following the progress of pupils, the individual classroom teachers and the administration will have formal procedures for marking progress and quantifying it. The role of the specialist will be to attempt to install an early-warning system so that any indication of a failure will be detected and interventions developed to get the student back on the successful track to course completion. This will rely heavily on the cooperation and sensitivity of the regular class teacher in the mainstream. There are a few issues about pupil progress that are controlled by the administration of the school and that should be considered here.

One policy that would be of assistance to LD students is a *reduced load* or *extended graduation* for qualified pupils. On the face of it, a sensible argument can be offered by demonstrating how a student with a reduction in academic demands would be able to capitalize on the resources of his or her learning abilities and attack a fewer number of courses in the same time frame as the average student. By permitting the student to earn sufficient credits for graduation over a longer span it may be possible to assist more of them toward the goal of graduation. There may be criticism of this practice in some circles, and many students may not wish to sever their identification with the group of students they accompanied to secondary school. The social identity with a particular senior class and a circle of friends cannot be easily dismissed. Nonetheless, these are options that may be available in some schools.

Another issue concerning pupil progress is the *minimum competency* test, an idea that has not been clearly thought out by those who would require its use. We have addressed this topic in another section because it has some implications for mildly handicapped students. Some have suggested (*Phi Delta Kappan*, February 1979, 60(6), 412) that the movement will quickly disappear because of massive court actions against it. Schools should assure that students are benefiting from their educational careers, but the testing movements as it is presently conceived promises to create more problems than it will solve, especially for mildly handicapped adolescents. If the specialist is to be involved with the competency test we would endorse the recommendation of Merle Steven McClung, of the Center for Law and Education, reported by Neill (1979), which states that schools should not set a uniform policy for special education students regarding the use of and awarding of a diploma on the basis of a competency test. The standards for passing and graduation can be included in the IEP of each handicapped student.

## ACCOMMODATION: REGULAR CLASS TECHNIQUES

The most salient feature of accommodation in the regular class is the characteristic pattern of circumventive strategies that permit the handicapped learner to achieve commensurate with the common expectation for all students. One or more actions that may be employed to bypass the learning disability may serve to assist the student toward the goal of learning about our culture and our world; and, in this capacity, accommodation is only one part of a total effort to educate the individual in conjunction with other actions, such as remediation. The focus of assistance to handicapped learners is widened beyond a restrictive preoccupation with only the learning disabilities.

The unfortunate experience of some students is that if they receive *only* remediation in the secondary school, they fail to learn to read or overcome underlying process deficits, and they fail to pass their classes. They end their school careers illiterate and uneducated. If the secondary program is limited only to account for basic skill deficits and/or basic psychological processes correlated with learning disabilities, students will have no assistance toward the goals of secondary education obtainable in mainstream classes. The use of accommodation in regular classes by mainstream teachers is of utmost importance. Most will not assume responsibility for improvement of basic skills but they can be instrumental in circumventing deficits in basic skills. Cooperation, mutual responsibility, and open exchange between the resource teacher and mainstream teachers are imperative.

The most crucial element in accommodation and compensatory teaching is successful implementation of these techniques in mainstream classes. Although the administration may adopt progressive policies and the resource teacher may be eager to consult with and support mainstream teachers, if the classroom door is shut to cooperation and mutual responsibility, little progress can be expected. The ability of the special teacher to elicit cooperation with mainstream teachers will be the deciding factor about program change; the teacher must patiently establish rapport with department heads and teachers, develop commonly accepted practices to assist students, and strive to get mainstream teachers to implement and refine circumventive teaching strategies. The more these practices become systematized and reduced to standard operating procedures, the more likely they will remain as permanent programmatic features with long-term benefits.

We have presented the reader with strategies for gaining the support and cooperation of mainstream teachers in various sections of this text so they will not be repeated here.

However, it should be reemphasized that the most important consideration is to avoid, in appearance and actuality, intensification of daily teaching and clerical burdens on mainstream teachers. The more that accommodation techniques reduce their anxieties and work load, the more likely will be acceptance and cooperation.

The component of regular class techniques encompasses a number of *teacher-controlled variables*. What follows are recommendations that may work with some teachers in various settings.

## TEACHER-CONTROLLED VARIABLES

Each teacher is trained in a discipline. Many courses, especially the academic ones, are founded on disciplines having a knowledge base; the task of teachers is to communicate knowledge to students in the form of facts and concepts. The state curriculum guide, the local curriculum guide, the course syllabus, and commercial materials are uniformly tied to the framework of each discipline. The following general observations may be made about courses/disciplines:

1. Although the nature of learning activities may vary from class to class, the knowledge contents of similar courses are based on invariant *key concepts* and *principles*.
2. Within each discipline there are several board concepts linked together to form the structure of the discipline.
3. Within this structure are subordinate concepts and facts that comprise the substance of lectures and reading or other assignments.

By extracting the key concepts and principles from the disciplines, the mainstream teacher and the special teacher can identify the precise targets of course work, the general structure and format of content, and the relationship of units, lectures, and assignments. The specialist will not be expected to specialize in any particular discipline, but an understanding of the general organization and intentions of each will enable teaching personnel to work together cooperatively because they will be able to communicate about a common purpose.

If the specialist and mainstream teachers have an understanding about the general nature of subject matter by identification of key concepts and principles, it is possible for the specialist to assume a more active role in directing and managing accommodatory techniques, assisting in mainstream class activities, and directing resource room activities related to survival in the mainstream. It should be recognized that, although the secondary curriculum is much more expansive, many resource teachers who work in middle schools and elementary schools that are departmentalized must deal with subject-matter specialization (language arts, science, etc.), which, although not as complex, is certainly similar to the challenge confronting the resource teacher in a junior or senior high school program. The remainder of this section deals with accommodation techniques that may be instigated by the resource teacher but that must be conducted by the mainstream teacher. The resource room is a support system, in large part, for accommodations in the regular class.

**Topical outline**

The mainstream teacher may prepare a topical outline of the course that reflects the general flow of course content. This would be predicated on key concepts and principles and the anticipated accomplishments of students as determined by the local curriculum guide. Some teachers do not provide students with a syllabus or other direction in the course, relying instead on daily assignments. Topical outlines would benefit all students, not just the handicapped student and the resource teacher, and they should be easy to supply.

The advantage of a topical outline is that it assists students in attempts to organize thoughts, notes, and information into a meaningful record to be used in the acquisition of course outcomes. A simple outline related to class lectures and intermediate objectives of units can be indispensable as a study guide because it imposes order on the factual information and data of daily lessons.

**Study guides**

A more formalized and demanding procedure than a topical outline is a study guide, which may be designed with specific objectives, assignments, and evaluative criteria. An elaboration of the study guide may be a written *learning contract*, which clearly identifies the major concepts that are to be obtained through study of specific content. It is worth noting that once such instruments are completed, they may easily be used with some modification for each student who subsequently enrolls for the course. Once the initial burden of developing a comprehensive study guide or learning contract is completed, it requires much less labor in subsequent efforts with other students. We have included examples of learning contracts in Chapter 9.

The learning contract would include the following minimum sections:

1. Specific objectives to be accomplished
2. Period of time during which the learning activities would be completed
3. Specific products of study such as book reports and experiments
4. Specific reading assignments (or negotiated alternatives) and other learning activities
5. Evaluative criteria (with pass/fail or letter grades associated with levels of successful completion)

**Technical vocabularies/glossaries**

Many nonhandicapped students at the secondary and college level encounter considerable difficulty in reading assignments and understanding lectures in many courses because terminology, jargon, and unfamiliar concepts must be learned and internalized before they become meaningful. The curious aspect about reading in content areas is that it is tied to a writing style unlike that of recreational reading or instructional materials used to teach reading. It is expository in nature, replete with major sections, subsections, changes in size and style of print, numerous graphs, and peculiar words and concepts. Most graduate students who have taken courses in research and statistics will recall the initial frustration caused by the unfamiliarity with statistical concepts and terms. As a student enters a new discipline, words appear with great frequency that are totally foreign or that have different meanings than in the vernacular.

In addition to varying degrees of ability to decipher new words in a course, most students will experience difficulty with terms and concepts. It is not necessary to read a term to learn its meaning and to be able to use it. Lists of terms available in glossaries may be used by tutors or placed on tape for students to simplify the definitional process involved in a body of knowledge. If the only manner by which a student can learn a new term, such as *plateau* or *water table*, is by reading it, then it is apparent that many students will fail. If the task is altered so that knowledge can be acquired by circumventing the deficit, education can proceed in spite of the limitations of the learner to gather information from printed matter. Mainstream teachers can be taught how to introduce and reinforce the understanding of new terms as a function of teaching reading in content areas.

## Advance organizers

As we have described the theory of Ausubel in relation to curriculum development, the term "advance organizer" has previously been introduced from his works to describe a process of mastery learning in curriculum areas. This term has also been adopted by some reading instructors for use in reading instruction with a similar purpose. Prereading questions are provided to the learner before he or she is induced to cover a reading section in a book. Presumably, the reader is cued to certain information that is required from the passage such as, "What is the major agricultural export of Bolivia?" Such questions reduce the task of the student to specific bits of information, shorten the reading time required to complete an assignment, and eliminate floundering about in a sea of paragraphs without a sense of purpose and with no expectations of subsequent responsibility for the information. Most persons will agree that textbooks are not very stimulating to read and that their major purpose is to present facts and concepts to the reader about the particular body of knowledge. Why not simply short-circuit the process for the slow reader? If a student learns that the Magna Charta was a major concession of the monarchy to commoners, which later became the underpinning of the U.S. Constitution, it should not concern us how the student learned it.

Advance organizers in a unit of study are incredibly simple to develop, and they can be related to traditional reading assignments, compressed reading matter, or to tape-recorded passages for students unable to read efficiently. An example of organizers for a unit on ancient Egypt follows:

1. What was the climate of the Nile valley?
2. How did the inhabitants make a living?
3. What were the major types of commerce?
4. How was the government organized?
5. What language(s) did the people speak?
6. What level of science did they develop?
7. What was the medium for trade: barter or money?

## Summaries of concepts

Another aid to students is the provision of summaries of content by mainstream teachers, which relate to the major concepts of a unit or course. Frequently, some teachers tend to be more interested in certain topics and will emphasize some aspects more than others. The textbooks and other printed matter may not embrace these emphases; hence the student may be at a disadvantage. It is also true that the most complex, abstract points of a unit are not understood by students. The complaint of a teacher that, "We covered that in class," is often surprising to students who attended more to the concrete aspects of the material than to the subtle, abstract qualities appreciated by the teacher. The ability to compare and contrast knowledge at highest levels of conceptual attainment requires nurturance and assistance that may be partly provided by the dissemination of summaries.

## Audiovisual aids

The variety of audiovisual aids available in schools to assist in the learning process is staggering; in light of this it is surprising how few teachers use much more than a piece of chalk. Some factors that might explain this are that some teachers do not know how to use equipment, others cannot interrelate it with class activities that may predominantly surround a lecture, and for others it may seem to be a lot of trouble when lecturing will suffice. The resource teacher may examine inventories to identify and locate what equipment and materials exist and endeavor to employ them in learning activities.

## Use of tape recorders

We have found the use of tape recorders as a substitute for notes to be unacceptable for most students. There is a tendency to lose attention in class because of total reliance on the machine. Studying with tapes is unwieldy because it is possible to tape as many as 20 to 25 hours of lecture in a single week. Students who have difficulty sitting through class in the first place are not likely to benefit much from sitting through the lecture again with the aid of a tape recorder. The best use of tape recording is in the initial presentation of information to students, as a substitute for books.

## Special texts

Special texts with a watered down vocabulary are generally available for certain subjects. Utilizing them is difficult, however. Some students would rather not possess them because of associated connotations. Many courses will not have alternative materials available. We recommend the use of *compressed* material, which is the distillation of materials into key concepts and principles, and important words and summaries.

A teacher who is currently involved with an in-service project associated with the University of Arkansas has utilized this technique at the secondary level to good measure. The objective is to reduce each two to three pages of a written text to one-half or one page of reading matter. This need not be done by the teacher. Students or volunteers may supply the labor to compress the major textbooks of several courses for use by students with reading problems as well as for the learning disabled. The amount of work presented to a student with compressed reading matter does not seem as overwhelming. It must be remembered that a typical student in high school may have as many as six or seven major textbooks per semester. Compressed material eliminates a lot of tedious work and improves attitudes toward reading; use by tutors is helpful in tutoring sessions and the material is easily transformed to audiovisual materials and to programmable learning machines.

## Alternative responding

Typical demands on the learner in terms of classroom performance are verbal responses in class, written responses, oral reports, and tests. Students receive grades for the qualtiy of their responses with greatest emphasis on tests. The inability to read, to speak articulately, or to write will hamper many mildly handicapped students. We endorse procedures that have been recognized as important by national testing bureaus, initially for blind students and now for students with certified learning disorders. Students should be permitted to supply tape-recorded responses or dictated transcripts for such assignments as book reports and should be permitted to have readers/writers for examinations.

We have discovered that if a resource teacher becomes involved in alternative testing, it is necessary to assure the teachers that cheating will not occur and that the test "won't get out." There is, of course, a real danger of this unless procedures are established that prevent tests from being compromised.

An interesting system was developed in a vocational-technical school by use of a programmable learning machine. Tests were placed on the machine with audio and visual presentation of questions. The student could respond by pushing the appropriate button to indicate his or her choice of answers. This eliminated the burden on teaching personnel, reduced the reading and writing demands on students, and satisfied the mainstream teachers. A by-product was that tests were improved in format, presentation style, and reliability by the specialists.

## Talking books

Talking books and other services for the blind are available to learning disabled students in some states where a psychologist is willing to certify them as dyslexic. The services are not that helpful because of delays in getting materials and the fact that many materials of importance in course work must be prepared at the local level to be maximally effective.

## Milieu

Milieu is a teacher-controlled variable in learning that interacts with other facets of teaching, making it difficult to measure its importance and effect in isolation. Milieu should be viewed as interwoven with teacher attitude, techniques, curriculum, teacher training, and teacher personality. The relationship of these factors to the environment as fostered by the teacher should be obvious. Change in teacher behavior cannot be accomplished solely through manipulation of milieu, but environmental factors should be considered in the accommodation process. Environmental factors include the definition of a "good" student, classroom rules, student-teacher interaction, student interaction, and physical space.

**Definition of a "good" student.** Teacher values and expectations set the tone for the classroom environment. The type of student desired by the teacher as a product of the program is probably the major determinant of the classroom atmosphere. The definition of a "good" student is related to the teaching style and the way in which the room is operated. Teaching styles produce definite effects on students, including the following results (Flanders, 1951, p. 110):

1. Teacher behavior characterized as directive, demanding, deprecating by the use of private criteria, and, in general, supporting of the teacher, elicits student behaviors of hostility toward self or the teacher, and withdrawal, apathy, aggressiveness, and emotional disintegration.

2. Teacher behavior characterized as receptive, problem oriented, evaluative, or critical by way of public criteria, and, in gen-

eral, student supportive, elicits student behaviors of problem orientation, decreased interpersonal anxiety, integration, and emotional readjustment.

Research results have been reported that indicate the existence of several types of teachers and students and that teacher effectiveness is enhanced by matching certain teacher types with certain student types (Bush, 1954; Heil et al., 1960). Bush (1954, p. 170) states that "a certain type of student tends to work successfully with one, rather than another, type of teacher," a belief long held by educators.

Research in the quantitative measuring and identification of teacher behaviors continues, but as yet this knowledge has not been utilized by practitioners responsible for teacher evaluation and student placement. Decisions as to section or grade are still based on policies and subjective, impressionistic reactions of administrators. The *Omega list* (Marsh et al., 1978) is an example of operational recognition of the effect of teacher behavior and expectations in placing students. In completing an Omega list, the following dimensions of the process of classroom interaction as identified by Spaulding (1965) should be considered:

- Means by which approval and disapproval are conveyed
- Manner in which teachers utilize their authority with students
- Emotional tone of the classroom
- Means by which teachers prefer to receive student information
- Types of student behavior that elicit approval or disapproval

**Classroom rules.** Behavioral standards are rarely consistent among classrooms even when general guidelines are dictated by school policy. The range of student behaviors observed reflects variance in tolerance for student interaction, social expectations, and standards for performance. Students typically can identify very clearly standards or rules for each class, even if they are unwritten. For example, students standing in a hallway were overheard discussing a particular class and the fact that having "junk" other than one's book on the desk during the lecture always resulted in negative attention from the instructor in the form of "watching," "picking on for questions," or confiscation of the item. We doubt if the teacher recognized this as a classroom rule, but the students certainly did!

Classroom rules and teacher behavior definitely affect pupil behavior as revealed in studies of dominative or socially integrative teacher behavior patterns (Anderson, 1937, 1939; Anderson & Brewer, 1946). Teachers whose behavior was primarily integrative had classes in which students demonstrated more initiative in their studies. The number and nature of the classroom rules as well as the manner in which they are enforced must be considered as integral in evaluating milieu and for considering accommodation.

**Student-teacher interaction.** The type and amount of student-teacher interaction is an important aspect of milieu. Researchers have measured the classroom climate based on teacher statements and questions (Mitzel & Rabinowitz, 1953; Withall, 1952). Teachers were found to differ significantly in their verbal behavior, producing different climates in the room. It is not unrealistic then to expect adolescents with academic and social problems to function better in a learner-supportive climate fostered by positive interaction with the teacher.

Student-teacher interaction can result in increased or decreased anxiety on the part of both parties, thus affecting the individual's performance as well as his or her attitude. Depending on the situation and the student, interaction with the teacher should be positive and consistent with the interaction allowed other students. Being overly solicitous of the student can be detrimental and interfere with student performance just as much as lack of attention and assistance.

**Student interaction.** The studies supporting the use of peer tutors illustrate the point that students learn from each other (Cloward, 1967; Erickson, 1971; Thomas, 1972). Spaulding (1965), the developer of the Coping Analysis Schedule for Educational Settings (CASES), has identified a behavioral category called integrative social interaction. It is described as mutual give/take, cooperative behavior, and studying or working together where participants are on a par. This type of behavior appears to be positively related to learning and motivation, making integrative social interaction among students a desirable educational goal.

Unfortunately, many secondary classes do not allow or foster peer interaction in the form of tutoring or group learning. The traditional classroom is teacher centered with little or no provision made for student interaction. When the resource teacher examines the regular class offerings for a possible mainstreaming placement, the amount and type of student interactions should be considered. Classroom visitations, student observations with an instrument such as CASES, and interviews with regular students provide useful insight into the student interaction nurtured in a classroom.

## APPROACHES TO INDIVIDUALIZATION IN THE MAINSTREAM CLASS

Individualized *instruction* and the individualized educational *plan* (IEP) are not synonymous. The IEP may specify the objectives, learning activities, and evaluative criteria for an individual student; however, all learning activities must be planned in accordance with variables controlled by mainstream teachers unless, of course, many of them are to occur in the resource room. Individualization in the mainstream must account for organization of the learning environment, delivery of efficient instruction, coordination of classroom activities, and simultaneous instruction of a number of pupils who may have different needs and problems (Gickling et al., 1979). What a student should learn may be determined by assessment and recommendations of various professionals and partly shaped by the curriculum and tradition, but how this will be accomplished in the educational environment can be a challenging problem to mainstream and resource teachers.

Individualized instruction is said to occur more frequently in elementary schools, primarily because children are engaged in individual seat work from 25% to 45% of the time (Adams & Biddle, 1970; Gump, 1967; Herbert, 1967); but seat work is not necessarily individualized instruction, especially if each child is sitting independently while working on the same page of a workbook. However, at least there is a time frame in the mainstream class that could permit individualization. It is much more difficult to find the time or to engineer the classroom so that the curriculum can be presented via an individualized approach in high school.

Individualized instruction, as conceived in the IEP, reveals the influence of behaviorism because learning objectives are prescribed in behavioral terms, the conditions of learning are specified, and the behavior to be learned is evaluated objectively. However, the utilization of behavioral principles in education, especially at the secondary level, has encountered problems because of the resistance of educators and the incongruity of a laboratory-based system of teaching for individuals and rigid group instructional arrangements. The problem of incongruity is further complicated by the preferred teaching style at the secondary level.

Large group instruction, limited individual work, and a predominant lecture method of teaching will not yield easily to innovation. Any alteration of this style is radical because the teacher, who has total control, will inevitably lose some degree of control with any change except that of removal of the student from the class for a period of time in the resource room. Although the student may progress with accommodatory techniques in the mainstream class and support from the resource room, the best efforts of the specialist would be the communication of concepts that will reorganize the learning environment of the mainstream class, enable the mainstream teacher to coordinate activities and deal simultaneously with a number of students and their accompanying problems, and individualize instruction.

The status quo affords comfort to the mainstream teacher; the routines of the day are clear, and covering predetermined quantities of work through lectures meets the expectations of administrators. The handicapped student who attends the resource room provides an expedient solution for the teacher. There is really no sense of sharing in the solution of educational problems of the student—the responsibility is shouldered by the resource teacher. If the resource teacher provides remedial reading instruction for the student, the mainstream teacher will be oblivious to the activities of the resource room. To combine scientific learning principles with instructional technology in order to replace the prevailing pattern of group instruction is a challenge, but one with extraordinary potential benefits for handicapped students. This is an ambitious undertaking and one that would be impossible without tremendous impetus for change at the level of the board of education and superintendency. It would be naive to presume that any individual teacher could possibly have that kind of impact. There are, however, some methodologies and concepts that may be borrowed from individualized educational systems to assist the resource teacher in working optimally in any setting.

There have been many plans and attempts to develop systems of individualized education, but they have not generally been embraced by institutions. The advent of technological innovations, programmed learning, and other scientific approaches to learning has enabled educators to revamp school organization to provide individualized education. The reasons for reluctance to change may be attributable to any number of factors, including tradition, lack of financial resources, and failure of teacher-training institutions to prepare teaching candidates appropriately.

Three highly sophisticated approaches to individualization have been developed for use with all students, primarily in elementary schools, and have been implemented successfully. These systems are: PLAN (Program for Learning in Accordance with Needs), marketed by the Westinghouse Corporation; IGE (Individually Guided Education), developed by the Wisconsin Research and Development Center; and Adaptive Environments for Learning, developed by the Learning Research and Development Center of the University of Pittsburgh. The common characteristics of these three systems have been reported by Briggs (1975):

1. They emphasize flexibility so that all children may be educated rather than focusing on the children who fit certain patterns of interests and aptitudes.
2. Each system uses a similar core of objectives.
3. Each system is humane because each treats students as individuals and does not view different rates of progress in some students as failure.
4. Each student is assessed to determine an entry point for instruction, and the instructional effort is designed for a particular student.

5. Sophisticated monitoring systems are used to follow the progress of the students.
6. Each system of individualization uses predesigned materials.
7. Each learner receives continuous feedback information.

As much as any system would be able to approximate these conditions in the development of instructional approaches, benefits to handicapped and nonhandicapped students would be realized. The resource teacher could not hope to alter the instructional practices of a secondary school to the extent of any of these systems, but subsystems utilizing these concepts are within reach.

Talmage (1975) has identified the components of traditional and individualized instructional systems (Table 12).

## Programming with a bivalent system

Synthesis of the characteristics of the traditional and individualized systems into an amalgamation or *bivalent system* may help to resolve problems in conceptualizing programming for secondary handicapped students in a school that is structured to resist innovations. The bivalent system is shown in Fig. 10-3. The student must typically enter the content course with a fixed entry point, fixed pace, and fixed termination and outcomes. To turn the system to the student's advantage, accommodation techniques may be applied in the classroom, support may be provided by the resource teacher to the mainstream teacher, and support may be provided to the student (study skills, tutoring, etc.). Although the student would be required to reach certain outcomes in the same time span as other students, he or she would be permitted to do so in alternative ways with reduced or eliminated reading, use of tapes and tutors, and alternative testing. The traditional system remains intact (it cannot be changed dramatically because of institutional rigidity), but it would be altered significantly to aid the student in mastery of the content and achievement of knowledge goals.

Simultaneously, remediation of basic skills such as reading and mathematics (or other types of remediation) may proceed in the resource program without the constraints of the traditional program. Variable entry, multiple routes for learners, and open-ended termination of remediation would be incorporated in an individualized program. The individualized program would continue until the learner reaches a terminal criterion (e.g., sixth or seventh grade competency), as in a criterion-dismissal program, or would continue indefinitely to any level of achievement possible throughout the student's secondary school career.

The significance of the bivalent system for handicapped learners should be apparent. The immediate needs of the student are accounted for, making resource room assistance of greater value to the student; retention in school can become an attainable goal; assistance is provided to the mainstream teacher that fully exercises the consulting role of the specialist; and long-term benefits can be derived after months and years of interaction with mainstream teachers, leading to more

**Table 12.** Components of traditional and individualized instructional systems according to Talmage (1975)

| Traditional | Individualized |
|---|---|
| Fixed outcomes for all learners | Criterion-referenced outcomes |
| Fixed entry points | Variable entry points |
| Fixed time and pacing | Variable pacing |
| Limited decision-making role of learner | Active decision-making role of learner |
| Large group instruction | Peer or individual grouping |
| Norm-referenced evaluation of learner | Criterion-referenced evaluation of learner |

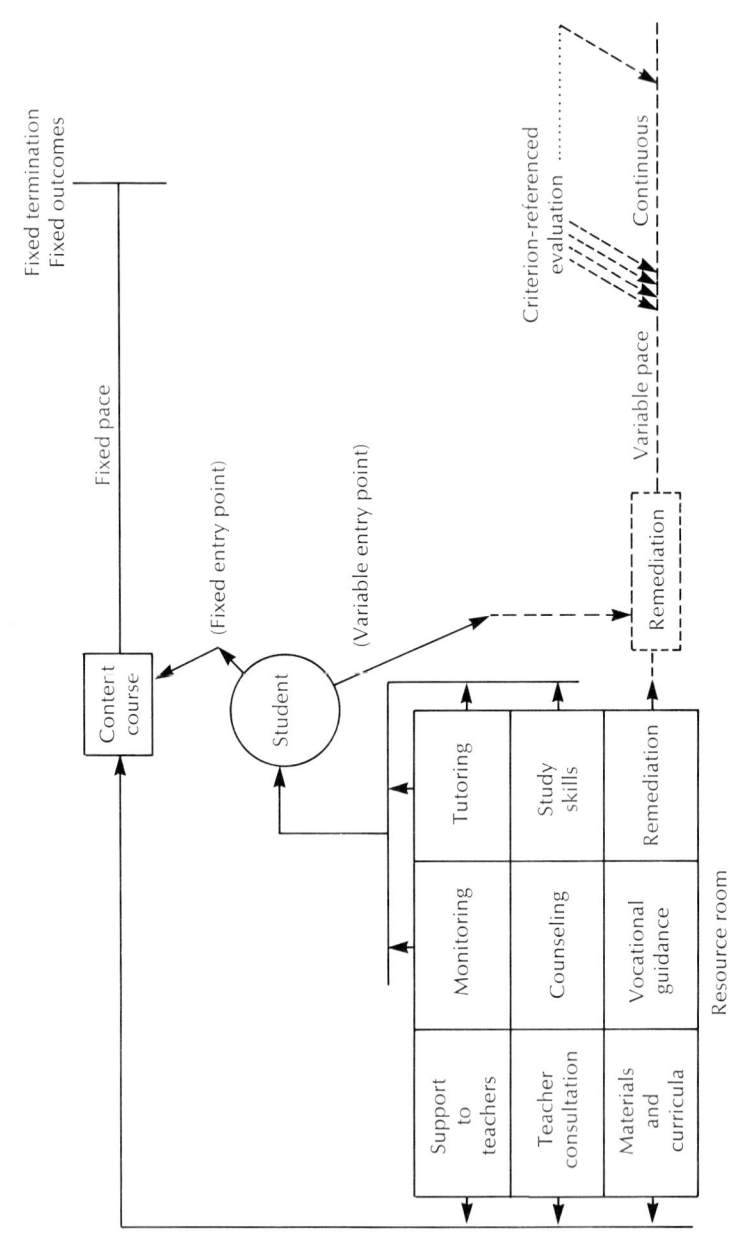

**Fig. 10-3.** A model of the bivalent system.

substantial changes in attitudinal development and instruction. Any combination of accommodative strategies may be used in conjunction with mainstream activities; any combination of backup support to aid the student in the resource room for mainstream class objectives may be used; and attention may be devoted to achievement in basic skills as well as process training, if that is an objective.

The key to programming success lies in careful planning and organization. Scheduling for individual students who enter the resource room must be tailored for a specific set of objectives; knowledge of the goals of content courses must be available; accommodation must be permitted in the content course; and learning units must be available for students that pertain to the fixed outcomes of the content course. Supplementary assistance may be in the form of aides, volunteer tutors, paid tutors, peer tutors, alternative instructional materials, and the use of available instructional hardware. Once the basic system is in place, and materials are developed, the major effort is concluded and future programming will entail modification for specific students, but not the same magnitude of preparation as in the initial developmental phase.

## Assessing objectives of content courses

Although there will be considerable variation among schools, there is a consistent pattern for teachers to emphasize knowledge objectives in the curriculum. As Bloom's taxonomy reveals, knowledge is the lowest order of cognitive activity in the *cognitive domain*. Curriculum guides may more ambitiously erect *synthesis* or *evaluation* of subject matter as outcomes for a course of study, but teacher-made tests and standardized achievement batteries put a premium on knowledge; that is, the ability to recall facts, methods and processes, principles, and generalizations.

Alternative methods of getting information (knowledge) to students who cannot read textbooks will not be a difficult process in a well-designed program. In fact, the materials used in a support program of tutoring and self-directed study for a subject may surpass actual teacher objectives of the course and more nearly approach analysis, synthesis, and evaluation.

The surest way to determine what a teacher expects of students is to examine copies of teacher-made examinations, inspect the general format, and categorize and determine the percentage of questions that require responding by classification within Bloom's taxonomy. If the resource teacher finds that a mainstream teacher emphasizes knowledge questions, a clue about preparing the student for examinations is apparent. Typically, tests in the objective mode (matching, multiple choice, and fill in the blank) are used by teachers because they require simple recall of knowledge and are easy to develop and score and because they directly relate to chapter assignments in textbooks.

## Selecting approaches to support students in the mainstream

In general, the approaches available to the resource teacher may be listed as follows:
1. Remediation of basic skills only
2. Development of a special resource curriculum leading to functional literacy and/or vocational skills
3. A bivalent system including assistance to the student in the mainstream and support and consultation to mainstream teachers in addition to remediation
4. Attempts to alter the learning environment of the mainstream class in addition to remediation and support

If the resource program is to be designed

in accordance with the choices listed in nos. 3 and 4 above, certain necessary preparatory steps will need to be taken. Aside from working closely with mainstream teachers in the implementation of accommodatory activities, the supports will need to be developed through purchase of new materials and equipment, utilization of existing materials and equipment, or development of remodeled mainstream classes. Any of these approaches will have to be sanctioned by the administration and supported by the teachers. Logically, the best chances to succeed with the more revolutionary approaches will be related to the number of adventurous, cooperative mainstream teachers that can be persuaded to participate through in-service education and personal contact.

Within any structure, however, basic planning will be necessary; Fig. 10-4 is a flowchart of important events in planning. The general process in Fig. 10-4 will apply to the simplest approaches to individualization as well as the more complex.

### Developing alternative learning units

There can be no doubt that the most tedious part of the process of assisting students in the mainstream will be the development of alternative learning units. Should the resource teacher attempt this much involvement, the direct cooperation of mainstream

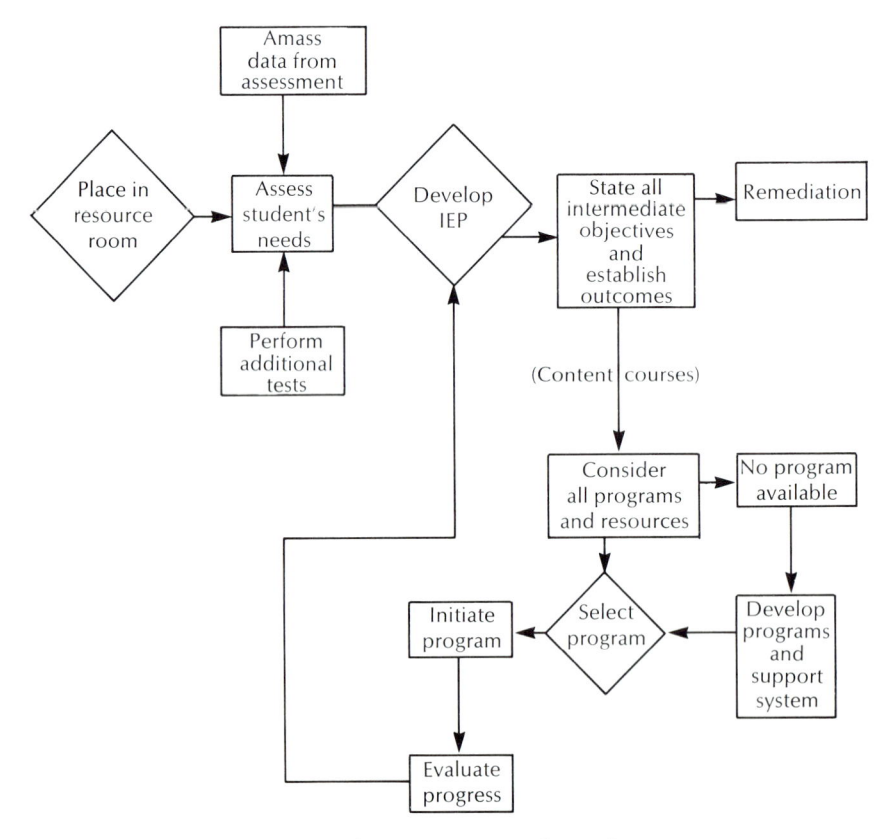

**Fig. 10-4.** Planning programs for student.

teachers and labor of volunteers (ACLD* members for example) will be required to select learning activities, sequence them, and develop media. The goals of learning activities should be to eliminate reading, involve small groups and peer dyads, and fully utilize existing hardware and audiovisual equipment available in the school. Assistance in establishing the sequence of learning activities may be necessary to assure that they are tied to the principal and subordinate objectives of the course of study.

*Association for Children with Learning Disabilities.

Ideally, classification by means of Gagne's taxonomy (1970) would impose an order on the linear format of the alternative learning experience. It should be remembered that, although this activity may seem to be overwhelming, it can be accomplished. Once it has, units will be perpetually available for students in succeeding classes, which will probably require only minor modification for maximum effectiveness. The facts and sequence of activities on a unit in American history are not likely to change unless someone finds serious errors in the historical record. The major task in a majority of courses

Content course

a
REQUIREMENTS
1. Objectives
2. Fixed outcomes
3. Outline
4. Course evaluations
5. Prevalent materials
6. Other data

b
AGREEMENT WITH MAINSTREAM TEACHER
1. Accommodative techniques in regular class
2. Alternative responding
3. Grading requirements
4. Assistance in development of alternative learning units

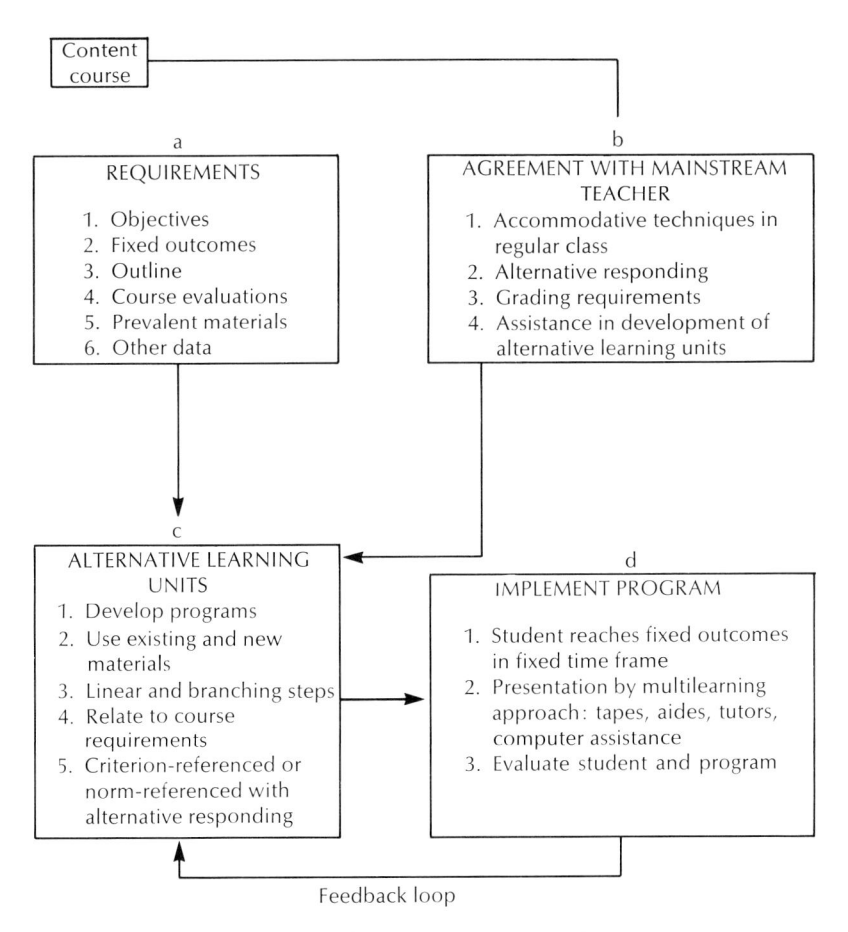

c
ALTERNATIVE LEARNING UNITS
1. Develop programs
2. Use existing and new materials
3. Linear and branching steps
4. Relate to course requirements
5. Criterion-referenced or norm-referenced with alternative responding

d
IMPLEMENT PROGRAM
1. Student reaches fixed outcomes in fixed time frame
2. Presentation by multilearning approach: tapes, aides, tutors, computer assistance
3. Evaluate student and program

Feedback loop

**Fig. 10-5.** Planning and preparing alternative learning units.

will be to accomplish the initial development of alternative learning units to supplement activities of the mainstream class. This is something that will undoubtedly take a great deal of time to complete and will not be available in the first one or two years. The resource teacher should carefully examine commercial materials that would eliminate large areas of unit development. The general steps for this process are found in Fig. 10-5.

### An interactional-learning model*

Previously, we have made the point that teachers generally present instruction to a class of students who are required to passively observe and interact about the subject matter when the teacher asks for a response. The environment, the conduct of students, the nature and pace of instruction, and virtually all other variables are controlled by the teacher. We have, from a practical point of view, defined such interactions as lecturing, although there are those who would contend that a lecture is strictly a verbal presentation by the teacher with *no* interaction by students except that of watching. We are not apologetic about our interpretation because we find the interaction of students to be so minimal that an occasional response to the teacher's inquiries does not substantially alter the fact that the teacher is lecturing. Consider the following excerpt from a social studies class:

**Teacher:** Our topic for today is British Columbia. British Columbia is Canada's Pacific province. It is very . . . uh . . . mountainous, containing the western slopes of the Rocky Mountains and the Selkirk and Coast ranges. There are many valleys and two large rivers. Can you name one of the rivers that flows into the U.S.?

**Student 1:** The Columbia.
**Teacher:** That's right. Another large river is the Fraser, which flows to the ocean near what city? (Pause) Come on, somebody knows. (Pause) Didn't you read your assignment. Yes!
**Student 2:** Vancouver.
**Teacher:** That's right. Vancouver is an important seaport, an island, and a city. The Canadian railway terminates in Vancouver. Most of the people who live near Vancouver work on farms, but there are many important industries associated with the general terrain. . . .

We consider this excerpt to be an example of common discourse in secondary classrooms. It is true that there is some interaction between students and the teacher, but it is extremely limited; there is no interaction between students. The teacher assumes total responsibility for the subject matter and parenthetical responses of students are inconsequential in the major activity that unfolds as the teacher continues to talk.

The rules of this activity are implied by the teacher: "I will ask occasional questions about the subject matter, but most of the time I will tell you about it. When I ask a question I want you to give me a brief, factual statement. Do not ask many questions of me and do not provide your own interpretations of issues and events." Hoetker and Ahlbrand (1969) have examined transcripts of classroom teaching dating back to the turn of the century, which indicate that this style of teaching existed then. It may be said that things have not changed much in the classroom for at least 80 years, and we could probably extend this backwards if we could find valid transcripts of classroom discourses of the 1700s.

Learning is enhanced when the program, not the teacher, directs the activities and the students are permitted to interact with each other. The program would consist of learning activities that are self-contained, presenting the students with tasks to perform each day. Activities would be predesigned on

---
*The interactional model and other in-class arrangements within the mainstream class emphasize approaches that may provide individualization under the direct control of regular teachers.

tapes or in written form for students to follow. The teacher is free to monitor activities and to work individually with students instead of lecturing.

The interactional model has several advantages: the lecture organization is dismantled, learning is not viewed as solely an encounter with textbooks and listening to the teacher, members of the class contribute to mutual learning of content, interpersonal alliances are propagated, learners with specific limitations are still able to get information, and the group process of learning allows the teacher to meet with individuals for specific instructional purposes. Moreover, the teacher need not be devoted to a particular method in order for the model to work because an amalgam of approaches, e.g., behavioral learning and discovery learning, may be used without violating the intention of the model—to promote interaction between learners.

Developing an interaction or group investigation system is initially demanding of the teacher's skill to organize the *program*, which consists of daily learning activities related to the curriculum embodied with the same content as that which the lecture would convey. Once the work is accomplished it can be used repeatedly in each succeeding year with minor modification and refinement.

The advantages to the adolescent are that learning becomes a group activity and responsibility, classroom participation will be much more interesting and relevant, and personal contact with students will forge interpersonal relationships. It may be difficult to get teachers to release some control of the learning environment to students. We

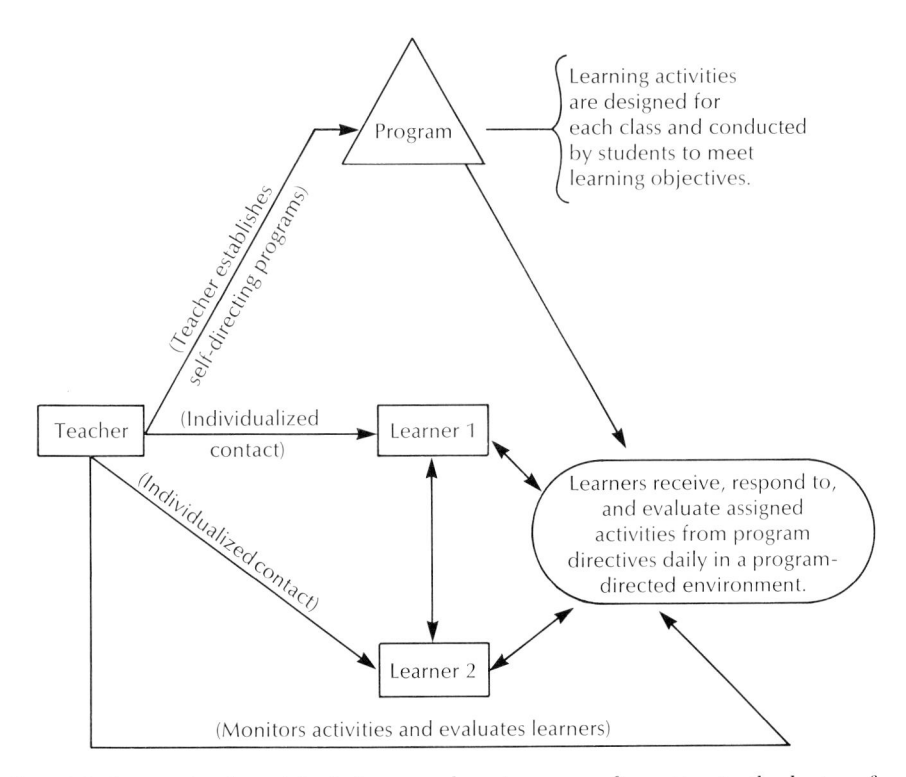

**Fig. 10-6.** Interactional model of classroom learning as an alternative to the lecture format. In a classroom interaction there will be learning groups comprised of two or more learners.

have mentioned the resistance to change and the long tradition of the lecture format punctuated with flurries of questions and answers, but some teachers will experiment if they know what to try. An example of this is given below. The basic model of interactional process is presented in Fig. 10-6.

**Example of an interactional program.** One of the authors served as a consultant in a high school program and assisted an English teacher in implementing an interactional model in the regular classroom. The purpose of the effort was to integrate learning disabled students into the mainstream, but a major by-product was favorable reactions from normal-achieving students, as well as from the teacher.

The district provided a curriculum guide for English, which specified the units of study for each six-week period, listing major concepts to be taught and assignments to be completed. With consultative assistance, the teacher developed learning centers, thereby reducing the number of students with whom he had to work on the more difficult concepts. This change is shown below.

*Old scheduling approach*
Monday: grammar (prepositional phrases)
Tuesday: composition (theme)
Wednesday: literature (interpretation)
Thursday: literature (interpretation)
Friday: composition (essay)

*Interactional approach*
*Center 1: grammar.* A taped lesson (15 minutes) reviews the use of prepositional phrases, giving extensive examples. A taped follow-up quiz requires students to listen to sentences and then circle the proper answer from the following:

1. The example does not include a prepositional phrase.
2. Example 1 includes a prepositional phrase.
3. Example 2 includes a prepositional phrase.

A key on the tape lists answers or teacher can grade later; student grading/recording of scores is preferred by most teachers.

A worksheet on prepositional phrases is included. An assignment is given: write ten original sentences containing prepositional phrases (underline these). (These papers are turned in for teacher review/grading.)

*Center 2: composition (theme).* A taped lesson (ten minutes) reviews the major considerations in writing a theme (this has been covered in detail earlier in the course) and gives instructions about the topic for the theme.

Sample themes are available at the center for student review. A checklist of considerations in grading is also posted, listing items such as:

1. Is your name on the paper?
2. Is it neatly written or typed on one side only?
3. Is the title clearly written or typed on outside?

The remaining time is provided for writing the theme. (A peer tutor could be assigned to this center for student assistance if needed.)

*Center 3: literature (interpretation).* A short story has been assigned for outside reading (LD students had this available on tape in the library). A worksheet is provided at the center requiring the following information:

1. Name of the story
2. List of major characters
3. Summary of the plot
4. Anything unusual about the story

The group assignment for this center is to collectively write a short story. It can be dictated into tape, typed by a student, or written in longhand by a designated recorder. It is to conform to criteria established in advance by the instructor.

*Center 4: literature (interpretation [instructor]).* A piece of literature has been assigned for outside reading and is available on tape as well. The instructor conducts the discussion of the author's meaning and analyzes the piece of work with the group.

*Center 5: composition (essay).* Sample short essays on various topics are available on tape at the center and in written form. Topical assignments can be selected from a list made available by the instructor.

Criteria for evaluation of essays are posted at the center. When equipment allows, essays are read onto tape rather than written. These are turned in for instructor grading.

The instructor in the English class covered exactly the same amount of material during that week as expected in a typical lecture class. However, rather than all 30 students having the same instructional sequence each day, six students attended each center. Students were given assigned groups in the beginning, indicating at which center to begin and in what order to rotate. For example, student A received a card on Monday with the following schedule: Monday, center 3; Tuesday, center 4; Wednesday, center 5; Thursday, center 1; Friday, center 2. Later the students became so responsible that they were only told that by Friday they must have completed all five centers and that no more than six students were permitted at a center; they were then left to organize their own schedules. This worked extremely well.

A reinforcement system was instituted, based on a contracting system. If a student completed the center assignment and met criteria for the assigned activity, reinforcement time was earned. The maximum amount of time per center was 50 minutes; if the student met criteria in 20 minutes, the balance of the period was spent in reinforcement activities. However, the emphasis was on meeting criteria or quality checks, not speed. The reinforcement area contained magazines identified as desirable by the students, games such as chess, high-interest reading materials, and radio/stereo equipment with earphones. Other reinforcers included time in the library, visits to the media center and, when possible, time in the gym. Obviously, reinforcers would vary with the group and the school system.

The English teacher was quite pleased with the performance of the students, attendance increased, tardiness decreased, and the need for general discipline was greatly reduced. Changing the instructional strategies used and restructuring the time frame within the classroom produced results that were quite gratifying to all parties. This is just an example of the interactional model as it could be used in a regular classroom.

**Modified lecture**

Initial contacts with mainstream teachers for the purpose of suggesting methods of altering the learning environment and structuring learning activities may need to be much less ambitious than the recommendation to completely change the instructional process as proposed in the interactional model. In reality, there are not likely to be many teachers who would be willing to alter their methods that significantly. Changes in that direction must accrue gradually and will spread as mainstream teachers influence their peers and successful programming occurs over a period of time. Therefore a modified lecture format may be attempted with willing teachers.

Modification entails the suspension of the lecture after a specified period of time. During the last part of the class period students would be permitted to cluster into groups for interactional activities directed by the teacher. These units would initially be prepared by the regular teacher and the resource teacher. Students would follow this general format:

1. An assigned task
2. Group interaction to complete the task

3. Evaluation
4. Report to teacher

## Guiding thoughts in developing individualized instruction

We have presented the reader with an extensive list of accommodatory techniques to be used in the regular classroom to aid the mildly handicapped student and have discussed issues and problems in individualization. We have noted that the principles of laboratory-based learning systems are difficult to apply in large group instruction; moreover, the nature of the secondary school's organization and trappings poses significant problems to the specialist. These reasons explain why some practitioners have elected to limit their involvement to the provision of criterion-referenced remedial attempts and/or vocational exploration. We have stressed the importance of engineering a system to support the student and the classroom teacher in the mainstream to maximize the effectiveness of accommodative techniques. We have gone one step further by suggesting that the specialist may be of assistance by introducing individualized educational concepts into the mainstream class.

A variety of approaches can be used, ranging from major programs that must be adopted by an entire school system, to more likely possibilities, such as the development of alternative learning units and restructuring of selected regular classroom environments. The major programs of individualization were said to be useful because they can guide the development of individual instructional techniques in special education. Teaching is a complex process that involves the learning environment, the style of teaching, the motivation and style of the learner, and interaction with subject matter. Much more needs to be learned about these variables, especially at the secondary level, but we can find direction and support from existing approaches.

Bloom (1978, pp. 564-566) has discussed three constructs about learning capabilities of students that should have some bearing on the issues of individualization and that may be helpful to planners. These constructs are:

1. There are good learners and there are poor learners.
2. There are faster and there are slower learners.
3. Most students become very similar with regard to learning ability, rate of learning, and motivation for further learning when provided with favorable learning conditions.

In considering these three constructs, Bloom makes the point that the correlation between measures of school achievement at grades 3 and 11 is about +.85; thus over an eight-year period the relative ranking of students in a class or school remains almost perfectly fixed. This should impress special educators who think that continued remediation, as a single effort, will be very fruitful at the secondary level. Although Bloom indicates that this relationship may be broken up, it will be done by programming or instruction adapted to each student's *needs* under conditions in which students believe that a new school situation is one in which they can start afresh, no matter how poorly the past record has been. Therefore there are poor learners who apparently learn more slowly but who may achieve high levels through *mastery learning* under conditions in which instruction is tailored to their needs and the presentation is unique and fresh. How often have we seen the frustration and boredom of adolescents who are subjected to another round of remedial reading, while at the same time they have more immediate needs and interests?

Encouragement may be gained from the research of Bloom, who demonstrates that students who have experienced individualized instruction and succeeded in an initial subject tend to learn subsequent courses in the same subject areas up to high levels with less need for extra time or help. That is, students who enroll in mastery classes in mathematics, science, reading, social studies, and so forth maintain new learning approaches in following courses in the same field with less need for special assistance or extra time. The amount of extra time needed by students, according to Bloom, is 10% to 15% more in order to learn the subject.

We would suggest that in secondary subjects where reading is eliminated or reduced, students may be able to master subject matter in the same real time as their nonhandicapped peers. This would enable specialists to permit students to learn subject matter through alternative approaches (presently an improbability for a student with seriously deficient reading skills) *and* to learn to read. About the importance of motivation and affect, we have made a considerable case for assisting students toward improved self-concepts and better mental health. Although some professionals will deemphasize the importance of affective factors or criticize the time spent working with students on these goals, we would suggest that success in achievement will lead to better adjustment, which in turn will lead to increased motivation to learn. As Bloom (1978, p. 568) states:

> To put it bluntly, repeated success in coping with the academic demands of the school appears to confer upon a high proportion of such students a type of immunization against emotional illness. Similarly, repeated failure in coping with the demands of school appears to be one source of emotional difficulties and mental illness. . . .

## ACCOMMODATION: RESOURCE ROOM TECHNIQUES

We have addressed many issues under several chapters describing the role of the resource teacher in provision of accommodation as well as assisting regular classroom teachers. The accommodation component includes teacher consultation, tutoring, extended counseling, direct support to teachers, monitoring, and study skills. Because we have thoroughly discussed tutoring, extended counseling, direct support to teachers, monitoring, and study skills in other chapters, we will provide a strategy for teacher consultation which is the key to any accommodative techniques that will be shared by professionals.

## Teacher consultation in accommodation

There are three aspects to be considered in teacher consultation as part of the accommodation process: learner characteristics/needs, the curriculum of the regular classroom subject, and the nature of the regular teacher (Fig. 10-7). Specific information on the abilities and problems of the individual student must be considered in making decisions about accommodation. The resource teacher must be able to interpret information about the learner and translate that into an estimate of the likelihood of success in the regular class. Consideration must be given to individual learner characteristics, including:

ACADEMIC FUNCTIONING: The resource teacher should utilize formal and informal assessment data collected during the placement process as well as performance information from contact with the student.

BEHAVIOR: The manner in which the student interacts with the external environment is typically of equal importance in predicting classroom success. The observational sampling of behavior required for the assessment process can provide valuable information in examining the student's coping or interactional patterns. The instrument described in Chapter 5, the Coping Analysis Schedule for Educational Settings (CASES), provides useful information in identifying and describing behavioral patterns in the classroom setting.

STUDY HABITS: Organizational skills and study habits should be evaluated as part of the preparation for accommodation. There is tremendous

**262** THE PROGRAM

variance in the manner in which students approach the task of studying. Some courses require that the students have specific skills in order to survive, and the resource teacher must acknowledge this requirement.

MOTIVATION AND INTEREST: Students with a particular interest or desire to participate in a class will have an increased chance at success. The resource teacher with good rapport with LD students has insight into their interests and can take that information into consideration in making program decisions.

Curricular demands vary among courses, making it necessary for the resource teacher to become familiar with the various courses being considered as part of the accommodation process. Attention should be given to

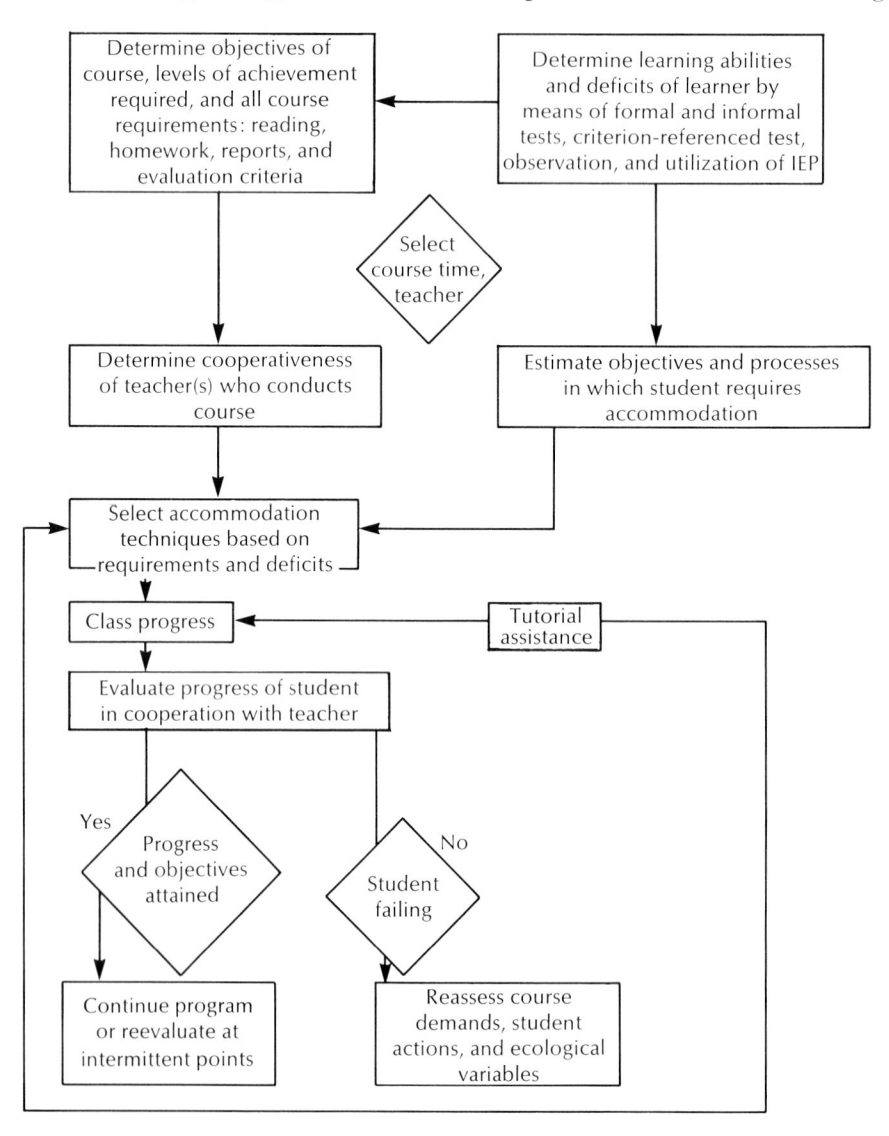

**Fig. 10-7.** Sequence of events for entry and exit in resource programming.

subject content and course structure, including the following factors:
- Course objectives
- Level of achievement required
- Topics included in course outline
- Number and type of tests and assignments required
- Modes of instruction used
- Evaluation criteria

The personality and attitudes of the regular teacher are extremely important in accommodation and must be examined realistically. Fig. 10-8 illustrates the teacher consultation process, including cooperative and circumventive efforts. The following narrative is an example of the implementation of the process as shown in Fig. 10-8, A; in this dialogue: the resource teacher (RT) and mainstream teacher (MT) are discussing a learning disabled student who is enrolled in the mainstream teacher's history class.

**RT:** I wanted to talk to you about Elizabeth in your second period history class. She is enrolled

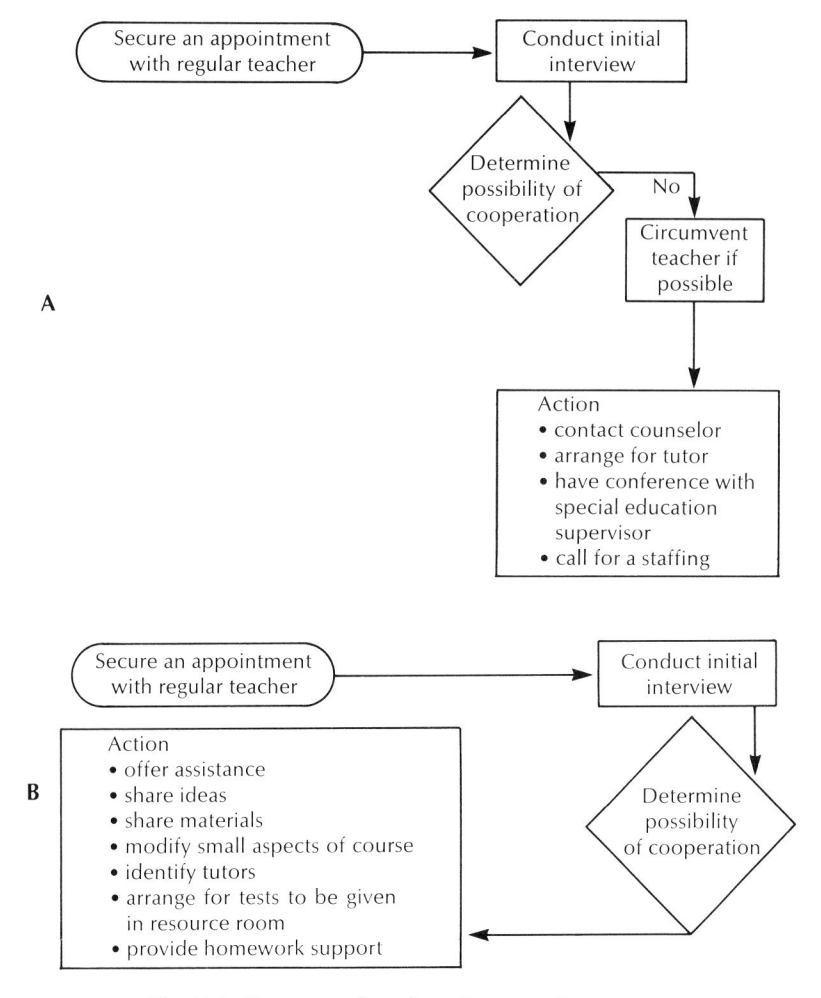

**A**

```
Secure an appointment  →  Conduct initial
with regular teacher         interview
                                  ↓
                         Determine
                         possibility of      No
                         cooperation   ────────→  Circumvent
                                                   teacher if
                                                   possible
                                                       ↓
                                                Action
                                                • contact counselor
                                                • arrange for tutor
                                                • have conference with
                                                  special education
                                                  supervisor
                                                • call for a staffing
```

**B**

```
Secure an appointment  →  Conduct initial
with regular teacher         interview
                                  ↓
Action                      Determine
• offer assistance          possibility
• share ideas     ←─────    of cooperation
• share materials
• modify small aspects of course
• identify tutors
• arrange for tests to be given
  in resource room
• provide homework support
```

**Fig. 10-8.** Two examples of teacher consultation process.

in my resource room, and the records indicate that she's having some difficulty with your class. I thought maybe this might be a good opportunity for us to talk about it.

**MT:** Yes, I would be glad to talk to you. She really is having a lot of trouble, and somebody needs to do something for her.

**RT:** Can you tell me some of the problems she is having in your class? I guess I don't have a clear understanding of what her difficulties are right now.

**MT:** Well, she just kind of, well, she is there every day. She sits in her seat and pays attention, but she never really does very well on the tests and most of her homework is not very good.

**RT:** Does she turn in the homework on time, and is she pretty prompt with most of the other assignments?

**MT:** Yes, she turns it in on time, but she might as well forget it because it is really not good.

**RT:** Do you think there is anything that I could do by working with you to help her complete the assignments and improve her performance in your class?

**MT:** Well, I really don't know what you can do. So I don't know how you can help. I know I can't help because I have just got too many kids to work with; there are 30 students in that class.

**RT:** Well, perhaps if you could give me your course outline and some of your course objectives as well as some indication of the kind of assignments perhaps I could, either through tutoring or accommodative services, try to keep her at least near the pace of the class and see that she gets the important points in the content. What do you think?

**MT:** Well, if I thought it would do any good I might do that, but I don't think you could help much because you don't know anything about history. I'm not being rude when I say that, but you're not trained in it, and it seems to me that Elizabeth's biggest problem is that the elementary school didn't do its job and I don't know why they expect us to have students like that in classes when they didn't learn to read.

The above conversation could have ended quite differently, as shown by the following dialogue (Fig. 10-8, *B*):

**RT:** I wanted to talk to you about Elizabeth in your second period history class. She is enrolled in my resource room and the records indicate that she's having some difficulty with your class. I thought maybe this might be a good opportunity for us to talk about it.

**MT:** Yes, I would be glad to talk to you. She really is having a lot of trouble, and somebody needs to do something for her.

**RT:** Can you tell me some of the problems she is having in your class? I guess I don't have a clear understanding of what her difficulties are right now.

**MT:** Well, she just kind of, well, she is there every day. She sits in her seat and pays attention but she never really does very well on the tests and most of her homework is not very good.

**RT:** Does she turn in the homework on time, and is she pretty prompt with most of the other assignments?

**MT:** Yes, she turns it in on time, but she might as well forget it because it is really not good.

**RT:** Do you think there is anything that I could do by working with you to help her complete the assignments and improve her performance in your class?

**MT:** Well, I really don't know what you do. So I don't know how you can help. I know I can't help because I have just got too many kids to work with; there are 30 students in that class.

**RT:** Well, perhaps if you could give me your course outline and some of your course objectives as well as some indication of the kind of assignments perhaps I could, either through tutoring or accommodative services, try to keep her at least near the pace of the class and see that she gets the important points in the content. What do you think?

**MT:** Sure, I would be glad to help in any way that I can and I would cooperate if you could give me an idea of what we could do to help her.

**RT:** Is there any time in your schedule when you could come to the resource room and see what materials I have available and how my program runs so we could work cooperatively?

**MT:** My preparation time is second period, and I am sure I could come down to your room sometime during second period on some day. What would be good for you?

**RT:** How about coming down second period this coming Thursday. We can talk a little bit then, and you can observe the program. That might help you have a clearer understanding of what I can do to help Elizabeth in your class. If you could give me a copy of your course outline, and the objectives perhaps I could formulate a few questions I might want to ask you if we could get together then after your visit. How about the possibility of you identifying a peer tutor that we could use to work with Elizabeth and with me.

**MT:** I can give you outlines and materials and I think I could find some people who might be able to help, but one thing that concerns me is, aren't you going to be trying to teach her how to read?

**RT:** Oh yes, Elizabeth is in a remedial reading group where we are working with specific reading skills. However, I think we can perhaps also help her by taking some of the main points and concepts that you're trying to get across in history and seeing if we can't provide some supportive instruction in that area. It seems to me that might be as beneficial, if not more so right now, in terms of your needs and Elizabeth's than just reading alone.

**MT:** Good, I'll come down on Thursday morning during the second period and visit with you. Maybe we can have a chance to get a cup of coffee.

At this point in the discussion between the resource teacher and the mainstream teacher, a decision point has been reached. After some experience with the mainstream teacher, it will be necessary to determine whether or not major modification of the instructional approaches used in the classroom can be implemented or if accommodation is the only approach to be provided to particular students. It is satisfactory if only accommodation is applied to students in the classroom; however, if the mainstream teacher becomes extremely cooperative and interested in experimenting with interactional models of learning, mastery learning, the use of the reinforcement system, materials modification, and the program-directed approach, significant change in the classroom will occur. The resource teacher will not only have an impact on one student in the class but will have left a legacy of educational change for all students in the program.

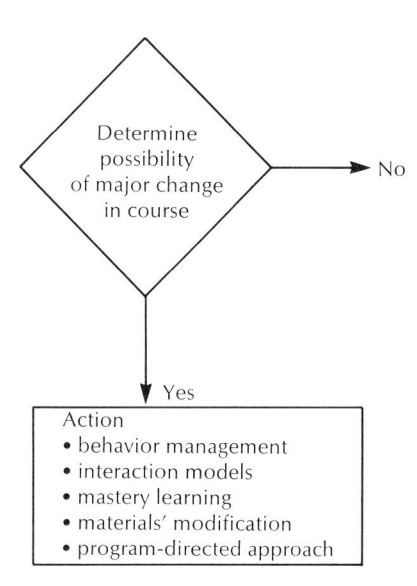

**Fig. 10-9.** Major course change.

Action
- behavior management
- interaction models
- mastery learning
- materials' modification
- program-directed approach

The specialist has skills and abilities as a technician and change agent in the learning environment which should transcend the present scope that is a heritage of the clinical teaching approach. Clinical teaching is an acceptable method of instruction for children in a one-on-one situation, but the role of the resource teacher is to extend his or her influences in as many ways as possible throughout the educational system.

After determining the extent of programming variance that might be permitted by a particular teacher, plans to assist the student more directly in the mainstream should be made in accordance with the steps in Fig. 10-7, which shows the steps for entry and exit from the mainstream course. This basic process could be used for the simplest approaches as well as the most complex.

## SUMMARY

In this chapter we have presented the basic elements of a comprehensive secondary program. Our view, as here presented, is that the relevance of education to disabled learners will not be enhanced nor really very meaningful if the efforts of the specialist to assist them are limited to the provision of remediation. In spite of the primary effects of learning disabilities, secondary effects include poor motivation, boredom, and attraction to interests beyond the school in the outside world. The drudgery of cycles of remedial programs throughout the years becomes totally aversive to most students in secondary school. In order to find education a fulfilling experience, it is necessary to assure that remediation is balanced with success experiences in the secondary program. To accomplish this we have suggested various ways of assisting the mainstream teacher to accommodate to the needs of students and have recommended support systems of the resource room that would directly support the student. A comprehensive approach to programming would increase the chances of success in remediation for those students who have the ability because they can receive an education while they approach literacy goals.

## REFERENCES AND READINGS

Adams, R. S., & Biddle, B. J. *Realities of teaching.* New York: Holt, Rinehart and Winston, 1970.

Anderson, H. H. An experimental study of dominative and integrative behavior of children of pre-school age. *Journal of Social Psychology*, 1937, 8, 335-345.

Anderson, H. H. The measurement of domination and social integrative behavior in teachers' contacts with children. *Child Development*, 1939, 10, 73-89.

Anderson, H. H., & Brewer, J. E. Studies of teachers' classroom personalities (II: Effects of teachers' dominative and integrative contacts on children's classroom behavior). *Applied Psychology Monograph*, 1946, 8, 128 pp.

Ausubel, D. P. *The psychology of meaningful verbal learning.* New York: Grune & Stratton, 1963.

Bloom, B. S. New views of the learner: Implications for instruction and curriculum. *Educational Leadership*, 1978, 35(7), 563-576.

Briggs, L. J. An instructional design theorist examines individualized instructional systems. In H. Talmage (Ed.), *Systems of individualized education.* Berkeley, Calif.: McCutchan, 1975.

Brutten, M. *Vocational education for the brain injured adolescent and young adult at the Vanguard School. International approach to learning disabilities of children and youth.* San Rafael, Calif.: Academic Therapy Publications, 1967.

Bush, R. N. *The teacher-pupil relationship.* New York: Prentice-Hall, 1954.

Cloward, R. D. Studies in tutoring. *Journal of Experimental Education*, 1967, 36, 25.

Erickson, M. R. *A study of a tutoring program to benefit tutors and tutees* (University Microfilm No. 71-16914). Ann Arbor, Mich.: University of Michigan, 1971.

Flanders, N. A. Personal-social anxiety as a factor in experimental learning situations. *Journal of Educational Research*, 1951, 45, 100-110.

Forell, E. R. No easy cure for reading disabilities. *Today's Education*, 1967, 65(2), 34-36.

Frauenheim, J. G. Academic achievement characteristics of adult males who were diagnosed as dyslexic in childhood. *Journal of Learning Disabilities*, 1978, 11(8), 476-483.

Gagne, R. M. *The conditions of learning* (2nd ed.). New York: Holt, Rinehart and Winston, 1970.

Gickling, E. E., Murphy, L. C., & Mallory, D. W. Teachers' preferences for resource services. *Exceptional Children*, 1979, 45(6), 442-449.

Glasser, R. The design and programming of instruction. In H. T. James et al. (Eds.), *The schools and the challenge of innovation* (Supplementary paper No. 28). New York: New York Committee for Economic Development, 1969, pp. 156-215.

Gump, P. V. *The classroom behavior setting: Its nature and relation to student behavior* (Final Report, Project No. 2453). Lawrence, Kan.: Midwest Psychological Field Station, University of Kansas, 1967.

Hass, G. *Curriculum planning: A new approach.* Boston: Allyn & Bacon, 1977.

Heil, L. M., Powell, M., & Feifer, I. *Characteristics of teacher behavior related to the achievement of children in several elementary grades.* Washington, D.C.: U.S. Dept. of Health, Education and Welfare, Office of Cooperative Research Branch, 1960.

Herbert, J. *A system for analyzing lessons.* New York: Teachers College Press, 1967.

Hoetker, J., & Ahlbrand, W. P. The persistence of the recitation. *American Educational Research Journal*, 1969, 6, 145-167.

Lehtinen-Rogan, L. E. How do we teach him? In E. Schloss (Ed.), *The educator's enigma: The adolescent with learning disabilities.* San Rafael, Calif.: Academic Therapy Publications, 1971.

Lerner, J. *Children with learning disabilities* (2nd ed.). Boston: Houghton Mifflin, 1976.

Maine, H. G. An experimental junior high school program. In J. I. Arena (Ed.), *Successful programming: Many points of view.* San Rafael, Calif.: Academic Therapy Publications, 1969.

Mann, L., Goodman, L., & Wiederholt, L. *Teaching the learning disabled adolescent.* Boston: Houghton Mifflin, 1978.

Marsh, G. E., II, Gearheart, C. K., & Gearheart, B. R. *The learning disabled adolescent: Program alternatives in the secondary school.* St. Louis: Mosby, 1978.

Massialas, B., & Cox, B. *Inquiry in social studies.* New York: McGraw-Hill, 1966.

Mitzel, H. E., & Rabinowitz, W. Assessing social-emotional climate in the classroom by Withall's technique. *Psychology Monographs,* 1953, 67(18).

Muehl, S., & Forell, E. R. A follow-up study of disabled readers: Variables related to high school reading performance. *Reading Research Quarterly,* 1973-74, 9(1), 110-123.

Neill, S. B. A summary of issues in the minimum competency movement. *Phi Delta Kappan,* 1979, 60(6), 452-453.

Page, W. R. *Instructional systems for students with learning disabilities: Junior high school program.* 1968. (ERIC Document Reproduction Service No. ED 035-138)

Reger, H., Schroeder, W., & Uschold, K. *Special education: Children with learning problems.* New York: Oxford University Press, 1968.

Schein, E., & Bennis, W. *Personal and organizational change through group methods.* New York: Wiley, 1965.

Siegel, E. *The exceptional child grows up.* New York: Dutton, 1974.

Silberman, C. E. *Crisis in the classroom.* New York: Random House, 1971.

Spaulding, R. L. *Achievement, creativity, and self-concept correlates of teacher-pupil transactions in elementary school classrooms.* Hempstead, N.Y.: Hofstra University, 1965. (Available from Institute for Child Development and Family Studies, San Jose State University, San Jose, Calif.)

Talmage, H. Instructional design for individualization. In H. Talmage (Ed.), *Systems of individualized education.* Berkeley, Calif.: McCutchan, 1975.

Thelen, H. *Education and the human quest.* New York: Harper & Row, 1960.

Thomas, J. L. Tutoring strategies and effectiveness: A comparison of elementary age tutors/college age tutors. *Dissertation Abstracts International,* 1972, 32, 3580A.

Wepman, J., Cruickshank, W. M., Deutsch, C. P., et al.: Learning disabilities. In N. Hobbs (Ed.), *Issues in the classification of children* (Vol. 1). San Francisco: Jossey-Bass, 1975.

Withall, J. Assessment of the social-emotional climates experienced by a group of seventh graders as they move from class to class. *Educational Psychology Measurement,* 1952, 12, 451.

Chapter 11
# REMEDIAL PROGRAMMING

A common and well-accepted purpose of special education is to provide mildly handicapped children and adolescents with remedial training in basic academic subjects or in underlying psychological processes thought to be important for learning. There may be many variations of remedial programming for mildly handicapped students, depending on the setting, the means by which students are classified for special education, and the influence of certification requirements for teachers in special education.

Although there has been sustained interest in the improvement of learning by treating processes or correlates of failure, the primary concern of special educators continues to be the remediation of reading deficiency and, to a lesser extent, skill development in arithmetic, spelling, and written expression. The goals of most school-based remedial programs appear to be (1) to assist students toward normal achievement in the acquisition of basic skills and/or (2) to promote functional literacy as a minimum competency in lieu of satisfactory remediation. The latter goal is quickly becoming more prevalent in secondary programs as students emerge from elementary schools lacking sufficient skill in reading, written expression, and mathematics necessary for independent functioning in the secondary curriculum.

Whereas there are some programs that emphasize compensatory approaches and others that immerse the student in vocational programming wherein reading and mathematic skills are taught incidentally with sequential tasks of the curriculum, to many educators there is a sense of extreme urgency about remediation with adolescents, compelling them to intensify the remedial effort. In the process, other goals of secondary education may be deemphasized in the belief that basic academic skills are more important than other skills. There will be wide differences in the importance attached to remediation at the secondary level, depending on many factors, the most important of which will be what abilities, deficits, and needs are ascribed to mildly handicapped students, and how they will be grouped for instruction.

## READING

If a learning disabled student has a significant discrepancy between his or her age and ability and academic achievement in basic reading skill and/or comprehension, if an emotionally disturbed or behaviorally disordered student has a similar disorder, and if a student has general academic deficiency because of mild mental retardation, a reading disability may be determined by a team of examiners. Remedial services may be provided in a resource room that specifically addresses reading deficits. The arrangement of the program will be determined by categorical or noncategorical influences in the school district and by the emphasis on integration of students in the mainstream or specific vocational programming available.

### Characteristics of disabled readers

Numerous characteristics and correlates of reading disabilities have been associated with the heterogeneous population of students regarded as mildly handicapped. There is no clear relationship between cause and effect in reading disorders; the many factors associated with reading disability in research account for a relatively small part of the total variance, leaving much unexplained. Table 13 is a compilation of the most common characteristics/correlates and the presumed effects on reading.

Although students in the mildly handicapped population may have many different characteristics that make generalizations impossible, Kirk et al. (1978, pp. 13-14) describe certain commonalities of two broad categories of handicapped learners—the slow learner and the disabled reader. They

**Table 13.** Factors related to reading behavior

| Factors related to reading behavior | Presumed effects on reading behavior |
|---|---|
| Central nervous system damage | Slight damage or dysfunction of the central nervous system is thought to interfere with learning and processing of information, thus impeding normal reading development. |
| Motoric abnormalities | Faulty motor development is thought to interfere with normal acquisition of integrities necessary for later learning; perceptual motor deficits are thought to account for problems experienced by children who cannot make stable reproductions of symbols and forms. |
| Hyperactivity | Hyperactivity is viewed as either a structural or learned behavioral pattern that interferes with attention, responding to the environment, strategic planning, and organization. |
| Perceptual disorders | Auditory discrimination, sound blending, visual discrimination, visual perceptual speed, and other perceptual constructs are used to explain a variety of basic disorders interfering with learning to read; perceptual disorders are inabilities to organize sensory stimuli and data necessary in the reading process at its most elemental level. |
| Attention | Disorders of attention, distractability, selective attention, and other constructs have been used to explain learning disorders. Students may not be able to attend to instruction or to engage in self-instructional learning. |
| Memory | Disorders of memory, primarily short-term auditory, visual, and kinesthetic, are thought to interfere with retention of associations necessary in beginning reading. |
| Language disorders | Severe language disorders are not typically associated with learning disabilities, but subtle language problems, evidenced by inability to structure or properly generate meaningful sentences, provide an inadequate foundation for learning. Impoverished language of EMR students is a general limitation. |
| Thinking disorders | Some students are thought to have difficulty in development of concepts, classifications, and abstract reasoning. The main effect of such disorders would be on comprehension and application of knowledge in the process of higher cognitive functioning. |
| Mixed dominance | Problems of mixed dominance or laterality have long been associated with reading disorders. In spite of the long-standing interest in this characteristic and the lack of research evidence to demonstrate a cause-effect relationship, it persists as an important correlate in the minds of some specialists. |
| Intermodal transfer | The ability to integrate modalities, changing visual and auditory stimuli into equivalents of another modality, or to transduce information has been associated with reading disabilities, leading to varying theories about training and instruction in reading. |

refer to the range of mentally retarded, learning disabled, and children with borderline intelligence who may make up part of the mildly handicapped group of students. They contend that these students may be grouped together for reading instruction because of the following commonalities:

1. Both groups deviate from the norm in the manner in which they learn.
2. The same diagnostic procedures and tests can be used for each group.
3. Treatment procedures overlap.
4. Correlates of reading failure found in one group are found in the other.

A considerable body of literature in learning disabilities has concerned a fundamental question, "Should remediation proceed from a basis of strengthening deficit processes or avoidance of them?" Reviews of research in which attempts have been made to train underlying processes (e.g., psycholinguistic functions, visual and auditory perceptual abilities), research that has primarily involved younger subjects, indicates that such training does not substantially alleviate dysfunctions; and it may be added that it does not enhance the ability to learn to read (Hammill & Larsen, 1974; Hammill & Wiederholt, 1973; Larsen & Hammill, 1975; Larsen et al., 1976; Newcomer & Hammill, 1976).

One of the most useful reviews of research in reading was contributed by Samuels (1973), who considered various variables in reading behavior and offered conclusions about the state of the art. Some important points of this review are:

1. Although some programs demonstrate the improvement of visual discrimination, there are inconsistent findings about the existence and significance of this skill.
2. Low-achieving students have a tendency to be more distractible.
3. Memory is associated with reading skill, and poor reading in some students may be assisted through improvement of visual memory.
4. Auditory discrimination is a complex and confusing construct; efforts to improve auditory discrimination may not be well conceived.
5. Most factors commonly associated with reading development (e.g., attention, visual-motor integration, memory, auditory and visual discrimination) have relatively low positive correlations with achievement.
6. Much of the research has been inadequately designed, poorly controlled, and has provided invalid results and conclusions.

The ability to read is dependent on many individual and environmental prerequisites, and it is apparent that numerous problems can interfere with learning; these factors may occur in different combinations. Separately, or in combination, they are not fully understood. To date, research about the correlates of reading disability and efforts to remediate students by training underlying processes are confounded and insufficient to give clear direction in teaching. In summary, it may be said that there are two basic types of remedial programs available to us, namely:

1. Approaches that focus on lack of skill or competence in a basic skill area and that utilize some specific approach to remediate or improve functioning in this area
2. Approaches based primarily on the remediation of an underlying process, a perceptual deficit, a receptive, integrative, or expressive language disorder, or some known or inferred organic dysfunction that is assumed to be the basic cause of the learning disability

Remediation for adolescents must proceed on the basis of pragmatic goals and not those that are highly theoretical, unvalidated, or otherwise dubious. The poor results of training in perceptual areas (i.e., attention, memory, and others) should indicate the need to exercise considerable caution in choices between process training and direct approaches. The training-benefit outcome is likely to be greater and certainly more relevant to students if approaches are chosen that emphasize remediation of basic-skill deficiencies, that is, reading fundamentals and comprehension.

The value of remediation as the only effort of a resource room may be inconsiderable. Remediation will diminish in importance with the age of a student. The inverse relationship is explained by the relevance of such instruction in the life of the student on a daily basis and whether or not it contributes to immediate needs. It is also explained by the fact that most seriously disabled readers, in view of present evidence, cannot be expected to make significant gains with known techniques. Students who are poor readers in elementary school tend to remain poor at the secondary level. Reading failure is a persistent, chronic problem with no easy cure (Muehl & Forell, 1973-1974). Spectacular successes of students at the secondary level are rare, isolated instances. Combining remediation with a compensatory effort may be more fruitful.

### Planning concepts in remediation

In general, the following guidelines may be useful for planning the remedial reading component of a resource room:

1. Because of equivocal and controversial research in process training with younger students and the paucity of research with adolescents, it is difficult to justify the investment of *time* and *resources* in this line of remediation with adolescents. The yield in terms of benefit to students is expected to be poor.

2. Programs based on learning strategies that are presumed to be applicable across a wide range of learning endeavors are not supported by research; hence, the outcomes are speculative and possible benefits are unknown.

3. Programs that are dedicated to remediation as the only component will sacrifice those students who do not benefit from remediation and detract from other worthy endeavors of a comprehensive approach such as compensatory and vocational programming.

4. Remediation must be justified in terms of accountability, relevance, expected outcomes, and demonstrable needs of students.

### Reading approaches

Although there has been an enormous amount of research about reading failure, there is no consistent unified picture of the cause-effect relationships of variables. In fact, the complexity of the reading process is such that the nature of normal reading development is not clarified by research. Developmental reading approaches provide an excellent contrast to remedial approaches. In the broad view of reading research, heuristic concerns will ultimately be of greatest importance but even with the limitations of current knowledge there is some illustrative guidance in following developmental trends to examine applicability of remedial approaches.

The most notable conclusions to date are those of Chall (1967), who examined the reading process thoroughly and concluded that:

1. Reading methods with a code emphasis (sound values of graphemes) tend to promote better reading achievement than methods with a meaning or whole-word emphasis.
2. The code emphasis puts a demand on accuracy, which lays the foundation for better word attack skills and vocabulary

and comprehension skills, although early reading gains are slow to develop.
3. Direct teaching of code-breaking techniques, that is, letter and sound relationships, is superior to methods that are less direct.
4. Students with poor aptitude and below-average abilities tend to perform better with a code-emphasis method.
5. Inferior comprehension and vocabulary development are associated with meaning-emphasis approaches.

Although there are some highly divergent methods used for developmental reading, most basal texts emphasize certain components of the reading process in accordance with developmental theories of textbook authors who stress, to varying degrees, phonics, structural analysis, sight vocabulary, vocabulary development, comprehension, and study skills. The sequence, time, and emphasis on certain skills, as well as other aspects of reading development, are determined logically by makers of basal series. Because reading is essentially little understood and processes in the learner are mostly unobservable, it is critical that practices of instruction be used with mildly handicapped adolescents that are efficient, tied to clear objectives, and interwoven with elements of motivation and feedback.

**Remedial reading approaches.** As a group, the reading failures exhibited by mildly handicapped adolescents appear to be quite similar to those of younger students. The sequence of skills assessed by formal and informal methods indicate that deficient word recognition skills, comprehension, and other correlates of reading failure are found in the older population, much as they are in elementary school pupils. This is not as surprising as it is instructive because of the tendency to seek new methods of reading instruction or a panacea for teenagers. The basic teaching strategies will be appropriate with this group as with others because, although certain remedial techniques may stress some aspects of reading more forcefully, the fundamental process of reading, when mastered, is common to proficient readers.

Although the group characteristics of adolescents may be similar to those of younger students, there are certainly some differences in the older population that must be considered as well as some probable differences that are as yet undetermined. One characteristic that must be assessed is the extent to which motivation will be a factor in reading development. Older students who have been subjected to remedial instruction for a number of years will become calloused to further attempts because of persistent failure. It becomes part of the self-concept to be a poor reader because of an undeniable record of failure. It is important to avoid methods that have been used before because exposure to familiar material cannot be encouraging. It is also important to differentiate between secondary students on the basis of criterion-referenced measures and to resist the tendency to classify students by group characteristics.

There are at least two types of reading behavior that will be found among most students in the resource room, although there will be considerable interindividual and intraindividual variability of skills and deficits. A portion of the students will be nonreaders, while others will have a command of decoding skills. Specific remedial programs will need to be used with nonreaders, and adaptations of developmental techniques will need to be used with students who have, to some extent, mastered certain aspects of reading development. Remediation, in both instances, means that the existing problem must be identified and alleviated through the prescription of a particular instructional sequence. In order to accomplish this, it is necessary to determine what skills the student has and those that must be developed. We have included a criterion-referenced review of reading skills that should be acquired in developmental reading between the fourth- and sixth-grade levels. The sixth-grade level is regarded by many to be roughly equivalent to "functional literacy." The skills included in the review do not, of course, correspond precisely with a particular grade level, but the review will serve as a system for developing outcomes for remediation. The criterion-referenced review of reading skills will aid in planning remedial programs because of the limitations inherent in most norm-referenced tests. The teacher may wish to use data from such instruments as diagnostic tests and informal inventories, but established outcomes give direction to planning, substance to objectives, and a clear understanding of the products and process of reading instruction.

We are recommending two general remedial reading plans, which must be individualized for each student in the program. The plans are based on the existence of two general groups of students, those who are nonreaders and those who have some basic skill development.

**Students with some basic skill development.** In planning to meet the needs of students who have some level of skill acquisition, the following general steps are recommended:

1. Assessment of reading skills/contrast with criteria
2. Specification of precise skills to be acquired
3. Sequencing of skills into manageable units for learning
4. Selection of materials, aids, and supports
5. Design of individual program—objectives and time frame
6. Implementation of the course of study
7. Evaluation design

**Students with marginal skill.** In using the term "marginal" reference is made to those students who are able to demonstrate acquisition of skill in reading but who are unable to read efficiently, with speed, or with sufficiency to attack the demands of the secondary curriculum. The areas to be included in remedial programming for such students are as follows:

1. *Structural analysis:* Structural analysis, a word attack skill, involves the use of parts of words to aid the learner. In general, this would include syllabication, root words, prefixes, suffixes, compounds, and apostrophes. Although there is association between patterns and sounds, the emphasis is placed on word recognition through analysis of the structure rather than by means of elements of sound.

2. *Phonics (phonetics):* The object of instruction in phonics is for the student to overlearn appropriate sound-symbol associations for use in decoding unfamiliar words. The emphasis is placed on the learning of consonants and vowels, consonant digraphs and vowel diphthongs, and irregular variations. Although there are rules that may be applied, many students are frustrated in remembering them. Some students experience difficulty in understanding words, although they can "sound them," if they must tediously apply rules or lack facility in deriving some meaning from a passage. There are excellent materials available to help teachers employ phonics in instruction, and many materials include them in a developmental sequence.

3. *Vocabulary development:* Students who read proficiently will experience continuous development of their vocabularies because they will encounter new words and expressions in reading that they are not likely to hear in conversation with peers or even teachers. It would be helpful to students with a poverty of words to receive direct instruction in vocabulary development for several reasons, including an improved speaking

vocabulary, a useful vocabulary for understanding content areas, and a vocabulary to aid in reading growth.

4. *Contextual clues:* Understanding words by their use in a sentence without knowing the meaning of the unfamiliar word is a skill that develops with reading. This is a guessing process that can be employed to infer the meaning of an unfamiliar word or to identify a word in the speaking vocabulary that has not been previously recognized in print. It may be of limited value to most students but should be considered as a method of word attack.

5. *Comprehension:* Although comprehension is the sine qua non of the reading process, it is not really understood by reading investigators because it is totally an internal activity of cognition. Literally, comprehension means "to understand what is read." Most developmental programs emphasize factual data in a passage, and the student is tested for comprehension by the challenge of correctly answering a series of questions. Some students who have visual perception deficits tend to perform well beyond the early stages of reading after decoding skills are established. Students who tend to have language-related problems, even though quite subtle, will often be able to decode efficiently but will falter as reading comprehension becomes more demanding, such as comparing, contrasting, and drawing inferences from a story or expository passage.

6. *Study skills:* Although many writers tend to separate study skills from basic reading skill, it is more realistic to consider them at the apex of basic skill development. Beyond the fourth-grade level of reading, most developmental materials or basal series add very few skills except some more refined techniques of reading. To a certain extent, study skills are introduced at each grade level and intensified through the eighth grade. Unfortunately, some developmental reading teachers ignore study skills with the emphasis on decoding abilities. Consequently, study skills should be carefully taught. They include the abilities to locate information, to use the dictionary and reference material, to use parts of a book, to outline, to take notes, and ultimately to do research papers.

**Reading in content areas.** One tremendous source of support to disabled readers is the assistance that can be provided by teachers in subject areas who emphasize *reading* in content. Teaching a student to read is not synonymous with reading in content areas; rather, it is a process of content-area instruction that demystifies the technical terminology of various disciplines. Herber (1979, p. 3) states that:

Reading is taught in content areas when subject-area teachers teach their students how to read what they are required to read as they read it. The instruction is provided by regular classroom teachers within regular subject-area classes as a natural part of the curriculum. This assures the simultaneous learning of course content and reading process, with neither being sacrificed to the other.

Subject-area teachers are not expected to teach developmental reading or remedial reading (e.g., word attack skills, phonics) but are expected to assist students in the identification, application, and comprehension of concepts and terms of the content. They learn to identify essential information, to build on prior knowledge with new information, and to improve general study skills. Because teaching reading is a skill that may be foreign to subject-area teachers, specialists will need to provide in-service training to improve the teachers' ability to synthesize course content and the reading process. It is apparent how valuable this would be to the segment of mildly handicapped students who participate in content classes.

**Special remedial techniques.** For the group of students in the secondary program who are seriously deficient in reading, who cannot decode, the preceding techniques will be of little value until some fundamental mastery of basic reading skill is achieved. The rate of gain for students is typically rather constant from the third grade of school. Most mildly retarded students are expected to reach second- to sixth-grade achievement on completion of school. LD students and emotionally disturbed students have no general expectations associated with their labels. Dramatic breakthroughs are not to be expected. The most severely reading disabled students are not likely to improve much beyond the earliest instructional levels. As they continue to fail, they become less motivated to attempt reading, and various emotional problems may be superimposed on the existing failure syndrome as a reaction to damaged self-esteem. Remedial reading at the secondary level with such students is difficult for the teacher because the chances of success are minimal, preoccupation with remedial reading detracts from other services that might be provided, and students may be resentful and hostile. Nonetheless, it may be decided to continue remediation. Individual assessment and planning will be absolutely essential if any progress is to be expected and fostered.

The specialized remedial techniques are familiar to specialists, but some discussion of them here will be important in order to consider some issues about their applicability and limitations in a secondary program.

***Fernald technique.*** The tracing technique developed by Fernald (1943) is highly touted and widely discussed but rarely used. It involves adherence to a few specific steps, but there is no accompanying program, which leaves development of lessons a major responsibility of busy teachers who may wish to select more structured approaches. The technique is extremely slow in development but can be easily adapted to meet individual needs of students and can be tied to a variety of reinforcement systems. Motivation is essential, and appropriate rewards can enhance pupil cooperation.

Briefly, (1) the teacher encourages the student to select a word he or she wants to learn; (2) the teacher transforms the word into written form (usually cursive) in a letter size large enough for the student to trace; (3) the pupil traces the word with the index finger while saying the word; (4) this process is repeated until the word can be written from memory. The teacher maintains a card file and constructs a story for the student by supplying essential words and typing the story line with the student's "words." The multisensory technique assists in development of a reading vocabulary and skill to attack new words. The initial stage relies on the visual, auditory, kinesthetic, and tactile sensations. Hence, the approach is commonly referred to as a VAKT technique. Ultimately, tracing is eliminated and the teacher ceases to produce written models of words. Many variations of the technique have existed, including those that incorporate considerable drill and phonics.

The obvious drawback to the Fernald technique is that it is tedious for both the teacher and the student. With motivation a key to success, the lack of it provides an infertile ground for instruction. The activities may seem childish to some "sophisticated" teenagers and others may be disappointed by minor successes over a long period of time.

***Gillingham approach.*** The Gillingham approach is a commercially available multisensory or VAKT technique that differs from the Fernald technique in that it stresses phonics, is highly structured, and has accompanying materials. Like the Fernald technique, it gradually builds on overlearned skills until the student is able to function with automatic responses. Phonograms and associated sounds are introduced, and instruction in writing them is introduced. The student must see, say, trace, and write the phonogram (in the air). Accompanying drill cards with key words and pictures are used to reinforce learning. After a series of phonetically compatible sounds, which can be combined into simple words, it learned, stories are presented that include these words. The approach has been successful with severely disabled readers, but it is extremely time consuming and lacks any emphasis on comprehension in early stages of reading. These factors could prove to be frustrating to some students who anticipate faster gains.

As with other VAKT approaches, simultaneous stimulation of input channels should be carefully considered to avoid distress to students who adversely react to overstimulation. Because independent reading is delayed until a large number of sound-symbol associations are made, and because the program may require two years, if successful, use of this approach must be weighed heavily against other variables in planning, such as the age of the student, years until completion of school, and other goals of education.

*Hegge-Kirk-Kirk remedial reading drills.* The Hegge-Kirk-Kirk method employs the use of drills to establish sound-symbol associations, closure, and left-to-right progression in the reading act. There are four parts, beginning with training in associating sounds with common consonants, short vowels, and regularly occurring consonant blends, diphthongs, and digraphs. The drills proceed with combinations of sounds learned in phase I; next more advanced and uncommon sounds included in whole words are introduced; and ultimately there is a concentration on word-building exercises and training in nonphonetic, sound-symbol associations and letters that are easily confused (e.g., *b* and *d*).

This method is recommended for use with students who have failed to learn after several years in school, but it is not to be regarded as a general method of instruction; rather, it is to be used with students who are stymied below the third-grade level in achievement. As soon as progress is made, the reading activities of the student are to be transferred to other reading techniques. This approach has been called a VAKT method because it emphasizes multisensory stimulation, but unlike other approaches, it integrates phonics with practice in actual words rather than prolonged practice with isolated sound-symbol associations. For this reason, the drills have attractive features for students at the secondary level. There is structure, rapid movement to meaningful content, and a measurable progression through a hierarchy of skills. Consequently, students are much more apt to be motivated.

*Development of reading skills.* Remediation of students who are retarded in reading at the higher levels, and reading instruction for those who achieve mastery of basic skills, will progress beyond the techniques listed above. As noted, word attack skills, phonics, structural analysis, and comprehension will be inherent parts of the remedial reading program. However, much of the emphasis is on decoding skills and cue reduction for word recognition. Consequently, stress is placed on oral reading behavior.

There has been a traditional belief that oral reading is a reflection of silent reading or a mechanism for the teacher to investigate silent reading. There is sufficient reason to believe that the functions of the central nervous system are quite different under each condition with a consequent effect on comprehension, the meaningful goal of the reading process. A considerable debate surrounds the issue of silent and oral reading. Kirk et al. (1978, p. 120) state that ". . . slow-learning or learning-disabled children should continue oral reading longer and at a higher grade level than is usually allowed with the average learner."

Reasons cited by Kirk et al. include the following: eye movement patterns have more fixations during oral reading; oral reading is the essential first step in reading; accuracy should be stressed rather than speed; oral reading enhances pronunciation and enunciation; and oral reading allows the teacher to gauge comprehension. They continue by asserting that reading disorders are caused by insistence on rapid transition to silent reading.

With secondary students, however, one could recommend the utilization of silent reading for isolation of meaningful content and subject-area comprehension as soon as possible. In the process of silent reading, an individual may ignore irrelevant information, grasp information from a few important clues, infer meaning from a passage, and attack reading matter in a stylized manner. By emphasizing study skills and using prereading questions, skimming, and so forth even poor readers will be able to attack content of various subjects with a predetermined plan. Although reading skills and speed may develop incidentally, literal and inferential comprehension must be emphasized. Adjusting reading rates for different types of reading is essential. However, speed will be less of a concern if a student knows what information to seek, how to analyze the content, how to record facts and concepts in an outline, and how to organize facts for recall. These are not simple skills by any means, but they are much more task relevant than persistent oral reading in content areas that slows the reader and involves the additional requirement of motor activity in the articulatory process as an extraneous detraction from reading. Oral reading may be emphasized in decoding and acquisition of basic reading skill but may be contraindicated when the objectives of reading switch from the process to specific outcomes, and from *learning to read* to *reading to learn*.

*Intensive remediation as a major program thrust.* To say anything less than that we must assist each student to reach his or her fullest capabilities, highest level of achievement, or (at least) functional literacy is heretical in educational circles. However, we must seriously consider the implications of such clichés if they are to be heralded as program goals. Some professionals adopt the position that remediation is the *only* approach to be used with LD adolescents. There can be no question that remediation should be *one* of the primary concerns of specialists; but the many other needs of the students pertaining to successful adjustment in the school environment and achievement in content courses should not be ignored. Retention in school and successful remediation depend greatly on a student's attitude, self-concept, and motivation, which are influenced by the total environment. The secondary specialist will find that the requirements of the principal, the needs of students, and the attitudes of regular classroom teachers will present a complex set of problems for handicapped learners. To restrict services to remediation can be a comfortable form of escapism from the responsibility to meet the immediate academic and personal-social needs of students and to assist mainstream teachers.

It is not surprising that the field has capped the secondary effort with remediation as a primary focus because of the tendency to imitate elementary-level programs and to resort to custom and authority for direction in solving problems. If we limit services to remediation, then we must consider some of the facts and assumptions underlying this practice:

1. There will be a narrow range of services (reading and arithmetic) for students who have many immediate needs that will not be addressed in this approach.

2. There is no overwhelming evidence that the field has been very successful in over-

coming the learning deficits of the majority of identified students.

3. Severe reading disability is likely to remain a persistent problem throughout the school careers and lives of affected students. The limited time in secondary school makes significant gains in remediation highly unlikely. It has been demonstrated that remediation over a period of many years will apparently not bring most severely disabled students up to grade-level expectations.

4. Motivation is a problem for adolescents who are veterans of many remedial approaches.

5. Students who make slow gains in achievement will most likely continue to progress at a slow pace.

6. The most stellar success stories of students who make dramatic achievement are rare instances not representative of the population of poor readers.

A follow-up study of disabled readers conducted by Muehl and Forell (1973-1974) and subsequent analysis by Forell (1976) challenge popular opinions about remediation of reading disabilities. The follow-up study was an examination of the academic careers of 43 children who had originally been referred to a reading clinic between the years of 1963 and 1965. The students were aged 8 to 15 at the time of diagnosis, all had normal intelligence as determined by the WISC, and each was free of gross sensory or neurological defects. During 1972, each subject was interviewed and administered a battery of tests that included three measures of reading. The findings indicated that *only* two subjects scored above the fiftieth percentile on reading tests and over half scored below the twentieth percentile. They had continued to have severe reading problems during junior and senior high school in spite of the remedial efforts of specialists in the reading clinic. The overwhelming conclusion was that severe reading disability is likely to remain with a student and not even years of tutoring are likely to contravene effects of the deficiency.

Similarly, Frauenheim (1978) examined the reading performance of 40 adult males who had been diagnosed as having primary reading retardation or developmental dyslexia. The mean age at diagnosis was 11 years 6 months, and the average age at the time of follow-up was 21 years 10 months. Tests that had been used with the subjects at diagnosis were utilized in the follow-up several years later. Of the 40 subjects, only one had an adult reading score above the sixth-grade level, and the average reading level was 3.6. It was indicated in this study that the age at which assistance began and adult reading level outcomes were not related. The fact that there was no relationship between the amount of special reading help and adult reading outcomes was interpreted to mean that the subjects had reached a plateau in reading development.

If we continue to amass research with similar conclusions, a major reassessment of the learning disabilities movement may need to be initiated or, at least, a major redirection. When efficacy studies in learning disabilities are conducted, as they have been in the field of mental retardation, it will be increasingly difficult to defend a separate funding base and professional actions if we must present evidence of successful remediation as the first line of defense. Many teachers will be defenseless on examination if they are persuaded by those who suggest that the only effort of the LD specialist at the secondary level is remediation of basic skills. Aside from the fact that such programming diminishes in importance to adolescents who are daily confronted with the need to compete in mainstream classes, there is little reason to believe the persistent reading problems of adolescents will improve much, even with massive doses of remediation over long periods of time. It is true that there are some rare cases of dramatic improvement, but the best evidence of this phenomenon is submitted in the form of testimonials from specialists in clinics who describe, anecdotally, the progress of these few students who, it must be said, are ordinarily highly motivated, tenacious persons that voluntarily seek the services of a clinic. Certainly, this type of student is not representative of the typical secondary school LD population, nor of reading clinics, judging from the large number of failures.

It is true that most secondary schools are not well equipped to handle students who cannot read, but this does not mean that the system cannot be altered. Adjusted programs in the content areas can provide successful learning opportunities to these students and the specialist can assume part of the responsibility for developing, managing, and monitoring these innovations. Reading need not be the only medium of learning available to any student, especially the mildly handicapped. Experiences with blind students in the mainstream prove this beyond any doubt. What is operating is a bias on the part of those who equate incompetence with reading deficiency in those students who have capable minds and 20/20 vision, and the narrow view of special educators who presume that learning cannot occur unless high levels of reading achievement are attained. Reading, to the "true believer" in the reading movement, can be used to justify the elimination of the opportunity to learn by summarily dismissing otherwise capable students from the mainstream of education, to undermine the process of acquiring basic concepts and knowledge about our culture transmitted to good readers in our schools, and to limit the opportunities of students through default by permitting prejudice against the poor reader to remain unchallenged. This kind of thinking leads ultimately to the following dubious concepts implicit in the proposals of some authorities about the purpose of the secondary program: (1) secondary content-area teachers cannot teach students who cannot read their textbooks; (2) students who cannot read proficiently must be channeled only into vocational course work; and (3) students who cannot read proficiently must be doomed to low-level jobs and serious underemployment.

We are not suggesting that remediation should be avoided in the secondary special education program but only that it should be one of a variety of options available to consumers of the program. Any program that becomes circumscribed by basic literacy goals will appear to fail unless substantial numbers of students make spectacular gains, an outcome that is not to be expected. Moreover, the remedial focus may become the only objective of the program, which would be unfortunate, indeed, in view of the exciting opportunities in the learning environment. Program options must be determined broadly by the many needs of students.

### Assessment of reading

Much of the formal task of assessment will be concluded in the diagnostic process used to place a student in the special education program. Teachers in remedial or compensatory resource rooms will have a greater need for information derived from diagnostic and informal tests because of the many limitations of standardized or formal tests. In general, it is necessary to establish that a significant discrepancy exists between the student's ability and actual reading performance. It is important to have a conceptualization of expected reading performance whether or not one uses a set criterion (e.g., three or more years in reading retardation) or significant differences between standard scores. We caution the practitioner to remember that most tests will be unable to provide information about *what* or *how* to teach.

Scores that commonly express perfor-

**Table 14.** Estimated reading levels for students by IQ, CA, and grade level

| IQ | Seventh grade<br>CA 12 | Eighth grade<br>CA 13 | Ninth grade<br>CA 14 | Tenth grade<br>CA 15 | Eleventh grade<br>CA 16 | Twelfth grade<br>CA 17 |
|---|---|---|---|---|---|---|
| 70 | 3.5 | 4.1 | 4.8 | 5.5 | 6.2 | 6.9 |
| 71 | 3.6 | 4.2 | 4.9 | 5.6 | 6.3 | 7.0 |
| 72 | 3.6 | 4.4 | 5.1 | 5.8 | 6.5 | 7.2 |
| 73 | 3.8 | 4.5 | 5.2 | 6.0 | 6.7 | 7.4 |
| 74 | 3.9 | 4.6 | 5.4 | 6.1 | 6.8 | 7.6 |
| 75 | 3.9 | 4.6 | 5.4 | 6.1 | 6.8 | 7.6 |
| 76 | 4.1 | 4.9 | 5.6 | 6.3 | 7.1 | 7.9 |
| 77 | 4.2 | 5.0 | 5.8 | 6.6 | 7.3 | 8.1 |
| 78 | 4.4 | 5.2 | 5.9 | 6.7 | 7.5 | 8.3 |
| 79 | 4.5 | 5.3 | 6.1 | 6.8 | 7.6 | 8.4 |
| 80 | 4.6 | 5.4 | 6.2 | 7.0 | 7.8 | 8.6 |
| 81 | 4.7 | 5.5 | 6.3 | 7.1 | 8.0 | 8.8 |
| 82 | 4.8 | 5.7 | 6.5 | 7.3 | 8.1 | 8.9 |
| 83 | 5.0 | 5.8 | 6.8 | 7.4 | 8.2 | 9.1 |
| 84 | 5.1 | 5.9 | 6.9 | 7.8 | 8.4 | 9.3 |
| 85 | 5.2 | 6.1 | 6.9 | 7.8 | 8.6 | 9.5 |
| 86 | 5.3 | 6.2 | 7.0 | 7.9 | 8.8 | 9.6 |
| 87 | 5.4 | 6.3 | 7.2 | 8.1 | 8.9 | 9.8 |
| 88 | 5.6 | 6.4 | 7.3 | 8.2 | 9.1 | 10.0 |
| 89 | 5.7 | 6.6 | 7.5 | 8.4 | 9.2 | 10.1 |
| 90 | 5.8 | 6.7 | 7.5 | 8.5 | 9.4 | 10.3 |
| 91 | 5.9 | 6.8 | 7.7 | 8.7 | 9.6 | 10.4 |
| 92 | 6.0 | 7.0 | 7.9 | 8.8 | 9.7 | 10.6 |
| 93 | 6.2 | 7.1 | 8.0 | 9.0 | 9.9 | 10.8 |
| 94 | 6.3 | 7.2 | 8.2 | 9.1 | 10.0 | 11.0 |
| 95 | 6.4 | 7.4 | 8.3 | 9.3 | 10.2 | 11.2 |
| 96 | 6.5 | 7.5 | 8.4 | 9.4 | 10.4 | 11.3 |
| 97 | 6.6 | 7.6 | 8.5 | 9.6 | 10.5 | 11.5 |
| 98 | 6.8 | 7.7 | 8.7 | 9.7 | 10.7 | 11.7 |
| 99 | 6.9 | 7.9 | 8.9 | 9.9 | 10.9 | 11.8 |
| 100 | 7.0 | 8.0 | 9.0 | 10.0 | 11.0 | 12.0 |
| 101 | 7.1 | 8.1 | 9.1 | 10.2 | 11.2 | 12.2 |
| 102 | 7.2 | 8.3 | 9.3 | 10.3 | 11.3 | 12.3 |
| 103 | 7.4 | 8.4 | 9.4 | 10.4 | 11.5 | 12.5 |
| 104 | 7.5 | 8.5 | 9.6 | 10.6 | 11.6 | 12.7 |
| 105 | 7.6 | 8.7 | 9.7 | 10.8 | 11.8 | 12.8 |
| 106 | 7.6 | 8.8 | 9.8 | 10.9 | 12.0 | 13.0 |
| 107 | 7.8 | 8.9 | 10.0 | 11.0 | 12.1 | 13.2 |
| 108 | 8.8 | 9.0 | 10.1 | 11.2 | 12.3 | 13.4 |
| 109 | 8.1 | 9.2 | 10.3 | 11.4 | 12.4 | 13.5 |
| 110 | 8.2 | 9.3 | 10.4 | 11.5 | 12.6 | 13.7 |
| 111 | 8.3 | 9.4 | 10.5 | 11.7 | 12.8 | 13.9 |
| 112 | 8.4 | 9.6 | 10.7 | 11.9 | 12.9 | 14.0 |
| 113 | 8.6 | 9.7 | 10.8 | 12.0 | 13.1 | 14.2 |
| 114 | 8.7 | 9.8 | 11.0 | 12.1 | 13.2 | 14.4 |
| 115 | 8.8 | 10.0 | 11.1 | 12.2 | 13.4 | 14.6 |
| ⋮ | ⋮ | ⋮ | ⋮ | ⋮ | ⋮ | ⋮ |
| 120 | 9.4 | 10.6 | 11.8 | 13.0 | 14.2 | 15.4 |
| ⋮ | ⋮ | ⋮ | ⋮ | ⋮ | ⋮ | ⋮ |
| 130 | 10.6 | 11.9 | 13.2 | 14.5 | 15.8 | 17.1 |

mance on achievement tests are the reading age score, the reading grade score, percentiles, and standard scores. Teachers who are thoroughly familiar with statistical properties of tests and methods of interpreting test data and profiles will be of great assistance to mainstream teachers because of the ability to provide useful information about students. It should be remembered that most secondary mainstream teachers will have only the most rudimentary training in using and understanding tests.

Although the determination of a significant discrepancy is essential in learning disabilities according to federal guidelines, there are many inaccuracies of any approach used to determine such discrepancies. Certainly care must be taken to assure that the classification systems are augmented with diagnostic and informal information. Standardized test scores will continue to be used after placement to measure gains in reading development, but they may disguise other forms of information or not indicate certain types of progress.

**Reading diagnostic tests.** A variety of reading diagnostic tests are commercially available. They generally provide either a wide range of measures in various subskills or assessment of specific skills such as oral reading or phonics. One of the most popular has been the *Durrell Analysis of Reading Difficulty* published by Harcourt Brace Jovanovich. The Durrell test is very comprehensive and may be recommended for use rather than an informal reading inventory (IRI) because the IRI is developed by the teacher with reference to a specific reading series or text. The reading demands of adolescents are much broader and instruction is likely to avoid basal texts because of the negative associations developed by students over the years.

**Criterion-referenced tests.** If functional literacy, defined by some as sixth-grade reading competency, is the only goal or one of many in the resource room, a criterion-referenced test (CRT) will be of greater utility than most standardized instruments for developing individualized instructional programs. The CRT focuses on specific objectives and outcomes. As noted previously, it is essential that instruction be devoted to skills that are generally associated with fourth- to sixth-grade reading and that are part of a developmental reading program. It should be noted that functioning at a sixth-grade level is much different than simply decoding words or passing a word recognition test that is equivalent to words found in a sixth-grade reader. It can be readily determined that reading skills of the middle grades are certainly not simple tasks.

**Review of reading skills.** A student who progresses through the fourth, fifth, and sixth grades should be able to perform the following general skills, which are ordered by increasing degrees of difficulty and generally associated with demands of basal texts and reading curricula that are predominant in schools. More refined tests may be developed, but these general sequential skills will aid the teacher in monitoring reading progress. The list below is a review of reading skills for grades 4 to 7.

1. Defines and gives examples or identifies examples of antonyms, synonyms, homonyms, and figures of speech.
2. Identifies root words.
3. Recognizes and explains the hyphen (e.g., twenty-two).
4. Can analyze prefixes (in, tri, em, per, post, ob, de, inter, super, trans, en, com, ab, dis, re, im, un, anti, mis).
5. Can analyze suffixes (ling, et, age, ance, ity, ment, ious, ant, ure, ence, eous, ent, wise, ly, ness, ish, ful, less, or, ours, ness, ward, al, hood, sp).
6. Can use accent clues and generalizations about syllabication; for example, the initial syllable is accented unless it is a prefix; endings that are syllables

are usually not accented; initial syllables (a, in, be, re, de) are commonly unaccented; when a vowel is followed by a consonant the next syllable begins with a consonant; divisions occur between compound words; and prefixes and suffixes are commonly syllables.
7. Can differentiate between main ideas and subideas.
8. Can recall the facts of a story or sequence of events.
9. Can recognize less complex figures of speech.
10. Identifies colloquialisms.
11. Interprets idiomatic speech.
12. Identifies the subject, predicate, direct object, and other fundamental parts of a sentence.
13. Complies with complex written instructions.
14. Places the comma appropriately in a sequence to separate items after an initial adverbial clause.
15. Skims to determine general content.
16. Uses prereading questions to find specific facts.
17. Is able to make inferences, judgments, and conclusions from a written passage.
18. Determines cause-and-effect relationships.
19. Predicts the outcome of a story.
20. In the process of oral reading, the student is able to scan ahead of his or her voice.
21. Interprets the meaning of basic illustrations.
22. Identifies facts that support a generalization.
23. Makes generalizations after accumulating facts.
24. Defines, identifies, and uses abstract words.
25. Analyzes a story by determining characters, actions, and results.
26. Uses hyphen in compound words.
27. Identifies inferential facts.
28. Distinguishes between irrelevant and relevant factual statements.
29. Uses tables, charts, and graphs to acquire information.
30. Uses the dictionary: guide words, pronunciation key, diacritical markings, accent marks, appropriate meaning.
31. Uses resource references: atlas, encyclopedia, and almanac.
32. Identifies vowel digraphs.
33. Explains and understands time relationships.
34. Summarizes information.
35. Identifies diphthongs.
36. Uses an index.
37. Makes an outline using main topic and ideas and subordinate concepts.
38. Distinguishes between objective and subjective statements.
39. Constructs various sentences using compound and abstract words, past participle, and future tense.
40. Reorganizes simple sentences into complex sentences; organizes a written paragraph with four or five supporting sentences.
41. Identifies regional and dialectical differences in grammar and speech.
42. Uses parts of book to locate information.
43. Finds books according to topics.
44. Uses a card catalog in the library.
45. Develops perfected cursive writing style.
46. Takes notes in class and can organize an outline with main ideas.
47. Identifies sensory imagery in written works.
48. Uses reference materials independently.
49. Can identify and describe the differences between various literary forms (e.g., fiction, nonfiction, poetry, biography).
50. Makes a brief written report from fac-

**284** THE PROGRAM

tual information taken from books and oral presentations.
51. Varies reading rate according to purpose and type of reading matter.
52. Identifies and understands all the parts of an expository book: headings, italics, and so forth.
53. Uses study guides.
54. Finds directions and identifies general information on map.
55. Locates information in a newspaper.

## Practical reading

In order for reading skills to be helpful to students who will ultimately be required to employ them in meeting daily demands, some practical application of reading should be made. There are infinite possibilities, many of which serve to motivate students because of the variety of interests that may be encompassed. Significant reading tasks performed by adults in daily routines have been determined by Murphy (1975, p. 52):

- Information about prices and weight
- Street and traffic signs
- Headlines in newspapers
- Writings on packages and labels
- Manuals and written instructions
- Forms, invoices, and accounting statements
- Tests, examinations, and written assignments
- Letters, memoranda, and notes
- Order forms
- Newspapers
- School papers and notes
- Bills and statements

The following materials are readily available in any community and can be used in a practical-reading emphasis:

- Advertisements
- Checkbooks
- Bills
- Amortization tables
- Blue Book (valuation)
- Blueprints
- Business letters
- Calendars
- Comic strips
- Contracts
- Employment applications
- Manuals
- Menus
- Tax forms
- Repair manuals
- Transportation charts
- Rental agreements
- Labels
- Instructions
- Diagrams
- Store catalogs
- Loan agreements
- Road maps
- Meters
- Paychecks
- Withholding forms
- Real estate documents
- Applications for licenses
- Traffic tickets
- Receipts
- Telephone directory
- Tickets
- Thermometer
- Newspapers
- Insurance forms
- Home mortgages
- Immunization records
- Warranties and guarantees
- Magazines
- Car titles
- First-aid manual
- Social Security forms

## STUDY SKILLS

One of the most basic goals of primary grade school teachers is to teach children to decode the printed page and to acquire the fundamental reading skills. Beyond the fourth grade, much of reading instruction involves extension, elaboration, and refinement of the processes learned in the first four grades. The concerns of special educators have also been to teach children to decode and acquire fundamental reading skills; but, because of the limited success with remediation beyond the initial stages of skill development, renewed efforts and alternative approaches are reiterated consecutively as students continue to fail. One area that has been neglected in regular education for non-handicapped students, and certainly by special educators who have been preoccupied with basic remediation, is study skills.

Study skills, as they are commonly called, are actually functional reading abilities or specific reading competencies enabling a pupil to study the content areas of the curriculum. Reading in textbooks is quite different from that which students typically encounter in basal series and other developmental materials. Most reading books are attractively displayed, have uniform type, are punctuated with colorful pictures and photographs, and have a predictability in content. Students are usually required to recall sequences and events about stories, make simple inferences, and relate descriptions after reading. Textbooks, on the other hand, are expository in nature, include many changes in type, are riddled with technical words and unfamiliar concepts, and are boring. The fact that texts are heavily weighted with facts and concepts, as well as being uninteresting, complicates the task of the learner. Study skills are essential for effective learning to occur because reading in the subject-matter areas is much more difficult than in reading classes.

It is apparent that study skills stand at the apex of reading abilities, the last to be mastered. Using them, the student is able to locate information, to interpret pictorial information, and to master the content of courses. Unfortunately, some students are able to complete the successful acquisition of skills in phonics, structural analysis, syllabication, and word meaning but lack adequate study skills. Part of the reason for inferior development of functional reading abilities can be attributed to the fact that they are not emphasized in regular classes nor by special education teachers.

It is not uncommon to find some reference to study skills in texts dealing with secondary subjects and reading in content areas. Typically the well-known SQ3R method of study is discussed, and it is presumed that study skills are more or less limited to adjusted reading rates. It seems that there is a presumption that study skills are only of concern in secondary schools. Actually, after the fundamental skills of reading are acquired by the fourth grade, the study skills are supposed to be stressed. Many students, however, are not introduced to a consistent, lawful process of instruction in study skills in regular classes. Successful gains in special education programs may lead a student back to the regular class during the elementary years with little or no attention paid to reading skills other than organized reading activities pertaining to remediation and the developmental sequence.

Study skills typically include the use of the dictionary and reference materials, locating information, and the organization of information through note-taking or outlining. We have organized study skills into *mechanical* and *critical reading skills*, which differentiate between reading in organized reading classes and that of reading in subject matter areas. Although both types are necessary for efficient learning in school subjects, the tasks are quite different. They are as follows:

| Mechanical | Critical reading |
| --- | --- |
| Recalling main ideas | Perceiving relationships |
| Locating main ideas | Drawing conclusions |
| Retelling a story | Making inferences |
| Recalling sequences | Interpreting feelings |
| Classifying information | Making judgments |
| Skimming | Comparing |
| Outlining | Contrasting |
|  | Making generalizations |
|  | Summarizing |

What we have called *critical reading* is the ability to transcend the more literal, mechanical aspects of decoding and comprehension. The cognitive structures of the more capable mildly handicapped adolescents that permit this are related to new skills of the mental processes—hypothetical, abstract reasoning and symbolism. The student is capable of very sophisticated processing of reading matter. The mechanical aspects are mastered, meaning is derived directly without attention to perceptual tasks of decoding, and high-order comprehension surpasses the more basic task of recalling factual information. Judgments are made, principles are identified, and generalizations are formed that relate to both the written passage and the experience of the reader. EMR students may not be expected to reach this level of attainment, but many ED and LD students, not able to read because of basic decoding deficits, are capable of processing the information with the same effect as in critical reading if they are provided with accommodation. In other words, the student is able to comprehend material without reading it (it is

**PRIMARY SKILLS FOR STUDY ASSIGNMENTS**

READING
- technical vocabulary
- SQ3R
- outlining
- note-taking

GRAPHICS
- charts
- diagrams
- tables
- graphs

**PRIMARY SKILLS FOR PRODUCTS**

FINDING SOURCES
- dictionary skills
- use of atlas
- encyclopedia
- other references
- library
  card catalog
  section, floor, shelf
  systems of classification

LOCATING SPECIFIC INFORMATION
- alphabetizing skills
- book parts
  title and author,
  title page,
  publication date,
  preface, headings,
  table of contents,
  introduction and summary,
  glossary, index,
  appendix

**LEARNING ACTIVITIES**

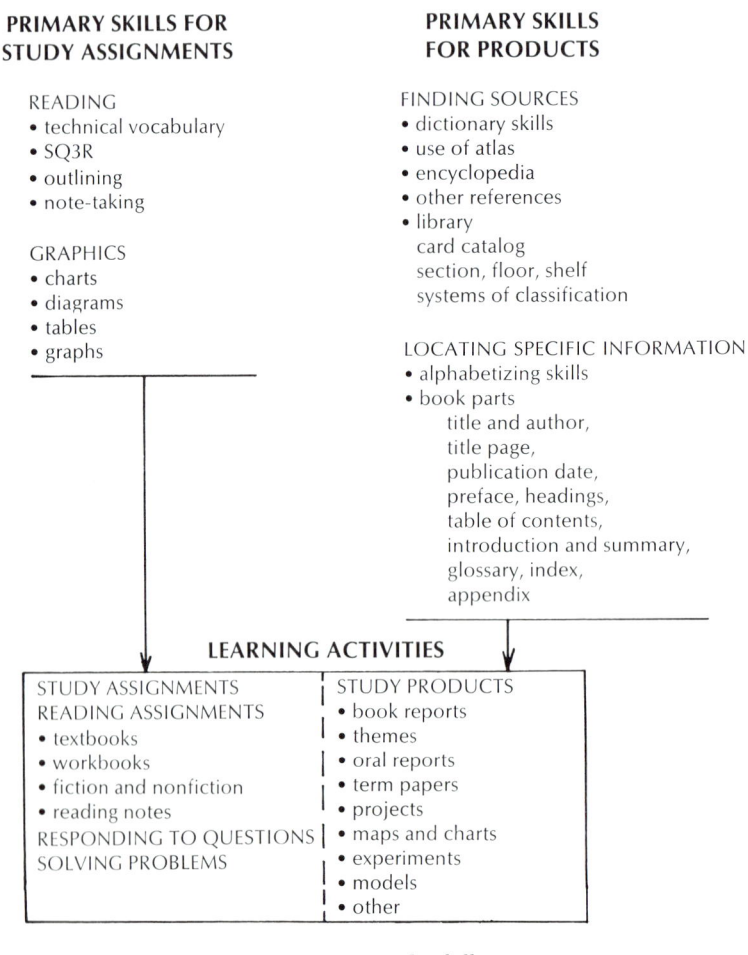

STUDY ASSIGNMENTS
READING ASSIGNMENTS
- textbooks
- workbooks
- fiction and nonfiction
- reading notes
RESPONDING TO QUESTIONS
SOLVING PROBLEMS

STUDY PRODUCTS
- book reports
- themes
- oral reports
- term papers
- projects
- maps and charts
- experiments
- models
- other

**Fig. 11-1.** Study skills.

read to the student or presented through another alternative approach). This, of course, is why students should be permitted to participate in the learning activities of the primary subject areas. They can learn subject matter although they may have difficulty with the preferred means of obtaining information.

Another important consideration in remediation that relates to these issues is that teaching students to decode is insufficient justification to eliminate them from resource services. It can be seen that the more complex reading skills and the application of reading in content areas will be demanding tasks deserving of support from specialists. Although a reader may be considered functionally literate with mastery of sixth-grade reading skills, this will not assure success in the school nor in society.

### Application of study skills

There are two general types of study skills: *primary skills for study assignments* and *primary skills for products*. Assignments and the creation of products are the major endeavors of homework, laboratory work, and in-school study. Both types are utilized by students in meeting the demands of course requirements on a daily basis and contribute significantly to successful completion of courses and earning passing grades. Simple decoding skills will not give the student this status of achievement in the secondary school. Fig. 11-1 represents the types of skills needed and the outcomes of study.

## ARITHMETIC AND MATHEMATICS

Specialists have assumed responsibility for assisting students with arithmetic disorders in the elementary grades, although this type of assistance has been much more restricted than in reading. At the secondary level there is a certain degree of anxiety about involvement in this area because of the complex and abstract nature of the mathematics hierarchy (algebra, trigonometry, and so forth). Some LD students will evidence specific disorders in arithmetic skills but not in reading, while others tend to have a superior facility for numerical symbolism but extremely deficient reading skills. In many cases the only problems that students have with arithmetic or mathematics are caused by their inability to read textbooks. The symbolic nature of mathematical statements enables some students to compensate for reading deficiency. In general, the basic goal is for all students to have functional skills in arithmetic. For students who have an interest or a real aptitude for higher mathematics, many of the accommodatory techniques and methods of assisting the mainstream teacher will be sufficiently supportive.

### Causes of arithmetic failure

Arithmetic disabilities have received very little attention (Marsh, 1976). Low achievement of EMR students in this area is consistent with a generally lower level of overall achievement. The causes of arithmetic failure have been likened to those that are correlated with learning disabilities in general. Until recently, the attentions of very few writers have been devoted to disorders of quantitative thinking (Chalfant & Scheffelin, 1969; Johnson & Myklebust, 1967). Factors that are thought to cause or to be associated with arithmetic failure are disorders of memory, spatial ability, visual perception, laterality and left-to-right orientation, and verbal ability. The paucity of research in this area, controversy about process training, and the limited understanding of arithmetic processes have caused attention to problems of arithmetic failure to be limited to rather direct remedial concerns.

For various reasons a distinction must be made between arithmetic and mathematics, according to Chalfant and Scheffelin (1969).

Arithmetic is the science of numbers and computation with them, more specifically addition, subtraction, multiplication, and division. Mathematics is the abstract science and study of quantity, form, arrangement, and magnitude. Arithmetic is concrete in nature; it deals with concrete entities, and the symbol system of arithmetic is not far removed from the actual manipulation of objects. Mathematics does not deal with concrete factors but is very abstract. We cannot presume that disorders of mathematics are similar to disorders of arithmetic, even though facility with computation is a prerequisite to mathematics. Until there is more research, it would be wise to treat arithmetic and mathematics differently and to recognize that other disorders may account for disabilities in mathematics.

## Characteristics of adolescents with arithmetic disabilities

In a study that is nearing conclusion (Marsh et al., 1979), we investigated the arithmetic disorders of elementary school children and adolescents who have been diagnosed as having arithmetic disabilities and have compared them with underachievers and normal achievers. Among a variety of interesting findings, the most interesting is that older and younger students are extremely deficient in computational abilities as well as underlying processes. There are very few differences between the younger and older groups, which confirms the findings of others who conclude that most problems in arithmetic are due to computational skill deficiencies (Otto et al., 1973); but we were impressed by the underlying difficulties with processes and the apparent inability to use visual symbols of arithmetic in various algorithms. It may be that computational deficiencies are the most common problems, but we believe that this may be partly an effect of achievement tests that are heavily weighted on computational skills with lesser emphasis on processes and underlying conceptualizations of the arithmetic process. In other words, for some students faulty computation may be symptomatic of more fundamental deficits that are not assessed with common instruments.

Planning to assist adolescents should proceed on much the same course as with plans to remediate younger students who have arithmetic disabilities. Assistance to students who experience mathematics disabilities may need to be very different because of different processes and causes of failure.

## Erecting arithmetic competencies

Students who manage to complete credits in mathematics at the secondary level sufficient to meet graduation requirements will often avoid any further involvement with mathematics, especially if they experience developmental problems with it or develop anxiety about the subject in general. Secondary mildly handicapped students are no exception, and those that have disabilities will most likely avoid elective enrollment in mathematics classes. Unless there is reason to believe that a student will excel in mathematics, most concerns of the specialist will be with those students who have serious disabilities in arithmetic. It should be noted that there is no trend for students to be referred at the secondary level for arithmetic or mathematics disabilities because many of them manage to pass a basic class, earn a credit, and avoid further involvement with mathematics classes. They are not likely to be detected by teachers or other school personnel because teachers in various content areas (e.g., language arts) will be little concerned about the arithmetic abilities of their students. In schools where competency examinations are used at specific grade levels there will be a greater chance of identifying students.

Students should be expected to develop functional abilities in arithmetic to be applied to daily living tasks and the demands of most common occupations. Actually, the level of skills in arithmetic necessary for daily functioning is probably quite low. At any rate, this should be a high priority of the specialist. To be consistent, we are recommending that achievement roughly equivalent to sixth-grade functioning should be satisfactory for most purposes.

The National Council of Teachers of Mathematics has issued a position statement on basic skills (1977) and has cautioned about the stress that might be placed on computational skills, an emphasis in special education due to the belief that most errors are the result of computational-skill deficiencies. As noted in our own research, because tests tend to measure computation and not processes, errors of computation may mask underlying conceptual disorders. In a study report by the National Council of Teachers of Mathematics, students were asked to determine 70% of 4200 votes that were cast in an election. Nearly half of the 13-year-old students and one out of five 17-year-old students applied the wrong arithmetic process (addition, subtraction, or division). The point was made that computational skills in isolation are ineffective; students must be given practical application and experience with arithmetic processes. The Council's statement on basic skills avoids specific grade levels and falls short of competency statements; ten areas are listed from their report:

1. Problem solving
2. Applying mathematics in everyday situations
3. Alertness to the reasonableness of results
4. Estimation and approximation
5. Appropriate computational skills
6. Geometry
7. Measurement
8. Reading, interpreting, constructing tables, charts, and graphs
9. Using mathematics to predict
10. Computer literacy

We are including computational skills that are generally associated with third- to seventh-grade abilities. This is not a fixed set of competencies; rather, it is a guide. It should be noted that other important aspects of arithmetic, such as geometric concepts, are not included due to the considerable emphasis on computation. The cautions of the Council, mentioned above, should be heeded in programming.

**Third-grade skills**

1. Given mixed sets of objects, the student can identify members and nonmembers.
2. The student can name or write the number for a given cardinal number.
3. Given any number (0-9,999), the student can accurately identify the place value of any given digit.
4. Given any number (0-9,999), the student can state the expanded notation (e.g., 4,716 = 4000 + 700 + 10 + 6).
5. The student can demonstrate multiplication as repeated addition, moves on a number line, or multiple sets.
6. The student can provide a definition of division as a rearrangement of sets or repeated subtraction.
7. The student can demonstrate that any number multiplied by one has a product equal to the number (e.g., 1 × □ = □).
8. The student can demonstrate that a number multiplied by 0 has a product of 0.
9. The student can apply a rule for addition and subtraction of numbers (0-9,999) in a horizontal and a vertical display.
10. The student can multiply one-digit numbers by 10 or 1000.

11. The student can divide a three-digit number by a one-digit number with no remainder.
12. The student can tell time to the minute.
13. The student can identify days, weeks, and months on a calendar.
14. Given an equation, the student can rearrange it into an inverse or reversible relationship (e.g., 21 + 16 = 37 and 37 − 16 = 21).
15. Given problems with missing addends, the student can perform subtraction to derive the missing value.
16. Given any coin, the student can state the value.
17. Given any coin, the student can identify it as a fraction of a dollar.

**Fourth-grade skills**
1. Given a verbal description of a number (0-999,999), the student can name the place value of each digit.
2. Given a number (0-999,999), the student can provide the expanded notation (e.g., 243,884 = 200,000 + 40,000 + 3,000 + 800 + 80 + 4).
3. Presented with a model of a fractional number, the student can provide the correct fraction expressed in numbers.
4. Given a fraction such as $\frac{4}{10}$, the student can give equivalent fractional names for the number.
5. Given a fraction such as $\frac{4}{10}$, the student can provide the simplest form (i.e., $\frac{2}{5}$).
6. Given a number, the student can round off to the nearest 10, 100, or 1000.
7. The student can demonstrate equivalency of transposed numbers in multiplication (e.g., 4 × 7 = 7 × 4).
8. Given three numbers, the student can demonstrate the associative property in multiplication by regrouping (e.g., [4 × 5] × 6 = 4 × [5 × 6]).
9. The student can demonstrate the distributive property in multiplication problems (e.g., 4 × 121 = 4[100] + 4[20] + 4[1] = 484).
10. The student can perform division, with no remainders, having a four-digit dividend and a two-digit divisor.
11. Given two numbers, the student can make equations for all basic functions (e.g., 24 and 4: 24 + 4 = 28; 24 − 4 = 20; 24 × 4 = 96; 24 ÷ 4 = 6).
12. Given a problem requiring the determination of length, weight, area, volume, or temperature, the student can describe the instrument used to measure and the corresponding unit of measurement.
13. The student can use liquid measures.
14. The student can tell time to the nearest second.
15. The student can describe weights of objects on scales in whole and fractional units.
16. The student can read temperatures on both scales.
17. The student can solve computational problems involving measures.
18. The student can make change in any combination less than $5.00.

**Fifth- through sixth-grade skills**
1. The student can multiply numbers using the vertical algorithm.
2. The student can solve for quotients using the long division algorithm and four-digit dividends and one-digit divisors.
3. The student can develop equivalent fractions (e.g., given $\frac{3}{4} = \frac{9}{12}$) and reduce to a simple term.
4. The student can convert improper

fractions to mixed numbers (e.g., $\frac{14}{3} = 4\frac{2}{3}$).

5. The student can compute sums and differences of decimal values (e.g., 4.3 + 3.64 = 7.94).
6. The student can determine costs, profits, and losses that do not require percentages or interest on a ledger.
7. The student can convert various measures into equivalencies (e.g., days to hours, hours to minutes; gallons to quarts, quarts to pints).
8. The student can express division quotients with remainders as mixed numbers or decimal values.
9. The student can express fractions with denominators of 10, 100, or 1000 in decimal form.
10. The student can express numbers in exponential form (e.g., $16 = 2^4$).
11. The student can perform division with a six-digit dividend and a two-digit divisor.
12. The student can determine an arithmetic average.
13. The student can describe units of time in centuries, decades, and years and can identify different time zones.
14. The student can determine products and quotients in problems having decimal fractions.
15. The student can interpret simple pie charts and line and bar graphs.

## Assessment of arithmetic disorders

The survey tests of achievement are usually inappropriate for students who have limited ability in arithmetic, especially if there is a complication of a reading disorder. For many students there will be only a few items on a test that they can understand sufficiently in order to be able to perform both the reading and required calculations. Therefore we recommend *diagnostic* testing and informal assessment. The most suitable diagnostic arithmetic test is the *KeyMath Diagnostic Arithmetic Test*, which can be used for remedial students above the sixth-grade level.

Informal procedures provide a rich source of information about how the student functions. The teacher should observe the student during the course of completing problems and (1) note the student's behavior, (2) ask the student to verbalize how the problem is attacked, and (3) inspect the effort to determine *what* kind of errors are made and *why*. The best approach is to use the comprehensive recommendations of Reisman (1978), who has excellent suggestions about the development of informal assessment techniques. Remediation cannot proceed without a complete analysis of the student's deficiencies and a clear notion of what objectives should be stressed. The sequence of events to occur in the teaching process is best determined by task analysis. The skill sequence of arithmetic is much more clearly discerned than that of reading and can be task analyzed much more easily.

To guide the specialist in developing informal assessment we have included the following areas, which are sequential in development but which, in some instances, may represent skills that emerge simultaneously. The areas of informal assessment are as follows:

1. *Cardinality*. The student may not have a concept of cardinality, that different sets of objects have different members. This skill would be developed in most adolescents.

2. *Ordinality*. The student may not have a concept of order, that fourth, fifth, or sixth represent values in a sequence. The lack of concepts may be evidenced by rote counting but lack of understanding.

3. *Symbolic association*. Although the student may have a concept of number (cardinality and ordinality), he or she may not be

able to associate symbols with the underlying concept (e.g., 7 = .......). Due to a visual memory deficit, the student cannot retain the image of the symbol (7).

4. *Symbolic confusion.* Some students confuse numbers although they have a concept of numeration. For example, 2 may be confused with 6, or 3 with 8, especially when written in the child's handwriting.

5. *Inability to group sets.* Given two sets (..) + (...) the student is unable to merge them into one unity or new set (.....). This usually means the student has a concept of ordinality but not of cardinality. The student may count by rote.

6. *Lack of a concept of place values.* The place values (units, tens, hundreds, and so forth) are not known. The student may have a concept of number, but symbolizing them as place values may not be understood. A more concrete step is usually required, such as use of an abacus or bundles of sticks, as:

$$\text{IIIIIIIII} + \text{IIIIIIIII} + \text{IIIIIIIII} + \text{I} = 31$$
$$\quad 10 \quad + \quad 10 \quad + \quad 10 \quad + 1$$
$$30 + 1 = 31$$

7. *Inability to dissociate sets (reversibility) or subtraction.* The student may be able to combine sets, or add (e.g., ... + .. = .....), but may be unable to reverse the process. The concrete form should be evaluated before computational errors are remediated, e.g.,

$$\begin{array}{r} 5 \\ -3 \\ \hline 1 \end{array}$$

8. *Inability to conceptualize multiplication and division.* Essentially, the same process as in no. 7 above is involved. The inability to represent multiplication and division in a concrete manner should be examined to check for concept attainment.

9. *Lack of mastery of computational skills or inappropriate application.* There are a variety of such problems, which require careful analysis to determine the error pattern:

$$\begin{array}{r} 21 \\ +32 \\ \hline 5\textcircled{2} \end{array} \quad \begin{array}{r} 27 \\ -14 \\ \hline 1\textcircled{2} \end{array} \quad \begin{array}{r} 2\backslash\!1 \\ \times\ \textcircled{4} \\ \hline 74 \end{array} \quad \begin{array}{r} 7 \\ 6\overline{)36} \\ 36 \end{array} \quad \begin{array}{r} (421)\ \text{Subtracts} \\ +634 \\ \hline 213 \end{array}$$

$$\begin{array}{r} 2\!\diagup\!1 \\ \times\ \diagdown\!3 \\ \hline 64 \end{array} \quad \begin{array}{r} 24 \\ \times\ 7 \\ \hline 48 \end{array} \text{(regroups and adds)} \quad \begin{array}{r} 56 \\ \times 40 \\ \hline 2240 \end{array}$$

10. *Incompletion of computational functions.*

$$\begin{array}{r} 40 \\ 9\overline{)364} \\ 360 \end{array} \quad \begin{array}{r} 24 \\ \times 6 \\ \hline 24 \end{array} \text{(does not carry; adds 2)}$$

11. *Confusion of null sets or use of 0.*

$$\begin{array}{r} 20 \\ -19 \\ \hline 19 \end{array} \quad 8 \times 0 = 8 \quad \begin{array}{r} 26 \\ -10 \\ \hline 10 \end{array} \quad \begin{array}{r} 40 \\ 10\overline{)40} \end{array}$$

12. *Regroups inaccurately.*

$$\begin{array}{r} 26 \\ +14 \\ \hline 31 \end{array} \quad \begin{array}{r} 462 \\ +286 \\ \hline 648 \end{array} \quad \begin{array}{r} 32 \\ +13 \\ \hline 55 \end{array} \quad \begin{array}{r} 43 \\ -8 \\ \hline 45 \end{array} \quad \begin{array}{r} 805 \\ -126 \\ \hline 779 \end{array}$$

13. *Cannot translate from word problem to basic algorithm.* This type of problem may be explained by inability to decode, inability to comprehend, or inability to extract numerical information from word problems. Memory may also be a factor, especially if word problems are read to the student.

• • •

We have found that some LD students tend to make significant errors in computational processes as additional visual information is added to a problem or as the process becomes somewhat more complex. Although such errors would be classified as computational, there are subtle differences that should be recognized, which can offer significant information. In comparison of LD students throughout elementary and junior high grades, the following transition points seemed to be ceilings for the students performing the problems. That is, while other students not classified as LD would tend to have wide dispersions across all types of increasingly difficult problems, LD students would tend to cluster at each point of transition. The following are examples of the types of problems that seemed to be transition points:

$$\begin{array}{r}12\\+8\\\hline\end{array}$$ (The complication is the need to regroup.)

$$\begin{array}{r}21\\+16\\\hline\end{array} \qquad \begin{array}{r}24\\+16\\\hline\end{array}$$ (This type of problem involves double columns; one is additive because of the need to regroup.)

$$\begin{array}{r}\$36\\+4\\\hline\end{array}$$ (Although students would solve the problem without the dollar sign, they tended to fail when it was added.)

$$\begin{array}{r}15.34\\-14.22\\\hline\end{array} \qquad \begin{array}{r}12.30\\+22.16\\\hline\end{array}$$ (Given numbers in four columns, many students were able to perform subtraction or addition accurately but the inclusion of decimal points tended to result in more errors.)

We assume that the reasons for errors in these types of problems occur because of the addition of a new perceptual element that is distracting and interferes with the computational process. This would not have been as impressive had there been a range of scores of LD students on either side of the cutoff scores, but there were not. At each successive level, LD students tended to cluster below each transitional point as a characteristic error pattern.

## Instructional approaches

Depending on individual student characteristics, a number of options may be available in remedial instruction. First, the school may have a suitable class for low-achieving students that follows a curriculum stressing acquisition of basic skills. If the class or teacher is judged not appropriate for a particular student, other options may be available. The second option may be that a remedial mathematics teacher is employed by the district to design individualized programs. Assuming that "territorial conflict" between the special teacher and the remedial teacher can be resolved and the student can meet eligibility criteria, this may be an appropriate placement. Lastly, the most likely approach will be for the special teacher to include the student in a program and design an individual plan. The program may consist of specific task analyses of instructional sequences tied to specific outcomes and may use either adapted materials or a commercial program. Whatever approach is used, learning activities that stress concrete examples, manipulatives where appropriate, and practical applications are the most beneficial.

## WRITTEN LANGUAGE DISABILITIES

Disabilities of written language may be classified as disorders of (1) handwriting, (2) spelling, and (3) written expression. Although they all represent skills expressed in written form, they are quite different skills. The importance of these skills in our verbally oriented society cannot be underestimated. However, critical decisions must be made about the time that will be devoted to each of these aspects of written behavior at the secondary level. As in other instances, no sweeping generalizations can be made because each case must be separately considered. Nonetheless, of the three categories, the most important, yet the most complex, is written expression, the ultimate skill of language development.

### Goals of written expression

A hierarchy of expressive skills must be used to aid in decisions about remediation of disabilities. As a general consideration, it is necessary to regard written expression problems as manifestations of a more widespread language deficit. EMR students have a decidedly lower level of language development than other students. Some secondary students are thought to have subtle language disorders, thinking disorders, and problems with verbal processing that may be most easily detected in written work. But, as Johnson and Myklebust (1967) have shown, expressive language is a skill that takes much longer to develop, following the tedious emergence of other aspects of language. If a student has problems with receptive and integrative language, then written expression or general verbal expression will be no better than the foundation. The preoccupation with expression may be misplaced if more fruitful remediation of prerequisite skills can provide the student with a stable language base. In some cases it is reasonable to expect that a student will not perform well if he or she spends little time in reading, writing, and developing more precise verbal skills.

As an encoding task, handwriting will not be comparable to decoding tasks such as reading or listening comprehension. Nondisabled adults are able to comprehend more in reading and listening than they are able to express orally or in written form. The goals of written expression must account for the presumptions that might be made about the following problems:

1. General expressive disorders of language
2. Problems with syntax, grammar, and impoverished vocabulary
3. Problems of written mechanics
4. Motor encoding problems (dysgraphia)

Assessment of written expressive disorders must include the following specific areas: formation of letters, words, and sentences; parts of speech; tenses; grammatical usage; word order; additions; substitutions; distortions; capitalization; use of the period, comma, question mark, apostrophe, hyphen, exclamation mark, and colon.

Goals for a specific student must be established after a complete evaluation of general writing behavior and written work. Written language is very complex and may be the most difficult achievement for mildly handicapped students. Expressive language, oral or written, will not be as sophisticated as receptive abilities, and the interference of learning problems may reduce the chances of success in this area, especially as school days draw to a close for the older student. If underlying problems are remediated and reading achievement proceeds well, a considerable investment in remediation of written expressive disorders may be warranted. The following general goals are recommended in ascending order:

1. Ability to write name (cursive), address, phone number, and other personally identifiable data.
2. Ability to complete a variety of forms accurately, such as job applications, insurance forms, and the short income tax form.
3. Ability to write a personal letter expressing simple ideas, feelings, and other personal expressions.
4. Ability to write a simple business letter.
5. Ability to write letters, reports, verse, and so forth, with abstract representation of thoughts, moods, ideas, concepts, and beliefs.

Kerrigan (1974) recommends the following teaching strategies to improve expressive writing in the use of themes.

1. Write a short, simple declarative sentence that makes one statement.
2. Write three sentences about the sentence in step 1 that are clearly and directly about the whole of that sentence, not just something in it.
3. Write four or five sentences about each of the three sentences in step 2.
4. Make the material in the four or five sentences in step 3 as concrete and specific as possible.
5. In the first sentence of the second para-

graph and every paragraph following, insert a clear reference to the idea in the preceding paragraph.
6. Make sure every sentence in your theme is connected with, and makes clear reference to the preceding sentence.

## The comprehensive language arts continuum

After determining a student's strengths and weaknesses in the area of reading, it is important to place those skills in the context of the comprehensive spectrum of language arts. Reading skills are important acquisitions; however, it is essential to develop auditory, spoken, and written language as parallel skills. To a great extent, each of these areas is dependent on the others.

The following comprehensive language arts continuum (Worth, 1979) is divided into four levels: the readiness level, the initial mastery level, the expansion level, and the independent level. No ages are assigned to the various levels since movement through the continuum depends a great deal on the student's cognitive maturity level. It is also important to note that while the skills do follow a sequential pattern, lack of mastery in one area will not necessarily impede progress in other areas.

With the exception of the readiness level, each level contains a section on listening and oral communication, vocabulary development, comprehension and study skills, and written communication. Since it is a preparatory level, the readiness level is divided into perceptual skills, listening and oral communication, and reading.

This continuum is designed to be used as a core of basic language skills. It is not intended to be an entire curriculum since all skills are built on previously learned skills, are reinforced, and continue to higher levels of sophistication.

I. Readiness level
  A. Perceptual skills
    1. Motor
      a. Locates body parts
      b. Traces shapes, numerals, letters; connects a series
      c. Repeats a rhythm made by tapping/clapping
      d. Follows oral directions to indicate left-right, front-back, up-down, over-under, above-below, and other locational directions
      e. Assembles simple puzzles
      f. Turns pages
      g. Matches colors, shapes, letters, and numerals
      h. Sorts small objects: buttons, beads, shells
      i. Copies shapes and letters of varying sizes
    2. Auditory discrimination
      a. Identifies common sounds
      b. Classifies sounds according to themes
      c. Identifies differences in pitch/volume
      d. Identifies rhyming sounds
      e. Identifies and produces words having same beginning sounds
      f. Identifies and produces words having same ending sounds
    3. Auditory memory
      a. Repeats a tapping sequence
      b. Repeats a stated sentence (of three or four words)
      c. Repeats a stated five-word sequence
    4. Visual discrimination
      a. Identifies similarities and differences
        (1) Objects
        (2) Shapes
        (3) Colors
        (4) Sizes
        (5) Numerals
        (6) Letters
        (7) Words
      b. Identifies missing parts
    5. Visual memory

a. Recalls following sequences
   (1) Objects
   (2) Colors
   (3) Symbols
b. Reproduces a design/shape pattern from memory
c. Repeats story facts in sequence
d. Performs three commands in sequence

B. Listening and oral communication
   1. Listening
      a. Responds to own name
      b. Listens to and follows directions
      c. Identifies the facts of the story through listening
   2. Oral communication
      a. Identifies by name common objects, animals, and colors
      b. Describes simple objects
      c. Speaks in sentences
      d. Retells a story
      e. Participates in conversations with a group
      f. Enunciates clearly and distinctly
      g. Uses appropriate speech patterns
      h. Gives simple directions/explanations

C. Written communication
   1. Handwriting
      a. Forms circles and straight lines

D. Reading
   1. Word study
      a. Letter recognition, upper and lower case
   2. Comprehension
      a. Identifies emotions such as happiness, sadness, and anger
      b. "Reads pictures"
      c. Identifies humor, excitement, and beauty in a story
      d. Can work independently for short periods of time

II. Initial mastery level
   A. Listening and oral communication
      1. Listening
         a. Identifies the main idea of story through listening
         b. Identifies the emotions of story through listening
      2. Oral communication
         a. Organizes short oral reports into introduction, body, and conclusion
         b. Gives short reports to small groups
      3. Oral reading
         a. Uses left to right eye movement without finger pointing
   B. Vocabulary development
      1. Word recognition
         a. Recognizes words with both capital and small letters at the beginning
         b. Is able to identify, in various settings, basic vocabulary words used in basal reading series
      2. Word study (phonics)
         a. Recognizes single initial consonants and can make their sounds
         b. Identifies single consonant sounds in final position
         c. Identifies single consonant sounds in medial position
         d. Recognizes short vowel sounds
         e. Recognizes long vowel sounds
         f. Identifies sounds of initial consonant blends
         g. Identifies common consonant digraphs
      3. Structural analysis
         a. Recognizes common endings: s, es, ed, ing, ly, er, est
         b. Identifies compound words
         c. Identifies common word families
         d. Identifies the number of syllables in familiar words
         e. Uses picture, context, and configuration
      4. Spelling
         a. Spells first and last name
         b. Spells simple words containing short and long vowel sounds
         c. Spells words of a given letter (word family) pattern such as -all, -at, -it, -en, -in, -an, and -ill
   C. Comprehension and study skills
      1. Reading comprehension
         a. Follows simple printed directions
         b. After reading a story, relates the main ideas
         c. Recounts the facts in a story (who, what, when, where, why, how)
         d. Identifies likenesses and differ-

ences in characters, times, and places
    e. Predicts outcome of a story
    f. Describes the sequence of events in a story using sentences
    g. Identifies the feelings of the characters in a story
    h. Reads silently without whispering vocalization
  2. Oral reading skills
    a. Uses correct pronunciation
    b. Uses correct phrasing (not word by word)
  3. Study skills
    a. Locates answers to simple questions in a story
    b. Alphabetizes by first letters
  D. Written communication
    1. Grammar and usage
      a. Identifies the use of capitals, periods, and question marks
      b. Identifies the use of exclamation points and quotation marks
      c. Identifies pronouns used to replace nouns in sentences
      d. Identifies a simple sentence
    2. Handwriting and composition
      a. Places body, hand, paper, and writing instrument in the proper position
      b. Copies words, numbers, and sentences
      c. Writes simple sentences
III. Expansion level
  A. Listening and oral communication
    1. Oral communication
      a. Gives reports substantiating a particular viewpoint
      b. Interprets/portrays a character or a scene illustrating a story
      c. Adjusts level of language to social/educational situations
  B. Vocabulary development
    1. Word recognition
      a. Identifies the 220 basic sight words (Dolch list)
      b. Identifies common contractions
      c. Identifies possessives
      d. Identifies multiple meanings of words
    2. Phonics
      a. Identifies vowel digraphs and diphthongs
      b. Identifies words with irregular vowel sounds
      c. Identifies ending blends and digraphs
      d. Identifies the two sounds of $c$ and $g$
      e. Identifies silent consonants
    3. Structural analysis
      a. Identifies root/base words
      b. Identifies the tense of verbs
      c. Identifies possessives
      d. Identifies contractions
      e. Divides words into syllables
    4. Spelling
      a. Spells words from a dictated word list
      b. Spells compound words
      c. Spells days of the week and months of the year
      d. Spells contractions
      e. Spells possessives
      f. Spells words with multiple spellings
  C. Comprehension and study skills
    1. Reading comprehension
      a. Identifies cause-and-effect relationships
      b. Categorizes people, places, and events
      c. Summarizes information
      d. Follows written directions to complete two- and three-step tasks
      e. Identifies irrelevant statements
      f. Distinguishes between fact and opinion
      g. Makes inferences
    2. Oral reading
      a. Uses proper voice intonation to give meaning
      b. Reads with adequate to good volume
      c. Has ability to convey meaning to listeners
    3. Study skills
      a. Locates information through use of titles, table of contents, and page numbers

- b. Identifies and uses resources found in the library
- c. Alphabetizes words by first two letters
- d. Uses the index
- e. Reads for a purpose: pleasure, skimming for information, general idea
- f. Identifies forms of mass media

D. Written communication
1. Grammar and usage
   - a. Identifies different types of sentences
   - b. Determines subject-verb agreement
   - c. Uses capital letters
   - d. Identifies the correct pronoun form: his, her, she, he, it
   - e. Identifies the common irregular plurals
   - f. Identifies comparative and superlative adjectives
2. Handwriting and composition
   - a. Demonstrates skills such as neatness, spacing between words and letters, alignment, and margins
   - b. Indents the first word in a paragraph
   - c. Writes answers to simple questions
   - d. Composes two or more related sentences
   - e. Transforms manuscript into cursive and written activities
   - f. Identifies and uses parts of a letter

IV. Independent level
A. Listening and oral communication
1. Oral communication
   - a. Participates in panel discussions and debates
   - b. Leads discussions

B. Vocabulary development
1. Word recognition
   - a. Recognizes unusual characteristics of words
   - b. Uses study skills to discover meanings and origins of self-generated vocabulary
   - c. Identifies word meanings through connotation and denotation

2. Structural analysis
   - a. Uses root words to form new words
3. Spelling
   - a. Identifies misspelled words
   - b. Spells words of varying vowel and consonant patterns
   - c. Uses spelling skills to locate words in the dictionary

C. Comprehension and study skills
1. Reading comprehension
   - a. Identifies information from charts, graphs, maps, etc.
   - b. Identifies propaganda techniques
   - c. Identifies author's purpose
   - d. Expands reading comprehension skills into reading in a variety of content areas
   - e. Identifies and generalizes story ideas
   - f. Skims to locate facts and details
   - g. Selects and rejects materials to suit a certain purpose
2. Oral reading
   - a. Participates in oral reading
3. Study skills
   - a. Uses note-taking skills
   - b. Uses a study formula in content area reading
   - c. Uses card catalogs and book classifications
   - d. Uses periodicals as sources of information
   - e. Adjusts reading rate for different purposes
   - f. Explores new areas and resources in specific interest areas

D. Written communication
1. Grammar and usage
   - a. Writes a variety of sentences and paragraphs independently
   - b. Uses vivid modifiers
   - c. Organizes information into an outline
   - d. Summarizes information
   - e. Writes reports on chosen topics
   - f. Initiates and records research to support self-generated theories
   - g. Records and evaluates personal happenings

## SUMMARY

One of the three models for teaching mildly handicapped secondary students is based on remediation. There are two general goals—to assist students toward normal achievement in acquisition of basic skills and to promote functional literacy as a minimum competency. The emphasis of most remedial programs is on reading, although mathematics and written expression will be important to a lesser extent. The practice of grouping all mildly handicapped students into a resource room for instruction at the secondary level will be determined by the type of certification for teachers and the extent to which a state classifies students by categorical labels. Hence, in some states, LD students will be in separate resource rooms while ED and EMR students will be educated in other separate programs.

The learning characteristics of the three categories of mildly handicapped students are extremely similar, and the instructional approaches will not differ greatly. However, programs that also serve the student in the mainstream through tutoring or through compensatory efforts will find the range of student levels and needs to be taxing of organizational ability. Remedial reading approaches will generally be directed to two major groups: the nonreader and the deficient reader, regardless of the categorical label that might be applied. Therefore remedial reading will be multifaceted, depending on the needs of each student. Specific remedial techniques were discussed as were study skills for use with students who may benefit from placement in the general curriculum.

Remediation of arithmetic disorders should focus on computational skills and application of those skills to daily needs. The disabilities of written expression were discussed with the notation that this would be the last verbal skill to develop. A range of goals was listed for the general population of mildly handicapped students.

### REFERENCES AND READINGS

Barbe, W. B. *Educators guide to personalized reading instruction.* Englewood Cliffs, N.J.: Prentice-Hall, 1961.

Chalfant, J., & Scheffelin, M. *Central processing dysfunctions in children: A review of research* (NINDS Monograph No. 9). Bethesda, Md.: U.S. Dept. of Health, Education and Welfare, 1969.

Chall, J. *Learning to read: The great debate.* New York: McGraw-Hill, 1967.

Fernald, G. M. *Remedial techniques in basic school subjects.* New York: McGraw-Hill, 1943.

Forell, E. R. No easy cure for reading disabilities. *Today's Education*, 1976, 65(2), 34-36.

Frauenheim, J. G. Academic achievement characteristics of adult males who were diagnosed as dyslexic in childhood. *Journal of Learning Disabilities*, 1978, 11(8), 476-483.

Fry, E. *Reading instruction for classroom and clinic.* New York: McGraw-Hill, 1972.

Gillespie, P. H., & Sitko, M. C. Reading problems. In L. Mann, L. Goodman, & J. Wiederholt (Eds.), *Teaching the learning disabled adolescent.* Boston: Houghton Mifflin, 1978.

Goodman, L., & Price, M. BEH final regulations for learning disabilities: Implications for the secondary school. *Learning Disability Quarterly*, Fall 1978, 1(4), 73-79.

Hammill, D., & Larsen, S. Relationship of selected auditory perceptual skills and reading ability. *Journal of Learning Disabilities*, 1974, 7, 282-291.

Hammill, D., & Wiederholt, J. Review of the Frostig Visual Perception Test and related training program. In L. Mann & D. Sabatino (Eds.), *First review of special education.* New York: Grune & Stratton, 1973.

Herber, H. L. Preface to a content-area reading program. *Reading*, January 1979, 5(1).

Johnson, O. J., & Myklebust, H. R. *Learning disabilities: Educational principles and practices.* New York: Grune & Stratton, 1967.

Kerrigan, W. J. *Writing to the point: Six basic steps.* New York: Harcourt Brace Jovanovich, 1974.

Kirk, S. A., Kliebhan, J. M., & Lerner, J. W. *Teaching reading to slow and disabled learners.* Boston: Houghton Mifflin, 1978.

*Language arts core of basic skills.* Ocala, Fla.: Marion County Public Schools, 1977.

Larsen, S., & Hammill, D. Relationship of selected visual perceptual abilities to school learning. *Journal of Special Education*, Fall 1975, 9, 282-291.

Larsen, S., Rogers, D., & Sowell, V. The use of selected

perceptual tests in differentiating between normal and learning disabled children. *Journal of Learning Disabilities*, February 1976, 9, 85-90.

Marsh, G. E., II. Teaching arithmetic and mathematics to children with learning disabilities. In B. R. Gearheart, *Teaching the learning disabled: A combination task-process approach.* St. Louis: Mosby, 1976.

Marsh, G. E., II, Gearheart, C. K., & Gearheart, B. R. *The learning disabled adolescent: Program alternatives in the secondary school.* St. Louis: Mosby, 1978.

Marsh, G. E., II, Lewis, M., & Jones, C. M. *An investigation of the arithmetic skills of students diagnosed as learning disabled.* Unpublished study, University of Arkansas, 1979.

Muehl, S., & Forell, E. A follow-up study of disabled readers: Variables related to high school reading performance. *Reading Research Quarterly*, 1973-1974, 9(1), 110-122.

Murphy, R. Assessment of adult reading competence. In D. Nielsen & H. Hjelm (Eds.), *Reading and career education.* Newark, Del.: International Reading Association, 1975, pp. 50-61.

Myklebust, H. R. Learning disabilities: Definition and overview. In H. R. Myklebust (Ed.), *Progress in learning disabilities* (Vol. 1). New York: Grune & Stratton, 1968, pp. 1-15.

National Council of Teachers of Mathematics. Position statement on basic skills. *Academic Teacher*, October 1977, pp. 18-20.

Newcomer, P., & Hammill, D. *Psycholinguistics in the schools.* Columbus, Ohio: Merrill, 1976.

Otto, W., McMenemy, R. A., & Smith, R. J. *Corrective and remedial teaching.* Boston: Houghton Mifflin, 1973.

Reisman, F. K. *A guide to the diagnostic teaching of arithmetic* (2nd ed.). Columbus, Ohio: Merrill, 1978.

Samuels, S. J. Success and failure in learning to read: A critique of the research. *Reading Research Quarterly*, 1973, 8, 200-239.

Spache, G. D., & Spache, E. B. *Reading in the elementary school.* Boston: Allyn & Bacon, 1969.

Wepman, J., Cruickshank, W. M., Deutsch, C. P., et al.: Learning disabilities. In N. Hobbs (Ed.), *Issues in the classification of children* (Vol. 1). San Francisco: Jossey-Bass, 1975.

Worth, M. *A comprehensive language arts continuum.* Unpublished paper, University of Arkansas, College of Education, 1979.

Chapter 12

# VOCATIONAL PROGRAMMING

Increasing numbers of secondary special education programs are adopting vocational models for mildly handicapped students. In spite of the trend, there is no clear direction about which models to use, which students to serve, and the relationship between special education and vocational education. This is complicated by the mainstreaming and noncategorical trends. The establishment of a special vocational program for handicapped students may have the effect of limiting training for a diverse population to a few possible jobs unless care is taken to assure that other options exist. The special education vocational program cannot afford to become a dumping ground for a segment of the school population regarded as unsuited to the general curriculum. Instead of being a viable option for some mildly handicapped students, it may become a major vehicle for shunting off unmotivated students who are unadjusted to the school setting into programmatic "containment."

Vocational success seems to be an implied promise of American education. All students are encouraged to remain in school with the expectation that on entering the work force, their potential for earned income will have a direct positive relationship to the number of years spent in school. It is true that there is a relationship between employment and years in school, better than that between employment and academic achievement, but the ability to obtain and hold a job is more directly related to other factors. For many students, possession of a high school diploma merely assures entrance to more advanced training that will ultimately lead to employment. Many other students will receive virtually all training for an occupation from an employer after being hired. The diploma is a device used to screen applicants. For most mildly handicapped students, vocational guidance and preparation are absolutely essential if they are to have quality lives.

Unfortunately, many of the mildly handicapped may be classified in the excess population described by Farber (1968), that is, a group that provides the bottom rung of the social-class ladder. They are important to the industrial society for establishment of social prestige and for selection in the available pool of candidates for jobs to make industry function. They also provide a source of income for the many helping professions who are paid for a variety of services to them. The greatest threat to mildly handicapped students in the future will be the changes wrought by technological and automated advances.

Many jobs that exist today will disappear. Many that will exist are yet unknown. It is clear that persons who may be able to secure employment will need more technical skills than ever before. There is a danger that many of the mildly handicapped will become technologically obsolete in the work force because the types of jobs they may hold will be replaced by automation, and they will compete with workers who have no impairments to the acquisition of skills to remain employable.

## VOCATIONAL EDUCATION

The growth of vocational education has mirrored the development of the American culture. When most jobs were associated with agriculture, which could be learned throughout childhood as a part of one's role in the family unit, and when many professions required liberal arts as a background for college entrance, there was little need for vocational education. As society became industrialized and urbanized, there was a concomitant need to prepare people to fill the many new types of jobs that emerged. The traditional course work of vocational education, such as home economics and industrial arts, existed for all students because of the practical skills that could be useful to any person on a daily basis. The development of vocational training in secondary schools to prepare students for specific jobs has occurred as a result of the beliefs that society needs trained nonprofessional workers and that guidance for non–college bound students who need vocational training benefits both the student and society.

The shifting nature of the work force is a problem for vocational education. As it becomes necessary to train large numbers of persons for specific occupations, vocational programs can respond by turning out so many candidates for available jobs that the demand ceases to exist. Technological changes can rapidly eliminate many jobs and rapidly create a demand for new ones, which causes the school to be out of step with the job market. Vocational education must continuously change to meet changing demands. This can be a difficult and expensive process. The general curriculum does not alter its content radically or frequently, building on what previously existed. Entire areas of the curriculum are not displaced as they must be in vocational education.

Another problem is that vocational education, and career education to some extent, is stigmatized by the types of students who have been placed in vocational programs. There is a long-held pecking order in the schools that accords higher status to the college preparatory sequence. Historically, the nonacademic, uncooperative, and handicapped have been placed in vocational education, which diminishes its prestige among teachers and students alike. To deny this is unrealistic in view of the fact that a major concern of special educators in the present mainstreaming trend is to improve the attitudes of regular teaching personnel and non-handicapped peers toward the handicapped.

Vocational educators have been no more willing nor better prepared to accept students who have poor academic abilities than are liberal arts teachers. Without strong support students with minimal academic competency will not necessarily fare any better in vocational education than in the general curriculum. This is the challenge to the special educator who works in a vocational model: to secure vocational training for mildly handicapped students that promises employment and satisfaction as aspects of postsecondary adjustment concerns.

The types of settings in which vocational programming may exist dictate what kinds of jobs will be included in the vocational training effort. Schools that are located in large, urban areas present different opportunities and disadvantages than those in smaller communities or rural areas. The selection of vocational education models depends on demographic characteristics, commitment of the school district to vocational education, resources available, and other factors. In general, there are high-cost training programs that require the investment of large amounts of funds and personnel. Vocational-technical high schools typify this kind. There are some high schools, large and comprehensive, that have enormous facilities for vocational education. Many schools must use some form of low-cost training that involves regular vocational course work, the use of work experience, work-study, and on-the-job training activities. Special education programs can be a part of or separated from any of these types of programs. Special educators may work in vocational settings or assume primary responsibility for managing specialized vocational programs for the handicapped.

## Objectives for planning vocational education of handicapped students

The Council for Exceptional Children (Davis & Ward, 1978, p. 2) has proposed the following objectives for vocational education of handicapped students:

1. Vocational education shall be available as a discrete element on a continuum of career education experiences provided for handicapped students to enable them to learn about and prepare for work.

2. Appropriate prevocational experiences shall be provided to prepare each handicapped student for placement in vocational education.

3. Every handicapped student shall have the opportunity to participate in a regular or special vocational education program in order to develop job-specific skills.

4. Vocational assessment shall be provided to determine the student's interests and vocational aptitudes in order to develop an appropriate individualized education program.

5. Supportive (related) services shall be provided as needed to maximize a handicapped student's potential for success in a regular or specially designed vocational education program.

6. Work experience options shall be available to help handicapped students bridge the gap between the school program and the world of work.

7. Vocational counseling and job placement and follow-up services shall be provided to assist handicapped students in securing and maintaining jobs suitable to their abilities and interests.

8. Appropriate work activities or sheltered employment training programs shall be provided to develop work skills for those students whose handicapping conditions are so severe as to prevent their immediate inclusion in occupational skill preparation programs.

With these objectives in mind, a number of related issues should be considered. Any secondary program that evolves as a separate curriculum and that emphasizes only one option (e.g., remediation only *or* vocational training only) may truncate opportunities for many students. Educational opportunities for mildly handicapped students should be expanded, not diminished. Personal and social development, remediation, assistance in the mainstream, and a wide range of career possibilities should be accounted for in planning. Vocational training should be a complementary part of the secondary school experience for adolescents. Decisions should be made about individuals rather than by categories; thus specific vocational tracks for the handicapped should be avoided. The plans for the future should also focus on satisfactory personal and social skills and relationships, enjoyable use of leisure time, civic responsibility, ability to remain viable in the work force, and occupational adjustment and economic independence.

## Planning the vocational program for handicapped students

The track record of education in providing for vocational adjustment of handicapped students is not very impressive (Viscardi, 1976). Schools must be mindful of the needs of handicapped students as indicated by these facts:

1. Only 4 million (36%) of the 11 million handicapped adults capable of competitive employment are working, but 74% of the nonhandicapped adult population is employed (Levitan & Taggart, 1976).

2. Many handicapped persons are underemployed, unable to secure jobs suited to their abilities (Razeghi & Davis, 1979). This is undoubtedly true in the case of many mildly handicapped students who leave school.

3. Employment opportunities are linked to the level of educational attainment, grades, and completion of training, as well as aspirations, and specific competencies for job-market entry. Without training there is a greater chance that job success will not be realized. Of the 13 million students served in vocational education in 1974, only 2% were handicapped (Staats, 1976).

4. It is obvious that handicapped students have fewer options, are trained for a limited range of occupational choices, and the jobs are usually low level (Davis & Weintraub, 1978; Razeghi & Davis, 1979; Staats, 1976).

5. Underemployment and unemployment are the greatest indications that schools fail to meet the needs of handicapped students (Shworles, 1976).

The legal bases for provision of career and vocational planning may be found in P.L. 94-142, P.L. 94-482, the Vocational Education Act of 1963 as amended in 1976, and Sections 503 and 504 of the Rehabilitation Act of 1973. States are mandated to spend 20% of federal vocational monies on disadvantaged pupils and 10% on the handicapped. These students are referred to as "special needs" students in the vocational education literature. Vocational education can quite legitimately be regarded as part of the individualized educational program (IEP) for secondary handicapped students. The implications of legislation for the handicapped are:

1. Services are extended to age 21, except in those states with contravening legislation.
2. Interagency cooperation and interdisciplinary agreement are necessary for adequate programming.
3. Career education must be systematically infused in the school curriculum.
4. Vocational education programs and services must be equally available to handicapped and nonhandicapped individuals.
5. Vocational programming is a high-priority need of handicapped students.

It is not clear who should be responsible for developing career education and the vocational curriculum for mildly handicapped students. Is it an additional responsibility for vocational educators or a continuation of responsibility for special educators? The lack of cooperation has historically been a serious problem in vocational preparation of the handicapped, and currently the trend continues with professional jealousies, competition, and hardened lines between professionals that detract from adequate services. However, the most significant factor in equalization of efforts for the handicapped and securing cooperation is related to funding and certification. Control of the purse strings determines the relationships of professionals as do state requirements for training of teachers who will work with the handicapped in vocationally oriented programs.

Planning must account for the myriad factors included in the laws and local circumstances. The following outline is provided as an aid in the development of a modified vocational education program.

I. Establish advisory committee
   A. Organize a representative body with members having a variety of expertise, to include vocational educators, special educators, general educators, support personnel, vocational rehabilitation counselors, parents, lay persons, local employers, handicapped students, and others
   B. Select a chairperson
   C. Select a recorder
   D. Charge the committee with the task of studying the problem
   E. Organize meetings, study and research sessions, and subcommittees
   F. Determine exact dates for completion of activities

II. Define target population
   A. Identify the population of mildly handicapped students
   B. Assess needs in vocational education
   C. Examine current vocational education programs in terms of ability to serve the students
   D. Estimate the number of students who could participate in regular vocational programs with no assistance
   E. Estimate the number of students who

could participate in regular vocational programs with support from special educators
- F. Estimate the need for modified or specialized vocational programs to meet the needs of students who cannot participate in regular vocational programs as presently constituted
- G. Identify the number and types of occupations that might be performed by the students in the target group
- H. Estimate the number of students who might benefit from postsecondary vocational programs and college training
- I. Identify the jobs available in the community or in nearby communities
- J. Match characteristics of the student population with job-market data
- K. Other

III. Review laws and regulations
- A. Review state laws and guidelines pertaining to special education, vocational education, rehabilitation, and so forth
- B. Review laws pertaining to child labor, child abuse, peonage, minimum wage, working conditions, and general school laws
- C. Summarize laws for target population as they relate to:
    1. Diagnosis
    2. Evaluation
    3. Treatment
    4. Training
    5. Education
    6. Sheltered employment
    7. Transportation
    8. Restrictions on replacement and training activities
    9. Other

IV. Determine demographic characteristics
- A. Use a map of the community and indicate population density
- B. Superimpose location of unit of interest (school, district)
- C. Locate junior and senior high schools, vocational-technical schools, and other facilities on map
- D. Locate and identify business and industrial job sites suitable for training and placement
- E. Determine rate of unemployment by categories
- F. Contact employers (surgey) and determine employer needs
- G. Other

V. Review resources
- A. Local sources
    1. School budget
    2. Possible private or nonprofit organizations
- B. State sources
    1. Rate and method of reimbursement for special education, vocational education, and support services
    2. Other
- C. Federal sources
    1. Vocational education acts
    2. Rehabilitation acts
    3. Titles of Elementary and Secondary Education Act
    4. Other
- D. Grants
    1. Bureau of Education for the Handicapped
    2. Bureau of Occupational and Adult Education
    3. Rehabilitation Services Administration
    4. State grants
    5. Private
    6. Other

VI. Space and equipment
- A. Estimate equipment needs
- B. Determine space needs and explore the possibility of rent-free or low-rent options

VII. Personnel needs
- A. Determine special education, vocational education, and supportive personnel needs
- B. Determine possibilities of contracting for services with other schools and agencies

VIII. Community services
- A. Determine scope and extent of community services
- B. Determine possible input of labor and trade unions
- C. Determine possible relationship with vocational-technical schools

D. Assess the nature and extent of existing vocational services in the schools and other settings
E. Estimate possibility of cooperative programming
F. Other
IX. Determine scope of programs
A. Propose the program types that might be used ranging from regular vocational placement to special or modified types
B. Project staff and personnel costs, space, and other significant costs
C. Estimate equipment needs and costs
X. Final report

## CAREER EDUCATION

Career education is a concept and a philosophy introduced to change the curriculum, improve schools, and enhance the lives of _all_ students by gradually and consistently introducing them to a widening experience of career exposure beginning in elementary school and extending, theoretically, throughout a lifetime. Hoyt (1976, p. 4) has provided the most widely accepted definition of career education: ". . . the totality of experiences through which one learns about and prepares to engage in work as part of her or his way of living."

A great deal has been written about career education and although only limited concrete effects of the movement have been realized in the school curriculum, considerable controversy has surrounded it. In essence, career education is an attempt to elevate vocational planning and career education to an equal footing with other parts of the general curriculum and to eliminate the social stratification of the curriculum. The societal objectives of career education are to help all individuals to develop a desire for work, to develop necessary work skills, and to engage in satisfying work that also benefits society. Therefore it is not synonymous with vocational training although many critics equate the two. The special education movement has embraced career education, and this may prove to be the downfall of the movement if it is to permeate the general curriculum. Career education may become viewed as a "special" program for the least capable students.

The problems thus far encountered by the career education movement are numerous. It has lower status in the minds of many educators, and professional groups and individuals have attacked it for such reasons as that it may undermine the goals of basic education, that it meets the needs of the establishment but not of individuals, and that it is a misguided attempt to solve serious social inequities without actually changing the society that creates them.

The success of the career education movement depends entirely on how it is defined and how it is evaluated. Although many are encouraged by the trend, especially those who are most interested in the welfare of handicapped students, its acceptance by general education remains undecided. As of this writing, the CEC has yet to adopt an official position statement on career education. Thus the development of career education programs in the schools is yet to be fully realized and the future is unclear. As a philosophy without tangible developments or major funding impetus on a broad scale, it remains as a higher ideal and a guiding concept for the rational evolution of a responsive educational system.

## CAREER PREPARATION

In general, the stages of career education are career awareness, orientation and exploration, and preparation. The awareness phase would be the focus of teachers in the elementary grades. Career orientation and exploration would encompass the junior high years in what has traditionally been referred to as the prevocational program. Career preparation, or vocational training, would consist of some type of training leading to immediate employment after school or deferred employment after further training. A variety of models may be used for career preparation.

## Goals of vocational training

There will be many goals and objectives proposed for career education both generally, such as those developed by Brolin and Kokaska (1979), and for specific training sequences. The diversity of the population of mildly handicapped students is such that broad goals should be stated for vocational training with more narrow goals and specific objectives identified for each student in the IEP and/or individualized written rehabilitation program (IWRP). The following goals are recommended for the mildly handicapped population in vocational training:

1. To be able to identify personal abilities
2. To develop individual areas of interest in accordance with abilities
3. To learn to compensate for physical and mental limitations
4. To develop control of emotional responses
5. To develop an appropriate emotional repertoire
6. To develop a positive self-image
7. To develop acceptable standards of dress and appearance
8. To develop an awareness of social interaction
9. To understand motives and needs associated with the behavior of others
10. To be able to adjust behavior appropriately to different settings
11. To complete formal school with a diploma
12. To develop occupational awareness
13. To establish realistic occupational goals
14. To secure employment or develop short-term plans for employment after graduation

## Vocational and career information

The resource teacher and the school counselor can collaborate with vocational educators by emphasizing career concepts and supplying vocational or occupational information. The main problem for mildly handicapped students is that many occupations will be closed to them, in spite of their abilities otherwise, because of their poor academic success, which leaves them with limited literacy skills and prevents them from obtaining degrees and certificates awarded in educational institutions. Degrees and certificates may not mean much more than that one has the permission to practice a trade or profession rather than implying competencies and skills. Nonetheless, without them, the candidacy pool for many occupations is restricted by the gate-keeping function of degrees and certificates. Many students are no less capable than blind persons who enter the work force, including the professions; but prejudice that equates handicapping conditions with incompetence will have the effect of limiting expectations and opportunities. Part of the task of the counselor, the special teacher, and other adults in contact with students will be to provide them with information about work and to encourage an interest in various possibilities. Although we may be skeptical about the career aspirations of certain students, it is imperative that each student be permitted to explore an interest without being forthrightly informed that he or she will never be able to succeed. Any enthusiasm, interest, or desire to investigate employment possibilities can have many benefits, including renewed motivation in school. A general set of guiding principles for the teacher (and others) is given below:

1. Do not force students to make career choices too early when they are not prepared to make such decisions.
2. Remember that psychological tests and other measures of school performance

(e.g., reading achievement) are not necessarily predictive of later success and achievement in the work force.
3. Students should be provided with numerous opportunities to explore occupational fields.
4. Counseling and work evaluation to direct the development of realistic ambitions should be conducted by those with training and skill in these activities.
5. Sexual stereotyping of occupations should be abolished.
6. Exposure to career options may open new vistas to students and provide the motivation to remain in school.

**Assessment of interests.** One method of assisting students in determining their interests is by means of tests and survey instruments. The purpose is to stimulate thinking about possible areas of employment, to quantify interest and aptitude in specific areas, and to motivate students to explore careers. Some typical instruments used with adolescents and adults are the *Kuder General Interest Survey* and the *Strong Vocational Interest Test*. The Kuder is a well-known test of vocational interests used with the general population. It is, however, difficult to use with students who cannot read efficiently because of its reliance on verbal skills. The Strong test has the same limitations as the Kuder.

Because of the dependence on reading of traditional tests, alternate pictorial tests have been developed for use with those who have either a limited reading ability or difficulty with verbal concepts. Although such instruments will be used with mildly handicapped students, there is a danger that lowered expectations may result because most of these tests will concern unskilled and semiskilled occupational interests. The following instruments present the examinee with pictorial illustrations of work situations, and the preferences or choices for particular types of work are elicited either by direct inquiry or by limited written instruction, depending on the instrument.

In the *Geist Picture Interest Inventory* various job activities are represented pictorially to assess the interests of the subject in 11 areas. The *Reading Free Vocational Interest Inventory* is a forced-choice test developed for use with the mentally retarded. As the name states, reading is not necessary to complete the test. The *Vocational Interest and Sophistication Assessment* is another reading-free instrument developed for use with the mentally retarded, but it has been used with LD students.

A variety of methods exist for assessment of vocational aptitude that (1) attempt to measure speed and accuracy of certain functions in work situations, (2) simulate work tasks, and (3) duplicate an exact work sample from a particular job.

**Aptitude tests.** There are several aptitude tests that have been used with the general population as well as with handicapped persons. Most of these require the subject to use a variety of tools, to assemble objects (e.g., nuts and bolts, place objects into holes), and to sort objects into categories. Some purport to measure specific skills, such as perception, speed, and accuracy, which are thought to be associated with a range of jobs. Some examples of tests in this category are the *Bennet Hand Tool Dexterity Test*, the *Crawford Small Parts Dexterity Test*, the *Purdue Pegboard*, and the *Minnesota Rate of Manipulation Test*.

One of the best known aptitude tests is the *General Aptitude Test Battery* (GATB), which provides measures in general learning ability, verbal aptitude, numerical ability, spatial aptitude, form perception, clerical perception, motor coordination, finger dexterity, and manual dexterity. The *Nonreading Aptitude Test Battery* (NATB) was developed to replace the GATB in use with subjects whose basic skill deficiencies would complicate performance on the former instrument.

**Work evaluation through simulation.** Formal development of hands-on activities to assess interests and potential of subjects has emerged in the form of work evaluation systems. Some schools have purchased these systems, but the cost would be prohibitive for many schools. The best known are the *Singer Evaluation System*, the *TOWER*, or *Testing, Orientation, and Work Evaluation in Rehabilitation*, and the *JEVS Work Samples*.

**Informal work samples.** Some teachers have developed work samples for use in a particular area because they reflect the types of jobs that might exist in the surrounding community and because they are usually quite inexpensive. Although standardization may be lost, insights about the ability of the subject to perform tasks in a work sample, coupled with standardized test information and clinical assessment, may be beneficial in motivation of students and work evaluation. In the most scientific approach, actual studies are conducted of a work situation, the sequence is duplicated for use as a sample, appropriate tools and materials are assembled, data are collected to determine norms for actual production units of paid employees, and other features, such as a scoring system, are developed. Some examples of work samples developed by teachers are:
- Processing credit card drafts
- Pricing groceries
- Operating a cash register
- Sorting mail
- Filing
- Small-engine assembly
- Use of office machines
- Performance of janitorial duties

The limitations of work samples relate to the fact that more sophisticated job tasks cannot be reproduced effectively without the need for physical space and significant amounts of money to purchase necessary equipment and materials. The use of work samples depends on the goals of the program. Therefore it may not be necessary to duplicate many tasks if the purpose is for evaluation of general work characteristics and attitudes.

**Developing a work interest.** Special educators may become involved, to varying degrees, in the actual vocational training efforts of the school. This depends on the local circumstances and the attitude about participation of handicapped students in the mainstream. If a separate vocational track is established for "special needs" students, then the bureaucratic patterns that follow may mean that all handicapped students will be excluded from liberal arts classes. Vocational mathematics, vocational English, and so forth will be used to substitute for other graduation credits, as has been done with the mentally retarded. In any event, the teacher can assist in the development of work orientation, work interest, and dissemination of work-related information. Some approaches that might be used are:
- Class discussion of students' interests
- Field activities, visitations
- Use of commercial films and workbooks
- Speakers
- Exploration of job clusters

**Job clusters.** Job clusters, or groupings of similar jobs into specific categories, can be used to understand the myriad jobs in the work force, to plan for curriculum development, and to evaluate the offerings of a school district in the area of vocational education. Job clusters in many schools reflect not only the jobs that may be obtained on high school graduation, but also the extent to which the school is willing to provide students with fundamental experiences that may be refined in community college, vocational technical school, and college. Of course, high school graduates are not able to immediately enter the work force for many jobs and certainly not as members of the professions that require graduate training; but exposure to some job clusters will enable students to make decisions, receive fundamental training, and be lead to the ultimate goals and ambitions for postsecondary adjustment. Job clusters are listed below. It should be remembered that the number of occupations included within clusters in a school district vocational program will be determined by the needs, size, and resources of the district, not to mention the business and industrial characteristics of the surrounding community. The 15 job clusters in vocational education are:

1. Agriculture and natural resources
2. Business and office
3. Communications and media
4. Construction
5. Consumer and homemaking education
6. Environment
7. Fine arts and humanities
8. Health
9. Manufacturing
10. Marine science
11. Marketing and distribution
12. Personal services
13. Public services
14. Recreation and hospitality
15. Transportation

## Vocational training

The *career education* movement would place work orientation experiences into the curriculum in the early grades and gradually build on them as students progress through the grades to secondary school. Ideally, active exploration would begin early and be emphasized in the junior high school with a formal prevocational program for all students. Prevocational training has been developed extensively for use with the mentally retarded as a precursor of vocational training that is to occur in high school. Otherwise, very little emphasis, outside of such work-study programs, can be found in most junior high school curricula. As a minimum, a comprehensive program would have a prevocational and a vocational training component. Schools should not overlook regular vocational courses in any sequence. The prevocational program provides exploratory experiences and enables school personnel to make comprehensive assessments of occupational interests and abilities prior to actual training. In accordance with the objectives of the prevocational program and the nature of materials used, a wide range of issues may be covered, including grooming, practical application of mathematics and reading, examination of work-related terminology, exposure to job applications and interviews, and a variety of other related activities. The general sequence of vocational education might be as follows:

- Prevocational training (exploration)
- Vocational evaluation
- Vocational training
- Placement
- Follow-up

Vocational training opportunities will vary, as noted above, in accordance with the resources of the school district. Many types of training programs may exist, as depicted in Table 15.

**Table 15.** Correlation of school-based and off-campus training

| School-based training | Off-campus training |
| --- | --- |
| Vocational education | Vocational technical school |
| Work experience | On-the-job training |
| Work-study | Off-campus work stations |

The following descriptions relate to the general program design of school-based training programs for the mildly handicapped. There are numerous examples that might be made, but the commonalities are noted as generalizations.

**Vocational education.** Many mildly handicapped students are enrolled in the regular vocational education courses of the school or vocational technical school and participate fully with nonhandicapped peers. Support for them may be in the form of consultation to vocational educators, as itinerant services, or as part of a combination special class (resource) and regular placement arrangement. The least handicapped students able to adjust to regular classes are most likely to be involved in this approach. The major problems of students, as in other classes of the general curriculum, will be to keep pace with instruction and reading content, pass examinations, and otherwise meet the demands of instruction. Many of the recommendations in Chapter 10 would be appropriate for assisting students in mainstream vocational classes. The school may have a variety of training areas associated with the 15 job clusters through which students are rotated for training, or other approaches, such as cooperative work education, may be used. In concept, the participation of students in vocational courses at this level is no different than that of any regular course of the general curriculum.

**Work experience.** Work experience is a program supervised by school-based vocational educators that enables students to have experiences in a work environment, either business or industry, through part-time employment. The major responsibility for vocational training is clearly that of vocational education personnel. As such, the programs are eligible for financial support from vocational monies, and the special educator can provide supportive services to teachers, students, and employers, which will be determined by the IEP.

**Work-study.** Work-study is a traditional arrangement developed primarily for the EMR student that was usually sponsored by an agreement between special educators and vocational rehabilitation. In many cases it appears that total responsibility for this approach is assumed by a special educator. At least in some states, this approach does not qualify for financial support from vocational education monies because it is not regarded as a vocational program. The work-study program has been criticized because it has been focused on training leading to dead-end jobs for a segment of the population unable to make rapid adjustments in the work force caused by technological change and economic trends. It should be remembered, however, that work-study programming was an innovation in its time when few other alternatives existed and it represented a professional response to handicapped students who were otherwise ignored by the system.

**Off-campus training.** Off-campus alternatives are similar to school-based programs except that local circumstances provide different options due to characteristics of the state or region.

**Vocational-technical schools.** There are area vocational technical schools, skill centers, and vocational high schools in various parts of the nation that have special facilities to house comprehensive training programs in vocational education. Handicapped students may be enrolled in these settings along with nonhandicapped students. In many cases, special education personnel are employed on the staff of the vocational school to assist students and may cooperate with special educators in the home schools. Some vocational schools house basic academic courses in the building.

**On-the-job training and off-campus work stations.** Under a variety of arrangements in special education or vocational education, students may be placed on locations in the community to receive vocational training. Part of this experience may be paid. Although these approaches might be classified as work experience, they may actually exist as components of work experience, vocational exploration, and as separate, limited training approaches. One of the problems in vocational programming, generally, is the confusion created by terminology. Different settings use terminology having multiple meanings.

• • •

The least restrictive environment for many mildly handicapped students should be regular vocational education. The fact that special programs exist does not mean that all special needs students should be placed in them. Many students can probably benefit from regular vocational education course work, and provisions of the compensatory models, explained in Chapter 10, would be as appropriate in vocational education as in the general curriculum. Placement in the regular vocational classroom could be supported by (1) consultation with the teacher, (2) itinerant services to the student, and (3) a resource room approach. In many settings where skill centers are utilized, the special educator is attached to the vocational staff to assist special needs students. Placement in work-study or cooperative education programs may be the least restrictive environment for other students, as determined by evaluation of student needs on an individual basis. In many cases, the type of program may be dictated by available resources. For example, in more rural areas, students must attend a skill center serving a wide geographic region in order to benefit from training. Thus bussing between the regular program and the vocational school is essential for all students.

The role of the special educator will vary from one setting to another and from one state to another in accordance with the types of vocational services that are provided. The role of a special educator who is employed to work in an existing vocational program should be apparent. Also, programs that employ the special educator for full responsibility, such as the work-study program, imply clear role functions. However, responsibility is frequently unclear in programs with secondary resource teachers.

### Role of the resource teacher

There may be arrangements in which a learning disabilities specialist is hired for the purpose of providing direct support in a vocational training program. In a more typical situation where the specialist is expected to perform the traditional role of a resource teacher, we recommend the arrangement given in Table 16.

**Table 16.** Support by resource teacher in vocational education

| Program level | Role of teacher |
|---|---|
| Prevocational | Provide career information, conduct classroom activities related to prevocational goals |
| Referral | Assist other professionals in collection of data, make observations, participate in assessment |
| Vocational evaluation | Conduct *only* those tests for which qualified to administer, supervise work experience activities, etc. |
| Vocational training | Provide support with academic work, assist with assignments, provide assistance to teachers, provide accommodation |
| Placement | Limited or no responsibility |
| Follow-up | Limited or no responsibility |

We recognize that some schools may elect to have vocationally oriented resource centers. This may be dictated by a great number of factors, including state certification requirements for teachers and reimbursement for special programs. It would seem to be very difficult for the resource teacher who is primarily responsible for remediation and academic subject areas to also conduct the primary vocational-training effort on behalf of students. To be fully trained in this area requires considerably more specialization and course work than would be ordinarily available in a preservice training program leading to certification in special education. There promises to be much confusion about the roles and functions of specialists in secondary programs due to the divergent tasks recommended by several authorities, the lack of clarity about the goals of secondary education, and the tenuous relationships between vocational education, special education, and vocational rehabilitation.

### Role of vocational rehabilitation

A variety of services can be provided to handicapped students by the state office of vocational rehabilitation. These might include assessment and evaluation, counseling and guidance, restoration services, the provision of special tools, transportation, and subsistence to prepare the student for employability. The heart of the rehabilitation process is the individualized written rehabilitation program (IWRP), which is similar to the IEP in education and which may be written jointly. According to Bitter (1979) the IWRP contains five primary service-related content areas, which represent a plan of action and a statement of mutual understanding. The five components are long-range employment goals, intermediate rehabilitation objectives, specific rehabilitation services, duration of services, and evaluation of progress.

### Vocational education and the future

Will special educators at the secondary level be tutors and remedial specialists, providing the major link to vocational education? The popularity of the resource-room model is indicated by its rapid spread at the secondary level. But the resource room, especially if it mimes its elementary counterpart, will not be as responsive as it could be to the needs of adolescents if the entire focus is on remediation or coping skills (also called learning strategies, progressive inclusion models, and so forth). If career education and vocational education are to be prominent in the secondary curriculum then universities will need to initiate new, innovative programs to properly prepare special educators to fulfill this role. Presently, this is not being done. Moreover, there seem to be some programs developing for categories of students that essentially adopt the old work-study model and apply it to a new population, such as LD students. Some of the materials produced in particular projects for vocational preparation of LD students are remarkable for their poor quality and low expectations of students. There can be little justification to relive some of the mistakes of the past because professionals with little or no training in vocational programming attempt to initiate special vocational programs for the handicapped, a well-intentioned but misguided effort. There must be cooperation between the various disciplines and agencies as well as a sensible division of labor.

## POSTSECONDARY TRAINING

As secondary programs are developed and expanded, it becomes obvious that a demand will also grow for postsecondary training. Presently, there are three major opportunities for those who do not acquire jobs in the work force on graduation: vocational technical schools, two-year or community colleges, and four-year colleges. Because the labels do not imply an ultimate level of performance or functioning, no predictions can be safely made about postsecondary adjustment.

Some handicapped students are intelligent, capable, and creative and have the aspiration to attend college. There are, of course, numerous case histories of some famous, and not so famous, persons who have managed to struggle through four years of college by means of ingenious coping devices. We are personally aware of an associate college dean who has learning disabilities but who is able to manage his duties with the assistance of an understanding secretary and a supportive wife. We are also aware of a practicing psychiatrist and a dentist who are taking remedial reading! The surprising fact is that they were able to survive some very rigorous training programs without assistance, not to mention the discouragement they must have felt when they were informed in high school that they should not pursue a college career. The point is that some LD students surpass the expectations of educators and LD authorities, and more would excel in many fields if they could benefit from assistance.

Generally, the options available to mildly handicapped students beyond high school are not much different than those for other students, just more limited. There should be much more consideration to the needs of mildly handicapped adolescents for postsecondary adjustment, not that nonhandicapped are less deserving but, by comparison, the needs of handicapped students are somewhat different. There is a consequent need for special attention of professionals to certain aspects of postsecondary adjustment. The career avenues for adolescents are:

1. Immediate employment in the work force
2. Attendance at a vocational technical school for specialized training
3. Attendance at a two-year college for specialized training
4. Attendance in a four-year college or university
5. Military enlistment
6. Unemployment
7. Involvement in the counterculture

### Employment in the work force

Many students who have no higher aspirations than to find a job will seek employment as soon as possible in some unskilled, semi-skilled, or skilled occupation. The job market may be more alluring than remaining in school so that many students will drop out in order to assume full-time employment. The initial appeal is, of course, the money that can be earned. If (as so many teenagers do) it is possible to stay in the parental home while working, the dollars seem to last longer and go farther—especially for the purchase of clothes and entertainment. As long as parents subsidize food and housing expenses, the financial rewards of employment in any job bring great satisfaction. As the tasks of assuming adult responsibility become inevitable, underemployment and job dissatisfaction begin to surface.

There are many persons who seem to survive without specialization (an ethic of lower-class workers), but the middle-class value system of high schools tends to revere employment that leads to long-term security, fringe benefits, and adequate economic resources. Although most educators would regard career selection and preparation as eminent considerations of the young, many young men and women seem to drift from one job to another without any planning. The purpose of a vocational training program is to equip students to enter the job market with a "work attitude," marketable skills, and greater chances of success. For special populations, these concepts are extolled but the efficacy of vocational programs will have to be validated on the evidence that they actually make a difference in assisting students to find and keep well-paying, satisfying jobs. Underemployment that plagues vocational adjustment of mentally retarded persons who are work-study graduates should cause us to pause and consider whether we are responsibly establishing goals for mildly handicapped students if we merely train them for dead-end jobs. For the present, there is sufficient reason to believe that some students would do as well (poorly) in vocational adjustment without any vocational training. Exemplary programs, elevated vocational goals, linkages with employers to eliminate bias, and workable follow-up systems will need to be developed. The postsecondary characteristics of the population will evidence higher unemployment, a greater frequency of underemployment, and more personal crises due to insecurity and uncertainty about the future.

## Attendance at vocational technical and two-year colleges

The academic and social deficits that interfere with school adjustment will continue to plague the mildly handicapped adolescent in postsecondary education. The plight of some students is described in the following excerpt (Reynolds, 1978, p. 6):

> Students who come to this vocational-technical school are not encouraged to apply if they have below-average academic, behavioral, or school attendance records; teachers in the various occupational areas have tremendous power to reject students they consider unpromising; little record keeping concerning student admissions and rejections is performed; the school has negotiated highly valued relationships with local unions and employers which put a premium on a standard, high-performing educational "product."

The inertia for special education programming has not existed beyond high school. The student who is admitted must surely have prior assistance and counseling because the likelihood of receiving special assistance, accommodation, and other compensating considerations is slim.

There are excellent opportunities in two-year colleges and vocational technical schools, but placement must be seriously considered to assure that opportunities the student seeks are realistic and attainable. Some community colleges offer special help to students, sometimes in the form of a continuation of remedial reading. A more pragmatic consideration is whether or not there is assistance toward the goal of vocational specialization, something that remedial reading will not ensure.

If the hope for advanced training through vocational technical schools is somewhat discouraging, one study (May et al., 1976) that surveyed the attitudes and opinions of vocational technical school administrators revealed that, although they were not prepared to offer services to LD students, *one third* of the respondents said they offered specific assessment information to their instructors to assist in training, *all* expressed a need for additional support services, most would admit LD students, and *half* were planning to expand services to LD students. A major weakness identified was that most instructors were trained in *specific trade skills* rather than instructional strategies and techniques.

Personal contact with professionals of various vocational schools reveals that the one-to-one nature of instruction and the interest of the instructors can facilitate the development of student skills that do not rely on academic performance. Some instructors devalue the importance of reading achievement. As a result, several fine training programs have evolved that circumvent a student's inability to read by modeling strategies and other compensations. However, such developments represent the personal commitment of an individual instructor rather than school policy.

**College programs as an option**

To some, college for LD students is unthinkable. Critics oppose their enrollment in college in the belief that such a concept is misleading and detrimental to overall programming (Schoolfield, 1978), but LD and some ED students go to college with or without assistance, and many of them make it in spite of incredible opposing odds. Some LD students should be given the opportunity to attend college because of their personal strengths and ability to succeed. Obviously this will not be an option for most; and, for those who try, the opportunities in careers will be limited. If a student is to be assisted, the following general points should be kept in mind:

1. Most colleges that admit students will have unconditional or open admissions policies, which should not be construed to mean that special assistance will be available.
2. Some small private colleges that advertise for LD applicants seem to be primarily motivated by the tuition money they will receive; many offer little or no assistance.
3. A college degree in many fields will not necessarily lead to employment, especially if the graduate has a learning disability.

This topic has been considered at greater length in a study reported by May (1976), who uncovered a number of facts about the limitations of college programs. The most striking finding is that, unlike public school programs, there are no special funds available: funds are from institutional budgets. It stands to reason that this will be a limiting factor in the future development of such programs.

It is noteworthy that college entrance examinations are now provided in an alternative form for learning disabled students, but the conditions of the test are noted on the student's record, which could have a biasing effect on an admissions officer. Therefore personal contact between the guidance counselor and college officers would be essential. The counselor would also be able to assist the college-bound student in many other ways, a suitable activity for any student who wishes to attend college. However, in the case of the LD student special attention to entrance requirements, routines of the course of study, and anticipated problems must be tediously examined. The student must be made aware of the stigmatization that will occur, especially if certain professors oppose the entrance of "nonacademic" students and if attendance in a study-skills class is demeaning in the college environment. Perhaps the most important key to success would be the selection of a college that has an academic support system and personal-social counseling.

Moorehead (N.D.) has developed a guide for college-bound LD students that includes a list of institutions said to accept LD students. Included is a list of skills necessary for performance in college, which includes reading, written communication, oral communication, social studies, clerical and study skills, mathematical abilities, and social adjustment factors.

The college-bound LD student may be rare; but it is expected that the number will increase as colleges (with dropping enrollments) invite them to apply with assurances of assistance and as society acknowledges that many of them have superior abilities that may be nurtured in a field with appropriate accommodations. The resource teacher and school counselors should temper student expectations with realistic information and aid them in their selections.

### Military enlistment

For some persons, enlistment in one of the branches of military service leads to a satisfactory vocational experience. The regimentation, limitations of opportunities, and restrictive nature make it unsuitable for many others. People who join to learn a trade are generally misled by the expectation that being in the service will be an inexpensive way to learn a skill that will lead to a secure civilian job after discharge. The crisis involving unemployed veterans is testimony to the fact that military training and experience do not lead to civilian jobs. If a student is able to enlist and wishes to remain in the service as a career, it may be said that this would be satisfactory postsecondary adjustment. However, we have known too many students who were misled by their own expectations and encountered serious adjustment problems because of the "hostile" nature of basic training, the structure, regimentation, and loss of personal freedom. Under such circumstances, persons with poor personal social skills and general immaturity may find that their enlistment becomes a nightmare because infractions in the military lead to incarceration, a dishonorable discharge, and complications in seeking civilian employment. Resource teachers and counselors should caution students, especially those with aggressive or resisting personalities, to carefully consider the military option.

### The counterculture as a "career" opportunity

Crime does pay! The chances of being apprehended, convicted, and sentenced for many crimes are not great. In the inner-city areas where youthful law offenders gain experience with the legal system, they learn that it is possible to "cop a plea" and be back on the street to continue commiting felonies. The point is that many LD and ED students are believed to become delinquents. It stands to reason that many such adults could become criminals. If secondary school looks like a dead end because of the insensitivity of personnel, the lack of relevance, and the unresponsiveness of programs to personal needs, a variety of antisocial pursuits may be more attractive and seem exceedingly rewarding.

The complex issues surrounding why persons use drugs or rob gas stations continue to be investigated and debated without any clear direction for prevention. A better school experience through the provision of counseling, career orientation, and accommodation to their needs may prevent these persons from choosing antisocial patterns in adult life. The secondary special teacher may not be able to accomplish much with adolescents who seem to be set in the wrong direction, but humane, responsive programming at the secondary level will save some.

## SUMMARY

In this chapter we have reviewed many issues pertaining to vocational training and postsecondary adjustment of students. It is clear that program development has been slow, vocational options are limited, and existing training notions are restricted to older models in special education that result in limited application to a diverse group of students.

A review of vocational training programs, assessment practices, and the roles of the teacher was presented. It was stated that the full responsibility for vocational training should not be shouldered by special educators. It was also noted that many issues in vocational training of students have not been resolved, an important one being that specialists at the secondary level have not yet determined what their roles will be in relationship to remediation, accommodation, and vocational training. Various postsecondary options for students were discussed, including vocational technical schools, colleges, and employment in the work force.

## REFERENCES AND READINGS

Abeson, A., & Zettell, J. The end of the quiet revolution: The Education for All Handicapped Children Act of 1975. *Exceptional Children,* 1977, *44,* 114-128.

Alper, S., & Retish, P. M. The influence of academic information on teachers' judgments of vocational potential. *Exceptional Children,* 1978, *44,* 537-538.

Bitter, J. A. *Introduction to rehabilitation.* St. Louis: Mosby, 1979.

Brolin, D., & D'Alonzo, B. Critical issues in career education for handicapped students. *Exceptional Children,* 1979, *45,* 246-253.

Brolin, D., & Kokaska, C. *Career education for handicapped children and youth.* Columbus, Ohio: Merrill, 1979.

Brolin, D., & Thomas, B. *Preparing teachers of secondary level educable mentally retarded students: A new model* (Final report). Menomonie, Wis.: University of Wisconsin-Stout, August 1972.

Colella, H. V. Career development center: A modified high school for the handicapped. *Teaching Exceptional Children,* 1973, *5,* 110-118.

Conner, J., & McAllister, E. *Pre-career and occupational training: A program description of a project in the public schools of Bryant, Arkansas, funded by Title IV-C.* ESEA, 1977.

Davis, S., & Ward, M. *Vocational education of handicapped students: A guide for policy development.* Reston, Va.: The Council for Exceptional Children, 1978.

Davis, S., & Weintraub, F. J. Beyond the traditional career stereotyping. *Journal of Career Education,* 1978, *5,* 24-34.

Farber, B. *Mental retardation: Its social content and social consequences.* Boston: Houghton Mifflin, 1968.

Fielding, P. (Ed.) *A national directory of four-year colleges, two-year colleges, and post-high school training programs for young people with learning disabilities.* Tulsa, Okla.: Partners in Publishing, 1975.

Gysbers, N. C., & Moore, E. J. Beyond career development—life career development. *Personnel and Guidance Journal,* 1975, *53,* 647-652.

Hansen, L. S. *An examination of the definitions and concepts of career education.* Washington, D.C.: U.S. Government Printing Office, 1977.

Hoyt, K. B. *An introduction to career education: A policy paper of the U.S. Office of Education.* Washington, D.C.: U.S. Government Printing Office, 1975.

Hoyt, K. B. *An introduction to career education: A policy paper of the U.S. Office of Education* (DHEW Publication No. [OE] 75-00504). Washington, D.C.: U.S. Government Printing Office, 1976.

Hoyt, K. B. *A primer for career education.* Washington, D.C.: U.S. Government Printing Office, 1977.

Jennings, W., & Nathan, J. Startling and disturbing research on school program effectiveness. *Phi Delta Kappan,* March 1977, pp. 568-572.

Levitan, S. A., & Taggart, R. *Jobs for the disabled.* Washington, D.C.: George Washington University Center for Manpower Policy Studies, 1976.

May, B. J., Armentrout, S. L., Rudy, R., & Clayton, D. P.L. 94-142 and vocational education: Parallel, picture and prophecy, *Journal of Career Education,* 1978, *5,* 53-62.

May, B. J., Rye, D., & Connors, J. *Survey of post-secondary educational services for LD students in Arkansas.* Unpublished manuscript, 1976. (Available from Graduate Education Building, Special Education Department, University of Arkansas, Fayetteville, AR 72701.)

Moorehead, S. *A guide to college bound LD students.* Columbus, Ohio: Project Expand, Child Service Demonstration Center, (N.D.).

Moorehead, S. *Project expand.* P.L. 91-230, OEC-0-74-8725. Columbus, Ohio: Project Expand, Child Service Demonstration Center, (N.D.).

Razeghi, J. A., & Davis, S. Federal mandates for the handicapped: Vocational education opportunity and employment. *Exceptional Children,* 1979, *45,* 353-359.

Reynolds, M. C. Career education and mainstreaming. *Journal of Career Education,* 1978, *5,* 4-15.

Schoolfield, W. R. Limitations of the college entry LD model. *Academic Therapy,* 1978, *13,* 423-431.

Schweich, P. D. The development of choices—an educational approach to employment. *Academic Therapy,* 1975, *10,* 277-283.

Shworles, T. R. Increasing the opportunities through vocational education. In J. E. Wall (Ed.), *Vocational education for special groups.* Washington, D.C.: American Vocational Association, 1976.

Sitlington, P. L., & Wimmer, D. Vocational assessment techniques for the handicapped adolescent. *Career Development for Exceptional Individuals,* 1978, *1,* 74-87.

Snider, R. Can we go back to the basics in the mainstream with career education for the handicapped? *Journal of Career Education,* 1978, *5,* 16-23.

Sontag, E. Specific learning disabilities program. *Exceptional Children,* 1976, *43,* 157-159.

Staats, E. B. *Training educators for the handicapped: A need to redirect federal programs.* Washington, D.C.: U.S. General Accounting Office, 1976.

Super, D. E. *Career education and the meanings of work.* Washington, D.C.: U.S. Government Printing Office, 1976.

U.S. Office of Education. *Improving occupational programs for the handicapped. A technical manual prepared by the Management Analysis Center, Inc. of*

*Washington, D.C. for the Bureau of Education for the Handicapped.* Washington, D.C.: U.S. Government Printing Office.

Viscardi, H. *Speech presented at the annual meeting of the President's Committee on Employment of the Handicapped.* Washington, D.C., April 30, 1976.

Whiteford, E., & Anderson, D. H. The mainstreaming of special needs students: Home ec. teachers are coping. *American Vocational Journal*, May 1977, pp. 42-44.

# Appendix A

# ASSESSMENT

## TESTS

Included in this section of Appendix A are tests that may be used with mildly handicapped students in junior and senior high school. The referral and assessment process is prescribed in most states, and there is a growing tendency for specific tests to be required, but the question of appropriateness and usefulness must be considered for each individual. Many of the tests listed here will be important to the multidisciplinary team in the diagnostic process of labeling students. Of greater significance is the aspect of assessment pertaining to daily lesson plans and short-range instructional objectives.

| Test | Publisher |
|---|---|
| American School Achievement Tests | Bobbs-Merrill |
| Auditory Perception Test-Visual Discrimination | Temple University |
| Ayres Space Test | American Guidance Service |
| Bender Gestalt Test | Western Psychological Services |
| Benton Revised Visual Retention Test | The Psychological Corporation |
| Bond-Balow-Hoyt Silent Reading Diagnostic Tests | Lyons & Carnahan |
| Botel Reading Inventory | Follett |
| Brigance Diagnostic Inventories | Curriculum Associates |
| Brown-Carlsen Listening Comprehension Test | Lyons & Carnahan |
| California Achievement Tests | California Test Bureau |
| California Psychological Inventory | Western Psychological Services |
| Cornell Index | The Psychological Corporation |
| Detroit General Intelligence Examination | Bobbs-Merrill |
| Detroit Tests of Learning Aptitude | Bobbs-Merrill |
| Devereau Behavior Rating Scale | Devereau Foundation |
| Diagnostic Reading Scales | CTB–McGraw-Hill |
| Doren Diagnostic Reading Test of Word Recognition Skills | American Guidance Service |
| Draw-A-Person Test | Western Psychological Services |
| Durrell Analysis of Reading Difficulty | Harcourt Brace Jovanovich |
| Forer Structured Sentence Completion Test | Western Psychological Services |
| Gates-MacGinitie Reading Tests | Western Psychological Services |
| Gates-McKillop Reading Diagnostic Tests | Western Psychological Services |
| Gordon Personality Inventory | Western Psychological Services |
| Goldman-Fristoe-Woodcock Auditory Skills Test Battery | American Guidance Service |
| Goldman-Fristoe-Woodcock Tests of Auditory Discrimination | American Guidance Service |
| Gray Oral Reading Tests | Western Psychological Service |

| Test | Publisher | Test | Publisher |
|---|---|---|---|
| High School Personality Questionnaire | Western Psychological Services | Rorschach Inkblot Test | Western Psychological Services |
| House-Tree-Person | Western Psychological Services | School Behavior Checklist | Western Psychological Services |
| Illinois Index of Scholastic Aptitude | Western Psychological Services | Self-Control Behavior Inventory | Nicholas Long, American University |
| IPAT Anxiety Scale Questionnaire | Western Psychological Services | Sequential Tests of Educational Progress | Educational Testing Service |
| KeyMath Diagnostic Arithmetic Test | American Guidance Service | Sixteen Personality Factor Questionnaire | Western Psychological Services |
| Leiter International Performance Scale | Stoelting | Slosson Drawing Coordination Test for Children | Slosson Educational Publications |
| Lincoln Diagnostic Spelling Test | Educational Records Bureau | Spache Diagnostic Reading Scales | California Test Bureau |
| Lincoln-Oseretsky Motor Development Scale | Western Psychological Services | Stanford Achievement Test | The Psychological Corporation |
| Metropolitan Achievement Tests | The Psychological Corporation | Stanford-Binet Intelligence Scale, Forms L and M | Houghton Mifflin |
| Monroe Diagnostic Reading Test | Stoelting | Stanford Diagnostic Arithmetic Test | Harcourt Brace Jovanovich |
| Nebraska Test of Learning Aptitude | University of Nebraska | Stanford Diagnostic Reading | Harcourt Brace Jovanovich |
| Nelson-Denny Reading Test | Houghton Mifflin | Symbol Digit Modalities Test | Western Psychological Services |
| Peabody Individual Achievement Test | American Guidance Service | Thematic Apperception Test | Western Psychological Services |
| Peabody Picture Vocabulary Test | American Guidance Service | Torrance Test of Creative Thinking | Western Psychological Services |
| Picture Story Language Test | Western Psychological Services | Verbal Language Development Scale | American Guidance Service |
| Picture Word Test | Western Psychological Services | Wechsler Adult Intelligence Scale | The Psychological Corporation |
| Prescriptive Reading Performance Test | Western Psychological Services | Wechsler Intelligence Scale for Children, Revised Edition | The Psychological Corporation |
| Psychoeducational Inventory of Basic Learning Abilities | Fearon Publishers | Wide Range Achievement Test | Western Psychological Services |
| Psychological Screening Inventory | The Psychological Corporation | Wide Range Achievement Test, Revised | Guidance Associates |
| Quick Neurological Screening Test | Academic Therapy | Woodcock Reading Mastery Test | American Guidance Service |
| Ravens Progressive Matrices | The Psychological Corporation | | |
| Rhode Sentence Completion | Western Psychological Services | | |

## THE ASSESSMENT PROCESS*

The following areas have been identified as potential areas of evaluation for any student suspected of having a handicapping condition:

I. Educational functioning
   A. Achievement in subjects
   B. Learning style
   C. Strengths and weaknesses
II. Social-emotional functioning
   A. Social/psychological
   B. Self-help skills
III. Physical functioning
   A. Visual
   B. Hearing
   C. Speech
   D. Motor/psychomotor
   E. Medical health
IV. Cognitive functioning
   A. Intelligence
   B. Adaptive behavior
V. Thinking processes
   A. Knowledge
   B. Comprehension
   C. Application
   D. Analysis
   E. Synthesis
   F. Evaluation
VI. Language functioning
   A. Receptive
   B. Expressive
   C. Nonverbal
   D. Speech
VII. Family
   A. Dominant language
   B. Parent-child interactions
   C. Social service needs
VIII. Environment
   A. Home
   B. School
   C. Interpersonal

## ASSESSMENT DOMAINS

I. Academic achievement
   A. Formal batteries
   B. Individual instruments
II. Intelligence tests
   A. Group
   B. Individual
III. Diagnostic tests
   A. Reading
   B. Mathematics
IV. Perceptual and motor tests
   A. Visual perception
   B. Auditory perception
   C. Perceptual-motor tests
V. Language assessment
VI. Adaptive behavior
VII. Tests of acuity
   A. Vision
   B. Hearing
VIII. Ecological assessment
   A. Checklists
   B. Rating scales
   C. Sociometric
   D. Observational
IX. Career education
   A. Aptitude tests
   B. Interest and attitude tests
   C. Career assessment
   D. Work evaluation and adjustment

---

*Walker, J. *Functions of the placement committee in special education.* Washington, D.C.: National Association of State Directors of Special Education, 1976.

## INDIVIDUAL EDUCATION PROGRAM: TOTAL SERVICE PLAN

Student's name: _____

School: _____ Date of entry: _____

Long-term goals:
1. _____
2. _____

| Short-term objectives | Support services | Person responsible | Percent of time | Start and end dates | Review date |
|---|---|---|---|---|---|
| | | | | | |

| Percent of time in regular class | Committee members present | Placement recommendation | Dates of meetings |
|---|---|---|---|
| | | | |

| Committee recommendations for specific procedures/techniques, materials, etc. | Objective evaluation criteria for each annual goal statement |
|---|---|
| | |

Appendix B

# SUGGESTED FORMS FOR COMPLIANCE WITH P.L. 94-142 FOR INDIVIDUAL PROTECTIONS AND PROCEDURAL SAFEGUARDS*

---

*These forms are reprinted from the *Referral, placement, and appeal procedures: Special education and related services*, Arkansas Department of Education, Division of Instructional Services, Special Education Section with the permission of Dr. Larry Rogers, Coordinator.

---

**PARENT NOTIFICATION OF REFERRAL**

Date: _____

Dear _____:

    Your child, _____, has been referred as possibly being able to benefit from special services. Such special services would provide extra assistance to help your child learn.

    We are holding a referral conference to discuss the educational needs of your child. We would like you to be there so that you can provide us with information about your child and also learn more about our services.

    We have scheduled a referral conference on _____ (date), at _____ in _____ of _____.

    Since we are required to see that children are best served as soon as possible, we will need to go ahead with the referral conference by _____ (date), if we do not hear from you.

    Please feel free to contact _____ (name) if you have any questions.

The phone number is _____.

    We are looking forward to hearing from you.

                                                                Sincerely,

                                                     _____
                                                     (principal's signature)

                                                     _____
                                                     (name of school)

## DOCUMENTATION OF PARENT NOTICES/CONTACTS

When means other than the suggested forms for notice to parents are utilized, documentation of the notice must be completed. Utilization of this or a similar form will provide the necessary documentation for a student's folder.

Type of communication used:
- ☐ Phone call
- ☐ Home visit
- ☐ School note sent home
- ☐ Other (describe) _____

Purpose of communication:
- ☐ Notice of referral conference
- ☐ Notice of referral conference decision
- ☐ Notice of evaluation conference
- ☐ Notice of evaluation conference decision
- ☐ Notice of annual review

Results of communication: _____
_____
_____

Comments: _____
_____

Date of communication: _____
Person making communication: _____
Approved: _____

## CHECKLIST FOR DUE PROCESS COMPLIANCE

Child's name: _____ Address: _____
Referring agent: _____ Team chairperson: _____

This checklist indicates that the above student meets all of the qualifications for placement in a program for exceptional children, as stipulated in the *Procedures for evaluation and placement: Special education and related services*, State Board of Education of Arkansas.

| | | |
|---|---|---|
| 1. Referral form | YES | NO |
| 2. Parent notification of referral form or documentation of notice | YES | NO |
| 3. Referral conference decision form | YES | NO |
| 4. Parent notification of referral conference decision form or documentation of notice | YES | NO |
| 5. Informed consent form | YES | NO |
| 6. Parent notification of evaluation conference or documentation of notice | YES | NO |
| 7. Evaluation conference decision form | YES | NO |
| 8. Parent notification of evaluation conference decision form or documentation of notice | YES | NO |
| 9. Consent: initial placement form | YES | NO |
| 10. Review notice or documentation of notice | YES | NO |
| 11. Individual education plan form | YES | NO |
| 12. Annual review report form | YES | NO |

The child may be placed only if all items listed above are marked YES.

Recommended placement: _____ School: _____
Placement date: _____ Teacher: _____
Date: _____

_____
(principal's signature)

## REFERRAL CONFERENCE DECISION

ID no.: _____

**Outcome of referral conference**

Student: _____
Birth date: _____ CA: _____ Referral conference date: _____
Attendees: _____

Referral conference decision:




Programming or review recommendations:




Professional(s) designated responsible: _____
Signature of principal/designee: _____
                                                                              (date)

## PARENT NOTIFICATION OF REFERRAL CONFERENCE DECISION

Date: _____

Dear _____:

The possibility of special education services for your child, _____, was discussed at a referral conference on _____.
The following decision was reached:



This decision was based on the following information:



_____ has been designated as responsible for seeing that the referral conference decision is carried out. Please contact this person if you have any questions or concerns. The telephone number is _____.
You have the right to a hearing if you disagree with this decision, and you have the right to review all relevant records maintained on your child. However, if you feel that different or additional services may be appropriate, or if you wish to bring further information about your child to us, please contact _____.

Sincerely,

_____
(principal's signature)

_____
(name of school)

## INFORMED CONSENT: RELEASE OF RECORDS
### (Name and address of school district)

**Information for parents or guardians**

It is the intent of this brochure to inform you that under regulations prescribed by State and federal law, your consent is required before this school district can deal with confidential information on your child in any of the following ways:

1. Disclose the information to anyone other than authorized personnel employed by this district;
2. Use the information for any purpose other than those stated below; or
3. Seek it directly from your child by formal evaluation. (Your refusal to consent to an evaluation does not prevent your child from receiving beneficial services.)

The Arkansas Department of Education is coordinating the collection of selected information items on physically, emotionally, and mentally handicapped children birth through twenty-one years of age for the purpose of determining present and future program and placement needs, and for statistical reporting. Information is sought by survey from this school district, the Divisions of Mental Retardation-Developmental Disabilities Services, Mental Health Services, Social Services, Rehabilitation Services, and Juvenile Services of the Department of Social and Rehabilitative Services, Easter Seal of Arkansas, and Arkansas Department of Health.

Information which could identify an individual child will not be collected or maintained beyond the level of the school district and will not be made available to any State level agency, except for such purposes as overall program monitoring. As a parent, you are guaranteed the right to inspect any such information which is subject to collection, to require the accuracy of such information, and to obtain copies. Access by any unauthorized person to information which would identify an individual child, without the informed consent of the parent, is expressly forbidden. Parents will be informed in their primary native language or other mode of communication unless it is clearly not feasible to do so. For individuals eighteen (18) years of age, or older, the above-stated rights pass to the individual.

The school district has the responsibility for the confidential maintenance of this information in locked storage and for the destruction of the information following the termination of services for the child. Parents will be notified prior to the entrance of this information and prior to the destruction of the data.

## INFORMED CONSENT: RELEASE OF RECORDS—cont'd
### (Name and address of school district)

Name of student: _____ Date of birth: _____

Address: _____ School: _____

Authorization is hereby granted to _____ for: (Mark one or more boxes.)
(name of district)

1. ☐ Conducting a formal evaluation of my child:

   _____
   (purpose of evaluation)

   _____
   (agency or person approved for conducting evaluation procedures)

2. ☐ Releasing the following information to a third party:

   _____
   (describe information to be released)

   _____
   (name of third party)

   _____
   (address)

   _____
   (city, state, zip code)

   Purpose of release: _____

3. ☐ Using the following information for other purposes:

   _____
   (describe information)

   _____
   (purpose)

I have read and I understand "Information for parents or guardians" on the first page of this form. I understand the purpose(s) for which my consent is being requested.

_____
(parent's signature)

_____
(date)

# EVALUATION CONFERENCE DECISION

ID no.: _____

## Outcome of evaluation conference

Student: _____
Birth date: _____ CA: _____
School: _____ District: _____
Evaluation conference date: _____ Location: _____
Attendees: _____
_____

Evaluations conducted, results, and evaluators:




Student eligibility for special education is certified by the establishment of this primary handicapping condition: _____ .

Signature of evaluator: _____

The above categorical statement *is a requirement* of Act 102 of 1973 as amended and Public Law 94-142 if a student is to receive special education benefits.

This is *not a statement of the student's general ability* but only involves the narrow area of public education.

This statement will be used only for determination of eligibility for special education services. There will be no *further reference* to this categorical statement during the delivery of educational services.

This categorical statement will be destroyed as soon as special service delivery is terminated.

Evaluation conference decision:




Programming recommendations:




Professional(s) designated responsible: _____
_____

Signatures of attendees: _____
_____

## PARENT NOTIFICATION OF EVALUATION CONFERENCE DECISION

Date: _____

Dear _____:

An evaluation of the learning needs of your child, _____, has been conducted in order to determine whether special education services would be beneficial. The results of the evaluation were reviewed at a conference, and the following decision reached:

This was based on the following information:

The recommended services for your child include _____.
(type of placement)

The detailed information which was used to arrive at this decision is available for your inspection.

_____ has been designated as responsible for seeing that the decision reached as a result of your child's evaluation is carried out. Consent is required for initial placement of your child in a special education program.

You have the right to obtain an independent evaluation of your child. You have the right to a hearing if you disagree with this decision. We feel that the decision made represents the most appropriate educational services for your child at the present time. However, if you feel that other services may be more suitable, or if you wish to provide us with additional information about your child, please contact _____.

Sincerely,

_____
(principal's signature)

_____
(name of school)

## PLACEMENT CONSENT

Date: _____

I, as parent or guardian of _____,

(check one)
☐ Authorize
☐ Do not authorize

placement in the _____ special education program. I understand that the need for this placement will be reconsidered and reviewed in terms of my child's progress at least annually.

_____
(parent's signature)

NOTE: This form is required only at initial placement; thereafter, the parent's signature on the annual updated IEP is sufficient to meet the consent requirements.

# INDIVIDUAL EDUCATION PLAN

1. Name or ID no.: _____
2. School district: _____
3. Building: _____ Principal: _____
4. Date plan developed: _____

Description of student's participation in regular educational program (detail of student's participation in the regular educational program if any; do not include lunch and recess):

_____
_____
_____
_____

Special education services provided (state specific services and amount of time spent in each):
1. _____
2. _____
3. _____
4. _____

## Long-range goals

Description of present level of functioning: _____
_____

Objective: _____

Date initiated: _____ Date completed: _____

| List long-range goals | Dates initiated | Dates completed |
|---|---|---|
| 1. | | |
| 2. | | |
| 3. | | |

## Short-range goals

Description of present level of functioning: _____
_____

Objective: _____

Date initiated: _____ Date completed: _____

| List short-range goals | Dates initiated | Dates completed |
|---|---|---|
| 1. | | |
| 2. | | |
| 3. | | |

*Continued.*

## INDIVIDUAL EDUCATION PLAN—cont'd

### Least restrictive setting

1. Circle the placement (service setting) that is least restrictive for this child based on data obtained during his/her evaluation and on the components of this plan:
   a. Regular class—indirect services
   b. Regular class—some direct instruction
   c. Regular class—maximum 3 periods per day in Resource Room
   d. Some instruction in regular class—minimum ½ day in self-contained class
   e. No instruction in regular class—self-contained class
   f. No instruction in regular class—special day service facility
   g. Residential school facility
   h. Hospital program
   i. Homebound instruction
2. List lesser restrictive placement or programming options that the plan developers considered and the reasons why those options were rejected (see continuum):
   Option: _____ Reason: _____
   Option: _____ Reason: _____
   Option: _____ Reason: _____
3. Describe program options and nonacademic services in which the child is participating:

   _____
   _____
   _____
   _____
   _____
   _____
   _____

### Parental participation

Describe the involvement of the parents in the development of this plan: _____

_____
_____
_____

### Signatures

Agreement to and acceptance of this individual education plan is so indicated by the signature of the persons involved in the development of this plan:

| | |
|---|---|
| (principal or designee) | (evaluation personnel) |
| (special education supervisor) | (parent) |
| (teacher [regular class]) | (counselor) |
| (special education provider) | (other) |

## ANNUAL REVIEW NOTICE

ID no.: _____

PURPOSE: To inform parents that the annual review of their child's educational placement is scheduled and to invite their participation, and to serve as annual notification of the parents' right to review school records.

Date: _____

Dear parent:

It has been almost one school year since your child was placed in his/her present educational program. In order to evaluate how well suited the program is to his/her needs, we have scheduled a review.

The review will take place on _____, _____, at _____
                                    (day)          (date)         (time)
at _____. We would like to invite you to be present during this
     (place)
review. If the scheduled time is not convenient, please contact me immediately so that another time can be arranged.

The following procedures will occur:




Within ten days after the review, you and your child's school principal will receive the findings and recommendations based on the annual review.

It is your right to (1) go over all records related to the annual review; (2) go over the procedures to be used in the review; and (3) be informed of the results of the review.

Sincerely,

_____
(signature of special education administrator
or school district superintendent)

_____
(telephone number)

## ANNUAL REVIEW REPORT

Conference date: _____
Attendees: _____
_____
_____

Progress to date:




Recommendations:




Comments:




Signature of chairperson of review team: _____
Parent signature: _____
Date of parent notification (if not in attendance): _____

# Appendix C

# INSTRUCTIONAL MATERIALS FOR MILDLY HANDICAPPED ADOLESCENTS

| Material | Company |
|---|---|
| *Reading* | |
| Action reading System | Scholastic Magazines |
| Activities for Reading Improvement | Steck-Vaughn |
| Activity-Concept English (ACE) | Scott, Foresman |
| Advanced Reading Skills | Reader's Digest Association |
| Adventure Series | Benefit |
| The American People: Parts I and II | Steck-Vaughn |
| Archie Multigraph Kit | Archie Enterprises |
| Bantam Paperbacks | Bantam Books |
| Be a Better Reader | Prentice-Hall |
| Be Informed Series | New-Readers Press |
| Breakthrough Series | Allyn & Bacon |
| Building Reading Skills in the Content Areas | Educational Activities |
| Classroom Reading Clinic | McGraw-Hill |
| Clues | Educational Progress Corp. |
| Contact Series | Scholastic Book Services |
| Countries and Cultures | Science Research Associates |
| Croft Skillpacks, Level II | Croft |
| Developing Reading Efficiency | Burgess |
| Developmental Reading Text Workbooks | Bobbs-Merrill |
| Diagnostic Reading Workbooks Series | Charles E. Merrill |
| Dimensions in Reading Series: Manpower and Natural Resources | Science Research Associates |
| Directions | Houghton Mifflin |
| Dolch Folklore of the World | Garrad |
| Double Action | Scholastic Book Services |
| Effective Reading | Globe |
| Forward, Back, Around | Curriculum Associates |
| Gaining Independence in Reading | Charles E. Merrill |
| Gates-Pearson Reading Exercises | Teachers College Press |
| Gillingham Materials | Educators Publishing Service |
| Go Reading in the Content Areas | Scholastic Book Services |
| Improve Your Reading Ability | Charles E. Merrill |
| Individualized Phonics | Teachers Publishing Corp. |
| Key Ideas in English: Levels 1, 2, and 3 | Harcourt Brace Jovanovich |
| Know Your World, Newspaper | American Education Publishers |
| Language Lab | Bowmar |
| McCall-Crabbs Standard Test Lessons in Reading | Teachers College Press |
| The Mott Basic Language Skills Program | Allied Educational Council of Chicago |
| Multiple Meanings | Curriculum Associates |
| New Goals in Reading | Steck-Vaughn |
| New Practice Readers | Webster Division/McGraw-Hill |
| New Streamlined English Series | New-Readers Press |
| News for You | New-Readers Press |
| Open Highways Program | Scott, Foresman |

| Material | Company | Material | Company |
|---|---|---|---|
| *Reading —cont'd* | | Step Up Your Reading Power | Webster Division/ McGraw-Hill |
| Pal Paperback Kit | Xerox Education Publications | Study Skills for Information Retrieval: Books 1, 2, 3, and 4 | Allyn & Bacon |
| Picto-cabulary Series | Dexter and Westbrook | | |
| Precise Word | Curriculum Associates | Study Skills Library | Education Development Labs |
| Rate and Comprehension Check Tests | Kingsborough Community College | Study Type Reading Exercises | Teachers College Press |
| Read-Understand-Remember Books | Allied Educational Council | Systems for Success | Follett |
| Reader's Digest Skill Builders | Reader's Digest | Target Programs | Field Enterprises Educational Publications |
| Reading Comprehension in Varied Subject Matter | Educators Publishing Services | Teenage Tales | Heath |
| Reading for Concepts A-H | McGraw-Hill | The Think Box | Benefit Press |
| Reading Development Kit C | Addison-Wesley | Timid Readings | Jamestown Publications |
| Reading Essential Series | Steck-Vaughn | | |
| Reading Improvement Material | Reader's Digest Services | Troubleshooters, I and II | Houghton Mifflin |
| Reading Incentive Lab 20 | Bowmar | Turning Point | McCormick-Mathers |
| Reading for Meaning Series | Lippincott | Vocabulary Improvement Practice | Harcourt Brace Jovanovich |
| The Reading Practice Program | Harcourt Brace Jovanovich | West Word Bound Book | Economy Publishers |
| Reading and Reasoning: Activity Cards | Schaffer | World of Vocabulary | Globe |
| | | *Writing* | |
| The Reading Skills Lab Program | Houghton Mifflin | Activity-Concept English (ACE) | Scott, Foresman |
| Reading Spectrum | Macmillan | Be Informed Series | New-Readers Press |
| Reading Success Series | Xerox Education Publications | Composition in Action | Science Research Associates |
| | Steck-Vaughn | Contact Series | Scholastic Book Services |
| Reading, Thinking and Reasoning | | Continuous Progress in Spelling | Economy Publishers |
| Reading/Thinking Skills | Continental Press | English for Everyday | Ideal Publishers |
| Reading Thinking Skill | Teachers Publishing Corp. | Everyday Reading and Writing | New-Readers Press |
| Reading for Understanding: General Ed. | Science Research Associates | Flub Stubs (Prescriptive Task Cards to Improve Writing Skills) | Creative Teaching Press |
| Reluctant Reader Series | Scholastic Book Services | Help Yourself to Better Handwriting | Educators Publishing Services |
| Remediation Reading (RR) | Modern Curriculum Press | Language Exercise Books | Steck-Vaughn |
| | | Lessons in Paragraphing | Curriculum Associates |
| SCOPE/Skills and SCOPE/Visuals | Scholastic Book Services | The Outlining Kit | Curriculum Associates |
| SCORE | Scholastic Book Services | Story Starters | Curriculum Associates |
| | | Systems for Success | Follett |
| Skillbooster Series | Modern Curriculum Press | Thirty Lessons in Notetaking | Curriculum Associates |
| Specific Reading Skills | Jones-Kenilworth | The Write Thing: Ways to Communicate | Houghton Mifflin |
| Specific Skills Series | Barnell Loft | | |
| The Spice Series, Vols. 1 and 2 | Educational Services | Writing Aids Through the Grades | Teacher College Press |
| SRA Reading Labs | Science Research Associates | Writing with Pictures | Prentice-Hall Media |

APPENDICES **341**

| Material | Company | Material | Company |
|---|---|---|---|
| *Mathematics* | | Merrill Mathematics Skill Tapes | Charles E. Merrill |
| Activities in Mathematics | Scott, Foresman | Michigan Arithmetic Program | Ann Arbor Publishers |
| Addition and Subtraction Facts | Teachers Publishing Corp. | Money Makes Sense | Fearon Publishers |
| Aftermath Series | Creative Publications | Number Concepts | Teachers Publishing Corp. |
| Applications in Math | Scott, Foresman | | |
| Arithmetic Fact Kit | Science Research Associates | Pacemake Practical Arithmetic Series | Fearon Publishers |
| Arithmetic in My World | Allyn & Bacon | Programmed Mathematic, Series II | Webster Division/ McGraw-Hill |
| Arithmetic Workbook | Dick Blick | Scott Geoboards | Creative Publications |
| Basic Algebra | Charles E. Merrill | Self-Teaching Arithmetic Books | Science Research Associates |
| Basic Essentials of Mathematics | Steck-Vaughn | SLAM (Simple Lattice Approach to Mathematics) | Prentice-Hall |
| Basic Mathematics | Charles E. Merrill | Sports in Things: High Interest Math Series | Educational Insights Publishers |
| The Buchnell Mathematics Self-Study System I | Webster Division/ McGraw-Hill | Steps to Mathematics, Books 1 and 2 | Steck-Vaughn |
| Coins and Bills | Developmental Learning Material | Synchromath Experiences | Rand McNally |
| Computations Skills Development | Science Research Associates | Tangle Table | Creative Publications |
| Consumer Related Mathematics | Holt, Rinehart and Winston | Tangramath | Creative Publications |
| Cues and Signals in Math, I and II | Ann Arbor Publishers | The Tapestry of Mathematics | Activity Resources Publishers |
| Developing Number Experiences | Holt, Rinehart and Winston | To Buy & Sell | Developmental Learning Materials |
| E.T.A. Curriculum Enrichment Material | Education Teaching Aids | Using Dollars and Sense | Fearon Publishers |
| Figure It Out | Follett | Winning Touch | University Publishing |
| Foundation Mathematics | Webster Division/ McGraw-Hill | Your Buying Power | Richards |
| Fractions | Ann Arbor Publishers | *Career development* | |
| Fun & Games; Activity Cards | Prentice-Hall Learning Systems | Career Planning Program | Houghton Mifflin |
| Good Times Again with Math | Prentice-Hall | COATS (Comprehensive Occupational Assessment & Training System) | Prep. Inc. |
| Good Times with Math | Prentice-Hall | Curriculum Materials for Vocational-Technical-Career Education | New Jersey Vocational Technical Lab |
| I.D.E.A.S. | Charles E. Merrill | Discovery Kit | Scholastic Book Services |
| Improving Your Ability in Mathematics | Harcourt Brace Jovanovich | Educating for Success | Queens College |
| Individualized Arithmetic Instruction | Love | Getting a Job | Fearon Publishers |
| Individualized Computational Skills | Houghton Mifflin | Handbook for Vocational Programs for the Handicapped | Bureau of Vocational Education, Maine State Dept. of Education |
| Math Lab | Benefit Press | | |
| Math Mystery Theatre | Imperial International Learning | Jerry Works in a Service Station | Fearon Publishers |
| Math Study-Scope | Benefit Press | JEVS Work Samples | Jewish Employment and Vocational Service |
| Math Workshop for Children | Encyclopedia Brittannica | | |
| Mathematics One and Two: Discovery and Practice | Harcourt Brace Jovanovich | MacDonal Vocational Capacity Scale | MacDonal Training Center Fd. |

| Material | Company | Material | Company |
|---|---|---|---|
| *Career development —cont'd* | | Vocational Instructional Materials for Students with Special Needs | N.W. Regional Educational Library |
| Making It on Your Own | Mafex Associates | The World of Work | New-Readers Press |
| McCarron-Dial Work Evaluation System | Dept. of Psychology, Indiana State University | WREST (Wide-Range Employment Sample Test) | Guidance Associates of Delaware |
| Micro-Tower ICD | Rehabilitation and Research Ctr. | *Teacher overview* | |
| New Readers Press | Division of Lauback Literacy International | Academic Activities for Adolescents with Learning Disabilities | Learning Pathways |
| Out of Work | New-Readers Press | Planning Individualized Education Programs in Special Education | Handicapped Learner Materials Distribution Center, Indiana University |
| Planning Meals and Shopping | Fearon Publishers | | |
| Real People at Work | Changing Times Education Service | | |
| Singer Vocational Education System | Singer Educational Division | Reading Diagnosis Kit & Reading Correction Kit | Center for Applied Research in Education |
| Special Education Career Development | Wisconsin Dept. of Public Instruction | Special Education Teachers Kit | Love |
| Step Method | The Psychological Corp. | Successful Learning Kit | Love |
| Vocational Education Development Project | Fox Valley Special Education Instructional Materials Ctr. | A Survival Manual: Case Studies and Suggestions for the Learning Disabled Teenager | Treehouse Associates |

# INDEX

## A

AAMD; *see* American Association for Mental Deficiencies
Abuse
  of adolescents, 50
  child; *see* Child abuse
Academic excellence, attitude of adolescents toward, 57
Academic programming and adjustment training, liaison between, 127
Accommodation, 191, 234
  administrative options in, 238-242
  or compensatory model, 149-151
  and compensatory programming, 231-267
  regular class techniques, 242-243
  resource room techniques, 261-265
  teacher consultation in, 261-265
Accommodative and compensatory techniques, 238-242
Accommodatory instruction, 221
Achievement, student, 100
Activity, intellectual, 40
Adaptive Environments for Learning, 250
Addiction, drug, 138
Adjustment training and academic programming, liaison between, 127
Adjustments, postsecondary, 219
Administration
  and organization of school, 77-90
  role of special educator with, 171-173
  special educator in, 152-153
Administrative issues that concern the special educator, 87-89
Administrative options in accommodation, 238-242
Administrator(s)
  characteristics of, 84
  and teachers' attitudes toward P.L. 94-142, 86
Adolescence, 27-28
  in America since 1790, 4-6
  cognitive structures of, 30-31
  developmental tasks of, 14, 28

Adolescence—cont'd
  and Oedipal complex, 29
  special problems in, 63-66
  tasks of, 63
  theories of, 28-33
Adolescents; *see also* Students
  abuse of, 50
  alienation and crime among, 33
  anti-intellectualism among, 32
  anxieties among, 64
  with arithmetic disabilities, characteristics of, 288
  attitudes toward academic excellence, 57
  cliques among, 59
  effects of
    back-to-basics movement on, 33
    changing adult roles on, 32
    environment of, 32-33
    sexual relations on, 32
  formal groups of, 56-59
  group characteristics of, 273
  group identification among, 56
  informal groups of, 59-63
  mildly handicapped, 7-10, 25-44
  modern social context of, 31-33
  self-concept of, 63
  social stratification among, 55-56
  subculture of, 6, 30, 60
Adult roles, changing, effects on adolescents, 32
Advance organizer model, 236, 245
Advocacy, 157-159
Affective first aid, 46, 128
Age or grade level grouping, 195
Agreements, written, in school organization, 81
Aides; *see* Paraprofessionals
Alcoholism, 67
  parental, 49-50
Algorithm, translation of word problem to, 292
Alienation and crime among adolescents, 33
Alternative learning models, 254

**343**

Alternative learning models—cont'd
  in regular classroom, 234-236
Alternative methods, 253
Alternative responding, 247
Alternative/modified curricula, 241-242
American Association of Mental Deficiency, 36, 116, 163
American Speech and Hearing Association, 132
  standards for school nurse, 134
Analysis
  cost, 206
  structural, 274
Anthropological view of student behavior, 70-71
Anti-intellectualism among adolescents, 32
Anxieties among adolescents, 64
Aptitude tests, 309-310
Arithmetic
  competencies, erecting, 288-291
  defined, 288
  disabilities, adolescents with, characteristics of, 288
  disorders, assessment of, 291-293
  failure, causes of, 287-288
  and mathematics, 287-292
ASHA; *see* American Speech and Hearing Association
Assessment, 112-121, 122, 321-324
  of arithmetic disorders, 291-293
  educational, 159-160
  environmental, and change, 127
  in expanded programming for mildly handicapped students, 132-134
  informal, 291-292
  of interests, 309
  objectives of content courses, 253
  of reading, 280-284
  role of nurse in, 135
Assigned period, 196
Assistant principals, characteristics of, 84
Association, symbolic, 291-292
Attendance, 105
  compulsory, laws for, 4, 5
  to lectures, 103
  at vocational technical and two-year colleges, 316-317
Attitudes
  faculty, 22
  parental, 52-55
  student, 20-21, 219
  of teachers, 102
  and temperament, 161-162
Audiologists, 132
Audiovisual aids, 246
Auditory discrimination, 271
Awareness of others, 132

## B

Back-to-basics movement, 106
  effects on adolescents, 33
Bargaining rights, teachers', as formal power, 85
Basic courses, 92-93
Basic curriculum, 7
Basic skills, 10-11
  remediation of, 251
Basics, back-to-, movement, 106
Battering, 50
BD; *see* Behaviorally disordered
BEH; *see* Bureau of Education for the Handicapped
Behavior
  conforming, of groups, 60
  dating and sexual, 60-61
  and interaction, student, 101
  management, 160, 225
  modeling, of teachers, 61
  modification, 123-124
  of regular teachers, 100-101
  ritual, of groups, 60
  student, 215-216, 248
    anthropological view of, 70-71
  of teachers, verbal, 248
  thinking, 40-42
  verbal, of teachers, 100-101
Behavioral characteristics of mildly handicapped, 39
Behavioral standards, 248
Behaviorally disordered, 38
Behavioral-personal-social dimension, 18-19
Benefits, cost, 206-207
Biological Sciences Curriculum Study, 95, 234, 235
Bivalent system, programming with, 251-253
Bloom's taxonomy, 40-41, 93, 253
Books, talking, 247
BSCS; *see* Biological Sciences Curriculum Study
Buckley Amendment, 83, 88
Budget
  apportionment of, 205
  constraints, 200-202
Bureau of Education for the Handicapped, 82
Bureaucratic and institutional inflexibility, 21-22

## C

CAI; *see* Computer-assisted instruction
Cannabis, 69
  defined, 68
Cardinal Principles of Education, Seven, 1
Cardinality, 291
CARE; *see* Computer Assisted Remedial Education
Career
  in counterculture, 318
  and vocational information, 308-311
Career education, 127, 307, 311

Career education—cont'd
  and survival skills, 233-234
Career preparation, 307-314
CASES; see Coping Analysis Schedule for Educational Settings
Categorical approach, 210, 232
CEC; see Council for Exceptional Children
Cells of Guilford model, 40
Change, environmental assessment and, 127
Child abuse, 50
Child Service Demonstration Centers, 115
Child-parent relations, 46-49
Child-rearing patterns, 47
Children, effects of divorce on, 50-51
Chlordiazepoxide, 135
Chronological age, student placement by, 235
Classroom
  culture of, 32
  engineered, 210
  interaction in, 248
  mainstream, 243
    individualization in, 249-261
  management strategies in, 225-230
  regular
    alternative learning models in, 234-236
    curriculum of, 262-263
    and resource room, instructional interface between, 99-100
    role of special educator in, 164-165
    teachers; see Teachers, regular
  rules, 248
  self-contained, 210-211
  systems used in, 226-230
  teachers, regular; see Teachers, regular
  techniques and accommodation, 242-243
Clinicians, speech and hearing, 132-134
Cliques among adolescents, 59
Clustered courses, 240
CMI; see Computer-managed instruction
Code emphasis, 272, 273
Codes, dress, 87
Cognition, 13; see also Cognitive development
Cognitive development, 13, 14-15, 26
Cognitive domain, 93, 253
Cognitive processes, 101
Cognitive structures of adolescence, 30-31
Colleges
  programs of, 317
  two-year and vocational technical, 316-317
Commission on the Reorganization of Secondary Education, 1
Communications, 219-225
  between special educators and mainstream teachers, 164

Communications—cont'd
  with paraprofessionals, 182-183
  parental, 176-180, 221
  in school organization, 80
  of special educator with regular teacher, 186
  written, 176
Community, special educator's relationships in, 189
Compensatory models, 8, 26, 149-151
  and accommodative techniques, 238-242
Compensatory programming and accommodation, 231-267
Competencies
  erecting arithmetic, 288-291
  grade-level, 289-291
Competency examinations, 106-107
  minimum, 242
Competency-based programs, 210
Comprehension, 275
Comprehensive language arts continuum, 295-298
Comprehensive programming, 195, 198-203
Compressed material, 246
Compulsory attendance laws, 4, 5
Computational functions, incomplete, 292
Computational skills, 288, 292-293
Computer Assisted Remedial Education, 224
Computer-assisted instruction, 224
Computer-managed instruction, 224
Computers, 224-225
Concepts
  in remediation, 272
  summaries of, 246
Conceptualization of multiplication and division, 292
Conferences, parent, 124-125, 173-176
Conflict in the family, 49-52
Conforming behavior of groups, 60
Confusion
  of null sets or zero, 292
  symbolic, 292
Congress, U.S., and school organization, 79
Constitution, U.S., and school organization, 78
Consultation
  model, 148
  as role of counselor, 121
  teacher, 153-156
  with teachers, management, 125, 127
Content courses, objectives of, 253
Contextual areas, reading in, 275
Contextual clues, 275
Contract bins, 228
Contracting, 226-229
Contracts
  continuing, 89
  learning, 244
  teachers', 89

Contracts—cont'd
    tenure, 89
    term, 89
Conversations, telephone, 180
Coordination, 19-20
    of program, 193-230
*Coping Analysis Schedule for Educational Settings*, 115, 249
Corporal punishment, 88
Cost, 205
    analysis, 206
    benefits, 206-207
    efficiency, 206
Council for Exceptional Children, 138, 163, 303-304, 307
Counseling, 160
    data collection in, 130-131
    individual and group, 130
    model, extended, 121, 122, 160
    parent, 124-125
Counselors, 183-185
    school guidance; *see* School guidance counselors
    vocational rehabilitation, special educator as, 189
Counterculture, 66-70
    as "career" opportunity, 318
Courses
    clustered, 240
    content, objectives of, 253
    credit for, and graduation policies, exceptions to, 240
    equilibrium of, 240
    requirements for, 103-104
    substitution, 240-241
    supplantation, 196, 241
    work in, 162-163
Criteria
    for determination of learning disabilities, 119
    evaluation, 203
Criterion-referenced measures of progress, 160
Criterion-referenced review of reading skills, 274
Criterion-referenced tests, 282
Critical reading skills, 285
Criticism of schools, 4
Cross-cultural theories of adolescence, 29
CRT; *see* Criterion-referenced tests
Culture, classroom, 32
Curricular patterns, 92-93
Curricular planning, 26-27
Curricular variations, 239-242
Curriculum, 235, 236-237
    alternative/modified, 241-242
    basic, 7
    considerations in special education models, 26
    development of, 160
    general, 7

Curriculum—cont'd
    and instruction in the secondary school, 91-108
    liberal arts, 1, 5
        reinforcement of, by law, 6
    parallel, 233
    of regular class, 262-263
    of secondary school, 92-93
    special, 11
    unitary, 15
Curve, 104-105

**D**

Daily lesson planning, 197-216
Daily problems in homework, 104
Darwin, evolutionary theory of, applied to adolescence, 28-29
Data collection in counseling, 130-131
Dating and sexual behavior, 60-61
Decision-making model, 130
Decision-making practice groups, 130-131
Delinquency, 66-67
    and learning disabilities, 139
DEM; *see* Discrepancy Evaluation Model
Deno's model, 16
Depression and suicide, 64-65
Development
    cognitive, 13
    curriculum, 160
    and functioning of program, variables in, 20-22
    interpersonal, 13
    personal, 12
    personnel, 238-239
    program, 42-43
Developmental tasks, 12-13
    of adolescence, 14, 28
    Havighurst's, 31
Deviancy as label, 52-53
Dexedrine; *see* Dextroamphetamines
Dextroamphetamines, 135
Diagnosis, educational, 159-160
Diagnostic and individual measurement of students, 159-160
Diagnostic tests, 291
    reading, 282
Diazepam, 135
Differences, individual, 31
Difficulty level, 204
Direct pupil services, 148-152, 161
Disabilities, learning, 7, 33-36
Disabled readers, characteristics of, 269-272
Discipline, 87-88
Discrepancy Evaluation Model, 218-219
Discrepancy, significant, defined, 114-115
Discrimination, auditory and visual, 271

Dismissal of teachers, 89
Dispositional placement, 16
Distractibility of low-achieving students, 271
Disturbance, emotional, 7, 38-43
Division and multiplication, conceptualization of, 292
Divorce, effects on children, 50-51
Dress codes, 87
Dress styles of groups, 59-60
Dropping out of school, 65
Drug abuse, 67-69
Drug addiction, 138
Drug overdose, 68
Drug therapy, 135, 138
Due process, 88, 218
Durability, 205
*Durrell Analysis of Reading Difficulty*, 282
Dynamic program, 19

### E

ECM; *see* Extended counseling model
Ecological variable, 237
Economics, token, 226
ED; *see* Emotional disturbance
Educable mentally retarded, 7, 36-38; *see also* Adolescents, mildly handicapped
   in self-contained classes, 210
Education; *see also* Schools
   career, 127
     and survival skills, 233-234
   purpose of, 1
   secondary
     goals of, 1
     overview of issues in, 3-24
     Seven Cardinal Principals of, 1
     special; *see* Special education
   vocational; *see* Vocational education
Education Commission of the States, 93
The Education for All Handicapped Children Act, 7, 9
Education for the Handicapped, Bureau of, 82
Educational agency, local, 81
The Educational Amendments of 1976, 9-10
Educational assessment, 159-160
Educational diagnosis, 159-160
Educational functioning, level of, 17-18
Educational models, 8-9, 12-15
Educational or psychological examiners, 185
Educational plan, individualized; *see* Individualized educational plan
Educational tracks of secondary school, 7
Educational unit, intermediate, 81
Efficiency, cost, 206
The Elementary and Secondary Education Act, 82, 85
Emancipation process and family conflict, 54-55

Emotional disturbance, 7, 38-43; *see also* Adolescents, mildly handicapped
   assessment issues in, 116-118
   in engineered classrooms, 210-211
   in self-contained classes, 210
Empathy of learning disabled students, 132
Employment in work force, 315-316
EMR; *see* Educable mentally retarded
Engineered classroom, 210
English, 95-96
Enlistment, military, 318
Enrollment procedures, 239
Environment, effects on adolescents, 32-33
Environmental assessment and change, 127
Environmental factors, 247
Equilibrium, course, 240
Equipment, 206-207
Erikson, neopsychoanalytic theories of, applied to adolescence, 29, 31
Evaluation, 128
   criteria for, 203
   program, 218
   of pupils, standardized, 159
   of subject matter, 253
   teacher-made, 160
   team for learning disabilities, 119
   work, through simulation, 310
Evolutionary theory of adolescence, 28-29
Examinations, competency, 106-107
Exceptions to course credit and graduation policies, 240
Existing materials, 200
Expansion level, 297-298
Experience, work, 312
Expressive skills, 293-294
Expulsion and suspension, 88
Extended counseling model, 121, 122, 125, 127, 128, 160, 183
Extracurricular activities, 105-106
Extra-time arrangement, 196

### F

Facilitator, special educator as, 188-189
Faculty attitudes, 22
Faculty communications, 219-221
Family
   conflict in, 49-52
   influences, 46-55
   nuclear, 46
   socialization through, 47
Family Education and Privacy Act, 142
Family Educational Rights and Privacy Act of 1974, 88
Fear of school, 63-64
Federal legislation, 82-84
   and state requirements, 218

Feedback to students, grades as, 218
Feedback training, 130
Fernald technique, 276
Field theory of adolescence, 29
Field trips and liability, 89
Fifth- and sixth-grade skills, 290-291
First aid
　affective, 46, 128
　and liability, 89
Flexible time, 210
Floor plans of resource room, 208, 209
Formal groups of adolescents, 56-59
Formal operational thought, 30-31, 39
Formal power, 84-85
Fourth-grade skills, 290
*Free and Inexpensive Learning Materials*, 200
Freud, Anna, 29
Freud, Sigmund, psychoanalytic theories of, applied to adolescence, 29
Frustration, tolerance for, 160-161
Functioning, educational, level of, 17-18

## G

Gagne's taxonomy, 255
GATB; *see General Aptitude Test Battery*
Gathering places of students, 60
Gaussian curve, 104-105
*Geist Picture Interest Inventory*, 309
*General Aptitude Test Battery*, 309
General curriculum, 7, 92
Gillingham approach, 276-277
Glossaries/technical vocabularies, 244-245
Goal statement/strategy planning, 127-128
Goals, 12-13
　of program, 203, 219
　of vocational training, 308
　of written expression, 293-295
GPA; *see* Grade point average
Grade or age level grouping, 195
Grade point average, 104, 106
　special education and, 167
Grade-level competencies, 289-291
Grading systems, 104-105
　for learning disabled or behaviorally disordered students, 217-218
Graduation
　extended, for learning disabled students, 242
　policies and course credit, exceptions to, 240
　requirements for, 106-107
Graphemes, 272
Grouping, sets, 292
Groups
　behavior of, characteristics of, 59-60
　counseling for, 130

Groups—cont'd
　dress styles of, 59-60
　evaluation sessions for, 128
　and identification among adolescents, 56
　practice, decision-making, 130-131
　presentations of, general guidelines for, 156-157
　ritual behaviors of, 60
Guidance counselor, school; *see* School guidance counselors
Guilford model, cells of, 40

## H

Hallucinogens, defined, 68
Handicapped
　flow of information to, 236
　legal bases for education, 9-10
　mildly, 7-10, 25-44
　　expanded programming for, assessment in, 133-134
　　expanded role of nurse in programming for, 135
　　prevalance of, 8
　　programming for, 122-132
　　services for, 122-132
　objectives for planning vocational education of, 303-304
　planning vocational program for, 304-307
Handwriting, 294
Havighurst, socialization theory of, applied to adolescence, 29-30
Hearing and speech clinicians, 132-134
Hegge-Kirk-Kirk remedial reading drills, 277
HELPS, 224
Homework, 104
Human services, 142

## I

IEP; *see* Individualized educational plan
IEU; *see* Intermediate educational unit
IGE; *see* Individually Guided Education
In loco parentis, 88
Independence, level of, 204-205
Independent level, 298-299
Individual and diagnostic measurement of students, 159-160
Individual and group counseling, 130
Individual differences, 31
Individual instruction, 195, 197-198, 228
Individual variable, 237
Individualization
　effect on schools, 4-5
　in mainstream class, 249-261
Individualized educational plan, 9, 15, 17, 83, 96, 149, 151-152, 185, 206, 208, 211, 214, 217, 218, 219, 224, 249, 251, 305, 308
　total service plan, 324

# INDEX

Individualized instruction, 195, 197-198, 228, 249
   development of, 260-261
Individualized instructional planning, model for, 15-23
Individualized written rehabilitation program, 308, 314
Individually Guided Education, 250
Inflexibility, institutional and bureaucratic, 21-22
Informal groups of adolescents, 59-63
Informal power in secondary school, 85-86
Informal reading inventory, 282
Information processing and information flow, 236-238
In-house sources of materials, 200
Input organization, 98
In-service programs, 188
Institutional and bureaucratic inflexibility, 21-22
Instruction
   accommodatory, 221
   and curriculum in the secondary school, 91-108
   individual, 195, 197-198, 228
      development of, 260-261
   individualized, 195, 197-198, 228, 249
   shared, 196
Instructional approaches, 293
Instructional interface between resource room and regular class, 99-100
Instructional materials, 339-342
Instructional planning, individualized, model for, 15-23
Instructional procedures, 17
Instructional techniques for mainstreaming, 97-98
Intellectual activity, 40
Intelligence, 40
   quotient, 36, 37, 115-116
Interaction
   and behavior, student, 101
   classroom, 248
   models of, 235
   peer, 249
   and role relationships of special education, 170-190
   student, 249
   student-teacher, 248-249
Interactional model, 195, 196-197
Interactional program, 258
Interactional-learning model, 256-259
Interest, assessment of, 309
Interface, instructional, between resource room and regular class, 99-100
Intermediate educational unit, 81
International Reading Association, 163
Interpersonal development, 13, 26
Interpersonal relationships, 14, 45-73
Interpretation, 172
IQ score, 36, 37, 115-116
IRA; see International Reading Association
IRI; see Informal reading inventory

Itinerant model, 148
IWRP; see Individualized written rehabilitation program

## J
Job clusters, 310-311
Judicial services/law enforcement, 139-142
Junior high school, 210
   replacement of, by middle school, 92

## K
*KeyMath Diagnostic Arithmetic Test*, 291
Knowledge, acquisition of, 93, 236-237
*Kuder General Interest Survey*, 309

## L
Labeling and parental attitudes, 52-54
Language arts, 95-96
   continuum, comprehensive, 295-298
Language disabilities, written, 293-298
Law enforcement/judicial services, 139-142
Laws
   compulsory attendance, 4, 5
   reinforcement of liberal arts curriculum by, 6
LD; see Learning diabilities; Learning disabled
LEA; see Local educational agency
Learner, 1-74
   characteristics/needs, 261-262
Learning
   machine for, programmable, 247
   mastery, 260-261
   models for, alternative, in regular class, 234-236
   strategies for, 272
   units, alternative, 254
   verbal, 98-99
Learning contract, 244
Learning disabilities, 33-36
   additional assessment procedures in, 118-120
   assessment issues in, 112-115
   and delinquency, 139
Learning disabled, 7, 211, 237; see also Adolescents, mildly handicapped
   or behaviorally disordered
      grade or age level grouping for, 195
      grading for, 217-218
   in college, 317
   compensatory models for, 232
   empathy for others, 132
   extended graduation for, 242
   and family relations, 48
   programs for, secondary, 232-234
   reduced load for, 242
   in self-contained classes, 210
   transition points for, 293

Lectures, 256-258
  attending to, 103
  modified, 259-260
Legal bases for educating mildly handicapped, 9-10
Legislation
  for educating mildly handicapped, 9-10
  federal, 82-84
Lesson planning, daily, 197-216
Letter grading system, 104
Liability, tort, 88-89
Liberal arts curriculum, 1, 5, 92
  reinforcement by law, 6
Librium; *see* Chlordiazepoxide
Life space, 29
Lighting of resource room, 208
Listening
  to lectures, 103
  as parental attention, 49
Load, reduced, for learning disabled students, 242
Local educational agency, 81, 83
Location of resource room, 208
Lockers and students, searching, 88

# M

Mainstream classes, 243
  individualization in, 249-261
  support of students in, 253-254
  teachers of, and specialist, 244, 250
Mainstreaming, 11-12
  instructional techniques for, 97-98
  and special education, interdependence of, 110
  and special educator, 96-99
  support for, 186
Management
  behavior, 225
  consulting with teachers, 125, 127
  personnel, special education, qualifications of, 82
  strategies for, classroom, 225-230
Management systems/information, 123-124
Marijuana, 69, 140
Mastery learning, 260-261
Mastery level, initial, 295-297
Materials, 199
  compressed, 246
  existing, 200
  instructional, 339
  money spent on, 200-202
  for parent conferences, 175
  priorities in selection of, 203
Mathematics, 95
  and arithmetic, 287-292
  defined, 288
  and reading remediation, 165-167

Mead, Margaret, cross-cultural theory of, applied to adolescence, 29
Meaning emphasis, 273
Mechanical reading skills, 285
Medication of students, 135, 138
Mellaril; *see* Thioridazine
Memory, 98, 271
Mental retardation
  assessment issues in, 115-116
  educable, 36-38
Mentally retarded, educable, 7
Methylphenidate hydrochloride, 135
Middle school to replace junior high school, 92
Milieu, 247-250
Military enlistment, 318
Minimum competency test, 242
"Missionary complex" in school organization, 80-81
Modeling behaviors of teachers, 61
Modeling in verbal learning, 99
Models
  advance organizer, 236
  alternative learning, in regular class, 234-236
  compensatory, 8, 26
    or accommodation, 149-151
    for learning disabled students, 232
  consulting, 148
  decision-making, 130
  defined, 15
  Deno's, 16
  educational, 12-15
    for special education at secondary level, 8-9
  extended counseling, 121, 122, 160
  Guilford, cells of, 40
  for individualized instructional planning, 15-23
  interactional, 195, 196-197, 235
  interactional-learning, 256-259
  itinerant, 148
  program, installation of, 19-23
  remedial, 8-9, 26, 151-152
  resource room, 9, 148
  special education, curriculum considerations in, 26
  vocational, 9, 26, 152
Money spent on materials, 200-202
Monitoring
  and record keeping, 216-224
  as function of computers, 224
Multiplication and division, conceptualization of, 292

# N

NAEP; *see* National Assessment of Educational Progress
NARC; *see* National Association for Retarded Citizens
Narcotics, defined, 68
NATB; *see* Nonreading Aptitude Test Battery
National Assessment of Educational Progress, 93, 94, 95

National Association for Retarded Citizens, 163
National Council of Teachers of Mathematics, 289
Needs, special, 9-10
Negligence, 88-89
Neurometrics to assess learning disabilities, 113
Noncategorical classification, 116
  problems of, 42
Noneducational therapies, 11
Nonreaders, 273
*Nonreading Aptitude Test Battery*, 309-310
Norm, work, 102
Normal curve, 104-105
Note-taking, 103-104
Nuclear family, 46
Null sets or zero, confusion of, 292
Nurse, school; *see* School nurse

## O

Objectives
  of content courses, assessing, 253
  for planning vocational education of handicapped students, 303-304
Observation in assessment of learning disabilities, 115, 119
Oedipal complex and adolescence, 29
Off-campus training, 312
Office of Education, 118
Omega list, 248
Operational approach to learning disabilities, 34-35
Operational thought, formal, 30-31
Operations of intellectual activity, 40
Oral reading, 277-278
Ordinality, 291
Organization(s)
  and administration of school, 77-90
  of input, 98
  parent, 180
  professional, 163-164
  and scheduling, 195-197
  of school, 78-84
  and unions, teachers', influence of, 102-103
Organizational patterns of special education, 81
Organizational skills, teacher, 214-215
Organizational structure, external, 82
Orton Society, 163
Others
  awareness of, 132
  learning disabled students' empathy for, 132
Outcomes, student, 205-207, 219
Outline, topical, 244
Outside sources of materials, 200
Overdose, drug, 68

## P

Parallel curriculum, 233
Paraprofessionals, 207, 208
  communication with, 182-183
  selection of, 180-181
  special educator's relationships with, 180-183
  supervision and utilization of, 182-183
  training of, 181-182
Parent Effectiveness Training, 123
Parent-child relations, 46-49
Parenting systems/information, 123
Parents
  alcoholism of, 49-50
  attention of, listening as, 49
  attitudes of, 52-55
  communication, 176-180
  conferences, 124-125, 173-176
  counseling, 124-125
  organizations, 180
  role of, 218
  role of special educator to, 173-180
  and student rights as formal power, 85
  support of, 176
  values of, 49
Participation in extracurricular activities, 106
Patterns, curricular, 92-93
Peer culture, 32
  influences of, 55-63
Peer interaction, 249
Peer tutors, 183
Perceptual training, 233
Personal development, 12, 13, 14, 26
Personality variables and the special educator, 160-162
Personal-social-behavioral dimension, 18-19
Personnel
  development of, 238-239
  supervisory, in special education, 81-82
  support, 121-142
    special educator's role to, 183-188
PET; *see* Parent Effectiveness Training
Phobia, defined, 63
Phonetics, 274
Phonics, 274
Physical policy, 218
Piaget, cognitive theory of, 39, 40
  applied to adolescents, 30-31
  applied to educable mentally retarded, 37
Pictorial tests, 309
P.L. 89-10, 82
P.L. 93-112, 10
P.L. 94-142, 7, 9, 11, 33, 82, 83, 85, 92, 118, 186, 305
  attitudes of administrators and teachers toward, 86
  compliance with, 325-338
P.L. 94-483, 9-10, 305

## 352 INDEX

Place values, 292
Placement, 17, 218
  by chronological age, 235
  dispositional, 16
PLAN; See Program for Learning in Accordance with Needs
Planning
  advance, for parent conferences, 174-175
  concepts in remediation, 272
  curricular, 26-27
  daily lesson, 197-216
  individualized instructional, model for, 15-23
  vocational, 127
    for handicapped, 304-307
Policies
  physical, 218
  school, 218-219
Population, target, 203-204
Postsecondary adjustments, 219
Postsecondary training, 314-318
Power
  formal, in secondary schools, 84-85
  informal, in secondary schools, 85-86
  and pressure groups, 86-87
  structure of secondary school, 84-87
Practical reading, 284
Practice groups, decision-making, 130-131
Pressure groups and power, 86-87
Prevocational training, 311
  for educable mentally retarded students, 152
Primary skills, 286, 287
Principals, 86, 87
  characteristics of, 84
  as formal power, 85
  role of
    in determination of role of school counselor, 121
    in school organization, 80
Principles of Education, Seven Cardinal, 1
Priorities in selection of materials, 203
Problems in resource rooms, 216
Procedures
  general, in assessment, 118
  instructional, 17
Process, 203-216
Process disorders, 113, 120
Process training, 272
Products
  of intellectual activity, 40
  primary skills for, 286, 287
Professional growth and training of special educator, 162-164
Professional organizations, 163-164
Professional schools, 5
Program for Learning in Accordance with Needs, 250

Programmable learning machine, 247
Programmatic approach to major developmental tasks of adolescence, 14, 15
Programming, 218
  academic, and adjustment training, liaison between, 127
  with bivalent system, 251-253
  compensatory, and accommodation, 231-267
  comprehensive, 195, 198-203
  for mildly handicapped students, 122-132, 135
    assessment in, 133-134
  remedial, 268-300
  vocational, 301-320
Programs
  coordination of, 193-230
  development of, 42-43
    and functioning of, variables in, 20-22
  dynamic, 19
  evaluation of, 218
  goals of, 203, 219
  in-service, 186
  model of, installation of, 19-23
  prevocational, for educable mentally retarded students, 152
  rationale for, 203
  relationship of student outcomes to, 205-206
  for secondary level, 191-320
  static, 19
Progress, student, 242
  criterion-referenced measures of, 160
  monitoring, 164
Propositional thought, 40
Protocol in school organization, 80
Psychoanalytic theories of adolescence, 29
Psychological or educational examiners, 185
Psychological process theory of learning disabilities, 112-113
Public relations, 156-157
Punishment, corporal, 88
Pupils; see Students
Push-out, defined, 65

## Q

Qualifications of special education management personnel, 82

## R

Rapport, establishing, 186
Rationale of program, 203
Readers, disabled, characteristics of, 269-272
Readiness level, 295-296
Reading, 96
  assessment of, 112, 280-284
  assignments in homework, 104

Reading—cont'd
  as basic skill, 10-11
  in contextual areas, 275
  and mathematics remediation, 165-167
  practical, 284
  remedial, 269-284
  skills of, 97
    critical, 285
    mechanical, 285
    review of, 282-284
*Reading Free Vocational Interest Inventory*, 309
Recognition, word, 274
Record keeping and monitoring, 216-224
Records, students', 88
Reduced load, 196
Regrouping, 292
Regular teachers; *see* Teachers, regular
Regulations, 87, 172
Rehabilitation Act of 1973, 305
The Rehabilitation Amendments of 1973, 10, 240
Rehabilitation, vocational, 314
Reinforcement area, 227
Reinforcers, 225-226
Related services, 17
Relationships, interpersonal, 14, 45-73
Release time, 196
Remedial area grouping, 195
Remedial models, 8-9, 26, 151-152
Remedial programming, 268-300
Remedial reading, 269-284
Remedial resource rooms
  grades in, 217
  teachers in, 211
Remedial techniques, special, 275-276
Remediation, 97, 233, 243
  of basic skills, 251
  intensive, as major program thrust, 278-280
  planning concepts in, 272
  in reading and mathematics, 165-167
Reorganization of Secondary Education, Commission on the, 1
Report, written, in assessment of learning disabilities, 119
Requirements
  course, 103-104
  graduation, 106-107
  state and federal, 218
Research, reading, 271, 279
Resource room, 20, 195, 211-214, 244, 250, 273
  assistance in, 251
  floor plans of, 208, 209
  grades in, 217
  lighting of, 208
  location of, 208

Resource room—cont'd
  model for, 9, 148
  problems in, 216
  and regular class, instructional interface between, 99-100
  remedial reading in, 269-284
  remediation in, 272
  scheduling of, 196, 208-210
  space in, 207-208
  teachers in, 250
    assessment of reading by, 280
    remedial, 211
    role in vocational and career information, 308-309
    role in vocational education, 313-314
  techniques and accommodation in, 261-265
  ventilation of, 208
Resource-consultant, 189
Resources, 199-200
  use of, 218-219
Responding, alternative, 247
Retarded, educable mentally, 7, 36-38
Reversibility, 292
Rights
  parental and student, as formal power, 85
  teachers' bargaining, as formal power, 85
Ritalin; *see* Methylphenidate hydrochloride
Ritual behaviors of groups, 60
Role relationships and interactions of special educator, 170-190
Roles, specified, 218
Rules, classroom, 248
Running away, 70

## S

Santa Monica Project, 211
Scheduling, 196
  and organization, 195-197
  of resource room, 208-210
Schools, 75-144; *see also* Education
  criticism of, 4
  dropping out of, 65
  fear of, 63-64
  guidance counselors, 121-132, 239
  high, 210
  junior high, 210
  nurse, 134-135, 138, 185
  phobia, 63
    treatment for, 63-64
  policies, 218-219
  professional, 5
  purpose of, 1
  secondary
    curriculum of, 92-93
    educational tracks of, 7

Schools—cont'd
  secondary—cont'd
    informal power in, 85-86
    instruction in, 91-108
    learning disabilities programs in, 232-234
    power structure of, 84-87
    program for, 191-320
  vocational-technical, 312
Science, 94-95
Scores
  IQ, 115-116
  test, 105
  Z, 104-105
SEA; see State education agency
Searching students and lockers, 88
Secondary education; see Education, secondary
Secondary schools; see Schools, secondary
Sedative-hypnotics, defined, 68
SEIMC/RMC; see Special Education Instructional Materials Centers and Regional Materials Centers
Self, development of, 47
Self-awareness, 131-132
Self-concept of adolescent, 63
Self-contained classes, 210-211
  special education programs for educable mentally retarded, grades in, 217
Self-control, 132
Sensoriphysical dimension, 19
Services
  for mildly handicapped, 122-132
  provided by school nurse, 135, 138
  related, 17
  support, 109-144
Sets, dissociation and grouping of, 292
Seven Cardinal Principles of Education, 1
Sexual and dating behavior, 60-61
Sexual drives and adolescence, 29
Sexual relations, effects on adolescents, 32
Shared instruction, 196
Sharing materials, 164
Sheltered workshop, 188
Shoplifting, 66
Significant discrepancy, 120
  defined, 114-115
Silent reading, 277-278
Simulation, work evaluation through, 310
Skills
  basic, remediation of, 251
  study, 127
Skills training, social, 131
Social context of adolescent, modern, 31-33
Social skills training, 131
Social stratification among adolescents, 55-56
Social studies, 93-94

Social training, 63
Social-behavioral-personal dimension, 18-19
Sociality, defined, 47
Socialization
  and extracurricular activities, 105
  theories of adolescence, 29-30, 31
  through family, 47
Solvents, defined, 68
Space in resource room, 207-208
Special assignments in homework, 104
Special curricula, 11
Special education
  career education in, 307
  educational models for, at secondary level, 8-9
  issues in, 10-12
  and mainstreaming, interdependence of, 110
  management personnel in, qualifications of, 82
  models, curriculum considerations in, 26
  organizational patterns of, 81
  overview of issues in, 3-24
  program(s), 303
    for educable mentally retarded, self-contained, grades in, 217
    problems of, 22-23
    students in, 167-168
    study skills and, 285
  supervisory personnel in, 81-82, 194
Special Education Instructional Materials Centers and Regional Materials Centers, 200-202
Special educators, 145-190
  administrative issues that concern, 87-89
  and formal groups, 57-59
  and mainstreaming, 96-99
  roles of, 139-142, 147-169, 183-188
  in vocational education, 310
Special needs, 9-10
Special problems in adolescence, 63-66
Special remedial techniques, 275-276
Special texts, 246
Specialist and mainstream teachers, 244
Speech and hearing clinicians, 132-134
Speech therapist, 185
SPSS; see Statistical Package for Social Sciences
SQ3R method of study, 285
Standardized evaluation of pupils, 159
Standards
  ASHA
    for school nurse, 134
    for speech and hearing clinicians, 132
  behavioral, 248
State and federal requirements, 218
State education agency, 83
State University College at Buffalo system, 224
Static program, 19

Statistical Package for Social Sciences, 224
Statistics in assessment of reading, 282
Stealing, 65-66
Stimulant, defined, 68
Storm and stress, 29
Strategies, 203-205, 214
    classroom management, 225-230
    learning, 272
Stress, storm and, 29
*Strong Vocational Interest Test*, 309
Structural analysis, 274
Students; *see also* Adolescents
    achievement of, 100
    attitudes of, 20-21, 219
    with basic skill development, 274
    behaviors of, 215-216
        anthropological view of, 70-71
        and interaction, 101
    gathering places of, 60
    "good," definition of, 247-248
    grades as feedback to, 218
    individual and diagnostic measurement of, 159-160
    interaction among, 249
    learning disabled, 237
        in college, 317
        compensatory models for, 232
        extended graduation for, 242
        reduced load for, 242
        transition points for, 293
    lockers, searching, 88
    low-achieving, distractibility of, 271
    in mainstream, support of, 253-254
    with marginal skill, 274-275
    medication of, 135, 138
    mildly handicapped
        assessment in, expanded programming for, 133-134
        expanded role of nurse in programming for, 135
        programming for, 122-132
    monitoring progress of, 164
    number of, 205
    outcomes, 205-206, 219
    and parental rights as formal power, 85
    placement of, by chronological age, 235
    progress of, 242
    records of, 88
    services for, direct, 148-152, 161
    in special education program, 167-168
    standardized evaluation of, 159
    tracking of, 216-217
Student-teacher interaction, 248-249
Study assignments, primary skills for, 286, 287
Study guides, 244
Study hall time, 196
Study of teaching, 100
Study skills, 127, 275, 284-287
Subculture, adolescent, 6, 30
Subject areas, 93-96
    grouping of, 195
Subject matter, 93
    influences of, 101-102
    synthesis or evaluation of, 253
Subject-centered curriculum, 92
Substitution of courses, 240-241
Subtraction, 292
Suicide and depression, 64-65
Supervision and utilization of paraprofessionals, 182-183
Supervisory personnel in special education, 81-82, 172-173, 194
Supplantation, course, 241
Support personnel, 121-142
    special educator's role to, 183-188
Support services, 109-144
Survival skills and career education, 233-234
Suspension and expulsion, 88
Symbolic association, 291-292
Symbolic confusion, 292
Synthesis of subject matter, 253
Systems for classrooms, 226-230

## T

Talking books, 247
Tape recorders, 246
Taped lessons, 215
Target population, 203-204
Tasks, developmental, 12-13
    of adolescence, 14, 28, 63
    for paraprofessionals, 182
Taxonomy
    Bloom's, 40-41, 93, 253
    Gagne's, 255
Teacher(s)
    and administrators' attitudes toward P.L. 94-142, 86
    attitudes of, 101
    bargaining rights of, as formal power, 85
    -consultant role, initiation of, 155-156
    consultation, 153-156
        in accommodation, 261-265
    contracts of, 89
    -controlled variables, 243-249
        milieu as, 247-250
    dismissal of, 89
    -made evaluations, 160
    mainstream, 250
        and specialist, 244
    management consulting with, 125, 127
    modeling behaviors of, 61
    organizational skills of, 214-215

Teacher(s)—cont'd
  organizations and unions of, influence of, 102-103
  regular, 99-103, 221, 263-265
    special educator's role to, 185-188
  regular and special education
    communication between, 164, 186
    sharing materials, 164
  resource room, 250
    assessment of reading by, 280
    role in vocational and career information, 308-309
    role in vocational education, 313-314
  role of
    in facilitating informal group acceptance, 61-63
    in family conflict, 51-52
  special education
    and formal groups, 57-59
    role of, 139-142
  -student interaction, 248-249
  unions as formal power, 85
  variables controlled by, 16-17
  verbal behavior of, 100-101, 248
Teaching strategies, 294-295
Teaching, study of, 100
Team, evaluation, for learning disabilities, 119
Technical vocabularies/glossaries, 244-245
Technology in assessment of learning disabilities, 113
Telephone conversations, 180
Temperament and attitude, 161-162
Tenure contracts, 89
Term contracts, 89
Termination of parent conferences, 175
Testing, diagnostic, 291
Tests, 34-35, 321-322
  aptitude, 309-310
  to assess learning disabilities, 115
  competency, 106-107
  criterion-referenced, 282
  diagnostic, reading, 282
  minimum competency, 242
  pictorial, 309
  scores of, 105
Texts, special, 246
Theories
  of adolescence, 28-33
  of learning disabilities, psychological process, 112-113
Therapist, speech, 185
Therapy
  drug, 135, 138
  noneducational, 11
  sessions, 121
Thinking behavior, 40-42
Thioridazine, 135
Third-grade skills, 289-290

Thought
  formal operational, 30-31, 39
  propositional, 40
Token economics, 226
Tolerance for frustration, 160-161
Topical outline, 244
Tort liability, 88-89
Tracing technique, 276
Tracks, educational, of secondary school, 7, 216-217
Training
  adjustment, and academic programming, liaison between, 127
  feedback, 130
  off-campus, 312
  on-the-job, 313
  of paraprofessionals, 181-182
  perceptual, 233
  postsecondary, 314-318
  prevocational, 311
  process, 272
  and professional growth of special educator, 162-164
  sequence of, for paraprofessionals, 181-182
  in social skills, 63, 131
  vocational, 311-313
    goals of, 308
Transition points for learning disabled students, 293
Translation from word problem to basic algorithm, 292
Tutors, peer, 183

**U**

Unions, teachers'
  as formal power, 85
  and organizations, influence of, 102-103
Unitary curriculum, 15
U.S. Congress and school organization, 79
U.S. Constitution and school organization, 78

**V**

VAKT techniques, 276, 277
Valium; *see* Diazepam
Values
  clarification of, 131-132
  defined, 49
  parental, 49
  place, 292
Variables
  in program development and functioning, 20-22
  teacher, 16-17
Ventilation of resource room, 208
Verbal behavior of teachers, 100-101, 248
Verbal learning, 98-99
Visual discrimination, 270
Vocabulary development, 274-275

Vocational adjustment coordinator, special educator as, 188
Vocational and career information, 308, 311
Vocational education, 7, 302-307, 312
Vocational Education Act of 1963 as amended in 1976, 305
*Vocational Interest and Sophistication Assessment*, 309
Vocational models, 9, 26, 152
Vocational planning, 127, 234
Vocational programs, 214, 301-320
Vocational rehabilitation, 314
Vocational rehabilitation counselor, special educator as, 189
Vocational technical and two-year colleges, 316-317
Vocational training, 311-313
   goal of, 308
Vocational-technical schools, 312
Volunteers, 228

## W

Wisconsin System of Instructional Management, 224
Word problem, translation to basic algorithm, 292

Word recognition, 274
Work
   evaluation through simulation, 310
   experience, 312
   force, employment in, 315-316
   interest, developing, 310
   norm, 102
   samples, informal, 310
   stations, off-campus, 313
Work-study, 312
Written agreements in school organization, 81
Written communication, 176
Written expression, goals of, 293-295
Written language disabilities, 293-298
Written report in assessment of learning disabilities, 119

## Y

Youth culture, 32

## Z

Z scores, 104-105
Zero or null sets, confusion of, 292

RESERVE

3115-7